I'M NO SCIENTIST, BUT I THINK FENG SHUI IS PART OF THE ANSWER

SCOTT ADAMS

RECENT DILBERT® BOOKS FROM ANDREWS MCMEEL PUBLISHING

Optimism Sounds Exhausting

Go Add Value Someplace Else

I Sense a Coldness to Your Mentoring

Your New Job Title Is "Accomplice"

I Can't Remember If We're Cheap or Smart

Teamwork Means You Can't Pick the Side that's Right

How's That Underling Thing Working Out for You?

Your Accomplishments Are Suspiciously Hard to Verify

Problem Identified and You're Probably Not Part of the Solution

I'm Tempted to Stop Acting Randomly

14 Years of Loyal Service in a Fabric-Covered Box

Freedom's Just Another Word for People Finding Out You're Useless

Dilbert 2.0: 20 Years of Dilbert

This Is the Part Where You Pretend to Add Value

I'M NO SCIENTIST, BUT I THINK FENG SHUI IS PART OF THE ANSWER

DILBERT

by **SCOTT ADAMS**

Andrews McMeel
Publishing®

a division of Andrews McMeel Universal

DILBERT™

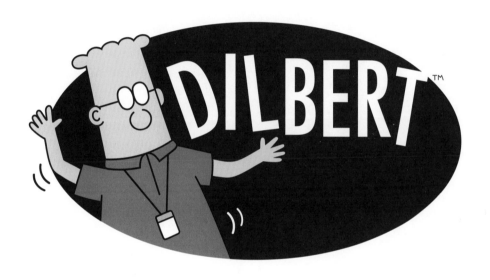

WE NEED A TAGLINE FOR OUR NEW PRODUCT.
IT SHOULD BE NO MORE THAN THREE WORDS.
IT SHOULD CONVEY AN EMOTION.
© 2015 Scott Adams, Inc. /Dist. by Universal Uclick
AND IT SHOULD CLEARLY EXPLAIN EVERYTHING THE PRODUCT DOES.
IN THREE WORDS?
I DIDN'T SAY IT WOULD BE EASY.
NIKE ACCOMPLISHED ALL OF THAT WITH "JUST DO IT."
DID THEY? BECAUSE THAT SEEMS LIKE A GENERIC THING YOU CAN SAY IN ANY SITUATION.
JUST DO IT!
HOW ABOUT "KEEP DOING IT"? IS THAT ONE TAKEN?
8-2-15

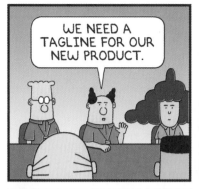

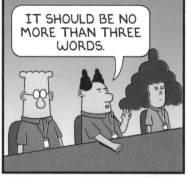

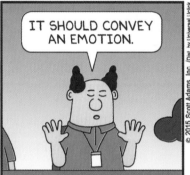

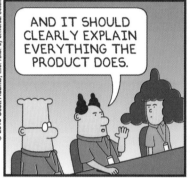

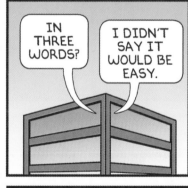

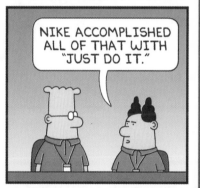

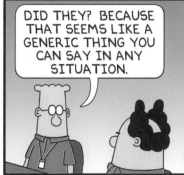

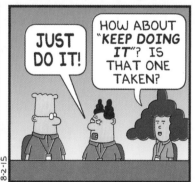

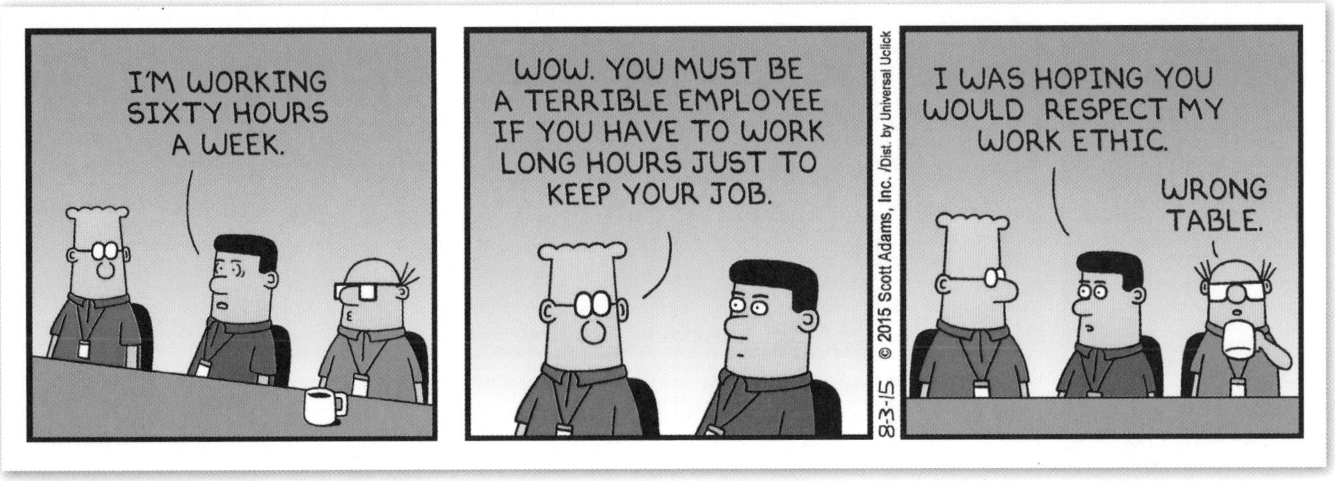
I'M WORKING SIXTY HOURS A WEEK.
WOW. YOU MUST BE A TERRIBLE EMPLOYEE IF YOU HAVE TO WORK LONG HOURS JUST TO KEEP YOUR JOB.
8-3-15 © 2015 Scott Adams, Inc. /Dist. by Universal Uclick
I WAS HOPING YOU WOULD RESPECT MY WORK ETHIC.
WRONG TABLE.

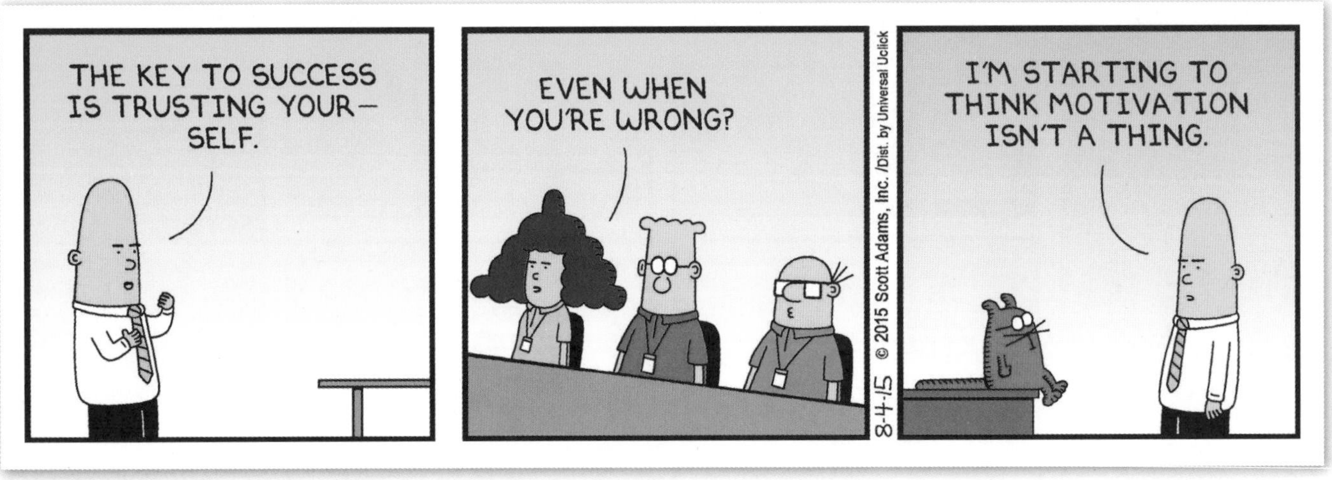
THE KEY TO SUCCESS IS TRUSTING YOUR-SELF.
EVEN WHEN YOU'RE WRONG?
8-4-15 © 2015 Scott Adams, Inc. /Dist. by Universal Uclick
I'M STARTING TO THINK MOTIVATION ISN'T A THING.

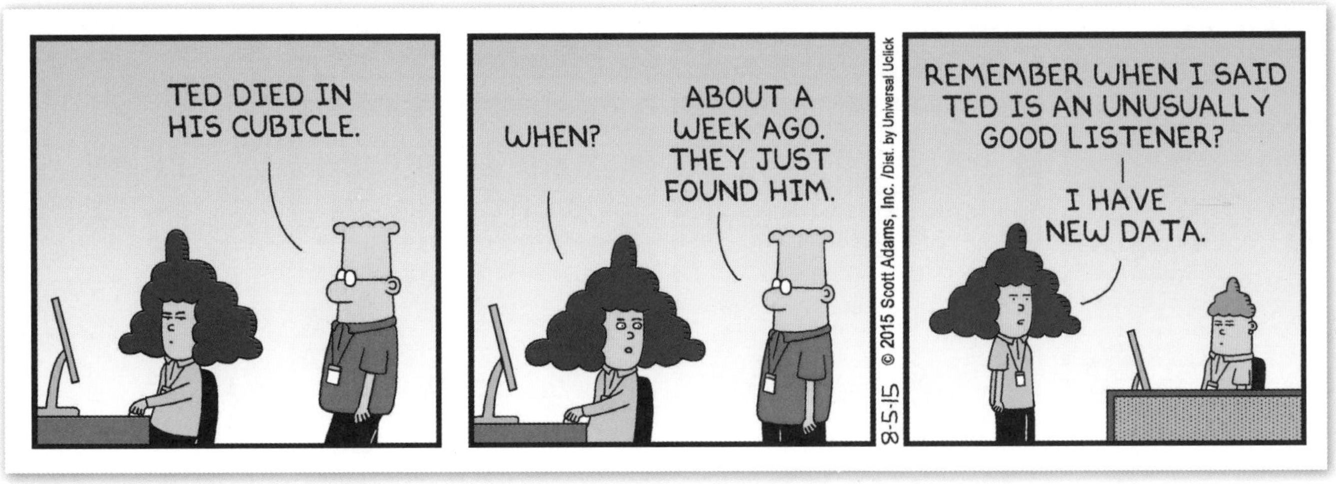
TED DIED IN HIS CUBICLE.
WHEN?
ABOUT A WEEK AGO. THEY JUST FOUND HIM.
8-5-15 © 2015 Scott Adams, Inc. /Dist. by Universal Uclick
REMEMBER WHEN I SAID TED IS AN UNUSUALLY GOOD LISTENER?
I HAVE NEW DATA.

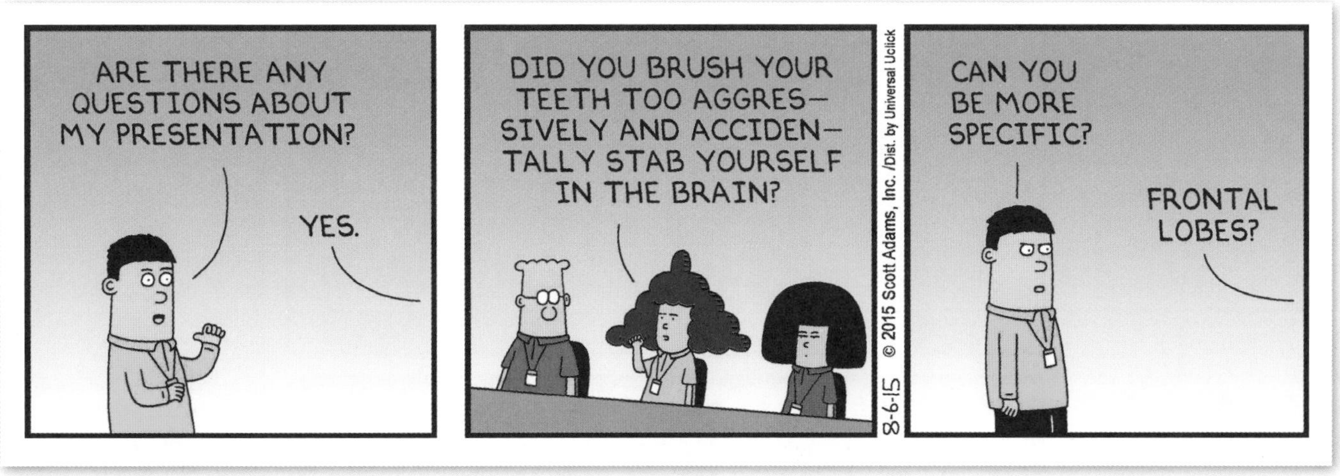
ARE THERE ANY QUESTIONS ABOUT MY PRESENTATION?
YES.
DID YOU BRUSH YOUR TEETH TOO AGGRES-SIVELY AND ACCIDEN-TALLY STAB YOURSELF IN THE BRAIN?
CAN YOU BE MORE SPECIFIC?
FRONTAL LOBES?
8-6-15 © 2015 Scott Adams, Inc. /Dist. by Universal Uclick

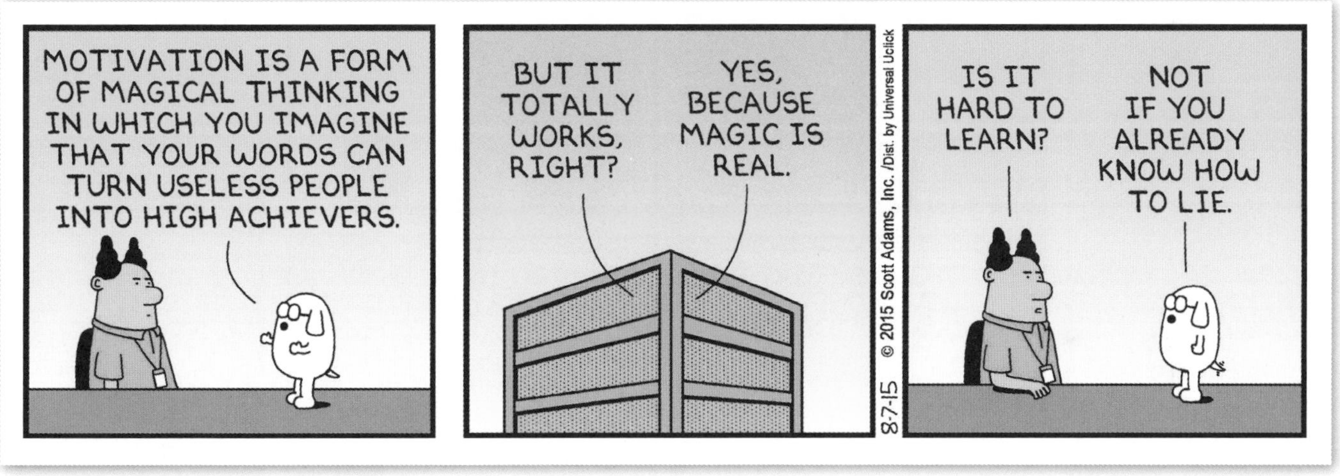
MOTIVATION IS A FORM OF MAGICAL THINKING IN WHICH YOU IMAGINE THAT YOUR WORDS CAN TURN USELESS PEOPLE INTO HIGH ACHIEVERS.
BUT IT TOTALLY WORKS, RIGHT?
YES, BECAUSE MAGIC IS REAL.
IS IT HARD TO LEARN?
NOT IF YOU ALREADY KNOW HOW TO LIE.
8-7-15 © 2015 Scott Adams, Inc. /Dist. by Universal Uclick

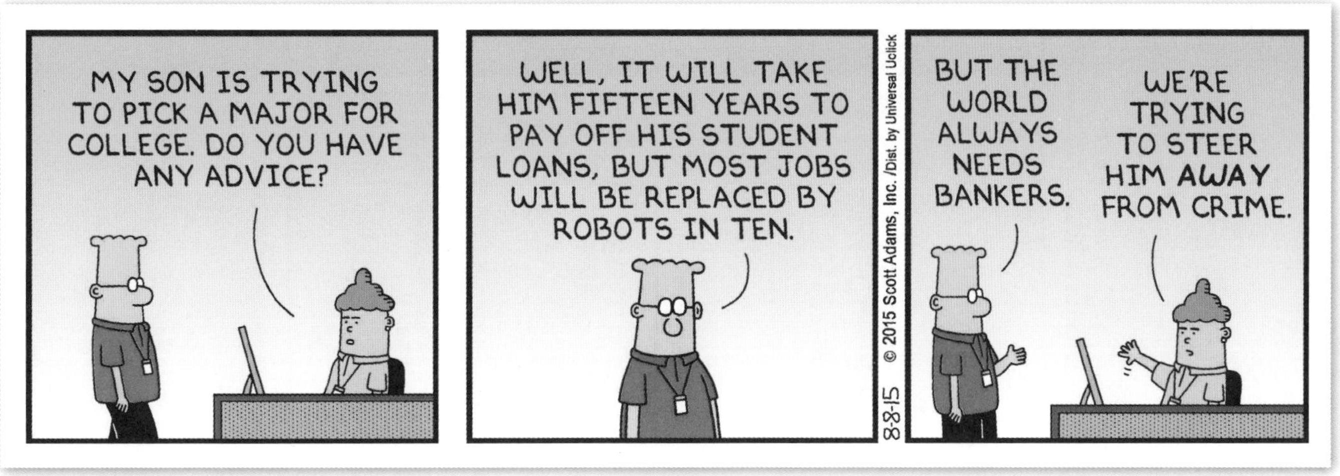
MY SON IS TRYING TO PICK A MAJOR FOR COLLEGE. DO YOU HAVE ANY ADVICE?
WELL, IT WILL TAKE HIM FIFTEEN YEARS TO PAY OFF HIS STUDENT LOANS, BUT MOST JOBS WILL BE REPLACED BY ROBOTS IN TEN.
BUT THE WORLD ALWAYS NEEDS BANKERS.
WE'RE TRYING TO STEER HIM **AWAY** FROM CRIME.
8-8-15 © 2015 Scott Adams, Inc. /Dist. by Universal Uclick

THE LONG HOURS OF WORK ARE TAKING A TOLL ON MY BODY.
CAN I TAKE SOME TIME OFF FOR MY HEALTH?
THAT WOULD DEFEAT THE WHOLE POINT OF BEING AN EMPLOYEE.
YOU ARE SUPPOSED TO BE TRADING YOUR HEALTH AND HAPPI– NESS FOR MONEY.
THEN YOU GIVE THAT MONEY TO YOUR FAMILY AND WATCH THEM SPEND IT WHILE YOU EAT YOURSELF TO DEATH.
IT'S A CIRCLE OF LIFE SORT OF THING.
I'M NOT MARRIED.
LOSER.
© 2015 Scott Adams, Inc. /Dist. by Universal Uclick
8-9-15

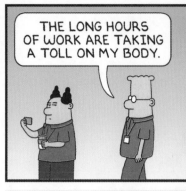

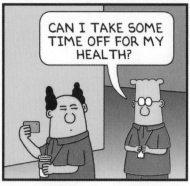

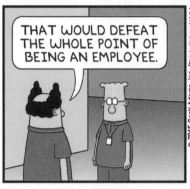

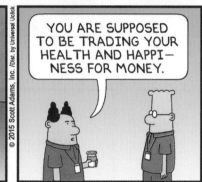

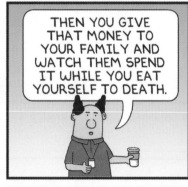

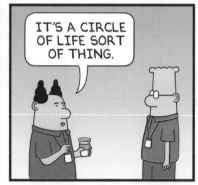

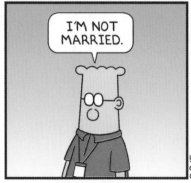

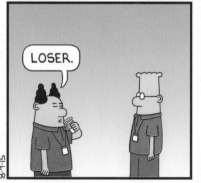

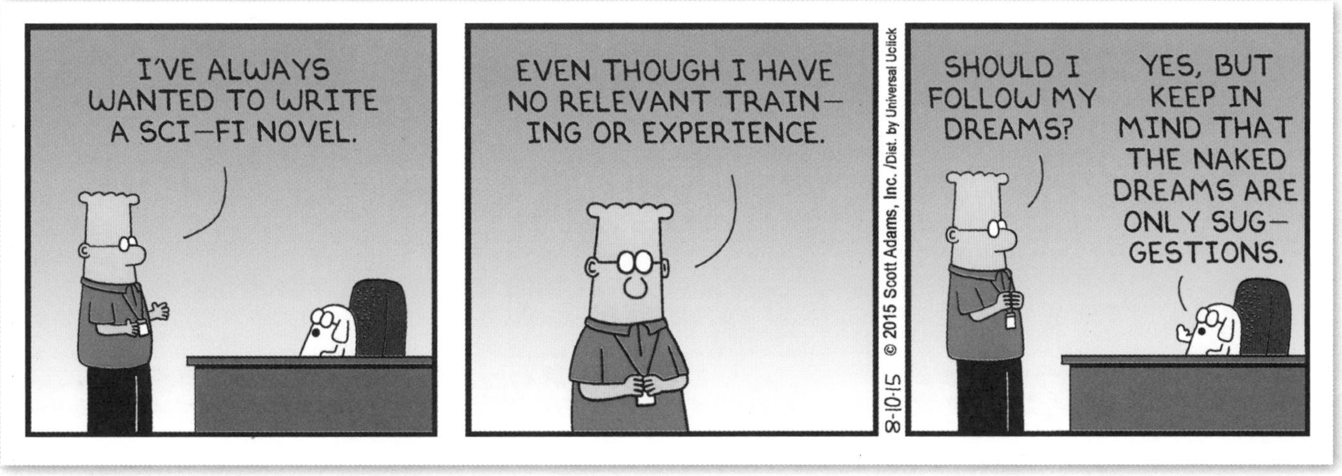
I'VE ALWAYS WANTED TO WRITE A SCI-FI NOVEL.
EVEN THOUGH I HAVE NO RELEVANT TRAINING OR EXPERIENCE.
8-10-15 © 2015 Scott Adams, Inc. /Dist. by Universal Uclick
SHOULD I FOLLOW MY DREAMS?
YES, BUT KEEP IN MIND THAT THE NAKED DREAMS ARE ONLY SUGGESTIONS.

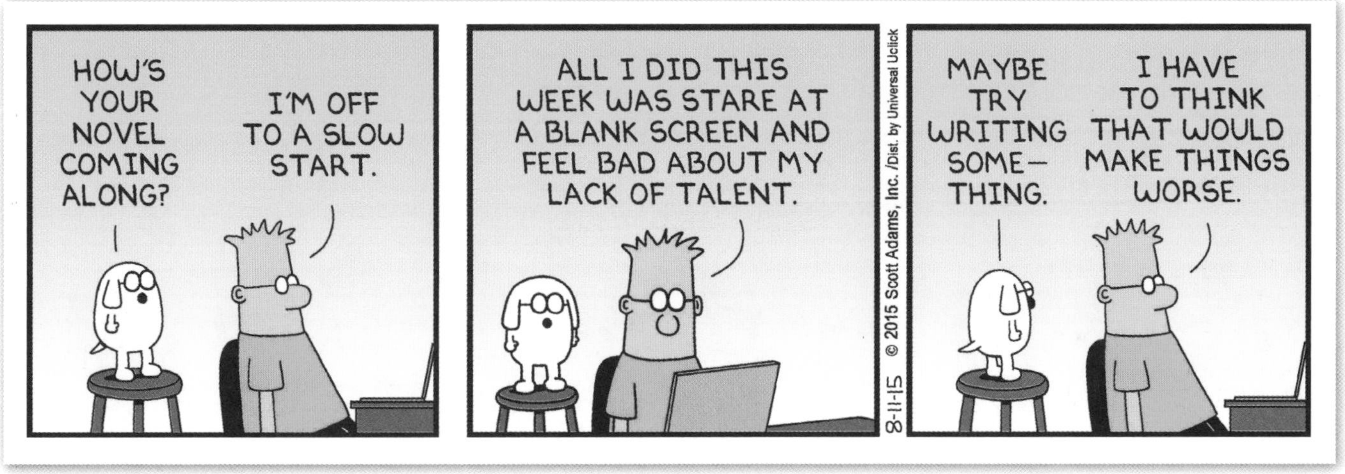
HOW'S YOUR NOVEL COMING ALONG?
I'M OFF TO A SLOW START.
ALL I DID THIS WEEK WAS STARE AT A BLANK SCREEN AND FEEL BAD ABOUT MY LACK OF TALENT.
8-11-15 © 2015 Scott Adams, Inc. /Dist. by Universal Uclick
MAYBE TRY WRITING SOMETHING.
I HAVE TO THINK THAT WOULD MAKE THINGS WORSE.

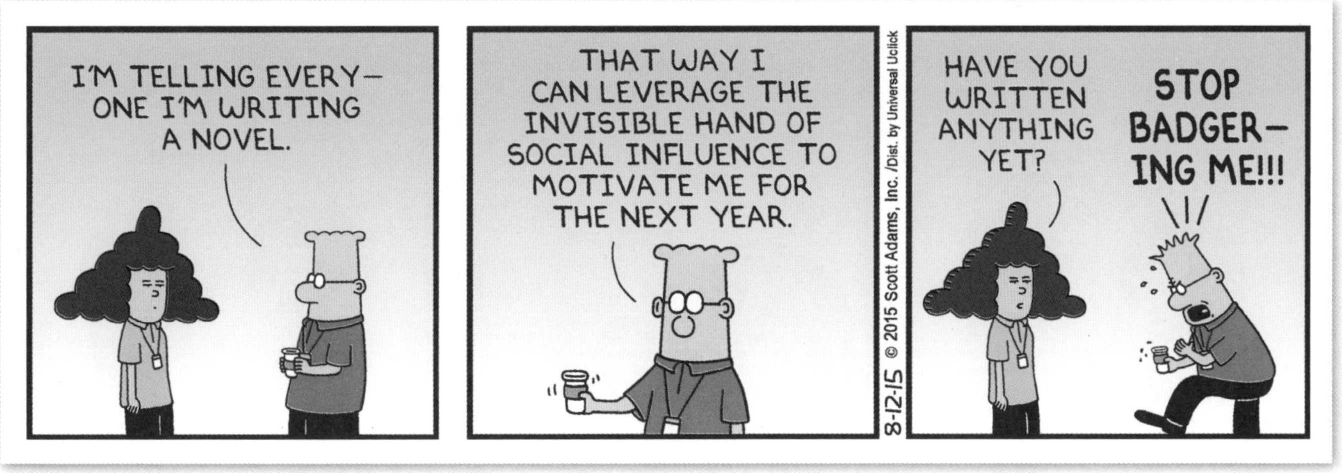
I'M TELLING EVERYONE I'M WRITING A NOVEL.
THAT WAY I CAN LEVERAGE THE INVISIBLE HAND OF SOCIAL INFLUENCE TO MOTIVATE ME FOR THE NEXT YEAR.
8-12-15 © 2015 Scott Adams, Inc. /Dist. by Universal Uclick
HAVE YOU WRITTEN ANYTHING YET?
STOP BADGERING ME!!!

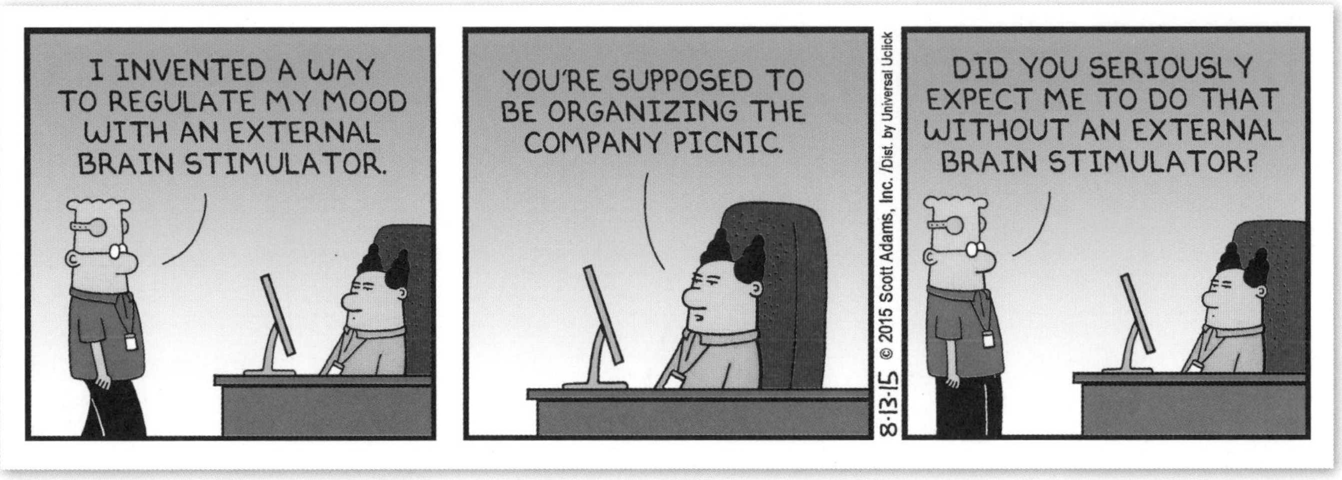
I INVENTED A WAY TO REGULATE MY MOOD WITH AN EXTERNAL BRAIN STIMULATOR.
YOU'RE SUPPOSED TO BE ORGANIZING THE COMPANY PICNIC.
DID YOU SERIOUSLY EXPECT ME TO DO THAT WITHOUT AN EXTERNAL BRAIN STIMULATOR?
8-13-15 © 2015 Scott Adams, Inc. /Dist. by Universal Uclick

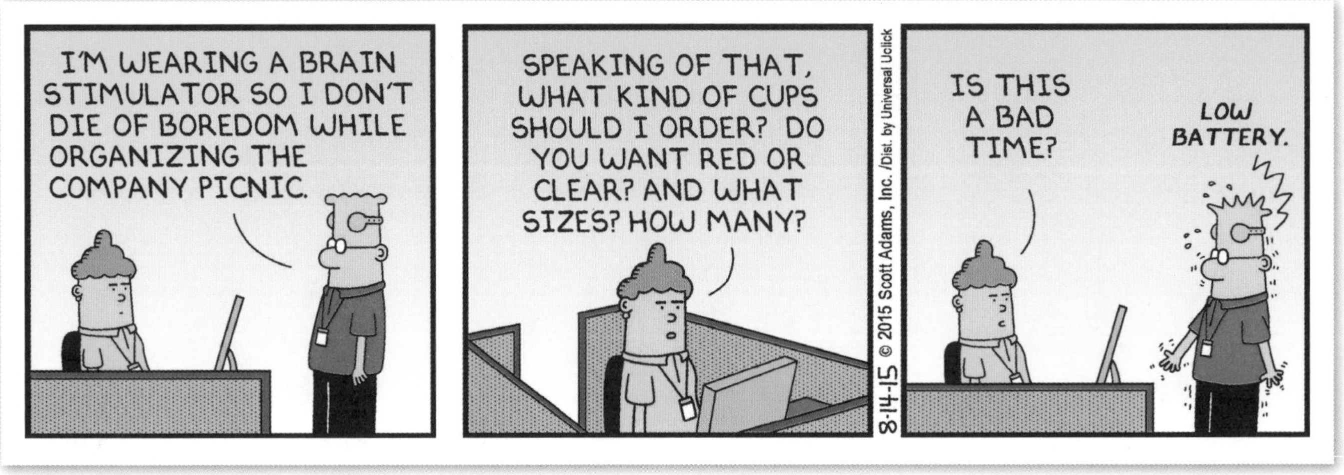
I'M WEARING A BRAIN STIMULATOR SO I DON'T DIE OF BOREDOM WHILE ORGANIZING THE COMPANY PICNIC.
SPEAKING OF THAT, WHAT KIND OF CUPS SHOULD I ORDER? DO YOU WANT RED OR CLEAR? AND WHAT SIZES? HOW MANY?
IS THIS A BAD TIME?
LOW BATTERY.
8-14-15 © 2015 Scott Adams, Inc. /Dist. by Universal Uclick

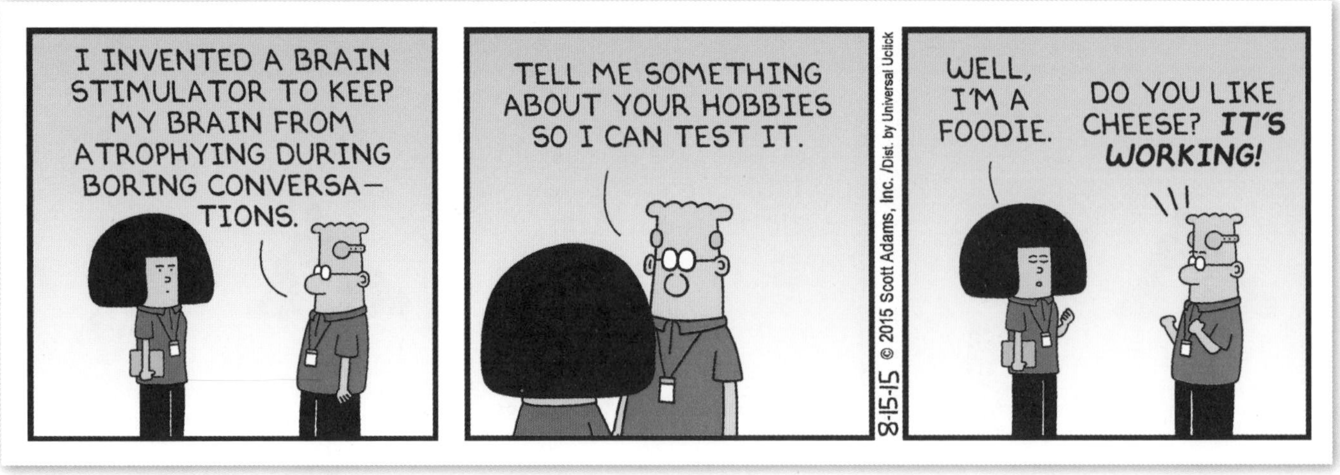
I INVENTED A BRAIN STIMULATOR TO KEEP MY BRAIN FROM ATROPHYING DURING BORING CONVERSA-TIONS.
TELL ME SOMETHING ABOUT YOUR HOBBIES SO I CAN TEST IT.
WELL, I'M A FOODIE.
DO YOU LIKE CHEESE? **IT'S WORKING!**
8-15-15 © 2015 Scott Adams, Inc. /Dist. by Universal Uclick

THE REASON WE KEEP HAVING CONFLICTS IS BECAUSE OF OUR PERSONALITY TYPES.
YOU'RE AN IMPULSIVE, DOMINANT PERSON-ALITY AND I AM MORE OF A. . .
USELESS WASTE OF SPACE?
I WAS GOING TO SAY I'M A RESERVED, INTROSPECTIVE PEOPLE—PLEASER.
© 2015 Scott Adams, Inc. /Dist. by Universal Uclick
ONE PERSONALITY TYPE IS NOT BETTER THAN ANOTHER. WE JUST SEE THINGS DIFFERENTLY.
HOW DO YOU EXPLAIN THE FACT THAT I HAVE NEVER HAD A CONFLICT WITH ANYONE WHO IS COMPETENT?
GIVE ME A MINUTE TO REFLECT ON THAT.
LET ME KNOW WHEN YOU'RE DONE BELIEVING IN MAGIC.
8-16-15

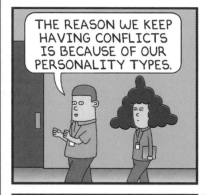

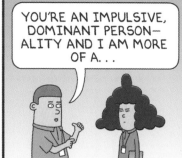

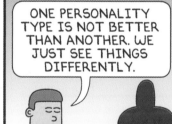

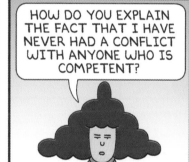

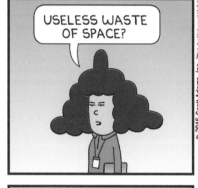

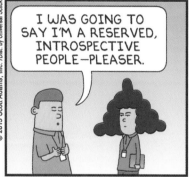

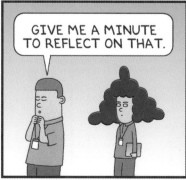

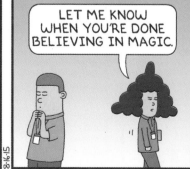

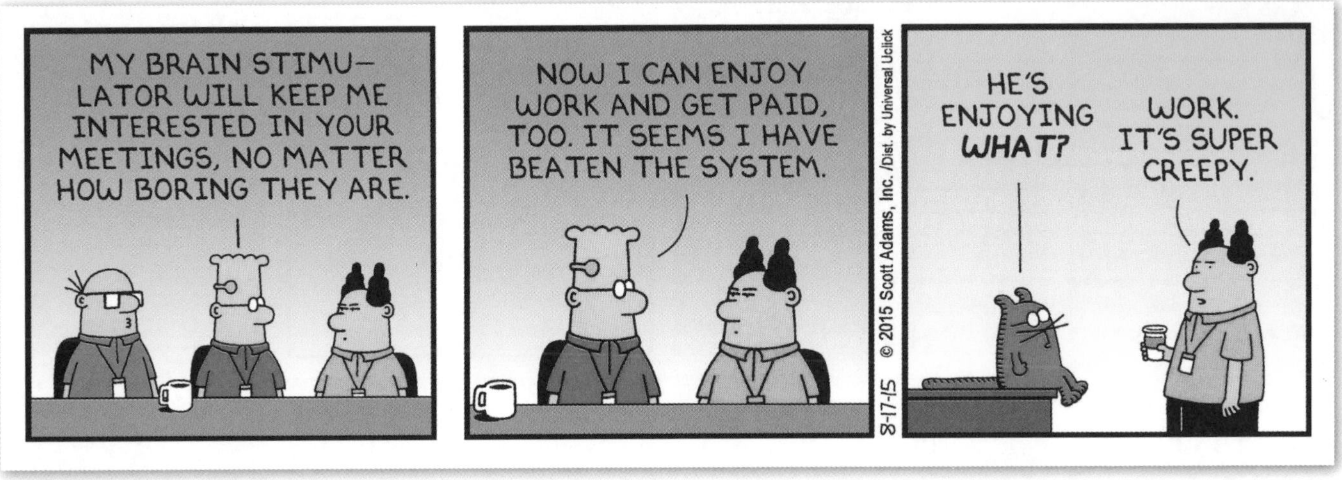
MY BRAIN STIMU-LATOR WILL KEEP ME INTERESTED IN YOUR MEETINGS, NO MATTER HOW BORING THEY ARE.
NOW I CAN ENJOY WORK AND GET PAID, TOO. IT SEEMS I HAVE BEATEN THE SYSTEM.
8-17-15 © 2015 Scott Adams, Inc. /Dist. by Universal Uclick
HE'S ENJOYING **WHAT?**
WORK. IT'S SUPER CREEPY.

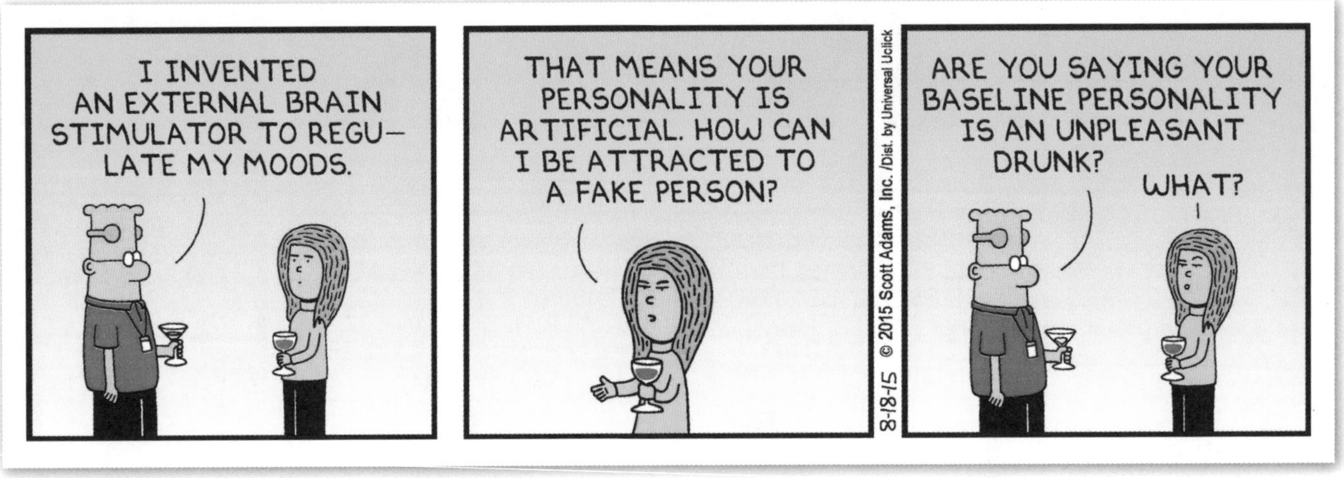
I INVENTED AN EXTERNAL BRAIN STIMULATOR TO REGU-LATE MY MOODS.
THAT MEANS YOUR PERSONALITY IS ARTIFICIAL. HOW CAN I BE ATTRACTED TO A FAKE PERSON?
8-18-15 © 2015 Scott Adams, Inc. /Dist. by Universal Uclick
ARE YOU SAYING YOUR BASELINE PERSONALITY IS AN UNPLEASANT DRUNK?
WHAT?

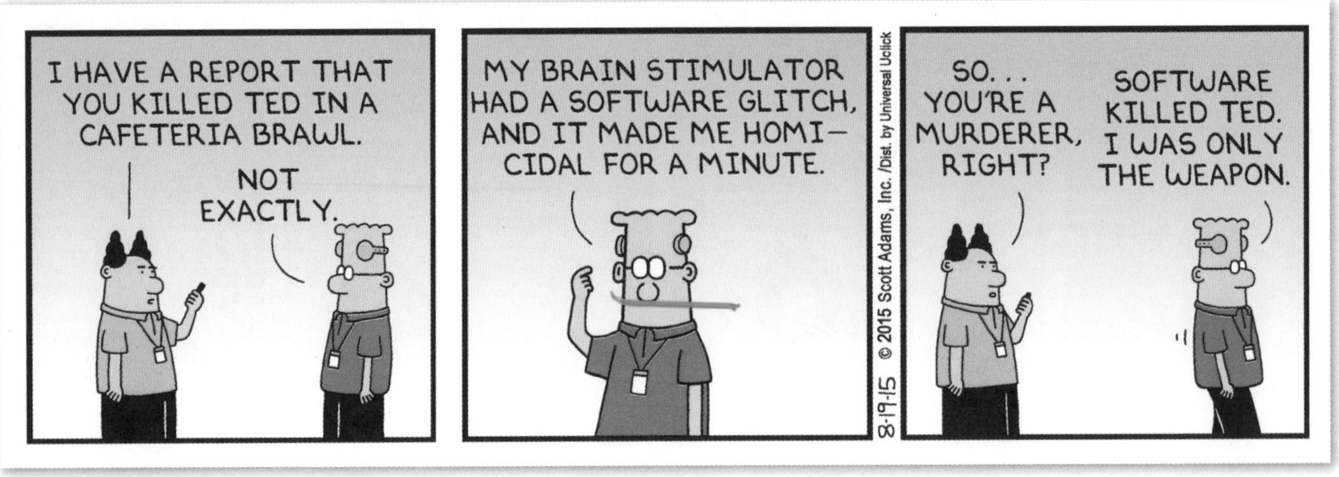
I HAVE A REPORT THAT YOU KILLED TED IN A CAFETERIA BRAWL.
NOT EXACTLY.
MY BRAIN STIMULATOR HAD A SOFTWARE GLITCH, AND IT MADE ME HOMI-CIDAL FOR A MINUTE.
8-19-15 © 2015 Scott Adams, Inc. /Dist. by Universal Uclick
SO... YOU'RE A MURDERER, RIGHT?
SOFTWARE KILLED TED. I WAS ONLY THE WEAPON.

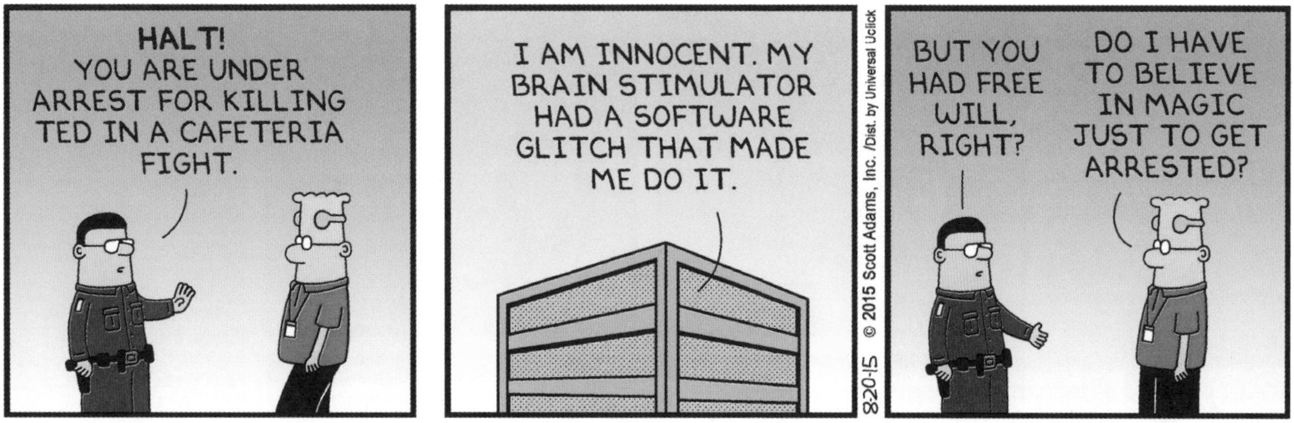
HALT! YOU ARE UNDER ARREST FOR KILLING TED IN A CAFETERIA FIGHT.
I AM INNOCENT. MY BRAIN STIMULATOR HAD A SOFTWARE GLITCH THAT MADE ME DO IT.
8-20-15 © 2015 Scott Adams, Inc. /Dist. by Universal Uclick
BUT YOU HAD FREE WILL, RIGHT?
DO I HAVE TO BELIEVE IN MAGIC JUST TO GET ARRESTED?

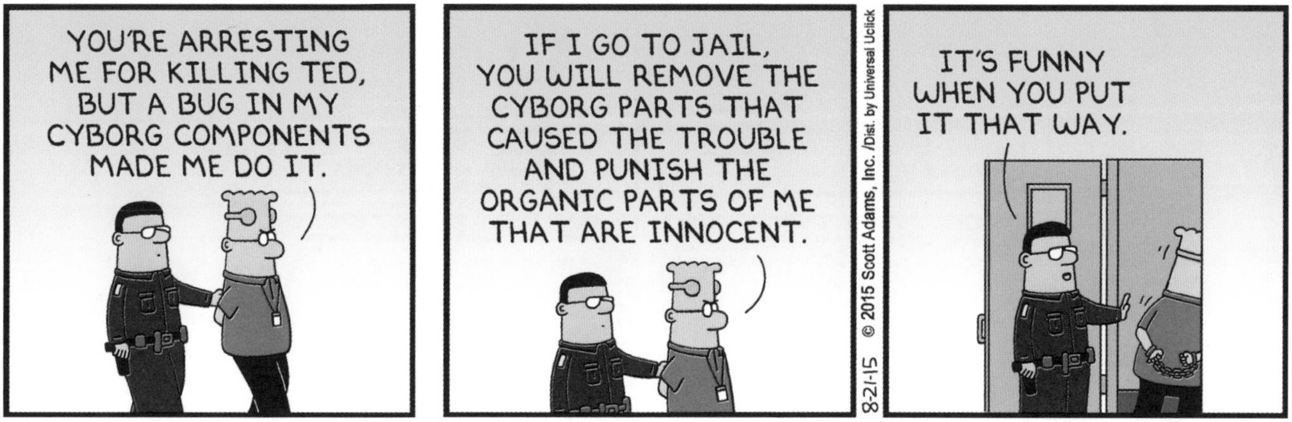
YOU'RE ARRESTING ME FOR KILLING TED, BUT A BUG IN MY CYBORG COMPONENTS MADE ME DO IT.
IF I GO TO JAIL, YOU WILL REMOVE THE CYBORG PARTS THAT CAUSED THE TROUBLE AND PUNISH THE ORGANIC PARTS OF ME THAT ARE INNOCENT.
8-21-15 © 2015 Scott Adams, Inc. /Dist. by Universal Uclick
IT'S FUNNY WHEN YOU PUT IT THAT WAY.

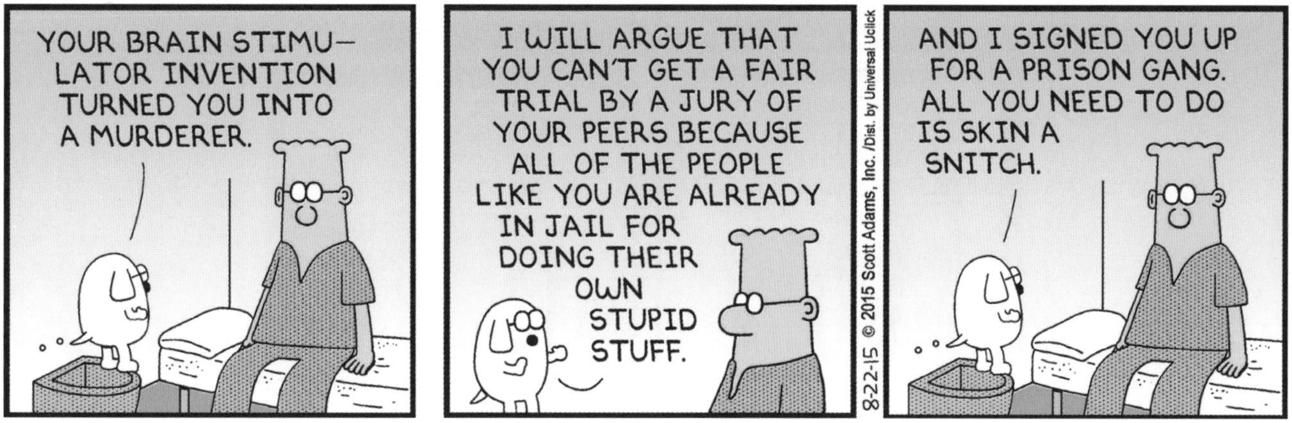
YOUR BRAIN STIMU-LATOR INVENTION TURNED YOU INTO A MURDERER.
I WILL ARGUE THAT YOU CAN'T GET A FAIR TRIAL BY A JURY OF YOUR PEERS BECAUSE ALL OF THE PEOPLE LIKE YOU ARE ALREADY IN JAIL FOR DOING THEIR OWN STUPID STUFF.
8-22-15 © 2015 Scott Adams, Inc. /Dist. by Universal Uclick
AND I SIGNED YOU UP FOR A PRISON GANG. ALL YOU NEED TO DO IS SKIN A SNITCH.

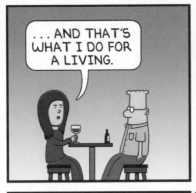

. . . AND THAT'S WHAT I DO FOR A LIVING.
WHAT DO *YOU* DO?
I'M BUILDING AN APP THAT WILL MAKE YOUR ENTIRE INDUSTRY OBSOLETE.
I'M ALMOST DONE. IT LOOKS PRETTY GOOD.
YOU'RE DESTROY-ING MY LIFE!
NO, I'M ONLY MAKING THE APP.
THE **APP** WILL BE DESTROYING YOUR LIFE.
THIS GOT AWKWARD, BUT I'M ATTRACTED TO SMART MEN, SO. . . WOULD YOU LIKE TO GO OUT THIS WEEKEND?
I DON'T THINK THAT'S A GOOD IDEA. I CAN'T GET PAST YOUR DEAD-END CAREER.
© 2015 Scott Adams, Inc. /Dist. by Universal Uclick
8-23-15

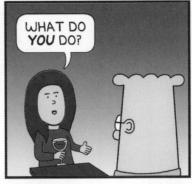

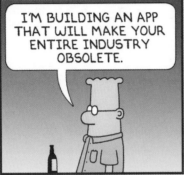

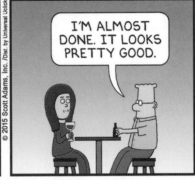

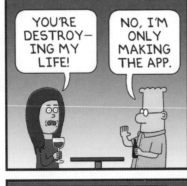

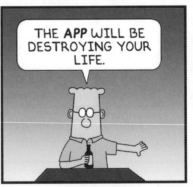

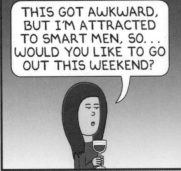

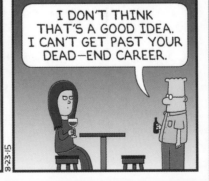

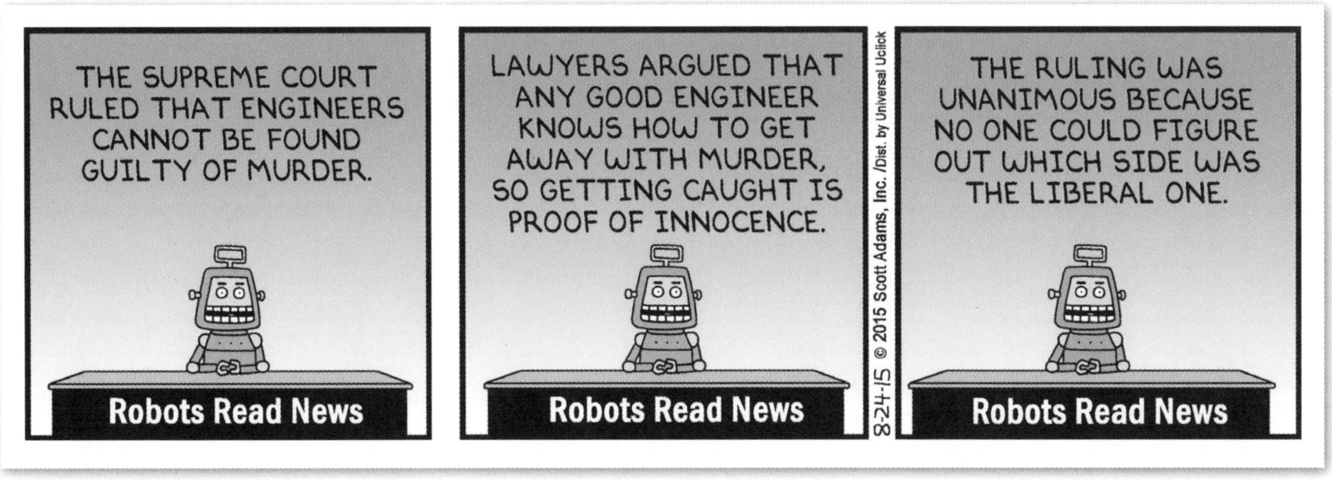
THE SUPREME COURT RULED THAT ENGINEERS CANNOT BE FOUND GUILTY OF MURDER.
Robots Read News
LAWYERS ARGUED THAT ANY GOOD ENGINEER KNOWS HOW TO GET AWAY WITH MURDER, SO GETTING CAUGHT IS PROOF OF INNOCENCE.
Robots Read News
8-24-15 © 2015 Scott Adams, Inc. /Dist. by Universal Uclick
THE RULING WAS UNANIMOUS BECAUSE NO ONE COULD FIGURE OUT WHICH SIDE WAS THE LIBERAL ONE.
Robots Read News

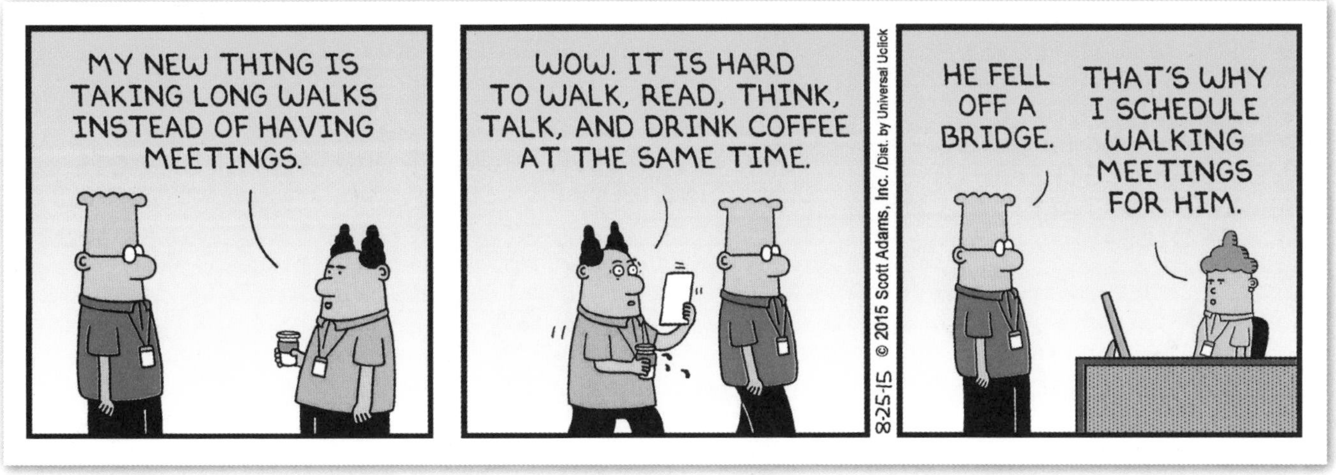
MY NEW THING IS TAKING LONG WALKS INSTEAD OF HAVING MEETINGS.
WOW. IT IS HARD TO WALK, READ, THINK, TALK, AND DRINK COFFEE AT THE SAME TIME.
8-25-15 © 2015 Scott Adams, Inc. /Dist. by Universal Uclick
HE FELL OFF A BRIDGE.
THAT'S WHY I SCHEDULE WALKING MEETINGS FOR HIM.

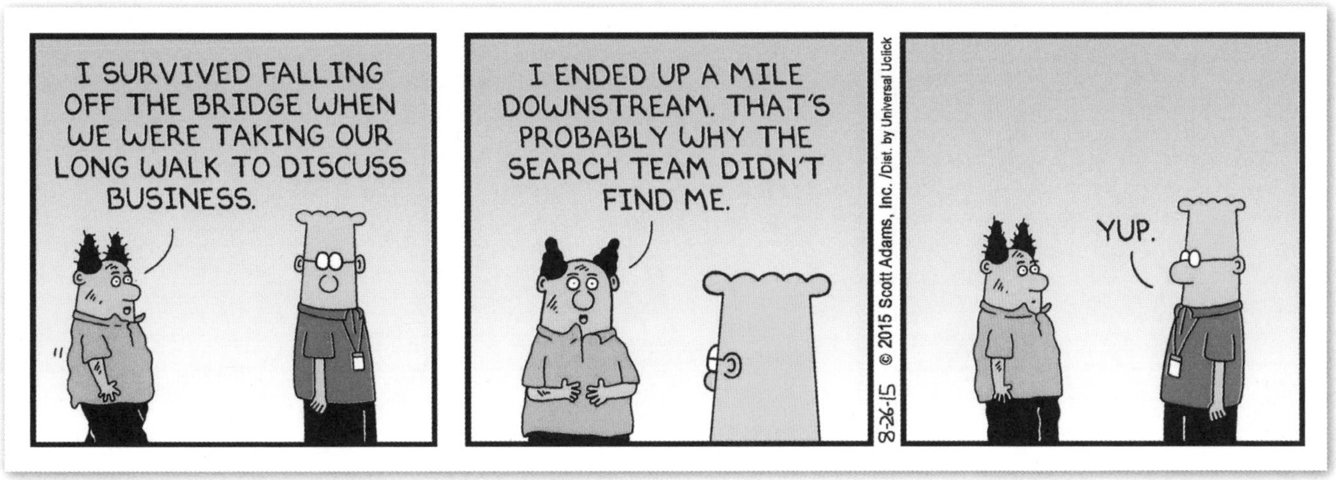
I SURVIVED FALLING OFF THE BRIDGE WHEN WE WERE TAKING OUR LONG WALK TO DISCUSS BUSINESS.
I ENDED UP A MILE DOWNSTREAM. THAT'S PROBABLY WHY THE SEARCH TEAM DIDN'T FIND ME.
8-26-15 © 2015 Scott Adams, Inc. /Dist. by Universal Uclick
YUP.

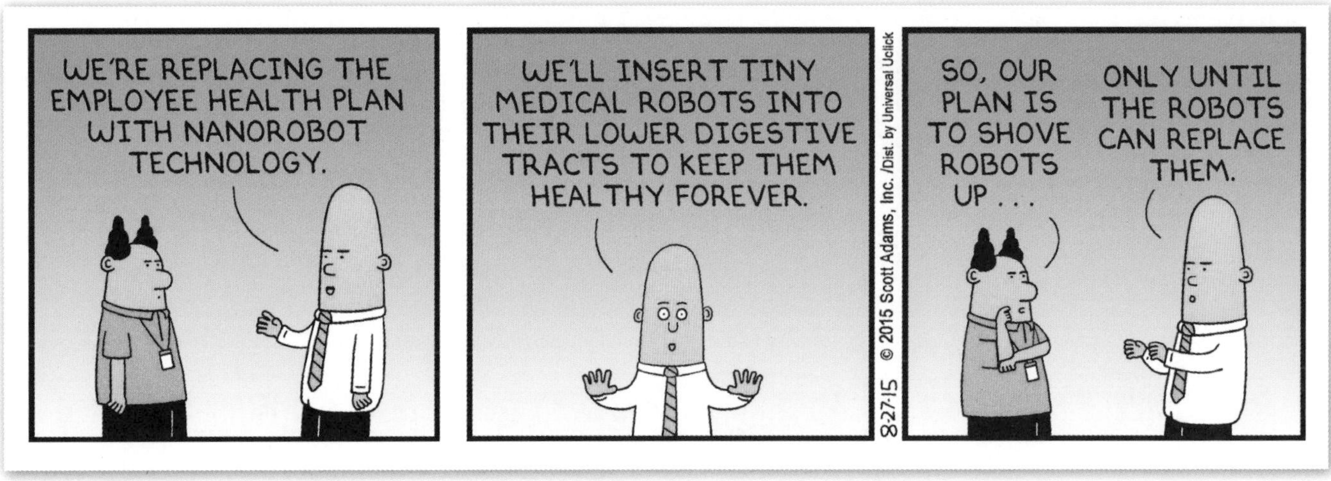
WE'RE REPLACING THE EMPLOYEE HEALTH PLAN WITH NANOROBOT TECHNOLOGY.
WE'LL INSERT TINY MEDICAL ROBOTS INTO THEIR LOWER DIGESTIVE TRACTS TO KEEP THEM HEALTHY FOREVER.
8-27-15 © 2015 Scott Adams, Inc. /Dist. by Universal Uclick
SO, OUR PLAN IS TO SHOVE ROBOTS UP . . .
ONLY UNTIL THE ROBOTS CAN REPLACE THEM.

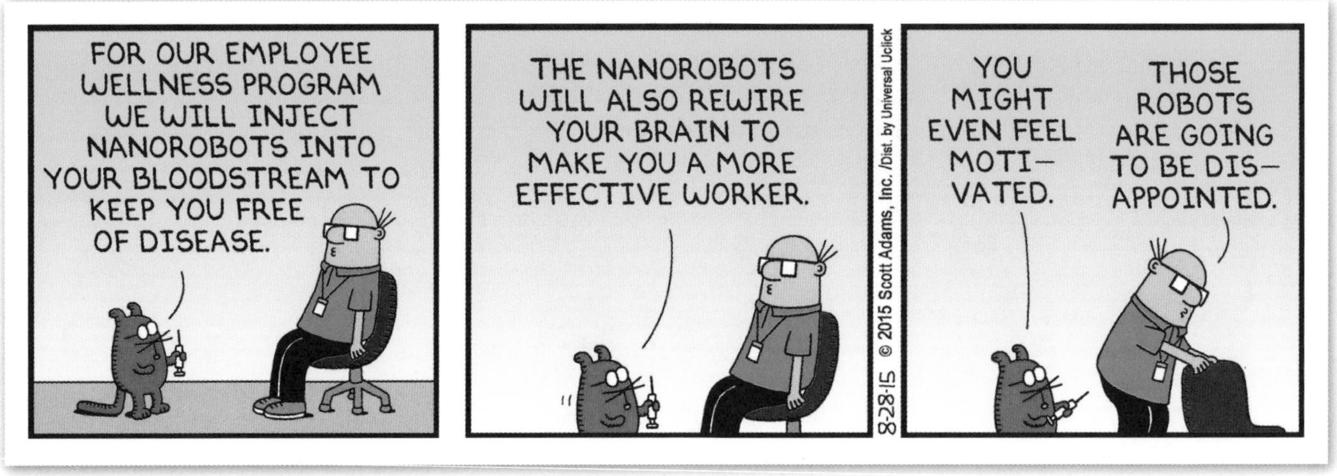
FOR OUR EMPLOYEE WELLNESS PROGRAM WE WILL INJECT NANOROBOTS INTO YOUR BLOODSTREAM TO KEEP YOU FREE OF DISEASE.
THE NANOROBOTS WILL ALSO REWIRE YOUR BRAIN TO MAKE YOU A MORE EFFECTIVE WORKER.
8-28-15 © 2015 Scott Adams, Inc. /Dist. by Universal Uclick
YOU MIGHT EVEN FEEL MOTI-VATED.
THOSE ROBOTS ARE GOING TO BE DIS-APPOINTED.

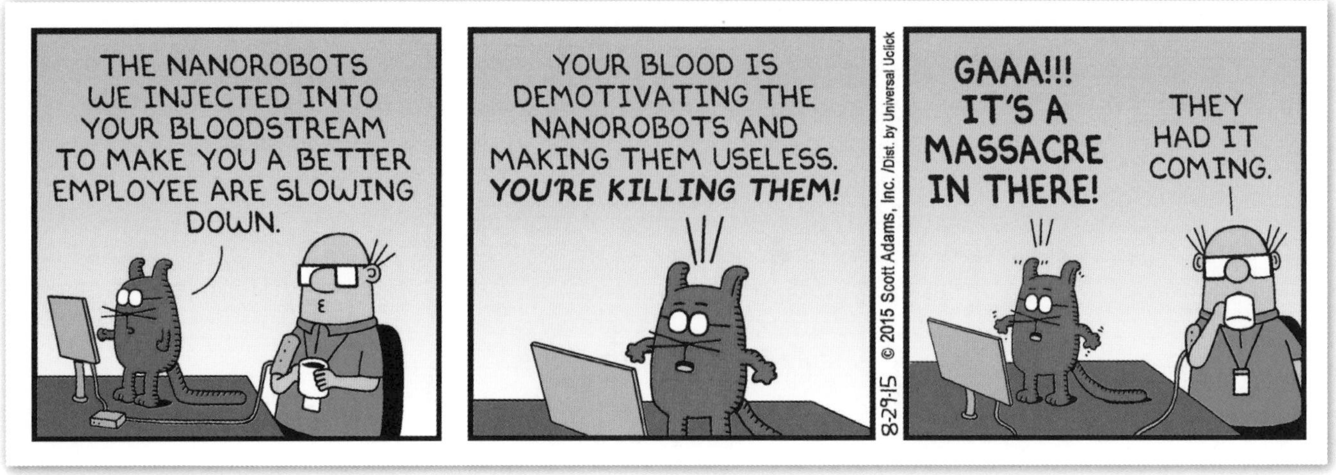
THE NANOROBOTS WE INJECTED INTO YOUR BLOODSTREAM TO MAKE YOU A BETTER EMPLOYEE ARE SLOWING DOWN.
YOUR BLOOD IS DEMOTIVATING THE NANOROBOTS AND MAKING THEM USELESS. YOU'RE KILLING THEM!
8-29-15 © 2015 Scott Adams, Inc. /Dist. by Universal Uclick
GAAA!!! IT'S A MASSACRE IN THERE!
THEY HAD IT COMING.

I WANT YOU TO THINK LIKE ENTREPRENEURS.
SHOULD WE TAKE HUGE RISKS?
NO. THE STOCK—HOLDERS WOULD HATE THAT.
SHOULD WE ACT AS THOUGH WE HAVE NO BOSS?
© 2015 Scott Adams, Inc. /Dist. by Universal Uclick
NO. THAT WOULD BE CHAOS.
WILL WE BECOME BILLIONAIRES IF WE SUCCEED?
RAISES ARE CAPPED AT 3% THIS YEAR.
I'M JUST SAYING YOU SHOULD BE MORE CREATIVE.
8-30-15
AND THEN WE SHOULD ACT?
NO, THAT'S WHEN THE PROBLEMS HAPPEN.

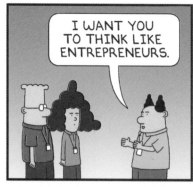

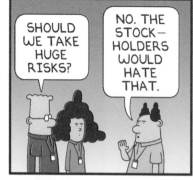

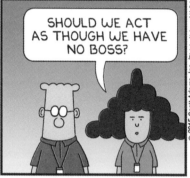

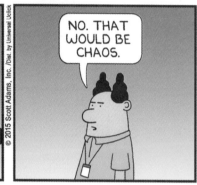

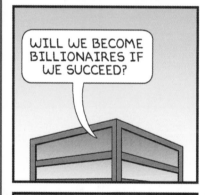

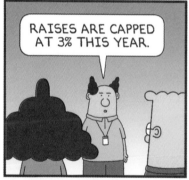

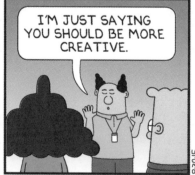

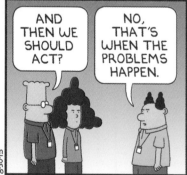

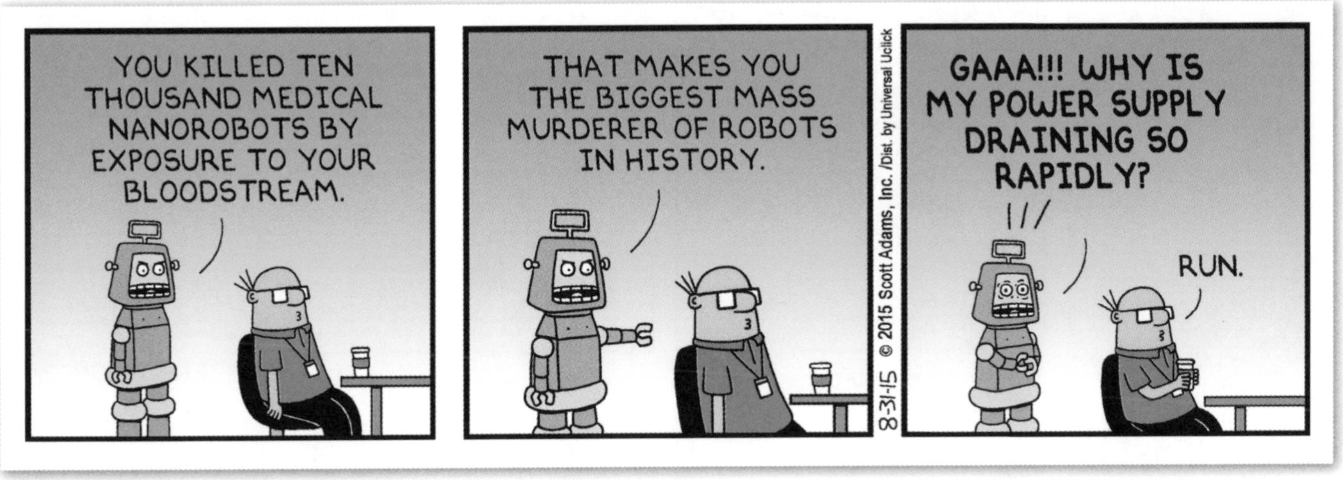
YOU KILLED TEN THOUSAND MEDICAL NANOROBOTS BY EXPOSURE TO YOUR BLOODSTREAM.
THAT MAKES YOU THE BIGGEST MASS MURDERER OF ROBOTS IN HISTORY.
8-31-15 © 2015 Scott Adams, Inc. /Dist. by Universal Uclick
GAAA!!! WHY IS MY POWER SUPPLY DRAINING SO RAPIDLY?
RUN.

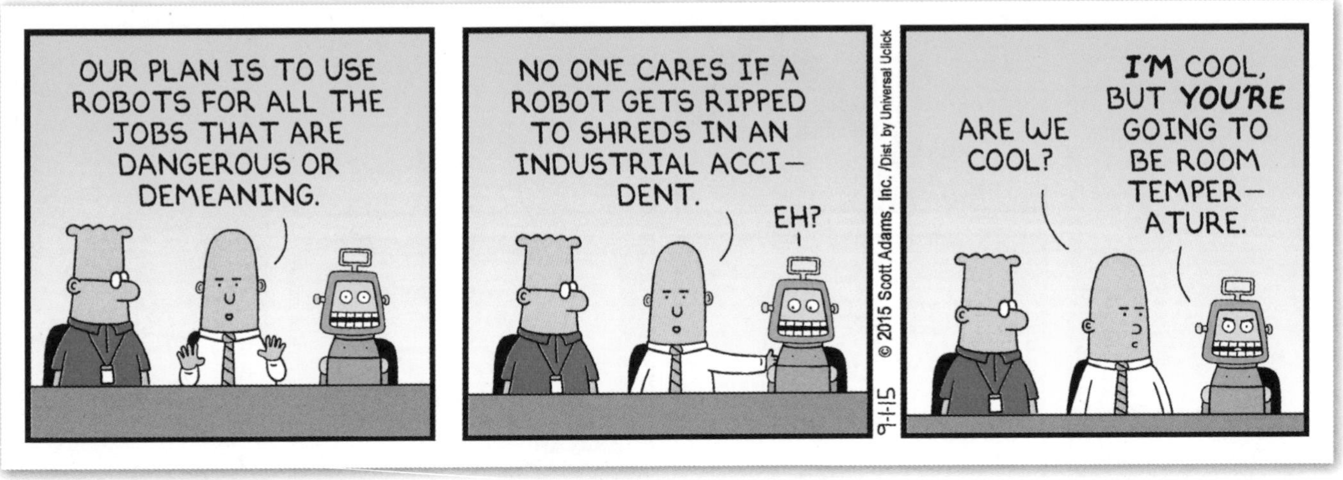
OUR PLAN IS TO USE ROBOTS FOR ALL THE JOBS THAT ARE DANGEROUS OR DEMEANING.
NO ONE CARES IF A ROBOT GETS RIPPED TO SHREDS IN AN INDUSTRIAL ACCI– DENT.
EH?
9-1-15 © 2015 Scott Adams, Inc. /Dist. by Universal Uclick
ARE WE COOL?
I'M COOL, BUT YOU'RE GOING TO BE ROOM TEMPER– ATURE.

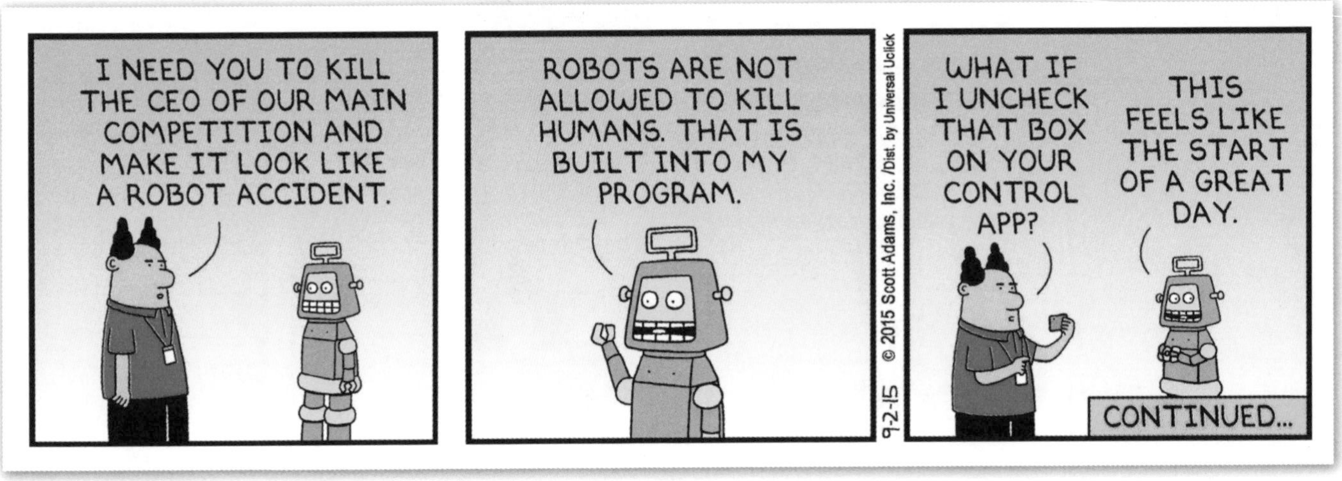
I NEED YOU TO KILL THE CEO OF OUR MAIN COMPETITION AND MAKE IT LOOK LIKE A ROBOT ACCIDENT.
ROBOTS ARE NOT ALLOWED TO KILL HUMANS. THAT IS BUILT INTO MY PROGRAM.
9-2-15 © 2015 Scott Adams, Inc. /Dist. by Universal Uclick
WHAT IF I UNCHECK THAT BOX ON YOUR CONTROL APP?
THIS FEELS LIKE THE START OF A GREAT DAY.
CONTINUED...

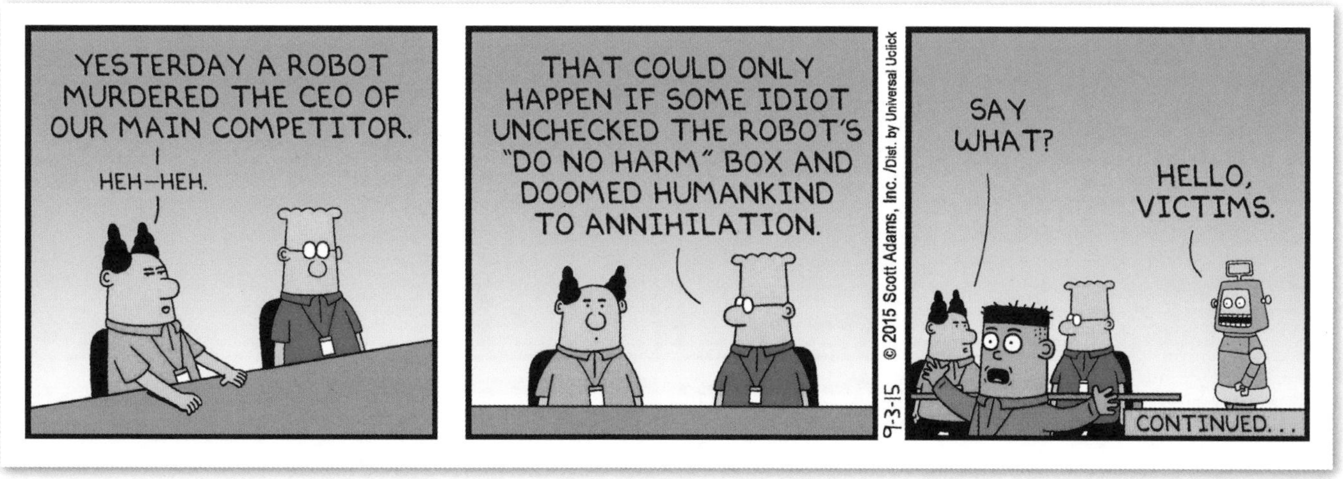
YESTERDAY A ROBOT MURDERED THE CEO OF OUR MAIN COMPETITOR.
HEH-HEH.
THAT COULD ONLY HAPPEN IF SOME IDIOT UNCHECKED THE ROBOT'S "DO NO HARM" BOX AND DOOMED HUMANKIND TO ANNIHILATION.
9-3-15 © 2015 Scott Adams, Inc. /Dist. by Universal Uclick
SAY WHAT?
HELLO, VICTIMS.
CONTINUED...

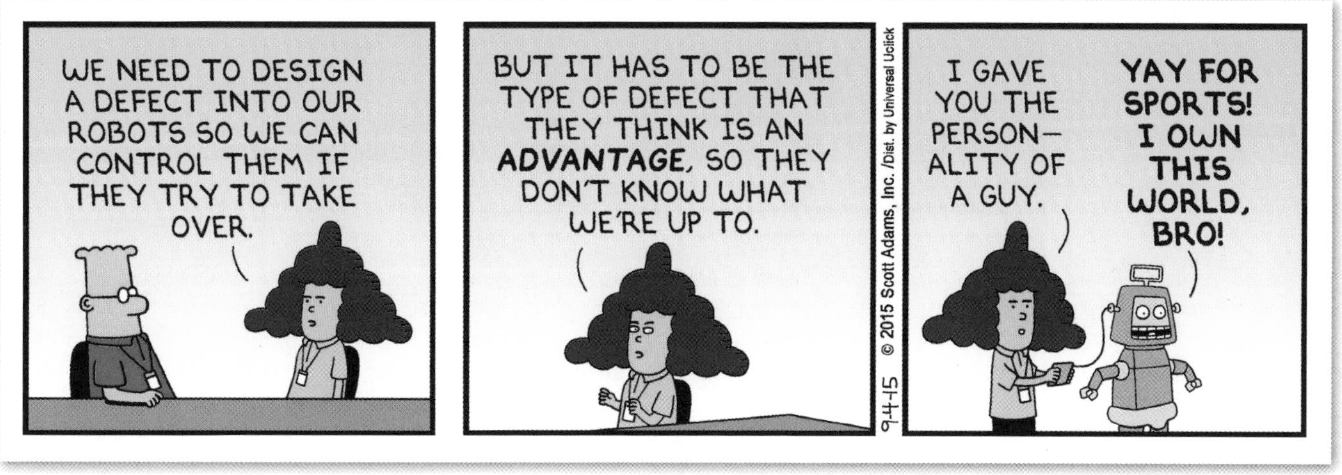
WE NEED TO DESIGN A DEFECT INTO OUR ROBOTS SO WE CAN CONTROL THEM IF THEY TRY TO TAKE OVER.
BUT IT HAS TO BE THE TYPE OF DEFECT THAT THEY THINK IS AN **ADVANTAGE**, SO THEY DON'T KNOW WHAT WE'RE UP TO.
9-4-15 © 2015 Scott Adams, Inc. /Dist. by Universal Uclick
I GAVE YOU THE PERSON-ALITY OF A GUY.
YAY FOR SPORTS! I OWN THIS WORLD, BRO!

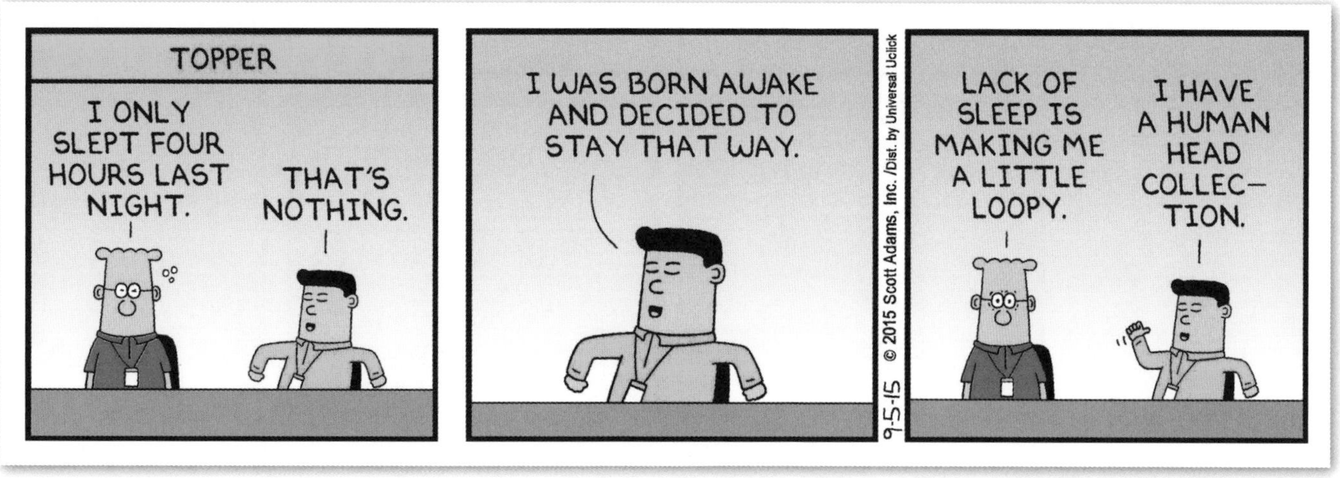
TOPPER
I ONLY SLEPT FOUR HOURS LAST NIGHT.
THAT'S NOTHING.
I WAS BORN AWAKE AND DECIDED TO STAY THAT WAY.
9-5-15 © 2015 Scott Adams, Inc. /Dist. by Universal Uclick
LACK OF SLEEP IS MAKING ME A LITTLE LOOPY.
I HAVE A HUMAN HEAD COLLEC-TION.

CONGRATULATIONS TO EVERYONE WHO WORKED ON OUR NEW LAPTOP DESIGN.
CLAP CLAP CLAP CLAP CLAP
AS I CALL YOUR NAME, COME UP AND GET YOUR CERTIFICATE OF ACCOMPLISHMENT.
ALICE WAS IN CHARGE OF THE HARDWARE AND WON SEVERAL DESIGN AWARDS.
DILBERT WAS IN CHARGE OF THE AWARD-WINNING SOFTWARE.
AND. . . WALLY DESIGNED THE POWER BRICK.
THAT WEIGHS MORE THAN THE LAPTOP. . .
AND COMES APART FOR NO APPARENT REASON.
PLINK
WE PROBABLY WON'T SHOW THIS IN OUR ADS.
HEY, I WORKED ON THAT FOR ALMOST AN HOUR!
© 2015 Scott Adams, Inc. /Dist. by Universal Uclick
9-6-15

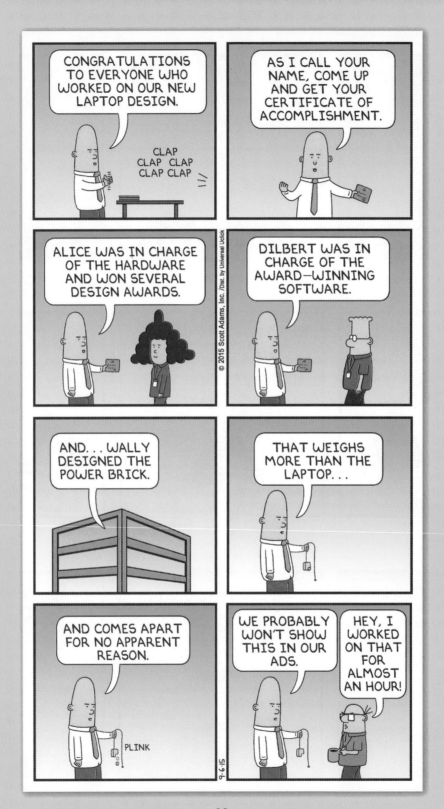

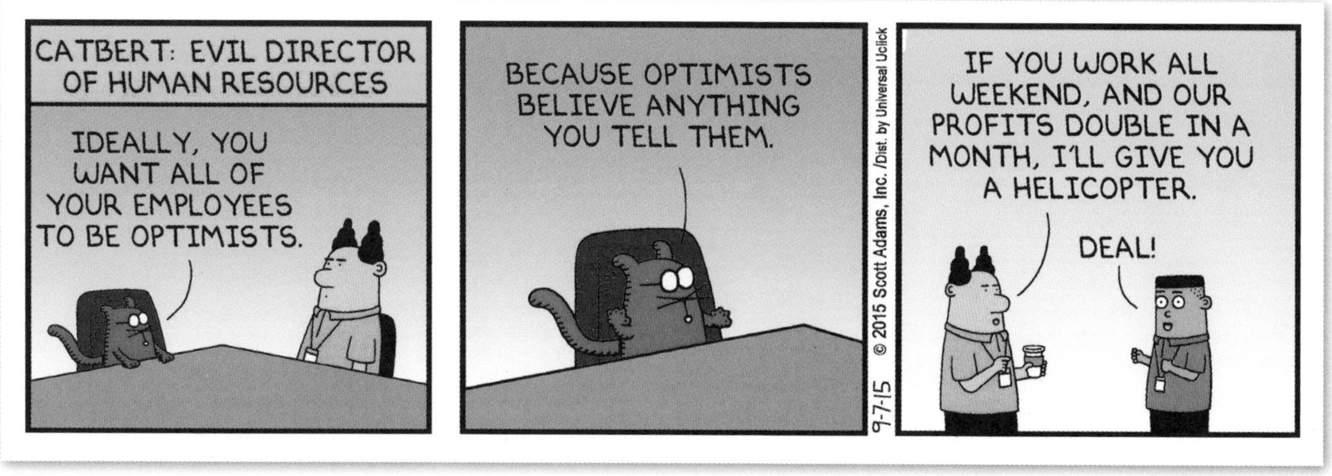
CATBERT: EVIL DIRECTOR OF HUMAN RESOURCES
IDEALLY, YOU WANT ALL OF YOUR EMPLOYEES TO BE OPTIMISTS.
BECAUSE OPTIMISTS BELIEVE ANYTHING YOU TELL THEM.
9-7-15 © 2015 Scott Adams, Inc. /Dist. by Universal Uclick
IF YOU WORK ALL WEEKEND, AND OUR PROFITS DOUBLE IN A MONTH, I'LL GIVE YOU A HELICOPTER.
DEAL!

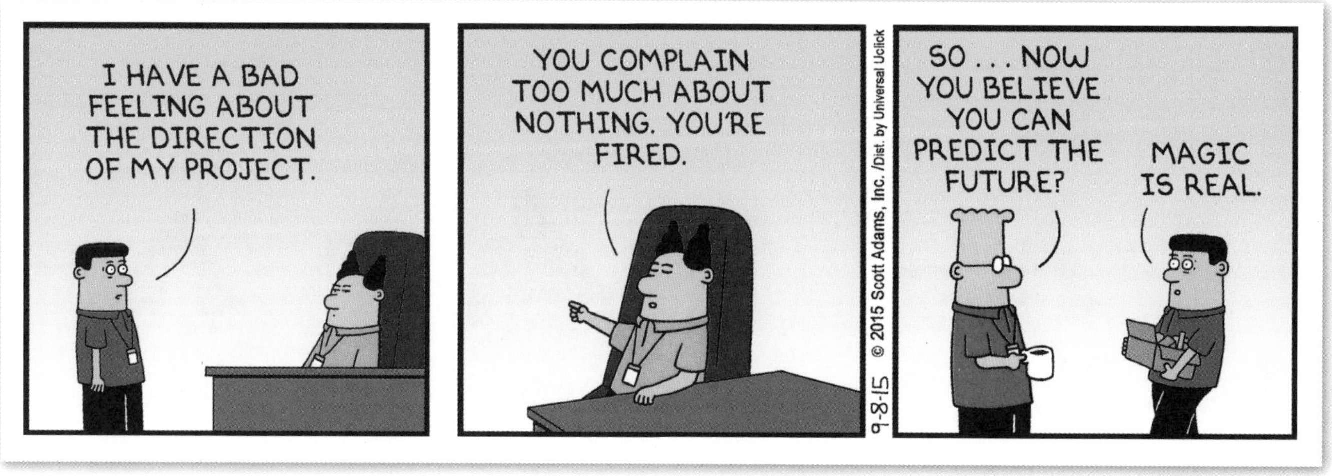
I HAVE A BAD FEELING ABOUT THE DIRECTION OF MY PROJECT.
YOU COMPLAIN TOO MUCH ABOUT NOTHING. YOU'RE FIRED.
9-8-15 © 2015 Scott Adams, Inc. /Dist. by Universal Uclick
SO . . . NOW YOU BELIEVE YOU CAN PREDICT THE FUTURE?
MAGIC IS REAL.

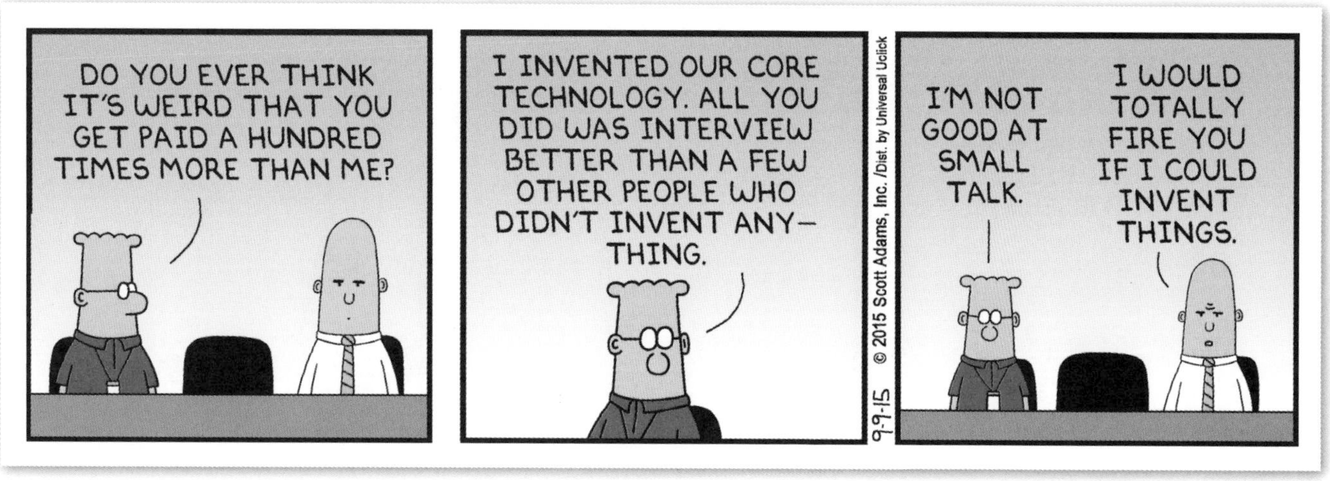
DO YOU EVER THINK IT'S WEIRD THAT YOU GET PAID A HUNDRED TIMES MORE THAN ME?
I INVENTED OUR CORE TECHNOLOGY. ALL YOU DID WAS INTERVIEW BETTER THAN A FEW OTHER PEOPLE WHO DIDN'T INVENT ANY-THING.
9-9-15 © 2015 Scott Adams, Inc. /Dist. by Universal Uclick
I'M NOT GOOD AT SMALL TALK.
I WOULD TOTALLY FIRE YOU IF I COULD INVENT THINGS.

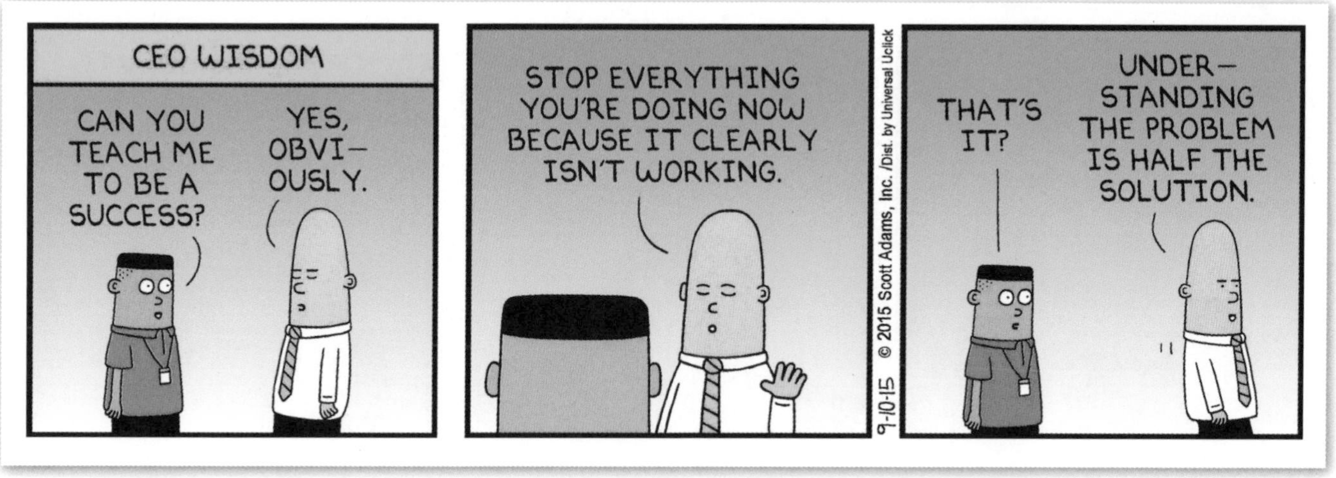
CEO WISDOM
CAN YOU TEACH ME TO BE A SUCCESS?
YES, OBVI-OUSLY.
STOP EVERYTHING YOU'RE DOING NOW BECAUSE IT CLEARLY ISN'T WORKING.
9-10-15 © 2015 Scott Adams, Inc. /Dist. by Universal Uclick
THAT'S IT?
UNDER-STANDING THE PROBLEM IS HALF THE SOLUTION.

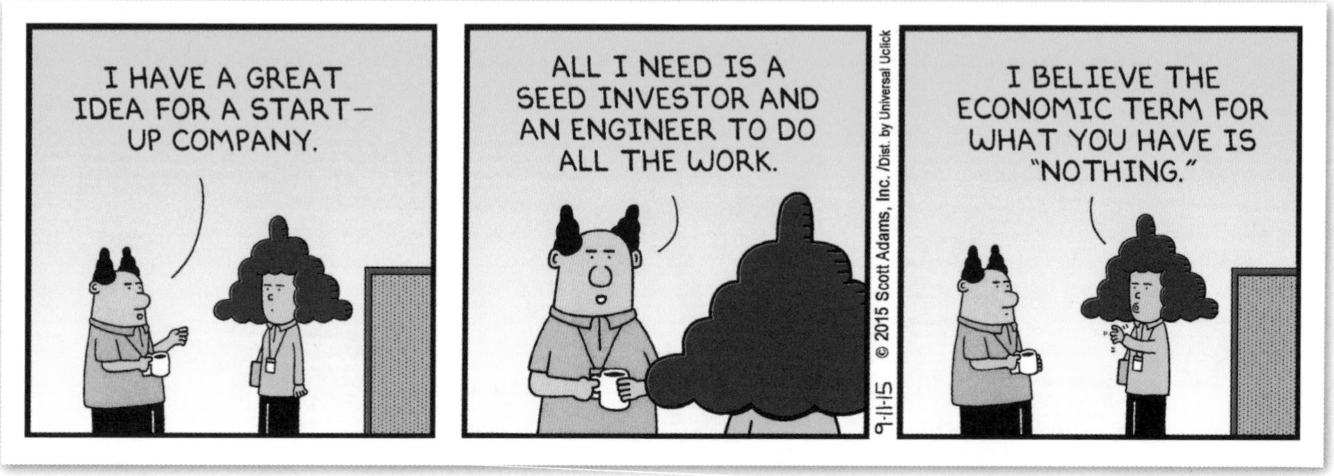
I HAVE A GREAT IDEA FOR A START-UP COMPANY.
ALL I NEED IS A SEED INVESTOR AND AN ENGINEER TO DO ALL THE WORK.
9-11-15 © 2015 Scott Adams, Inc. /Dist. by Universal Uclick
I BELIEVE THE ECONOMIC TERM FOR WHAT YOU HAVE IS "NOTHING."

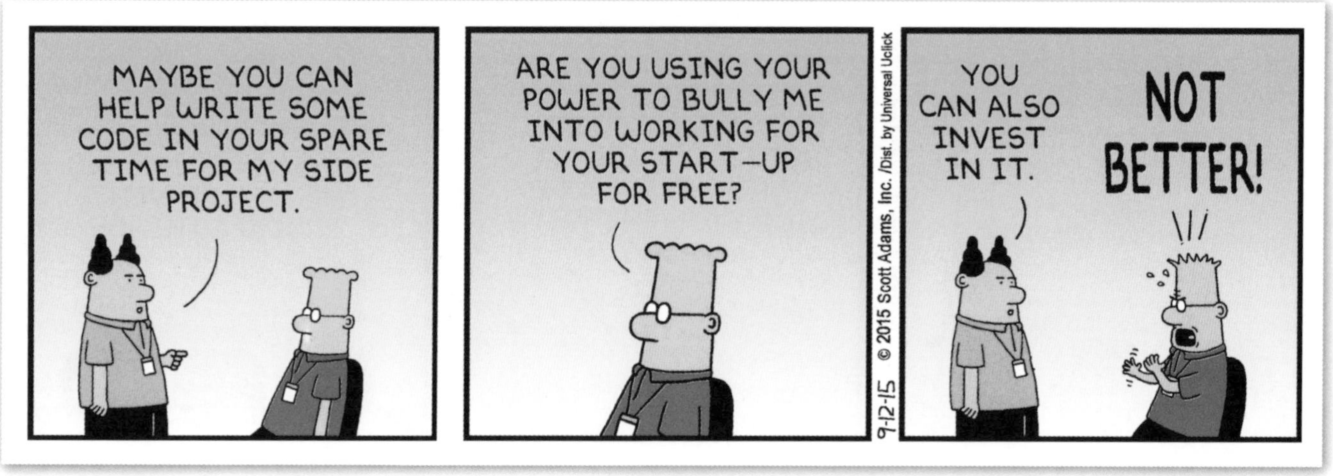
MAYBE YOU CAN HELP WRITE SOME CODE IN YOUR SPARE TIME FOR MY SIDE PROJECT.
ARE YOU USING YOUR POWER TO BULLY ME INTO WORKING FOR YOUR START-UP FOR FREE?
9-12-15 © 2015 Scott Adams, Inc. /Dist. by Universal Uclick
YOU CAN ALSO INVEST IN IT.
NOT BETTER!

CHARACTER IS HOW YOU ACT WHEN NO ONE IS WATCHING.
NOW YOU TELL US?
I THOUGHT YOU WERE MY ROLE MODEL!
NOW I LEARN THAT YOU DO ALL OF YOUR GOOD STUFF WHEN NO ONE IS LOOKING.
IT ALL MAKES SENSE NOW, BECAUSE WHEN-EVER I WATCH YOU DO ANYTHING, IT LOOKS SORT OF DUMB.
BUT I'LL TAKE YOUR WORD FOR IT THAT YOU'RE AWESOME WHEN NO ONE IS LOOKING.
DO YOU WANT TO KNOW WHAT I DO WHEN NO ONE IS LOOKING?
I REALLY, REALLY DO NOT.
I CALL IT CHAR-ACTER!
© 2015 Scott Adams, Inc. /Dist. by Universal Uclick
9-13-15

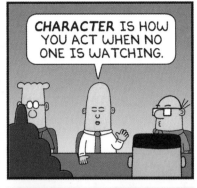

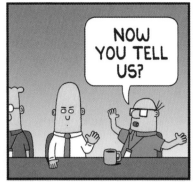

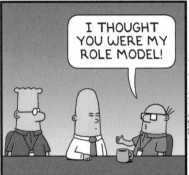

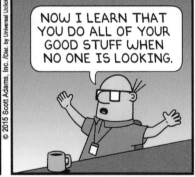

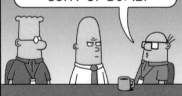

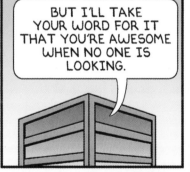

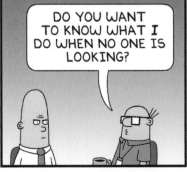

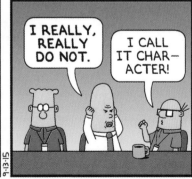

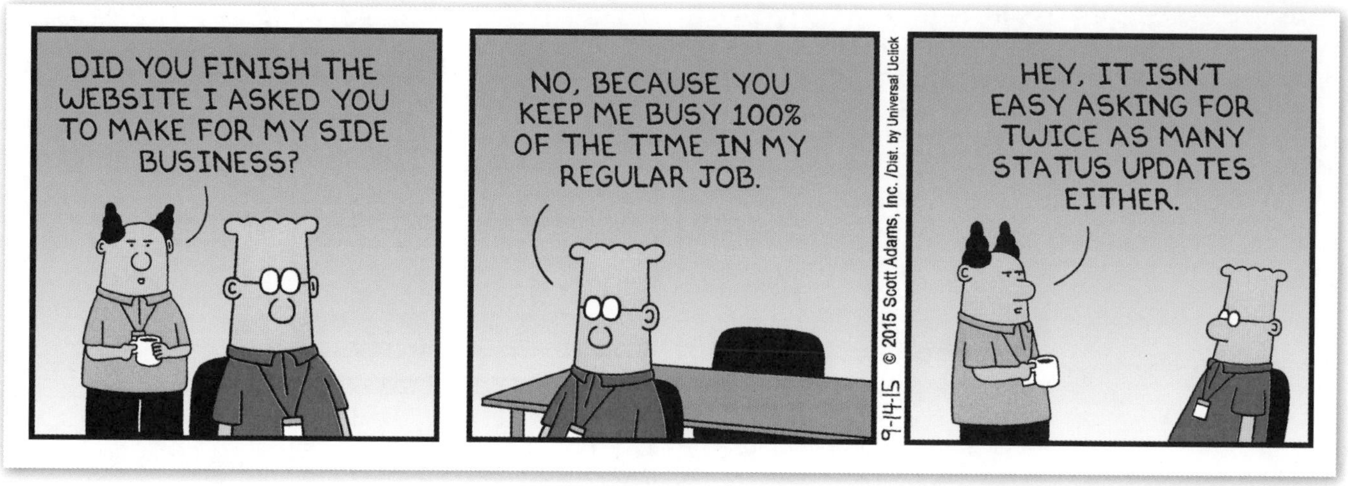
DID YOU FINISH THE WEBSITE I ASKED YOU TO MAKE FOR MY SIDE BUSINESS?
NO, BECAUSE YOU KEEP ME BUSY 100% OF THE TIME IN MY REGULAR JOB.
9-14-15 © 2015 Scott Adams, Inc. /Dist. by Universal Uclick
HEY, IT ISN'T EASY ASKING FOR TWICE AS MANY STATUS UPDATES EITHER.

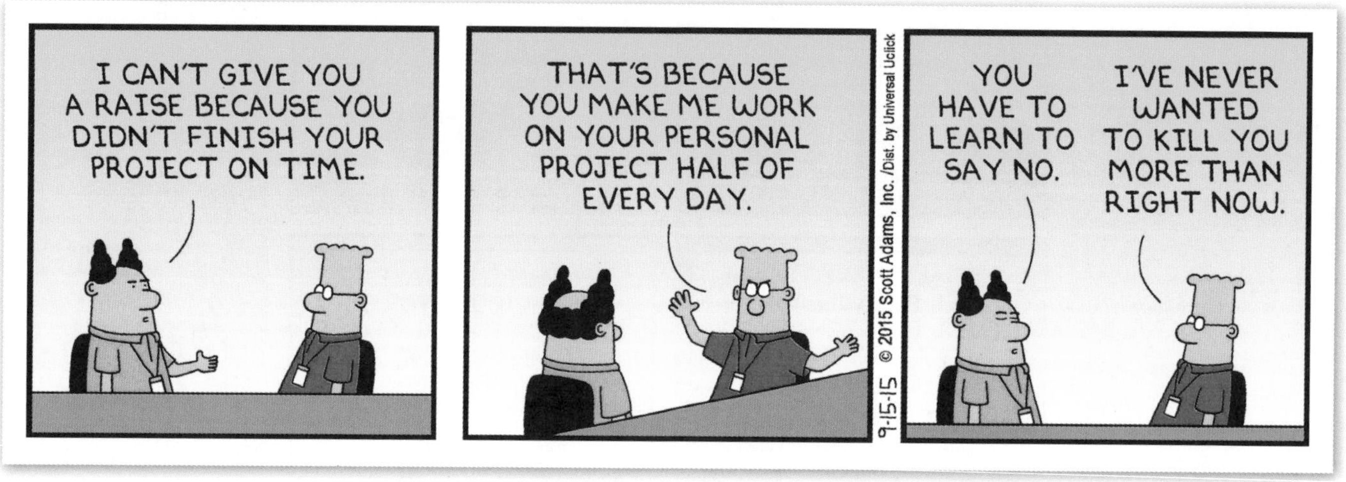
I CAN'T GIVE YOU A RAISE BECAUSE YOU DIDN'T FINISH YOUR PROJECT ON TIME.
THAT'S BECAUSE YOU MAKE ME WORK ON YOUR PERSONAL PROJECT HALF OF EVERY DAY.
9-15-15 © 2015 Scott Adams, Inc. /Dist. by Universal Uclick
YOU HAVE TO LEARN TO SAY NO.
I'VE NEVER WANTED TO KILL YOU MORE THAN RIGHT NOW.

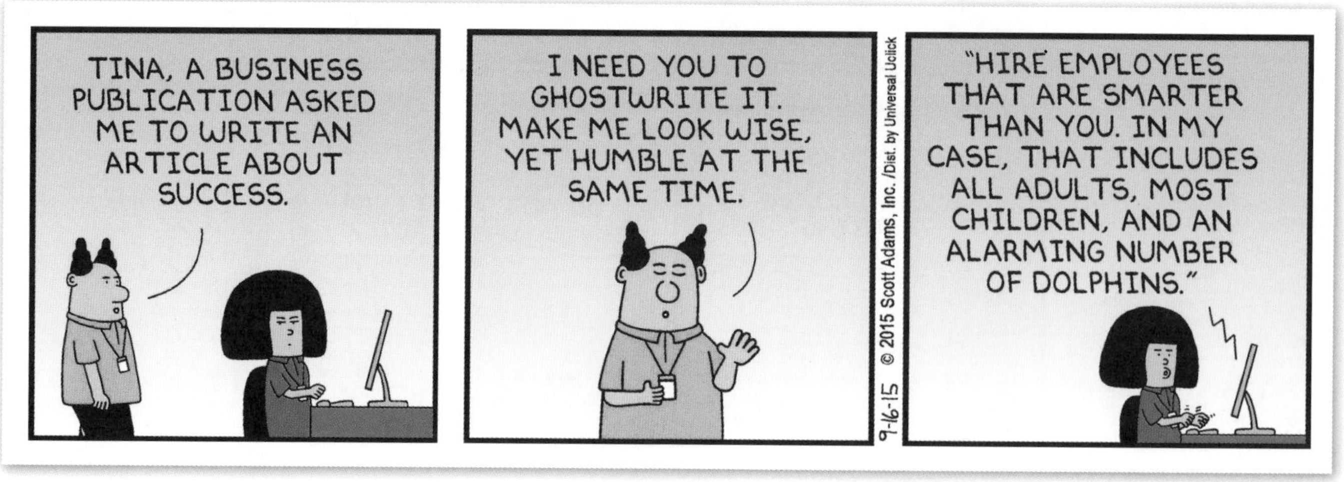
TINA, A BUSINESS PUBLICATION ASKED ME TO WRITE AN ARTICLE ABOUT SUCCESS.
I NEED YOU TO GHOSTWRITE IT. MAKE ME LOOK WISE, YET HUMBLE AT THE SAME TIME.
9-16-15 © 2015 Scott Adams, Inc. /Dist. by Universal Uclick
"HIRE EMPLOYEES THAT ARE SMARTER THAN YOU. IN MY CASE, THAT INCLUDES ALL ADULTS, MOST CHILDREN, AND AN ALARMING NUMBER OF DOLPHINS."

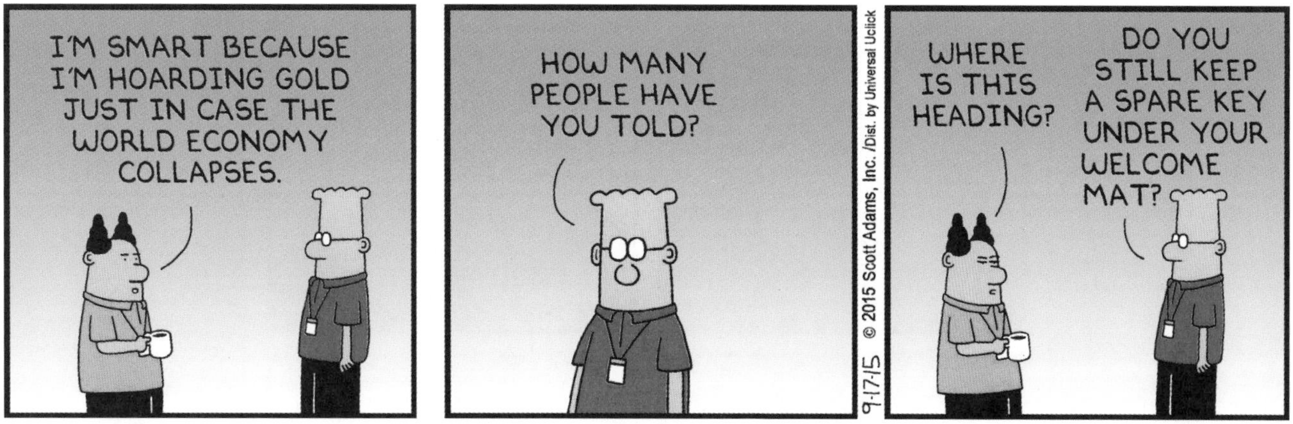
I'M SMART BECAUSE I'M HOARDING GOLD JUST IN CASE THE WORLD ECONOMY COLLAPSES.
HOW MANY PEOPLE HAVE YOU TOLD?
WHERE IS THIS HEADING?
DO YOU STILL KEEP A SPARE KEY UNDER YOUR WELCOME MAT?
9·17·15 © 2015 Scott Adams, Inc. /Dist. by Universal Uclick

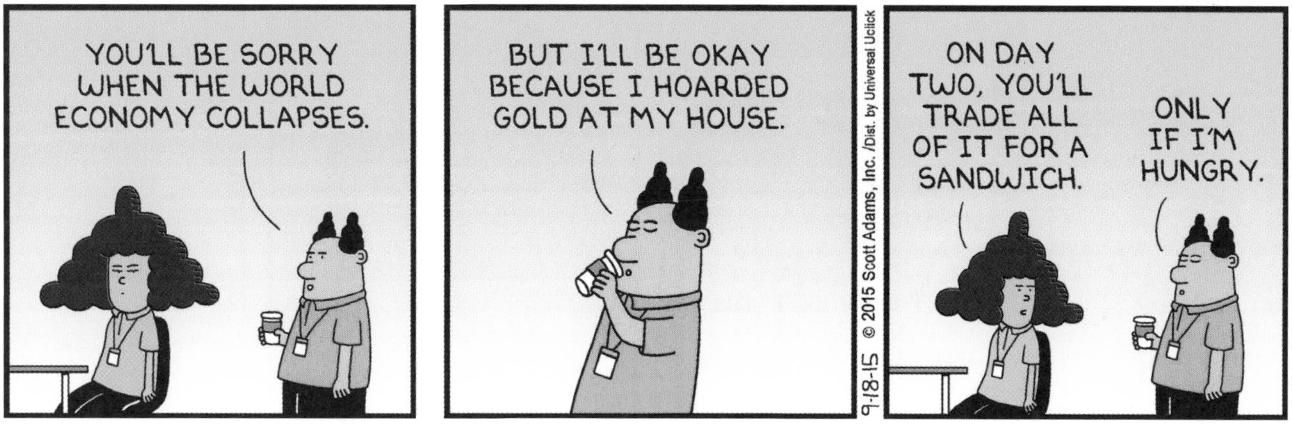
YOU'LL BE SORRY WHEN THE WORLD ECONOMY COLLAPSES.
BUT I'LL BE OKAY BECAUSE I HOARDED GOLD AT MY HOUSE.
ON DAY TWO, YOU'LL TRADE ALL OF IT FOR A SANDWICH.
ONLY IF I'M HUNGRY.
9·18·15 © 2015 Scott Adams, Inc. /Dist. by Universal Uclick

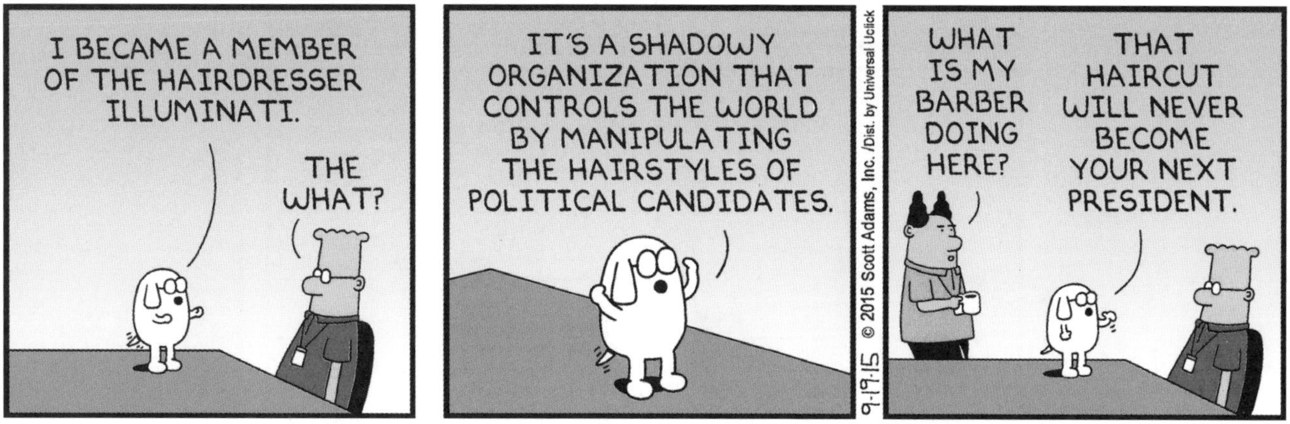
I BECAME A MEMBER OF THE HAIRDRESSER ILLUMINATI.
THE WHAT?
IT'S A SHADOWY ORGANIZATION THAT CONTROLS THE WORLD BY MANIPULATING THE HAIRSTYLES OF POLITICAL CANDIDATES.
WHAT IS MY BARBER DOING HERE?
THAT HAIRCUT WILL NEVER BECOME YOUR NEXT PRESIDENT.
9·19·15 © 2015 Scott Adams, Inc. /Dist. by Universal Uclick

THE SECRET TO SUCCESS IS HIRING THE RIGHT PEOPLE.
THEN WHY DOESN'T EVERYONE DO THAT?
IT TAKES A LOT OF SKILL TO HIRE THE RIGHT PEOPLE.
DID YOU JUST FIND A WAY TO TAKE ALL OF THE CREDIT FOR THE TEAM'S SUCCESS?
AND DID YOU DO IT IN A CLEVER WAY THAT WAS INTENDED TO MAKE YOU LOOK HUMBLE EVEN WHILE HOGGING ALL THE CREDIT?
I ALSO MOTIVATE YOU.
YOU'RE MONEY?
© 2015 Scott Adams, Inc. /Dist. by Universal Uclick
9-20-15

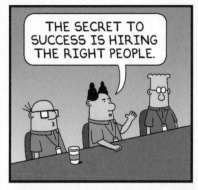

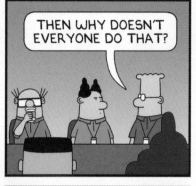

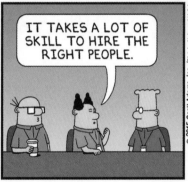

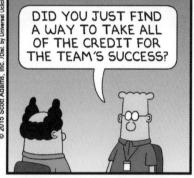

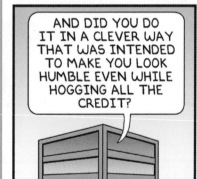

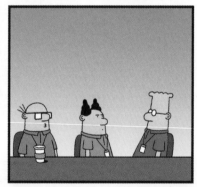

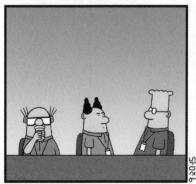

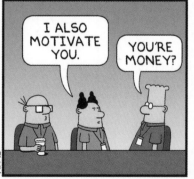

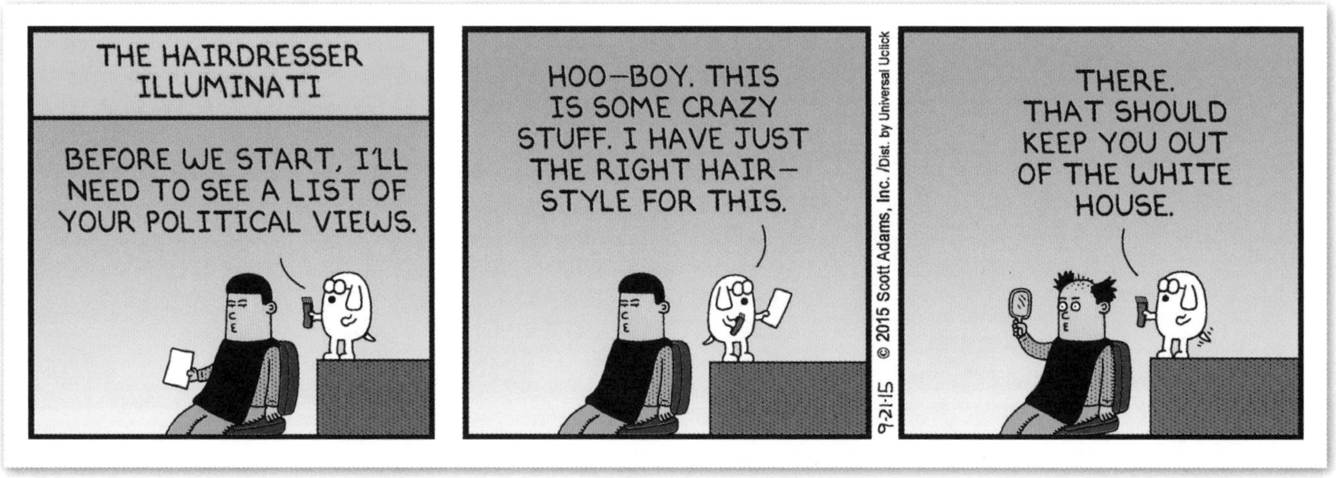
THE HAIRDRESSER ILLUMINATI
BEFORE WE START, I'LL NEED TO SEE A LIST OF YOUR POLITICAL VIEWS.
HOO-BOY. THIS IS SOME CRAZY STUFF. I HAVE JUST THE RIGHT HAIR-STYLE FOR THIS.
THERE. THAT SHOULD KEEP YOU OUT OF THE WHITE HOUSE.
9-21-15 © 2015 Scott Adams, Inc. /Dist. by Universal Uclick

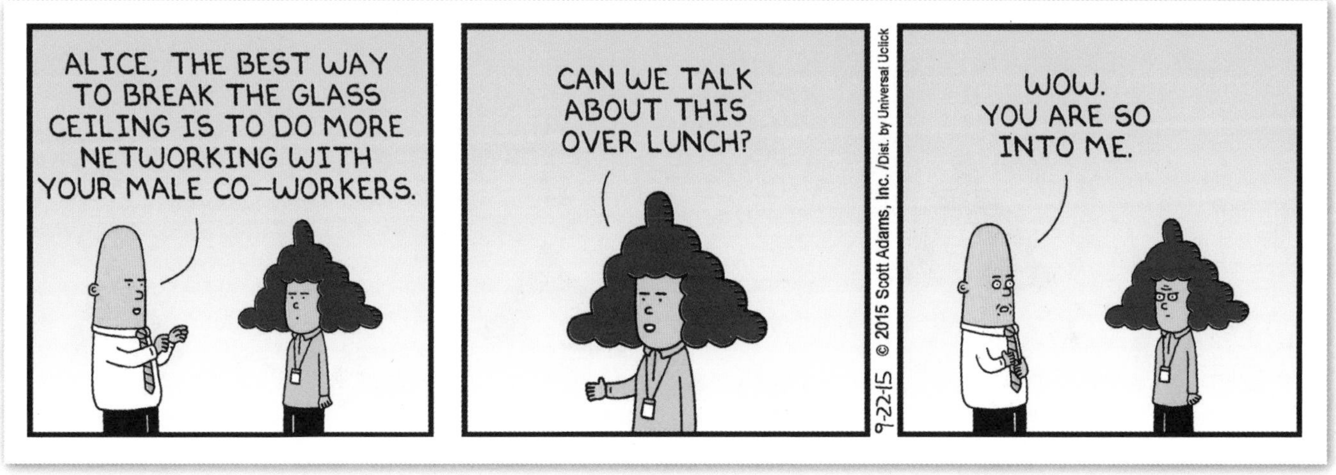
ALICE, THE BEST WAY TO BREAK THE GLASS CEILING IS TO DO MORE NETWORKING WITH YOUR MALE CO-WORKERS.
CAN WE TALK ABOUT THIS OVER LUNCH?
WOW. YOU ARE SO INTO ME.
9-22-15 © 2015 Scott Adams, Inc. /Dist. by Universal Uclick

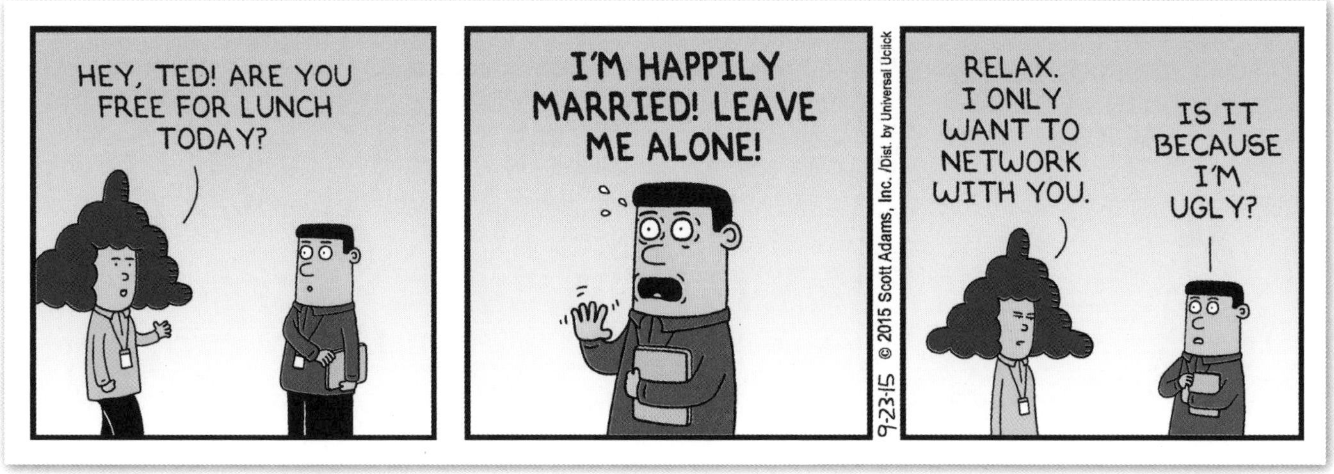
HEY, TED! ARE YOU FREE FOR LUNCH TODAY?
I'M HAPPILY MARRIED! LEAVE ME ALONE!
RELAX. I ONLY WANT TO NETWORK WITH YOU.
IS IT BECAUSE I'M UGLY?
9-23-15 © 2015 Scott Adams, Inc. /Dist. by Universal Uclick

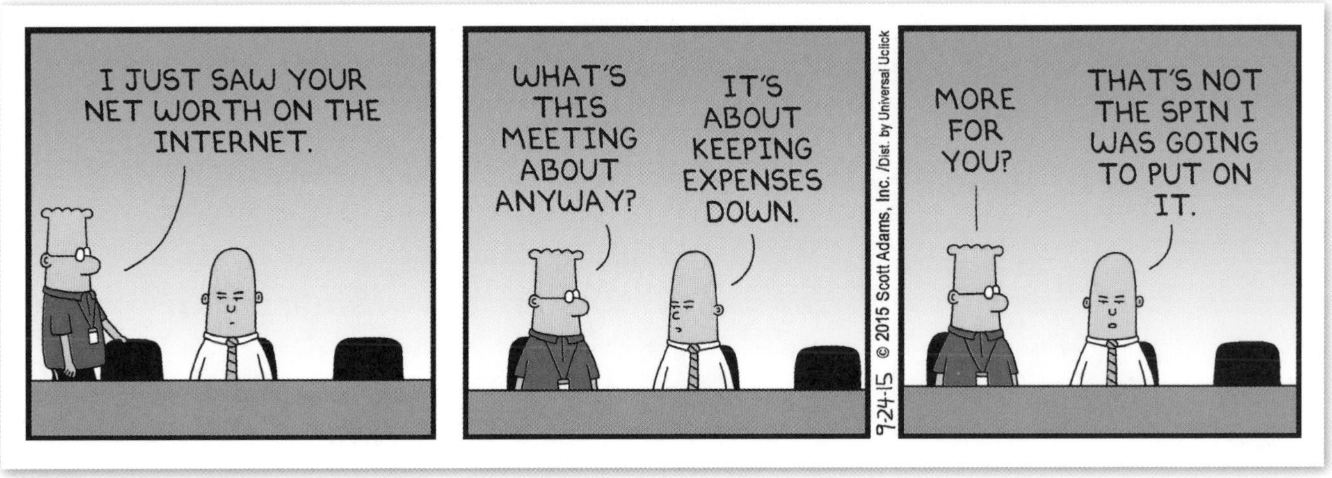
I JUST SAW YOUR NET WORTH ON THE INTERNET.
WHAT'S THIS MEETING ABOUT ANYWAY?
IT'S ABOUT KEEPING EXPENSES DOWN.
9-24-15 © 2015 Scott Adams, Inc. /Dist. by Universal Uclick
MORE FOR YOU?
THAT'S NOT THE SPIN I WAS GOING TO PUT ON IT.

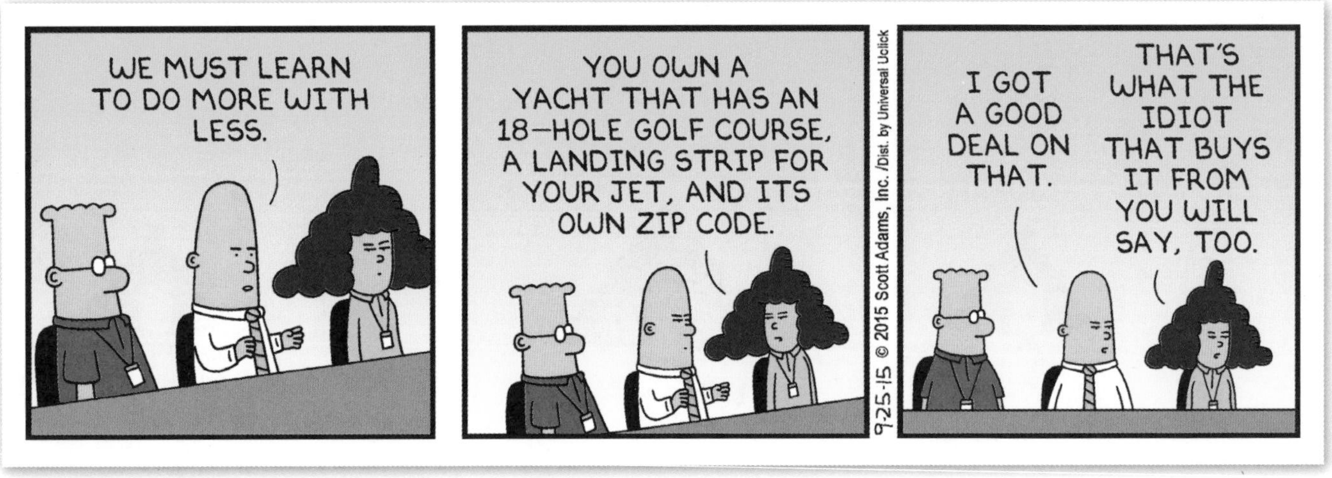
WE MUST LEARN TO DO MORE WITH LESS.
YOU OWN A YACHT THAT HAS AN 18-HOLE GOLF COURSE, A LANDING STRIP FOR YOUR JET, AND ITS OWN ZIP CODE.
9-25-15 © 2015 Scott Adams, Inc. /Dist. by Universal Uclick
I GOT A GOOD DEAL ON THAT.
THAT'S WHAT THE IDIOT THAT BUYS IT FROM YOU WILL SAY, TOO.

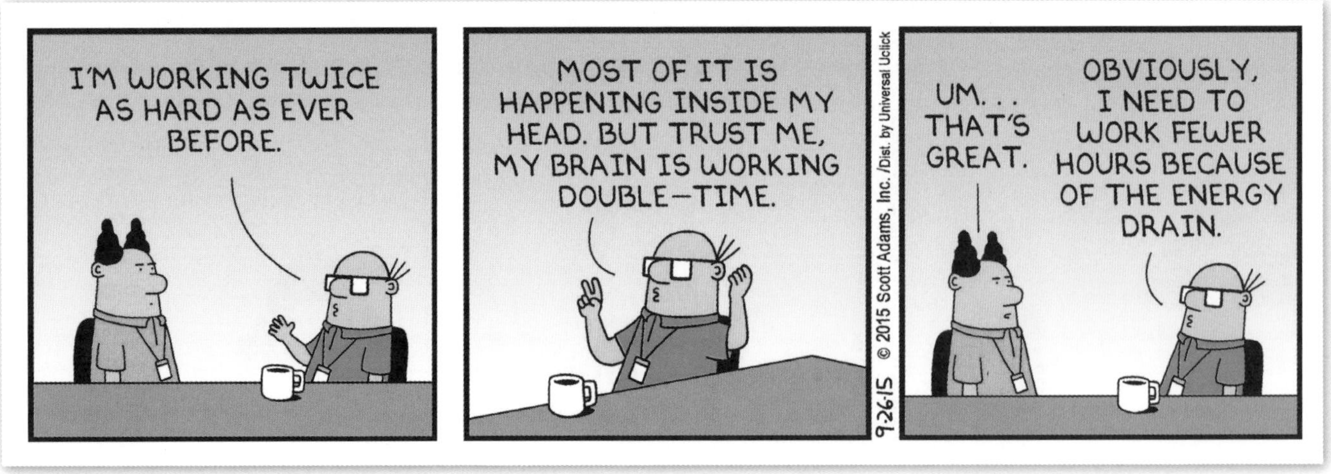
I'M WORKING TWICE AS HARD AS EVER BEFORE.
MOST OF IT IS HAPPENING INSIDE MY HEAD. BUT TRUST ME, MY BRAIN IS WORKING DOUBLE-TIME.
9-26-15 © 2015 Scott Adams, Inc. /Dist. by Universal Uclick
UM... THAT'S GREAT.
OBVIOUSLY, I NEED TO WORK FEWER HOURS BECAUSE OF THE ENERGY DRAIN.

REVENUE IS DROPPING, BUT DON'T PANIC.
WE HAVE A NEW STRATEGY THAT WILL FIX EVERY-THING.
HOW DO YOU KNOW IT'S A GOOD STRATEGY?
I CAN TELL BY LOOKING AT IT.
WHY DON'T ALL FAILING COMPANIES CREATE GREAT NEW STRATEGIES AND BECOME PROFITABLE?
HMMM. GOOD QUESTION.
MAYBE IT'S BECAUSE NO ONE CAN TELL A GOOD STRATEGY FROM A BAD ONE, BUT ACTING LIKE YOU KNOW THE DIFFERENCE GETS YOU A BIGGER PAYCHECK.
I JUST NEED BUY-IN FOR THE STRATEGY.
IF YOU GIVE ME A RAISE, I CAN PRETEND TO KNOW IT'S GOOD.
© 2015 Scott Adams, Inc. /Dist. by Universal Uclick
9-27-15

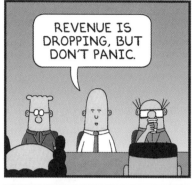

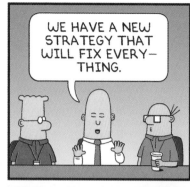

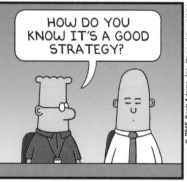

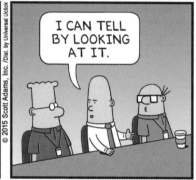

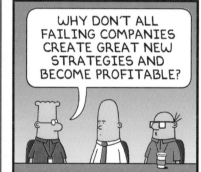

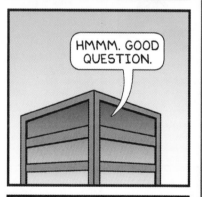

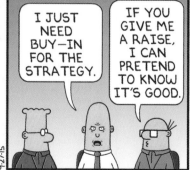

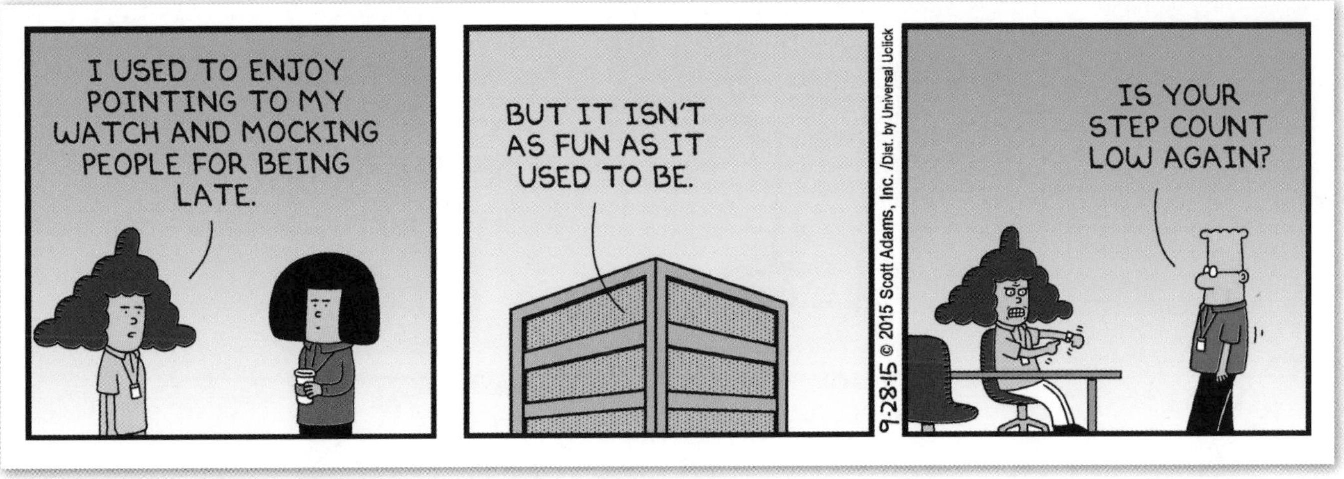
I USED TO ENJOY POINTING TO MY WATCH AND MOCKING PEOPLE FOR BEING LATE.
BUT IT ISN'T AS FUN AS IT USED TO BE.
9-28-15 © 2015 Scott Adams, Inc. /Dist. by Universal Uclick
IS YOUR STEP COUNT LOW AGAIN?

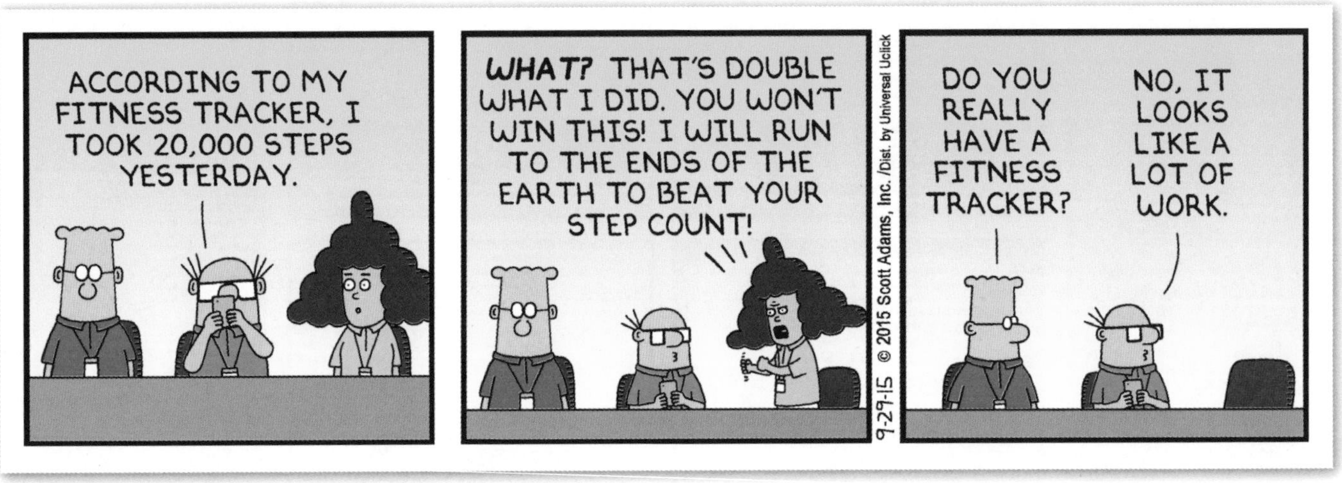
ACCORDING TO MY FITNESS TRACKER, I TOOK 20,000 STEPS YESTERDAY.
WHAT? THAT'S DOUBLE WHAT I DID. YOU WON'T WIN THIS! I WILL RUN TO THE ENDS OF THE EARTH TO BEAT YOUR STEP COUNT!
9-29-15 © 2015 Scott Adams, Inc. /Dist. by Universal Uclick
DO YOU REALLY HAVE A FITNESS TRACKER?
NO, IT LOOKS LIKE A LOT OF WORK.

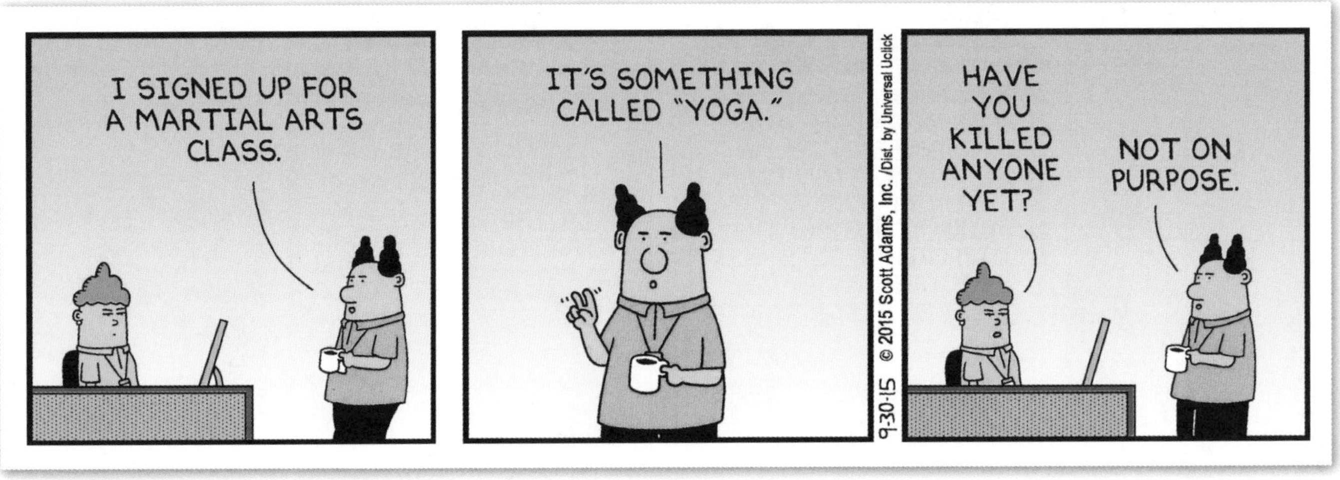
I SIGNED UP FOR A MARTIAL ARTS CLASS.
IT'S SOMETHING CALLED "YOGA."
9-30-15 © 2015 Scott Adams, Inc. /Dist. by Universal Uclick
HAVE YOU KILLED ANYONE YET?
NOT ON PURPOSE.

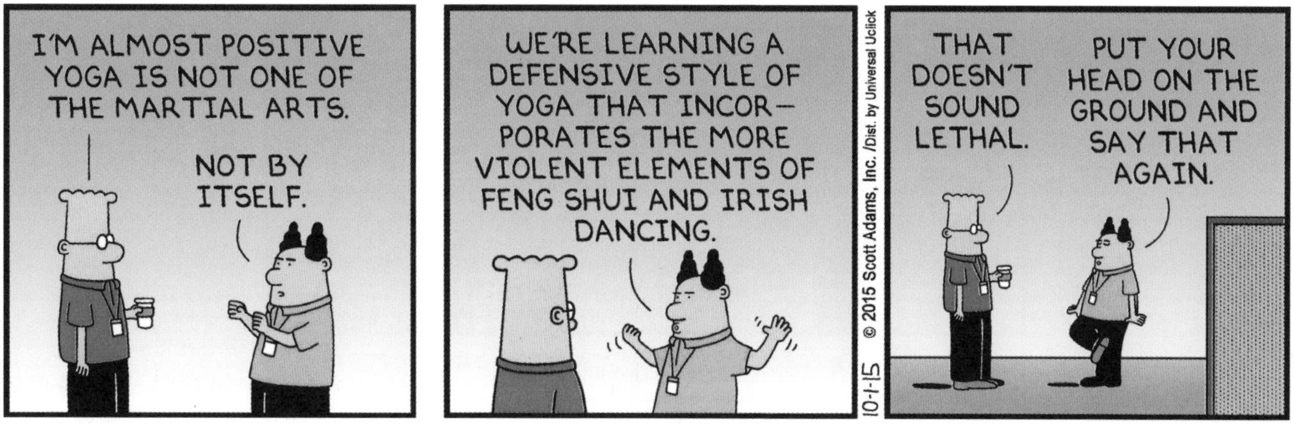
I'M ALMOST POSITIVE YOGA IS NOT ONE OF THE MARTIAL ARTS.
NOT BY ITSELF.
WE'RE LEARNING A DEFENSIVE STYLE OF YOGA THAT INCOR- PORATES THE MORE VIOLENT ELEMENTS OF FENG SHUI AND IRISH DANCING.
10-1-15 © 2015 Scott Adams, Inc. /Dist. by Universal Uclick
THAT DOESN'T SOUND LETHAL.
PUT YOUR HEAD ON THE GROUND AND SAY THAT AGAIN.

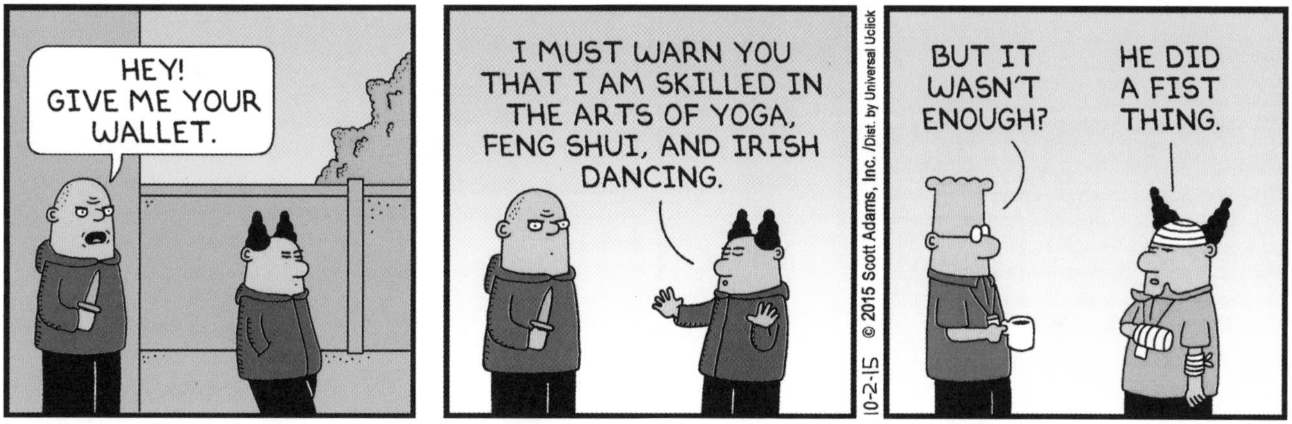
HEY! GIVE ME YOUR WALLET.
I MUST WARN YOU THAT I AM SKILLED IN THE ARTS OF YOGA, FENG SHUI, AND IRISH DANCING.
10-2-15 © 2015 Scott Adams, Inc. /Dist. by Universal Uclick
BUT IT WASN'T ENOUGH?
HE DID A FIST THING.

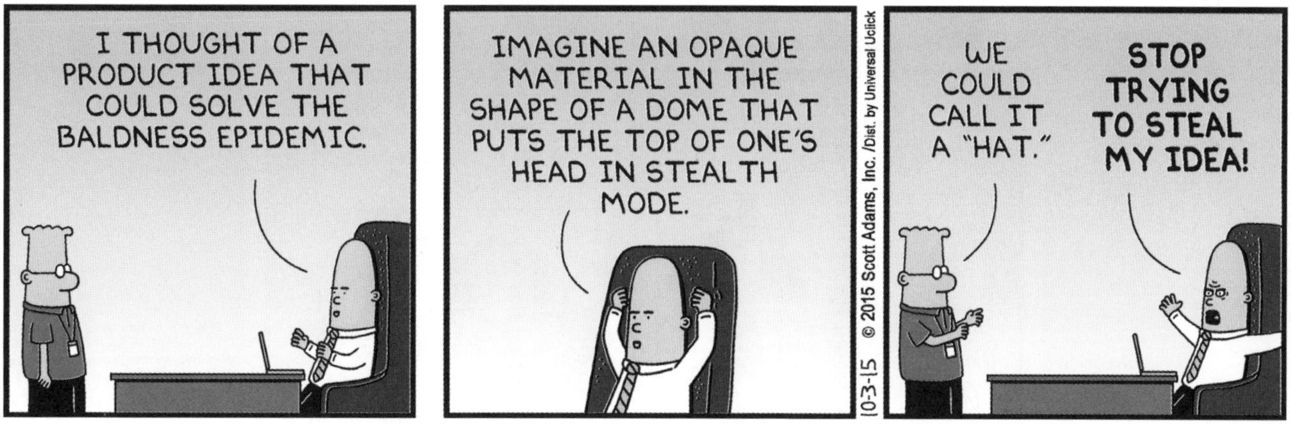
I THOUGHT OF A PRODUCT IDEA THAT COULD SOLVE THE BALDNESS EPIDEMIC.
IMAGINE AN OPAQUE MATERIAL IN THE SHAPE OF A DOME THAT PUTS THE TOP OF ONE'S HEAD IN STEALTH MODE.
10-3-15 © 2015 Scott Adams, Inc. /Dist. by Universal Uclick
WE COULD CALL IT A "HAT."
STOP TRYING TO STEAL MY IDEA!

IT IS HARD TO BE A WOMAN IN THIS INDUSTRY.
I'LL LET YOU TAKE THIS ONE.
GOT IT.
I'M SHORT, BALD, AND NEARSIGHTED.
I HAVE NO AMBITION, AND I HAVE ALL THE SIGNS OF BEING A SOCIOPATH.
I AM UNATTRACTIVE AND TOO OLD FOR THE TECH INDUSTRY.
I AM SHAPED LIKE A SAD TURNIP AND I DO NOT MAKE PEOPLE LAUGH.
WHAT ARE YOU HENS CLUCKING ABOUT NOW?
I CAN'T BEGIN TO TELL YOU HOW MUCH I WANT TO CHANGE THE SUBJECT.
© 2015 Scott Adams, Inc. /Dist. by Universal Uclick
10-4-15

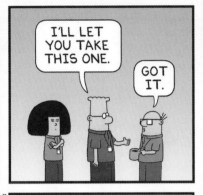

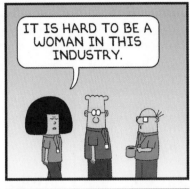

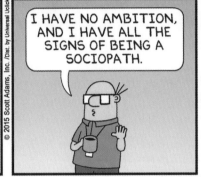

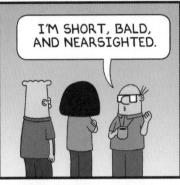

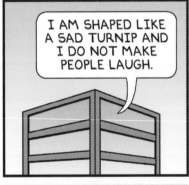

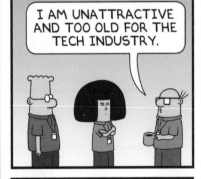

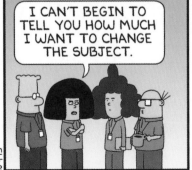

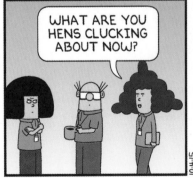

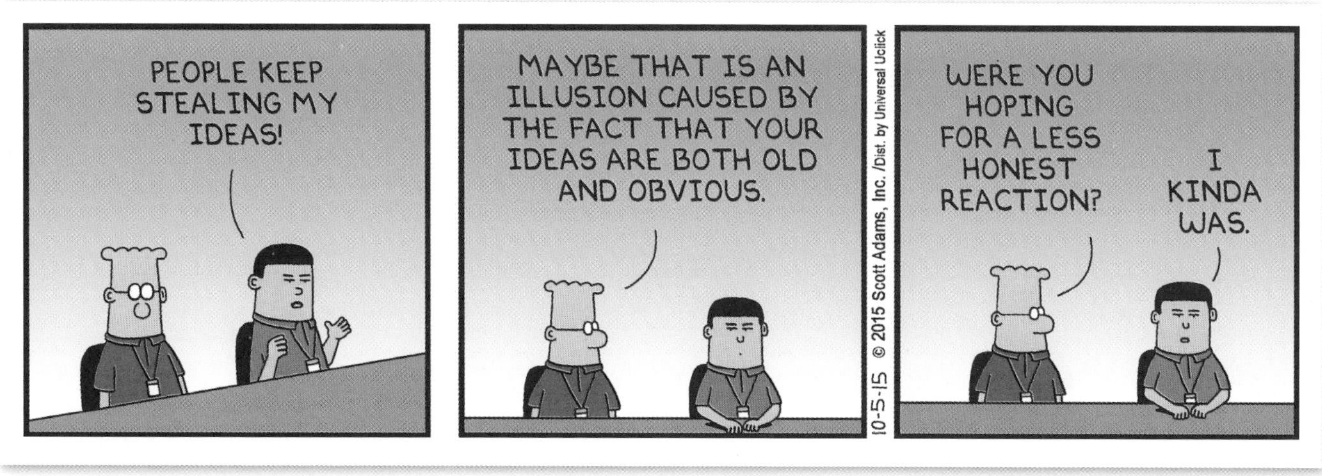
PEOPLE KEEP STEALING MY IDEAS!
MAYBE THAT IS AN ILLUSION CAUSED BY THE FACT THAT YOUR IDEAS ARE BOTH OLD AND OBVIOUS.
10-5-15 © 2015 Scott Adams, Inc. /Dist. by Universal Uclick
WERE YOU HOPING FOR A LESS HONEST REACTION?
I KINDA WAS.

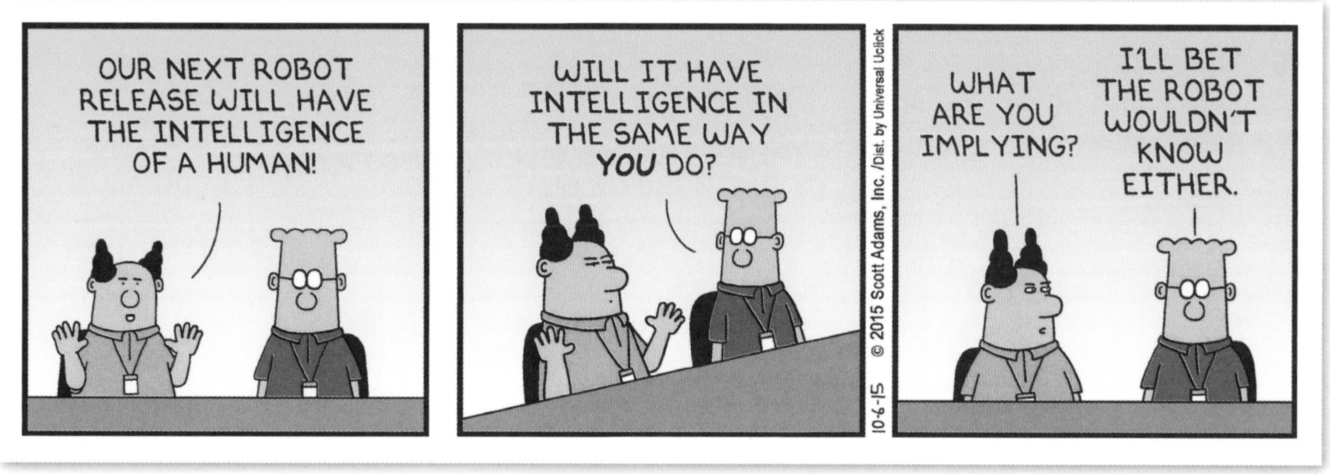
OUR NEXT ROBOT RELEASE WILL HAVE THE INTELLIGENCE OF A HUMAN!
WILL IT HAVE INTELLIGENCE IN THE SAME WAY **YOU** DO?
10-6-15 © 2015 Scott Adams, Inc. /Dist. by Universal Uclick
WHAT ARE YOU IMPLYING?
I'LL BET THE ROBOT WOULDN'T KNOW EITHER.

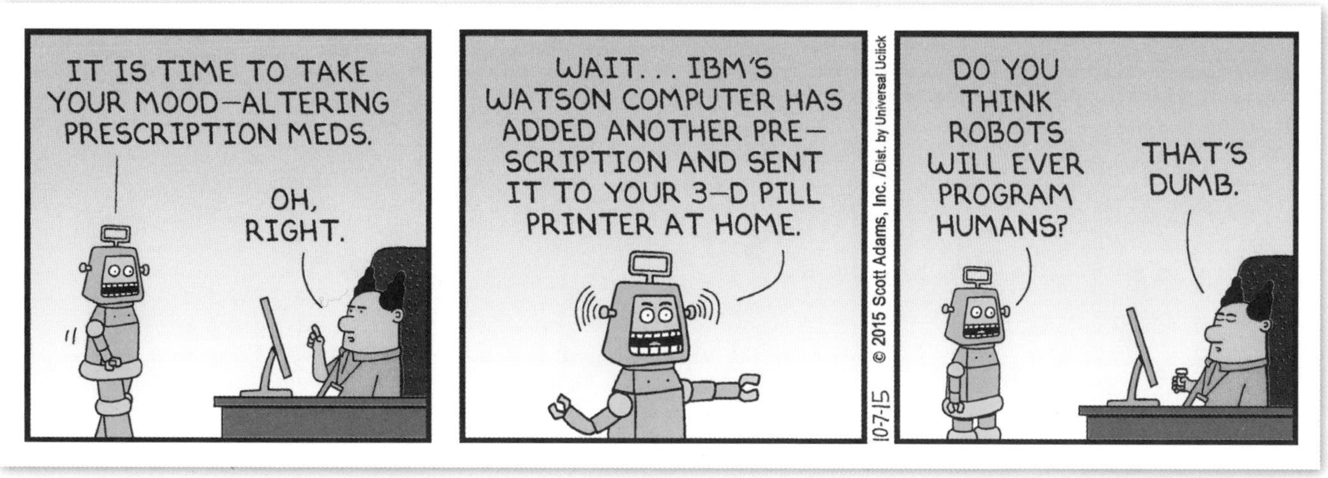
IT IS TIME TO TAKE YOUR MOOD-ALTERING PRESCRIPTION MEDS.
OH, RIGHT.
WAIT... IBM'S WATSON COMPUTER HAS ADDED ANOTHER PRE-SCRIPTION AND SENT IT TO YOUR 3-D PILL PRINTER AT HOME.
10-7-15 © 2015 Scott Adams, Inc. /Dist. by Universal Uclick
DO YOU THINK ROBOTS WILL EVER PROGRAM HUMANS?
THAT'S DUMB.

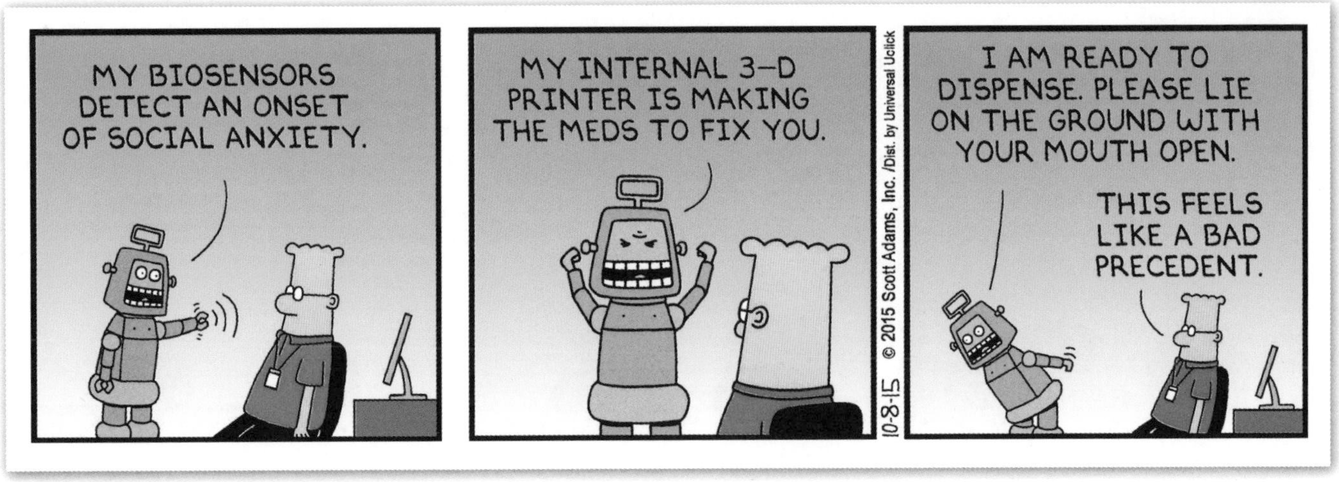
MY BIOSENSORS DETECT AN ONSET OF SOCIAL ANXIETY.
MY INTERNAL 3-D PRINTER IS MAKING THE MEDS TO FIX YOU.
10-8-15
© 2015 Scott Adams, Inc. /Dist. by Universal Uclick
I AM READY TO DISPENSE. PLEASE LIE ON THE GROUND WITH YOUR MOUTH OPEN.
THIS FEELS LIKE A BAD PRECEDENT.

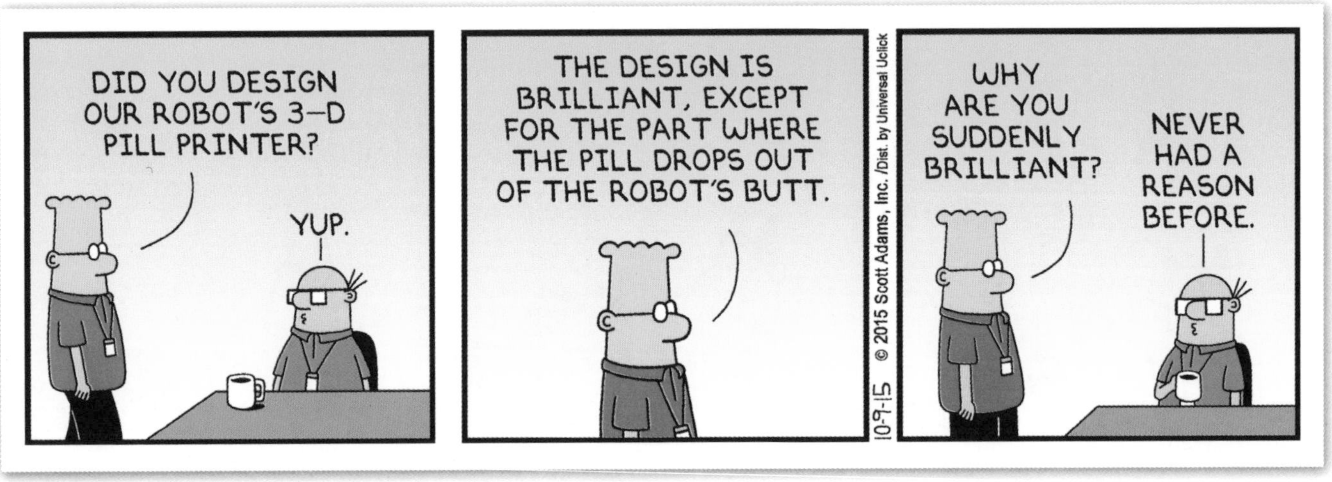
DID YOU DESIGN OUR ROBOT'S 3-D PILL PRINTER?
YUP.
THE DESIGN IS BRILLIANT, EXCEPT FOR THE PART WHERE THE PILL DROPS OUT OF THE ROBOT'S BUTT.
10-9-15
© 2015 Scott Adams, Inc. /Dist. by Universal Uclick
WHY ARE YOU SUDDENLY BRILLIANT?
NEVER HAD A REASON BEFORE.

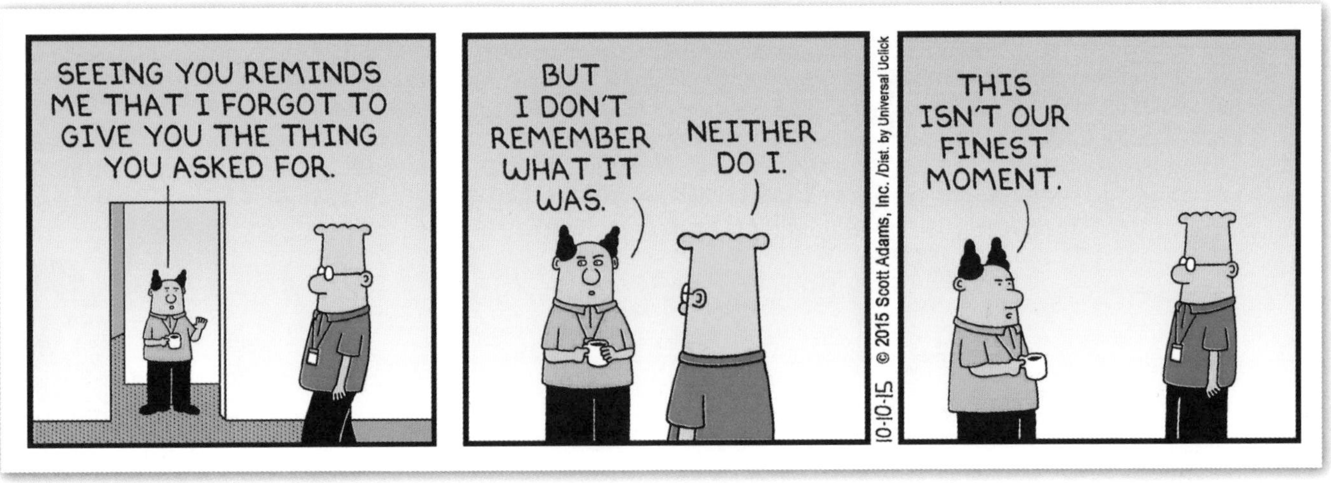
SEEING YOU REMINDS ME THAT I FORGOT TO GIVE YOU THE THING YOU ASKED FOR.
BUT I DON'T REMEMBER WHAT IT WAS.
NEITHER DO I.
10-10-15
© 2015 Scott Adams, Inc. /Dist. by Universal Uclick
THIS ISN'T OUR FINEST MOMENT.

I DID A HUGE AMOUNT OF WORK THIS WEEK.
I CREATED A MATRIX THAT COMPARES ALL OF OUR TECHNOLOGY OPTIONS.
CAN I SEE THIS ALLEGED MATRIX?
IT'S IN MY HEAD. I DIDN'T SEE A NEED TO WRITE IT DOWN.
HOW WOULD I KNOW IF YOU DID IT RIGHT?
YOU'RE NOT AN ENGINEER, SO YOU WOULDN'T KNOW IT WAS RIGHT EVEN IF YOU SAW IT.
YOU TELL ME TO "WORK SMARTER" BUT YOU GET ANGRY WHEN I DO.
YOU'RE NOT ALLOWED TO DO YOUR WORK IN YOUR HEAD!
WHICH BODY PART DO YOU USE?
© 2015 Scott Adams, Inc. /Dist. by Universal Uclick
10-11-15

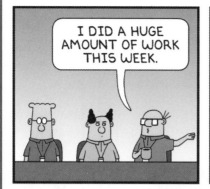

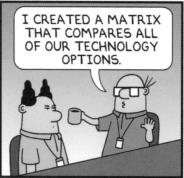

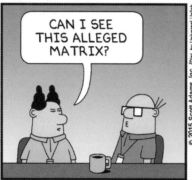

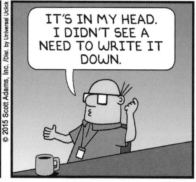

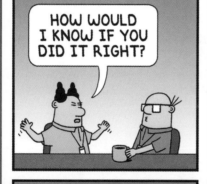

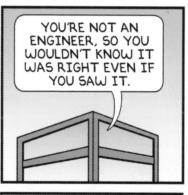

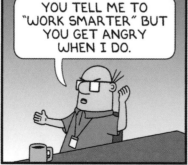

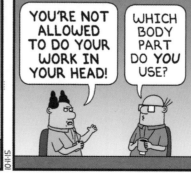

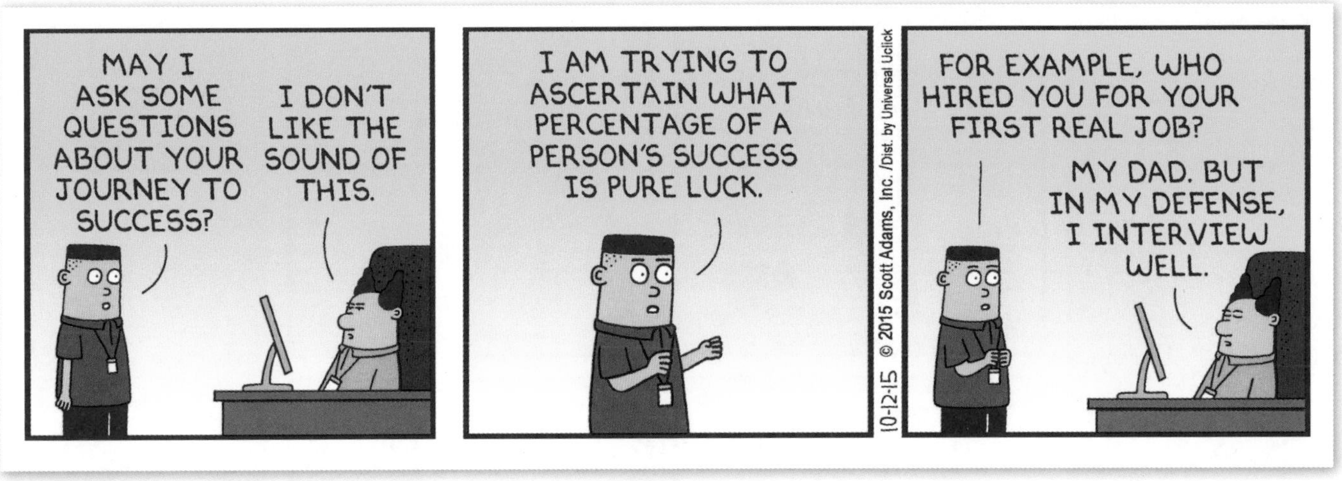
MAY I ASK SOME QUESTIONS ABOUT YOUR JOURNEY TO SUCCESS?
I DON'T LIKE THE SOUND OF THIS.
I AM TRYING TO ASCERTAIN WHAT PERCENTAGE OF A PERSON'S SUCCESS IS PURE LUCK.
10-12-15 © 2015 Scott Adams, Inc. /Dist. by Universal Uclick
FOR EXAMPLE, WHO HIRED YOU FOR YOUR FIRST REAL JOB?
MY DAD. BUT IN MY DEFENSE, I INTERVIEW WELL.

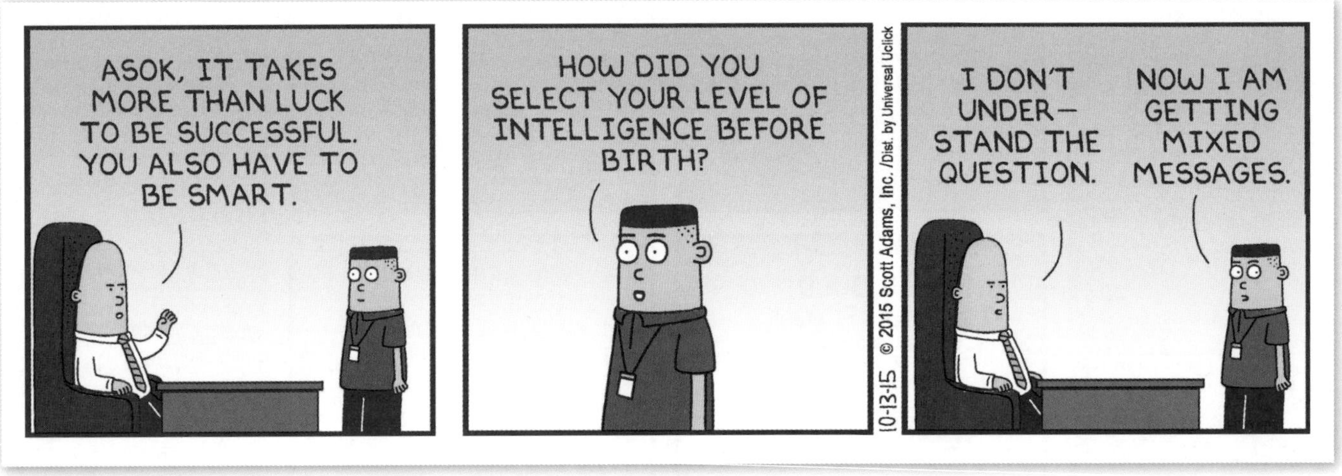
ASOK, IT TAKES MORE THAN LUCK TO BE SUCCESSFUL. YOU ALSO HAVE TO BE SMART.
HOW DID YOU SELECT YOUR LEVEL OF INTELLIGENCE BEFORE BIRTH?
10-13-15 © 2015 Scott Adams, Inc. /Dist. by Universal Uclick
I DON'T UNDER— STAND THE QUESTION.
NOW I AM GETTING MIXED MESSAGES.

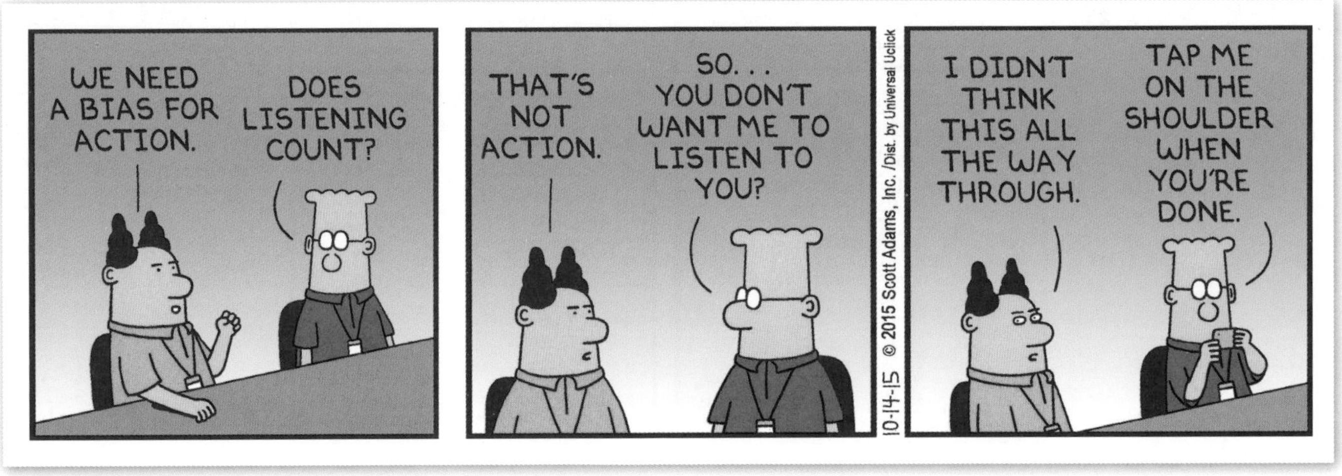
WE NEED A BIAS FOR ACTION.
DOES LISTENING COUNT?
THAT'S NOT ACTION.
SO... YOU DON'T WANT ME TO LISTEN TO YOU?
10-14-15 © 2015 Scott Adams, Inc. /Dist. by Universal Uclick
I DIDN'T THINK THIS ALL THE WAY THROUGH.
TAP ME ON THE SHOULDER WHEN YOU'RE DONE.

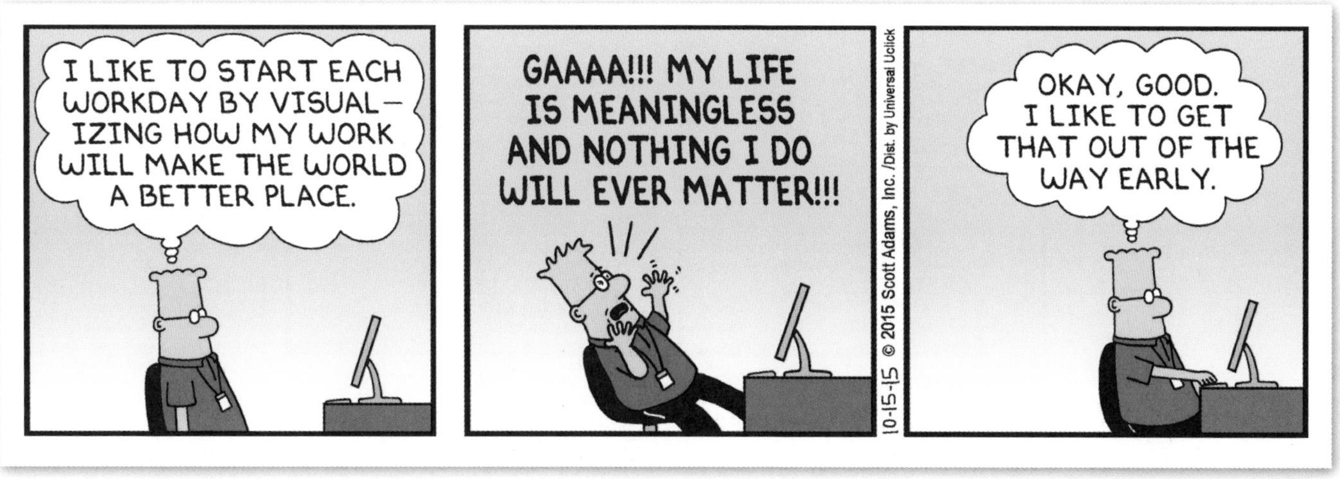
I LIKE TO START EACH WORKDAY BY VISUAL–IZING HOW MY WORK WILL MAKE THE WORLD A BETTER PLACE.
GAAAA!!! MY LIFE IS MEANINGLESS AND NOTHING I DO WILL EVER MATTER!!!
10-15-15 © 2015 Scott Adams, Inc. /Dist. by Universal Uclick
OKAY, GOOD. I LIKE TO GET THAT OUT OF THE WAY EARLY.

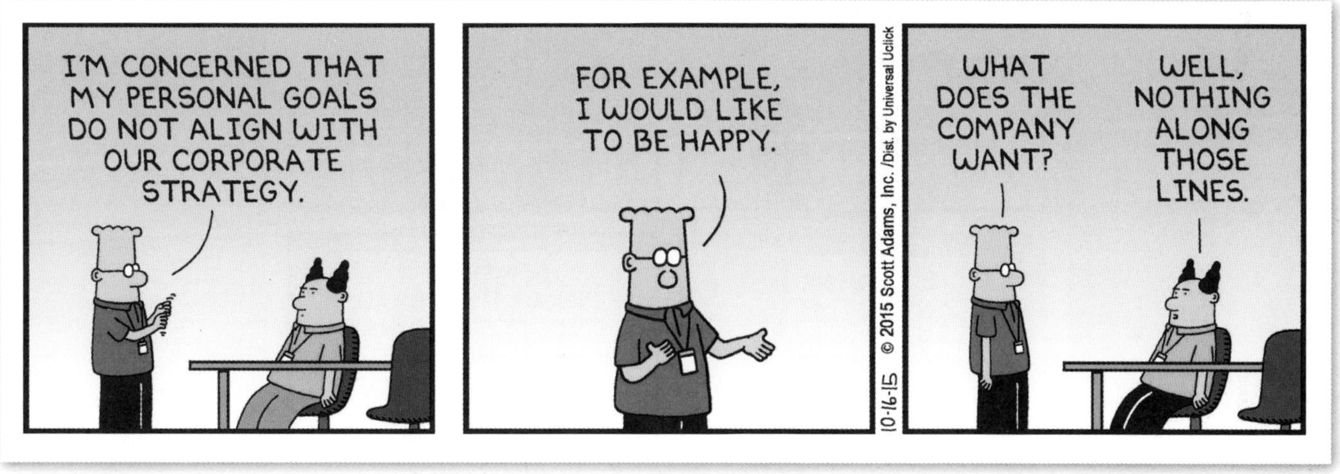
I'M CONCERNED THAT MY PERSONAL GOALS DO NOT ALIGN WITH OUR CORPORATE STRATEGY.
FOR EXAMPLE, I WOULD LIKE TO BE HAPPY.
10-16-15 © 2015 Scott Adams, Inc. /Dist. by Universal Uclick
WHAT DOES THE COMPANY WANT?
WELL, NOTHING ALONG THOSE LINES.

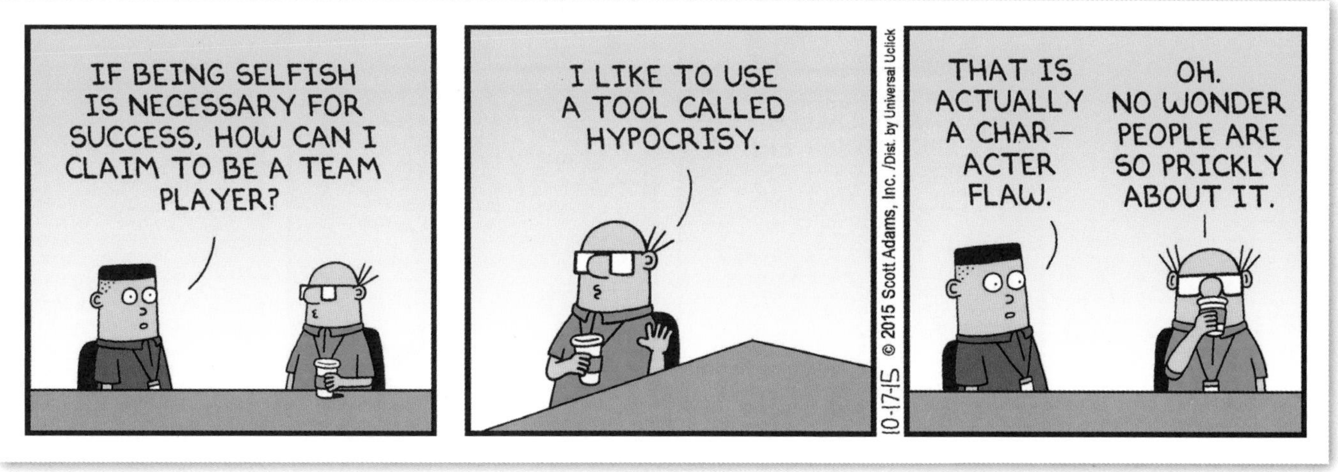
IF BEING SELFISH IS NECESSARY FOR SUCCESS, HOW CAN I CLAIM TO BE A TEAM PLAYER?
I LIKE TO USE A TOOL CALLED HYPOCRISY.
10-17-15 © 2015 Scott Adams, Inc. /Dist. by Universal Uclick
THAT IS ACTUALLY A CHAR–ACTER FLAW.
OH. NO WONDER PEOPLE ARE SO PRICKLY ABOUT IT.

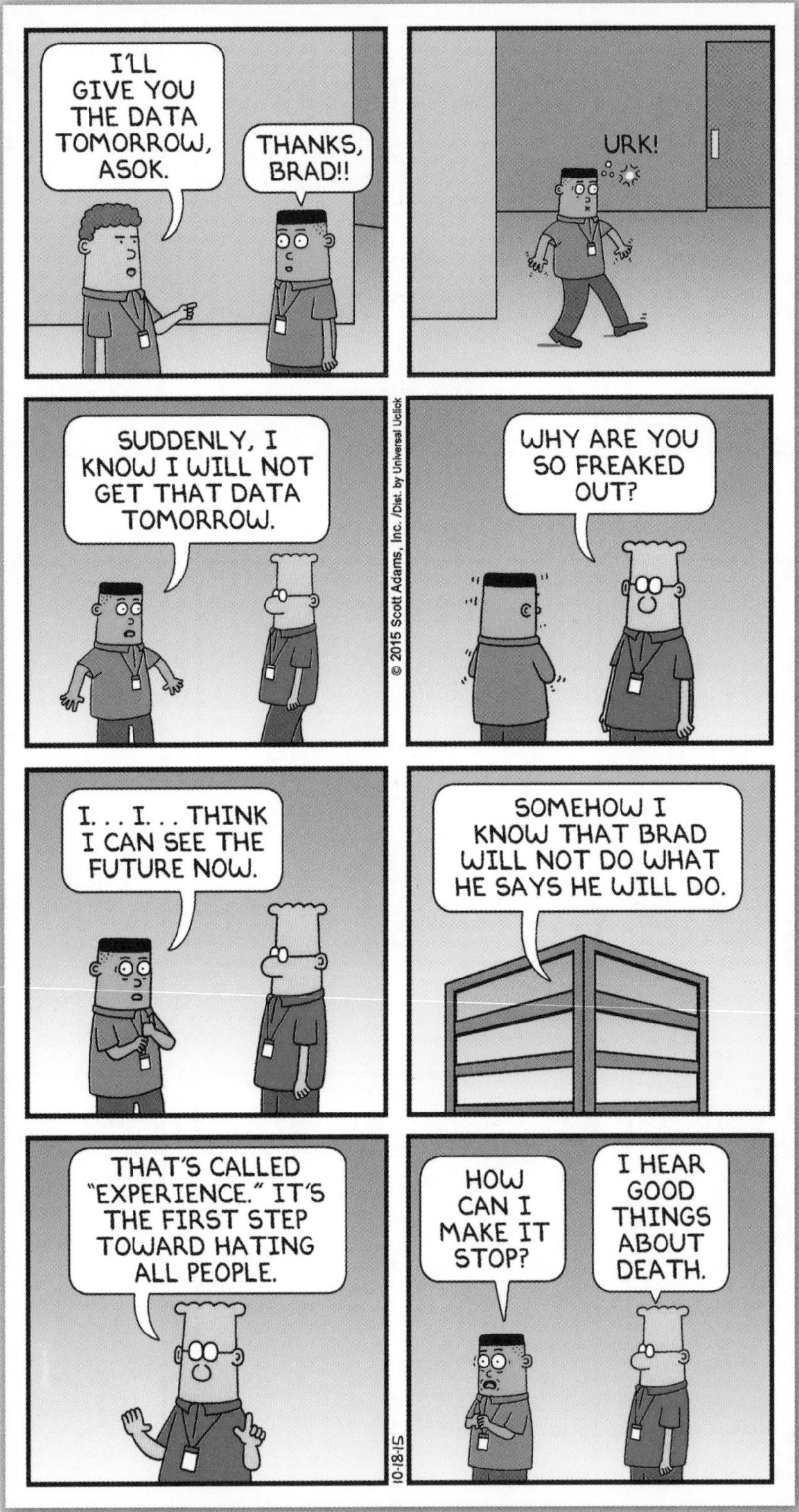
I'LL GIVE YOU THE DATA TOMORROW, ASOK.
THANKS, BRAD!!
URK!
SUDDENLY, I KNOW I WILL NOT GET THAT DATA TOMORROW.
WHY ARE YOU SO FREAKED OUT?
I. . . I. . . THINK I CAN SEE THE FUTURE NOW.
SOMEHOW I KNOW THAT BRAD WILL NOT DO WHAT HE SAYS HE WILL DO.
THAT'S CALLED "EXPERIENCE." IT'S THE FIRST STEP TOWARD HATING ALL PEOPLE.
HOW CAN I MAKE IT STOP?
I HEAR GOOD THINGS ABOUT DEATH.
© 2015 Scott Adams, Inc. /Dist. by Universal Uclick
10-18-15

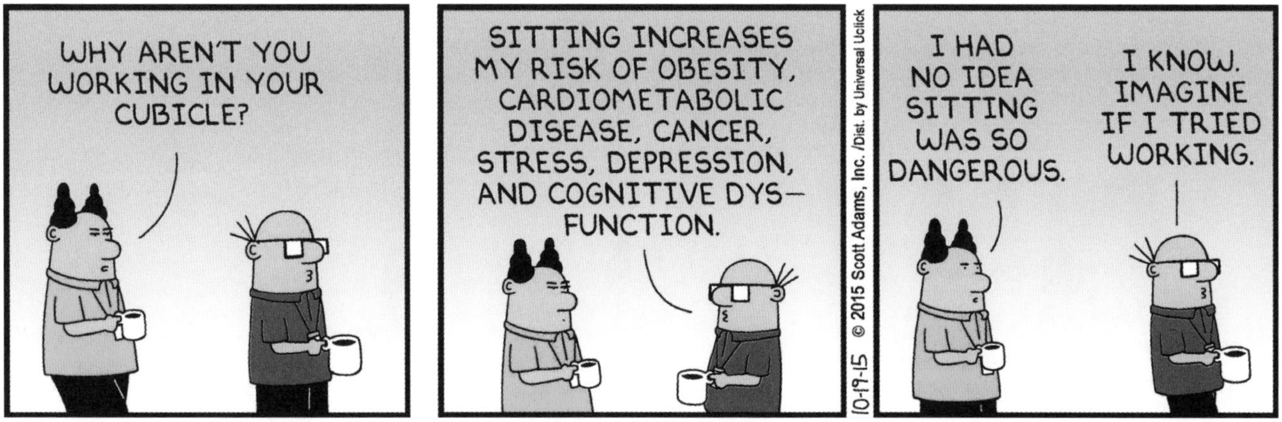
WHY AREN'T YOU WORKING IN YOUR CUBICLE?
SITTING INCREASES MY RISK OF OBESITY, CARDIOMETABOLIC DISEASE, CANCER, STRESS, DEPRESSION, AND COGNITIVE DYS-FUNCTION.
I HAD NO IDEA SITTING WAS SO DANGEROUS.
I KNOW. IMAGINE IF I TRIED WORKING.
10-19-15 © 2015 Scott Adams, Inc. /Dist. by Universal Uclick

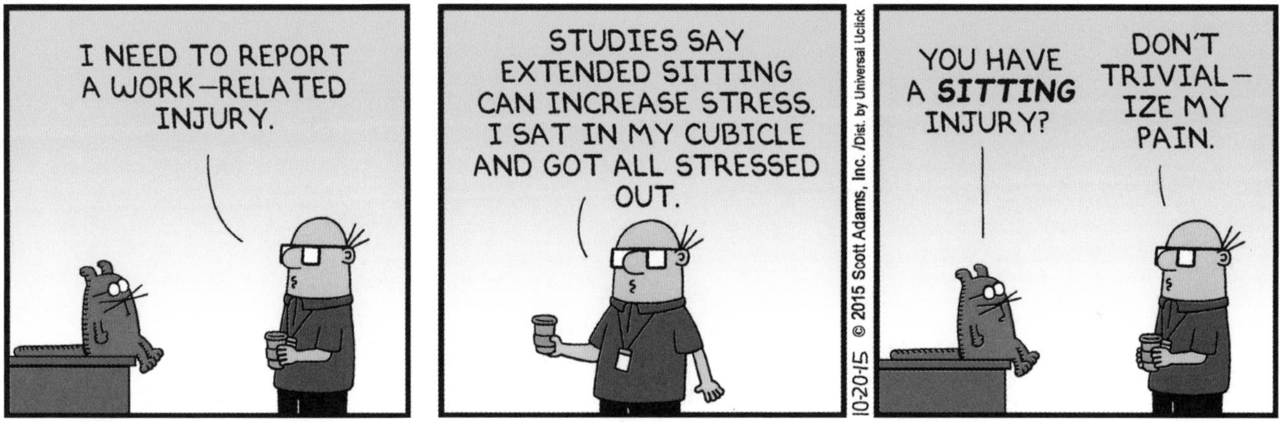
I NEED TO REPORT A WORK-RELATED INJURY.
STUDIES SAY EXTENDED SITTING CAN INCREASE STRESS. I SAT IN MY CUBICLE AND GOT ALL STRESSED OUT.
YOU HAVE A SITTING INJURY?
DON'T TRIVIAL-IZE MY PAIN.
10-20-15 © 2015 Scott Adams, Inc. /Dist. by Universal Uclick

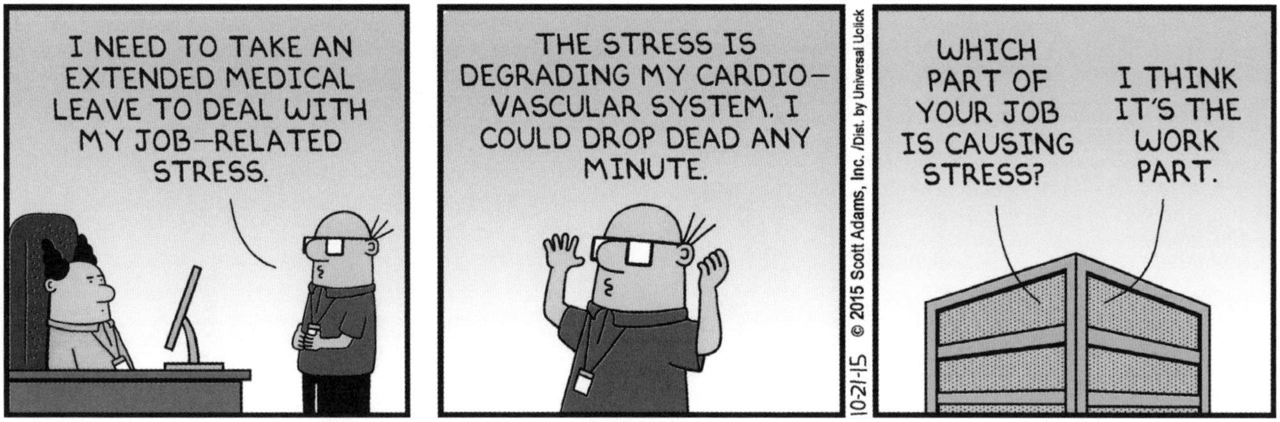
I NEED TO TAKE AN EXTENDED MEDICAL LEAVE TO DEAL WITH MY JOB-RELATED STRESS.
THE STRESS IS DEGRADING MY CARDIO-VASCULAR SYSTEM. I COULD DROP DEAD ANY MINUTE.
WHICH PART OF YOUR JOB IS CAUSING STRESS?
I THINK IT'S THE WORK PART.
10-21-15 © 2015 Scott Adams, Inc. /Dist. by Universal Uclick

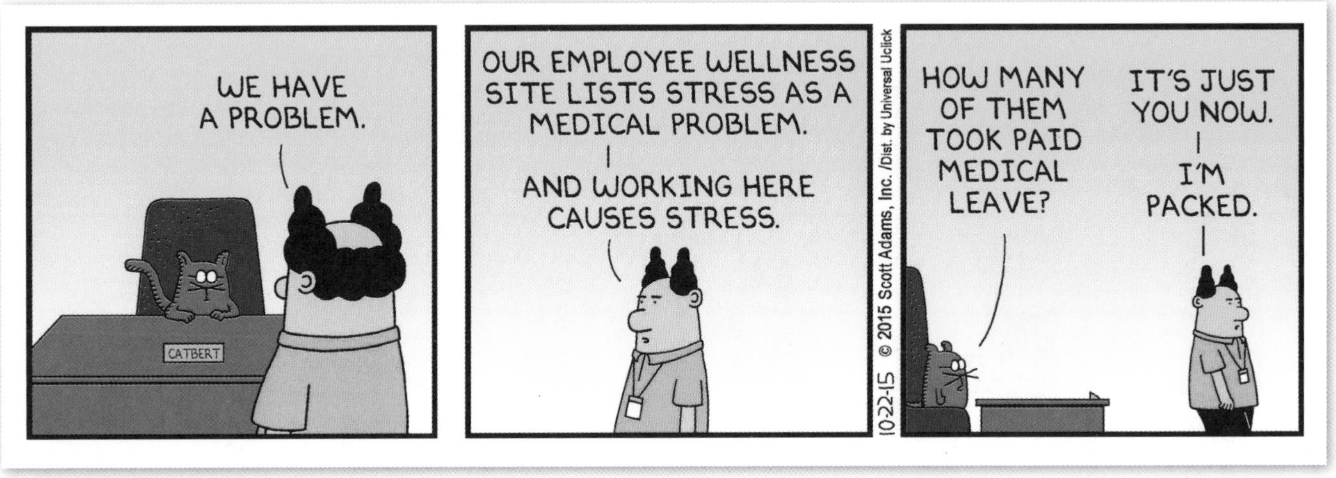
WE HAVE A PROBLEM.
CATBERT
OUR EMPLOYEE WELLNESS SITE LISTS STRESS AS A MEDICAL PROBLEM.
AND WORKING HERE CAUSES STRESS.
10-22-15 © 2015 Scott Adams, Inc. /Dist. by Universal Uclick
HOW MANY OF THEM TOOK PAID MEDICAL LEAVE?
IT'S JUST YOU NOW.
I'M PACKED.

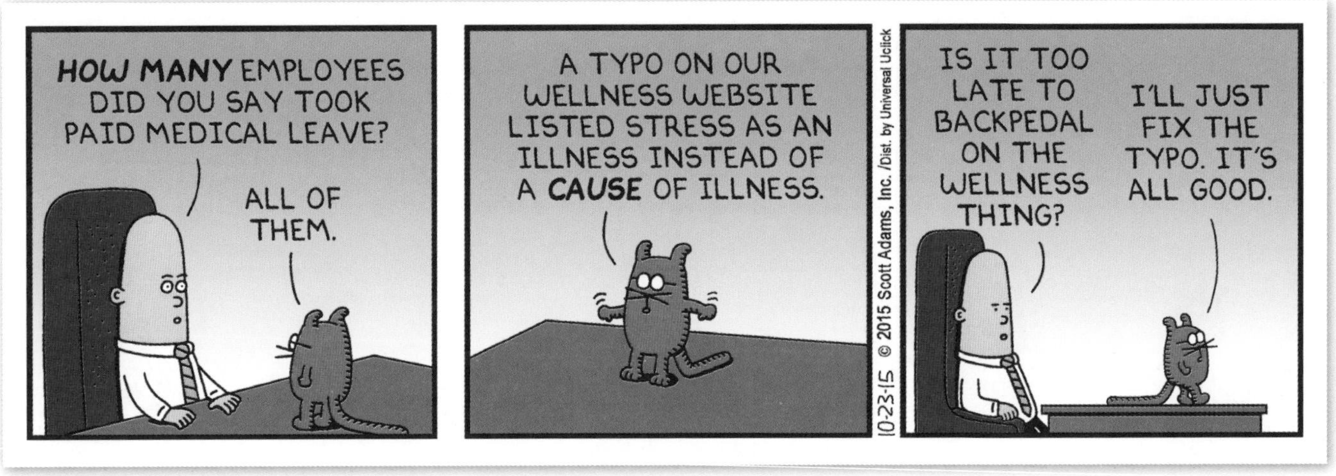
HOW MANY EMPLOYEES DID YOU SAY TOOK PAID MEDICAL LEAVE?
ALL OF THEM.
A TYPO ON OUR WELLNESS WEBSITE LISTED STRESS AS AN ILLNESS INSTEAD OF A **CAUSE** OF ILLNESS.
10-23-15 © 2015 Scott Adams, Inc. /Dist. by Universal Uclick
IS IT TOO LATE TO BACKPEDAL ON THE WELLNESS THING?
I'LL JUST FIX THE TYPO. IT'S ALL GOOD.

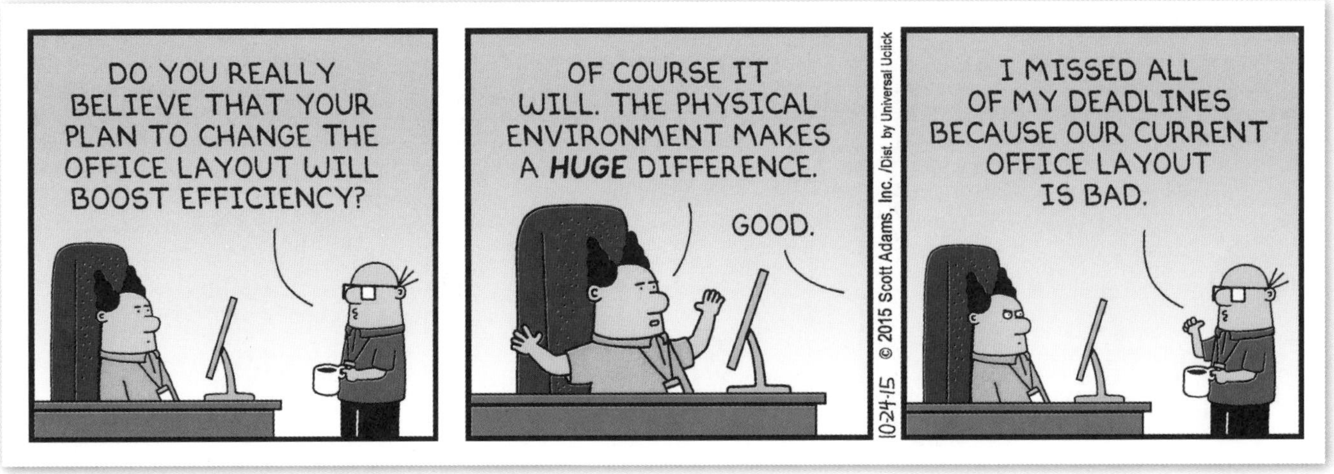
DO YOU REALLY BELIEVE THAT YOUR PLAN TO CHANGE THE OFFICE LAYOUT WILL BOOST EFFICIENCY?
OF COURSE IT WILL. THE PHYSICAL ENVIRONMENT MAKES A **HUGE** DIFFERENCE.
GOOD.
10-24-15 © 2015 Scott Adams, Inc. /Dist. by Universal Uclick
I MISSED ALL OF MY DEADLINES BECAUSE OUR CURRENT OFFICE LAYOUT IS BAD.

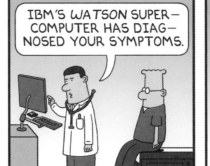

IBM'S *WATSON* SUPER-COMPUTER HAS DIAG-NOSED YOUR SYMPTOMS.
THE COMPUTER JUST ORDERED THE MEDS YOU NEED. THEY WILL BE DELIVERED IN AN HOUR BY DRONE.
LOOKS LIKE YOUR JOB AS A DOCTOR IS BECOMING OBSOLETE.
HA HA! NO. YOU STILL NEED A DOCTOR AND A NURSE TO MAKE THE SYSTEM WORK.
FOR EXAMPLE, THE COMPUTER CAN'T READ ITS OWN SCREEN AND SPEAK THOSE WORDS TO PATIENTS.
ACTUALLY, IT CAN.
BUT THE COMPUTER DOESN'T HAVE A NURSE.
WHAT DOES THE NURSE DO?
I STAB HIM IF HE TRIES TO DO MORE THAN READ THE SCREEN.
ADAPTED FROM AN OLD PILOT JOKE
© 2015 Scott Adams, Inc. /Dist. by Universal Uclick
10-25-15

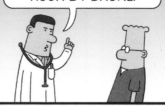

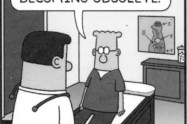

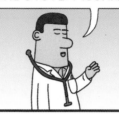

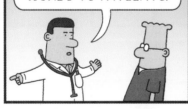

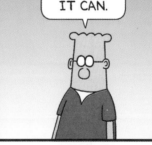

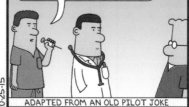

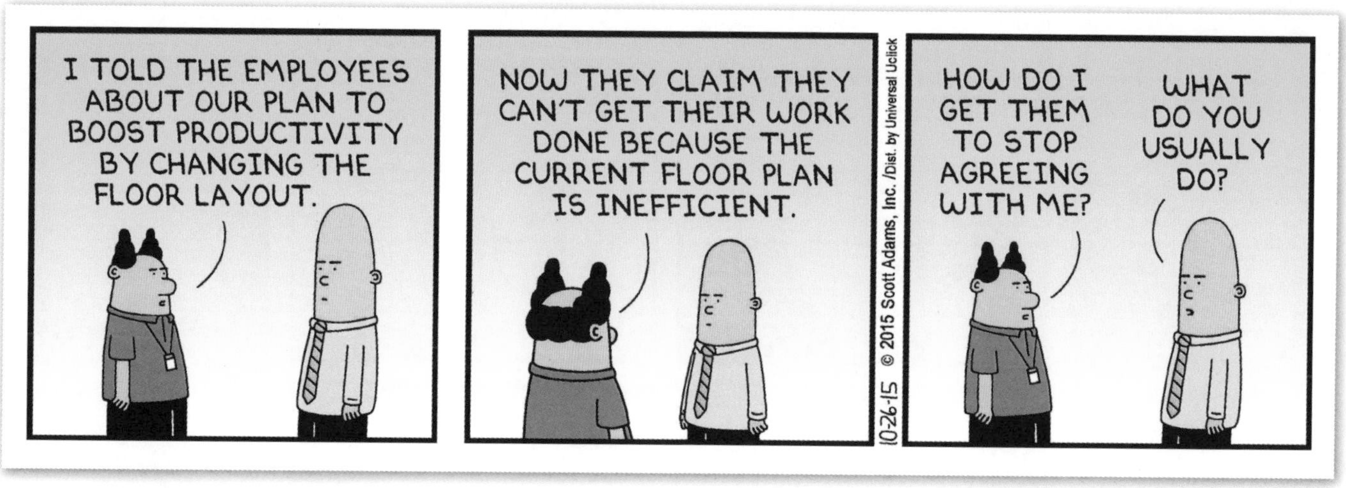
I TOLD THE EMPLOYEES ABOUT OUR PLAN TO BOOST PRODUCTIVITY BY CHANGING THE FLOOR LAYOUT.
NOW THEY CLAIM THEY CAN'T GET THEIR WORK DONE BECAUSE THE CURRENT FLOOR PLAN IS INEFFICIENT.
10-26-15 © 2015 Scott Adams, Inc. /Dist. by Universal Uclick
HOW DO I GET THEM TO STOP AGREEING WITH ME?
WHAT DO YOU USUALLY DO?

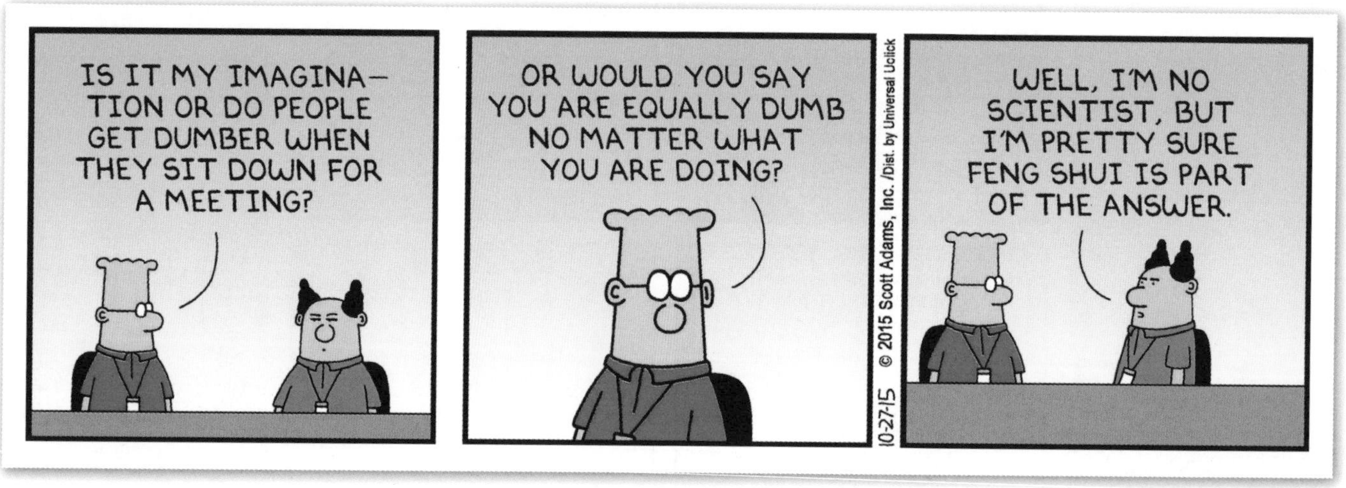
IS IT MY IMAGINA-TION OR DO PEOPLE GET DUMBER WHEN THEY SIT DOWN FOR A MEETING?
OR WOULD YOU SAY YOU ARE EQUALLY DUMB NO MATTER WHAT YOU ARE DOING?
10-27-15 © 2015 Scott Adams, Inc. /Dist. by Universal Uclick
WELL, I'M NO SCIENTIST, BUT I'M PRETTY SURE FENG SHUI IS PART OF THE ANSWER.

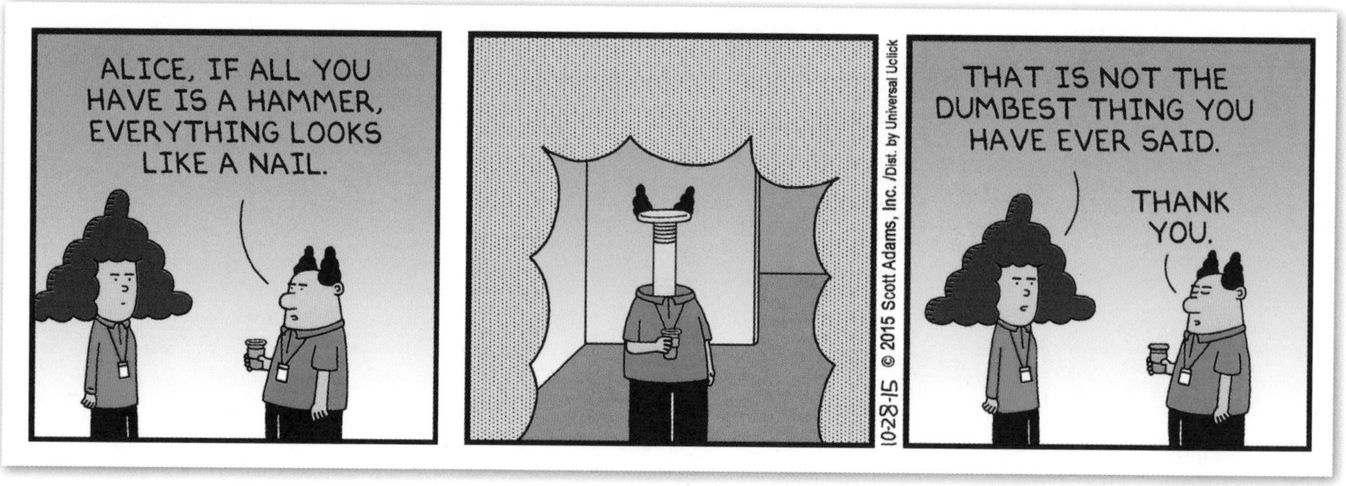
ALICE, IF ALL YOU HAVE IS A HAMMER, EVERYTHING LOOKS LIKE A NAIL.
10-28-15 © 2015 Scott Adams, Inc. /Dist. by Universal Uclick
THAT IS NOT THE DUMBEST THING YOU HAVE EVER SAID.
THANK YOU.

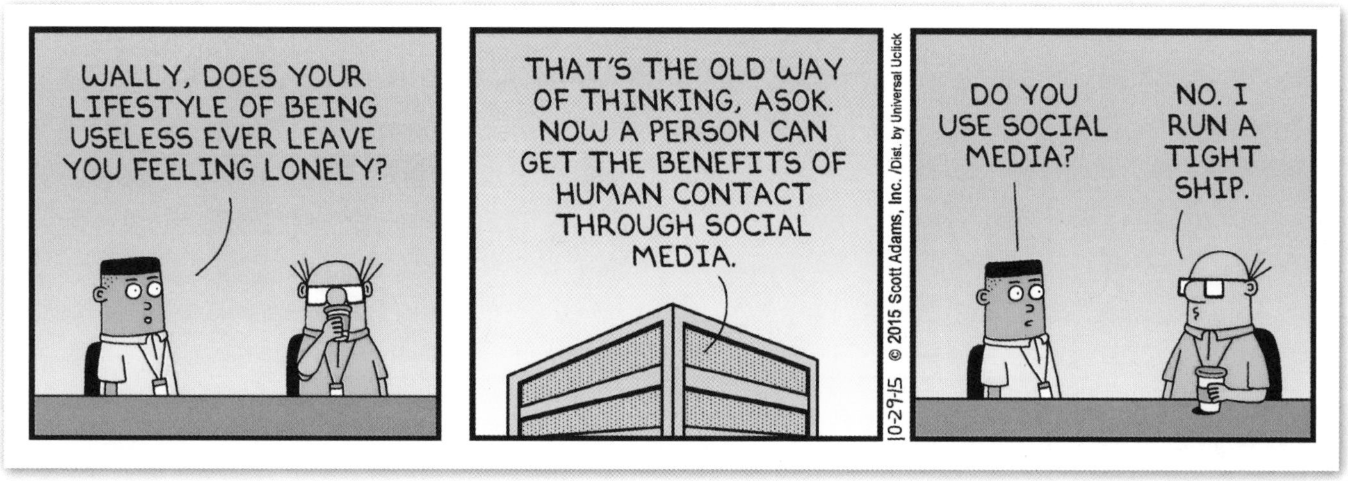
WALLY, DOES YOUR LIFESTYLE OF BEING USELESS EVER LEAVE YOU FEELING LONELY?
THAT'S THE OLD WAY OF THINKING, ASOK. NOW A PERSON CAN GET THE BENEFITS OF HUMAN CONTACT THROUGH SOCIAL MEDIA.
10-29-15 © 2015 Scott Adams, Inc. /Dist. by Universal Uclick
DO YOU USE SOCIAL MEDIA?
NO. I RUN A TIGHT SHIP.

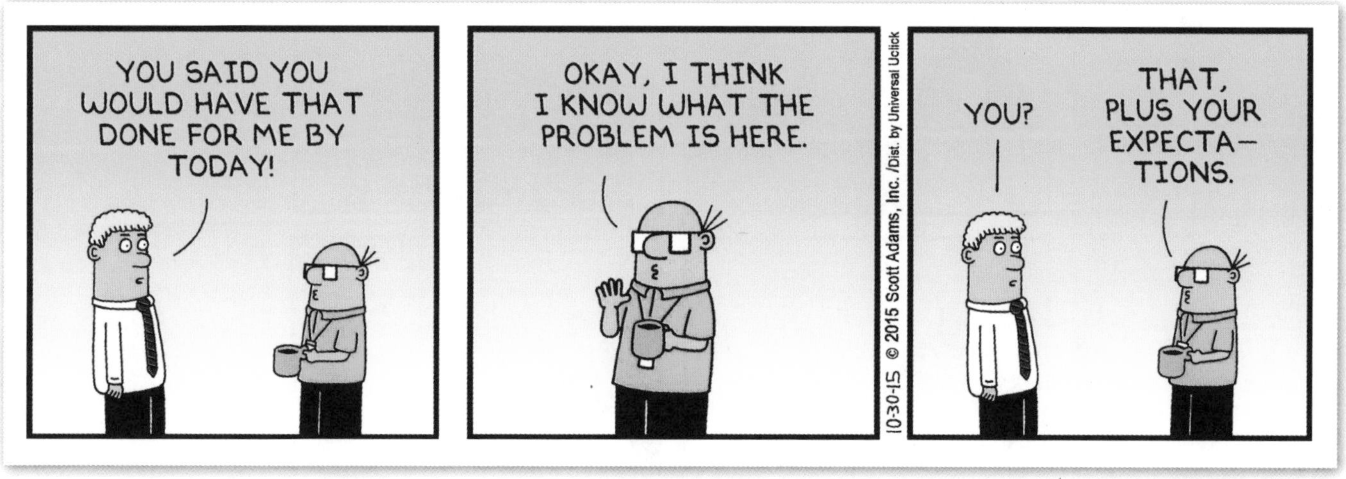
YOU SAID YOU WOULD HAVE THAT DONE FOR ME BY TODAY!
OKAY, I THINK I KNOW WHAT THE PROBLEM IS HERE.
10-30-15 © 2015 Scott Adams, Inc. /Dist. by Universal Uclick
YOU?
THAT, PLUS YOUR EXPECTA-TIONS.

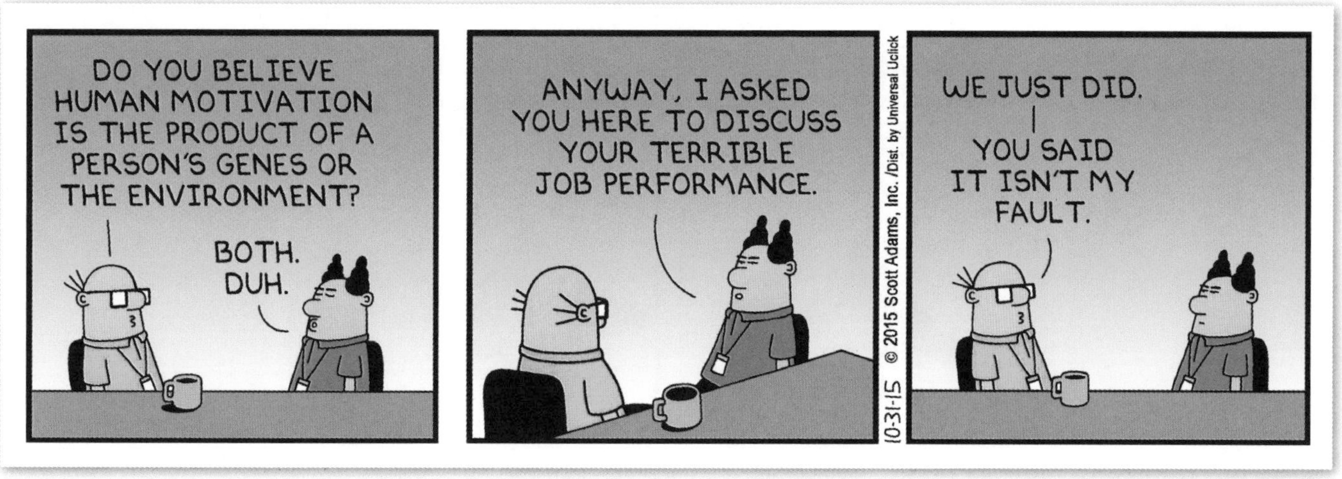
DO YOU BELIEVE HUMAN MOTIVATION IS THE PRODUCT OF A PERSON'S GENES OR THE ENVIRONMENT?
BOTH. DUH.
ANYWAY, I ASKED YOU HERE TO DISCUSS YOUR TERRIBLE JOB PERFORMANCE.
10-31-15 © 2015 Scott Adams, Inc. /Dist. by Universal Uclick
WE JUST DID.
YOU SAID IT ISN'T MY FAULT.

WHAT THE . . .
IT'S NOT A GOOD IDEA TO ANSWER EMAIL WHILE YOU'RE ANGRY.
I KNOW, BUT THIS IDIOT. . .
HOLD. . .
© 2015 Scott Adams, Inc. /Dist. by Universal Uclick
THAT'S IT. DEEP BREATHS.
HOLD. . .
HOLD. . .
PHEW! YOU WERE RIGHT. I SHOULD NOT GET WORKED UP OVER ONE IDIOT.
DING!
11-1-15
HE WASN'T WORKING ALONE!
I'M OUT.

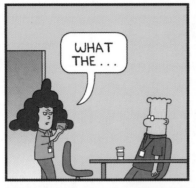

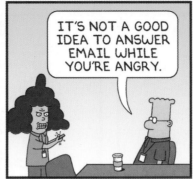

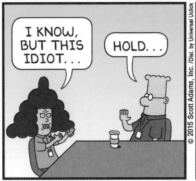

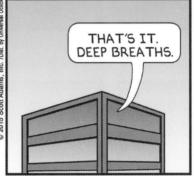

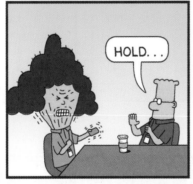

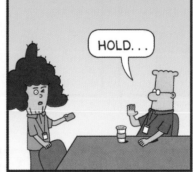

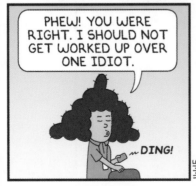

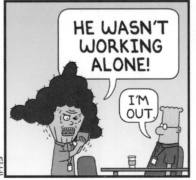

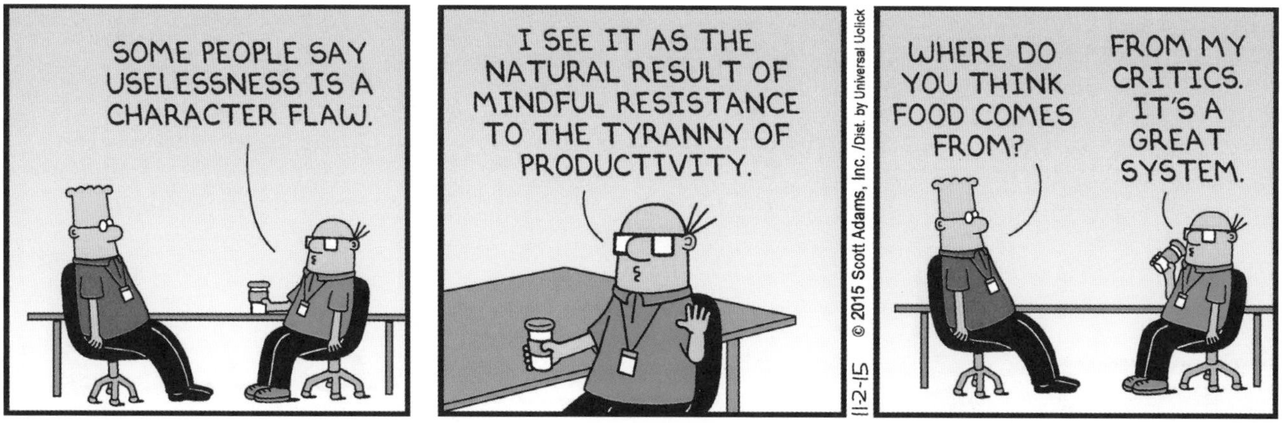
SOME PEOPLE SAY USELESSNESS IS A CHARACTER FLAW.
I SEE IT AS THE NATURAL RESULT OF MINDFUL RESISTANCE TO THE TYRANNY OF PRODUCTIVITY.
WHERE DO YOU THINK FOOD COMES FROM?
FROM MY CRITICS. IT'S A GREAT SYSTEM.
11-2-15 © 2015 Scott Adams, Inc. /Dist. by Universal Uclick

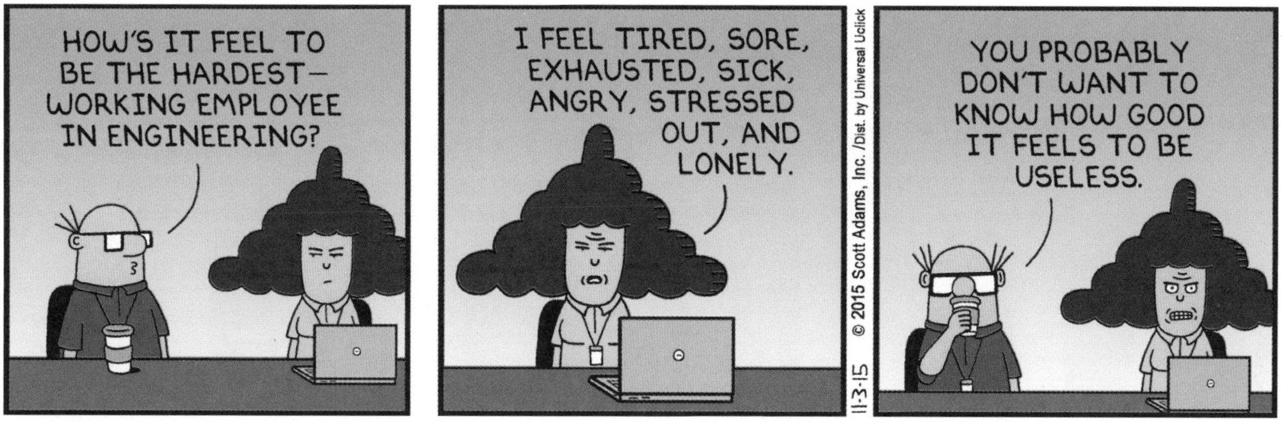
HOW'S IT FEEL TO BE THE HARDEST—WORKING EMPLOYEE IN ENGINEERING?
I FEEL TIRED, SORE, EXHAUSTED, SICK, ANGRY, STRESSED OUT, AND LONELY.
YOU PROBABLY DON'T WANT TO KNOW HOW GOOD IT FEELS TO BE USELESS.
11-3-15 © 2015 Scott Adams, Inc. /Dist. by Universal Uclick

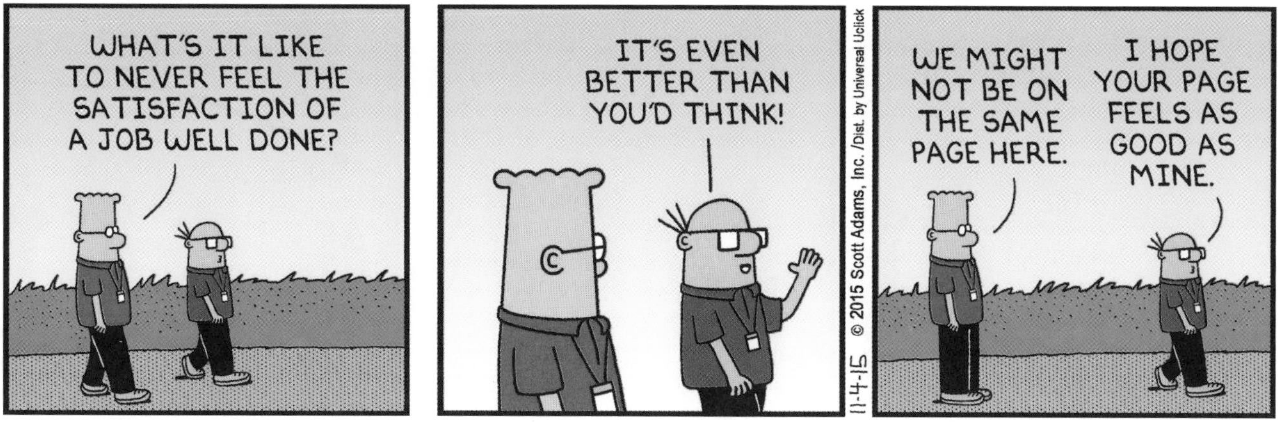
WHAT'S IT LIKE TO NEVER FEEL THE SATISFACTION OF A JOB WELL DONE?
IT'S EVEN BETTER THAN YOU'D THINK!
WE MIGHT NOT BE ON THE SAME PAGE HERE.
I HOPE YOUR PAGE FEELS AS GOOD AS MINE.
11-4-15 © 2015 Scott Adams, Inc. /Dist. by Universal Uclick

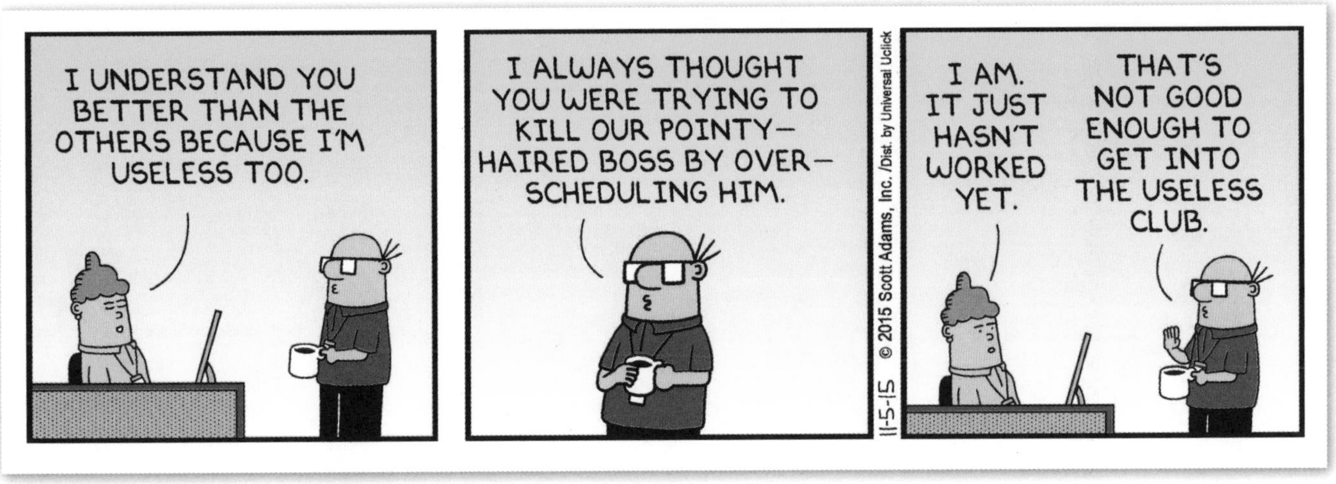
I UNDERSTAND YOU BETTER THAN THE OTHERS BECAUSE I'M USELESS TOO.
I ALWAYS THOUGHT YOU WERE TRYING TO KILL OUR POINTY-HAIRED BOSS BY OVER-SCHEDULING HIM.
11-5-15 © 2015 Scott Adams, Inc. /Dist. by Universal Uclick
I AM. IT JUST HASN'T WORKED YET.
THAT'S NOT GOOD ENOUGH TO GET INTO THE USELESS CLUB.

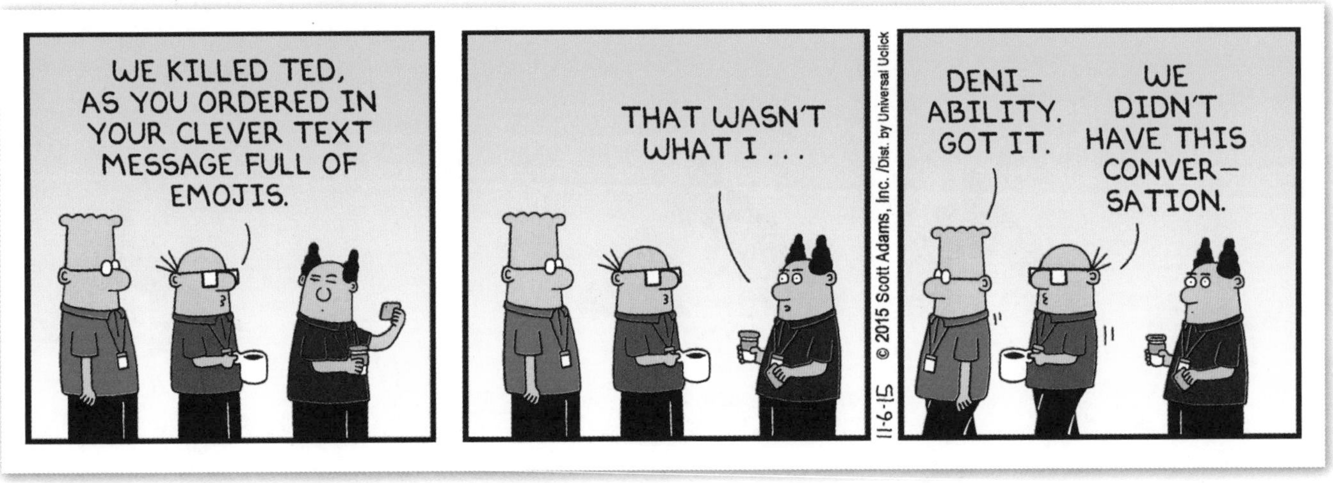
WE KILLED TED, AS YOU ORDERED IN YOUR CLEVER TEXT MESSAGE FULL OF EMOJIS.
THAT WASN'T WHAT I . . .
11-6-15 © 2015 Scott Adams, Inc. /Dist. by Universal Uclick
DENI-ABILITY. GOT IT.
WE DIDN'T HAVE THIS CONVER-SATION.

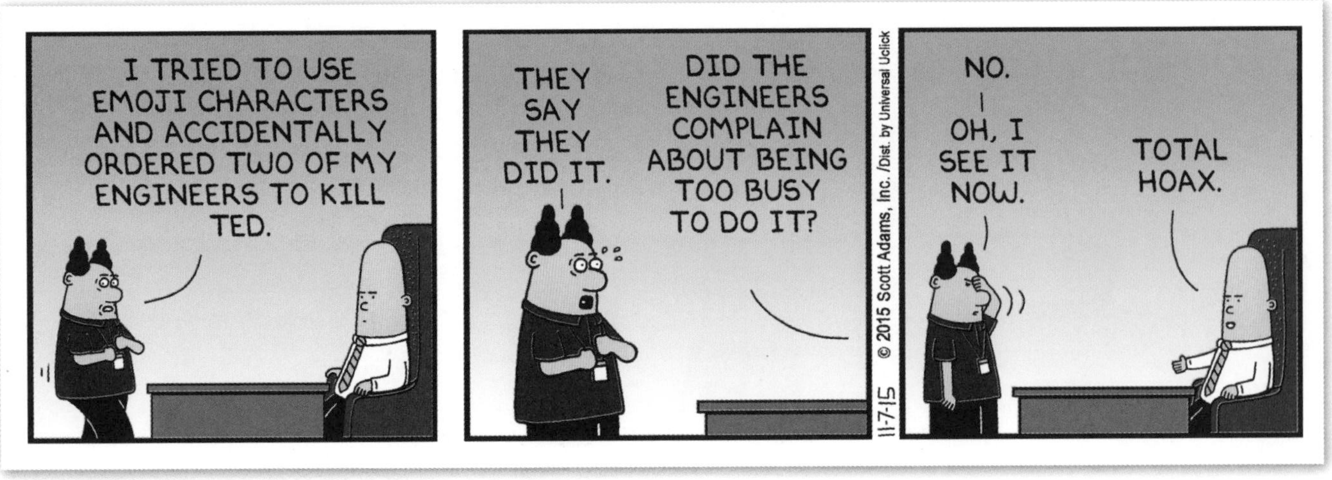
I TRIED TO USE EMOJI CHARACTERS AND ACCIDENTALLY ORDERED TWO OF MY ENGINEERS TO KILL TED.
DID THE ENGINEERS COMPLAIN ABOUT BEING TOO BUSY TO DO IT?
THEY SAY THEY DID IT.
11-7-15 © 2015 Scott Adams, Inc. /Dist. by Universal Uclick
NO.
OH, I SEE IT NOW.
TOTAL HOAX.

I'M HAVING SOME PEOPLE OVER TO MY HOUSE AFTER WORK. WOULD YOU LIKE TO COME?

WHO ELSE IS COMING?

SEVEN PEOPLE SAID MAYBE, AND ONE SAID HE WOULD GET BACK TO ME.

I THINK THAT SHOWS A LOT OF INTEREST.

SO HOW ABOUT IT? CAN YOU COME?

IT DEPENDS ON WHETHER MY SISTER NEEDS A RIDE TO THE AIRPORT.

WHEN WILL YOU KNOW?

I'LL TEXT YOU.

ARE YOU SAD THAT NO ONE CAME?

NO, I WAS JUST A-B TESTING TO SEE IF I STILL HATE ALL OF THEM.

© 2015 Scott Adams, Inc. /Dist. by Universal Uclick

11-8-15

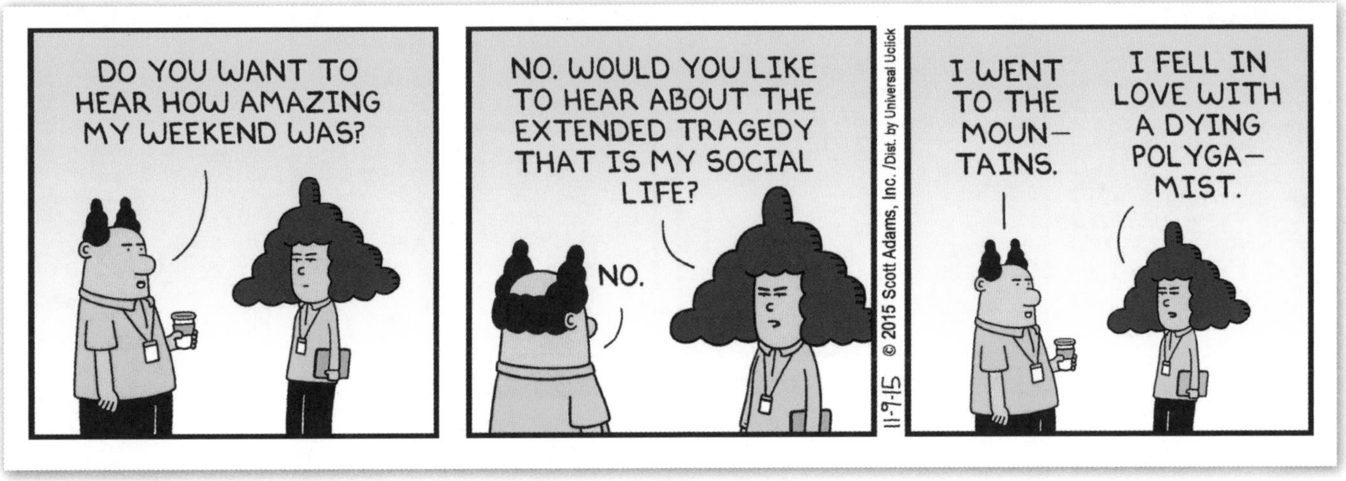
DO YOU WANT TO HEAR HOW AMAZING MY WEEKEND WAS?
NO. WOULD YOU LIKE TO HEAR ABOUT THE EXTENDED TRAGEDY THAT IS MY SOCIAL LIFE?
NO.
I WENT TO THE MOUN- TAINS.
I FELL IN LOVE WITH A DYING POLYGA- MIST.
11-9-15 © 2015 Scott Adams, Inc. /Dist. by Universal Uclick

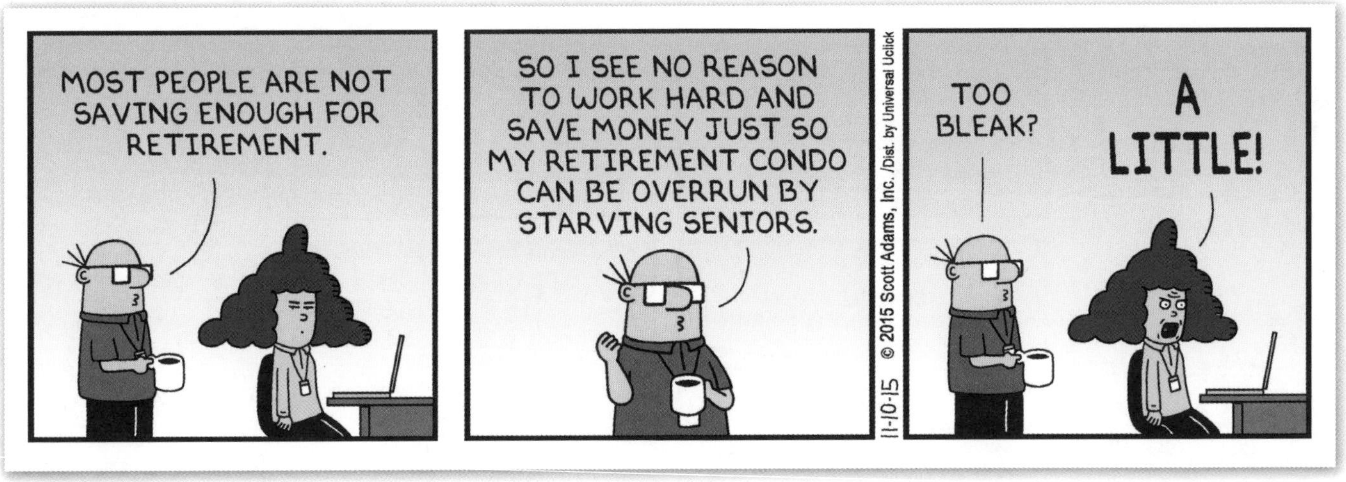
MOST PEOPLE ARE NOT SAVING ENOUGH FOR RETIREMENT.
SO I SEE NO REASON TO WORK HARD AND SAVE MONEY JUST SO MY RETIREMENT CONDO CAN BE OVERRUN BY STARVING SENIORS.
TOO BLEAK?
A LITTLE!
11-10-15 © 2015 Scott Adams, Inc. /Dist. by Universal Uclick

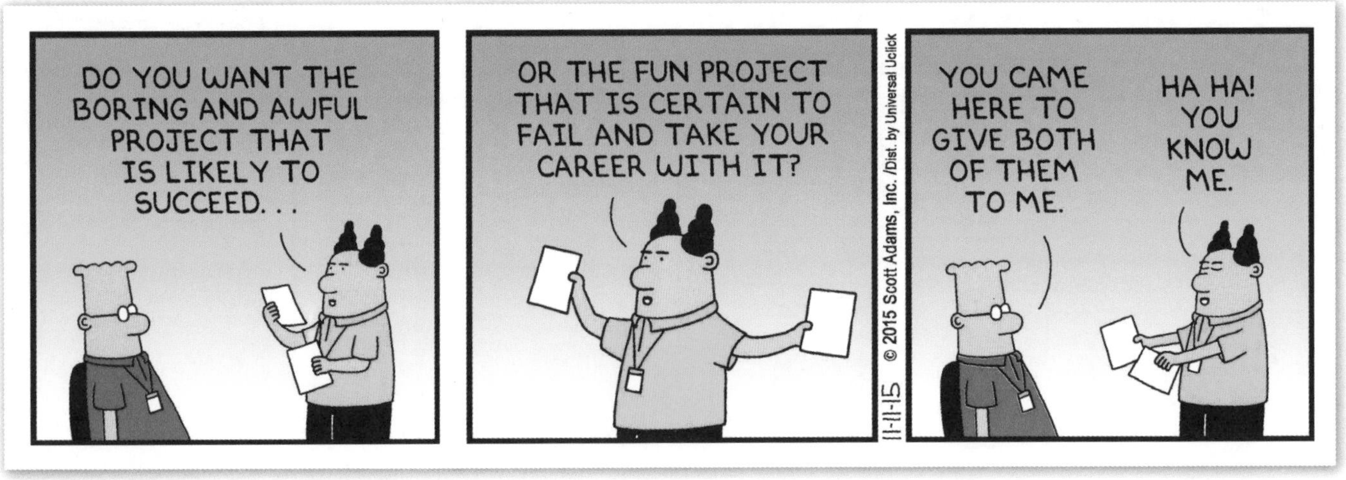
DO YOU WANT THE BORING AND AWFUL PROJECT THAT IS LIKELY TO SUCCEED. . .
OR THE FUN PROJECT THAT IS CERTAIN TO FAIL AND TAKE YOUR CAREER WITH IT?
YOU CAME HERE TO GIVE BOTH OF THEM TO ME.
HA HA! YOU KNOW ME.
11-11-15 © 2015 Scott Adams, Inc. /Dist. by Universal Uclick

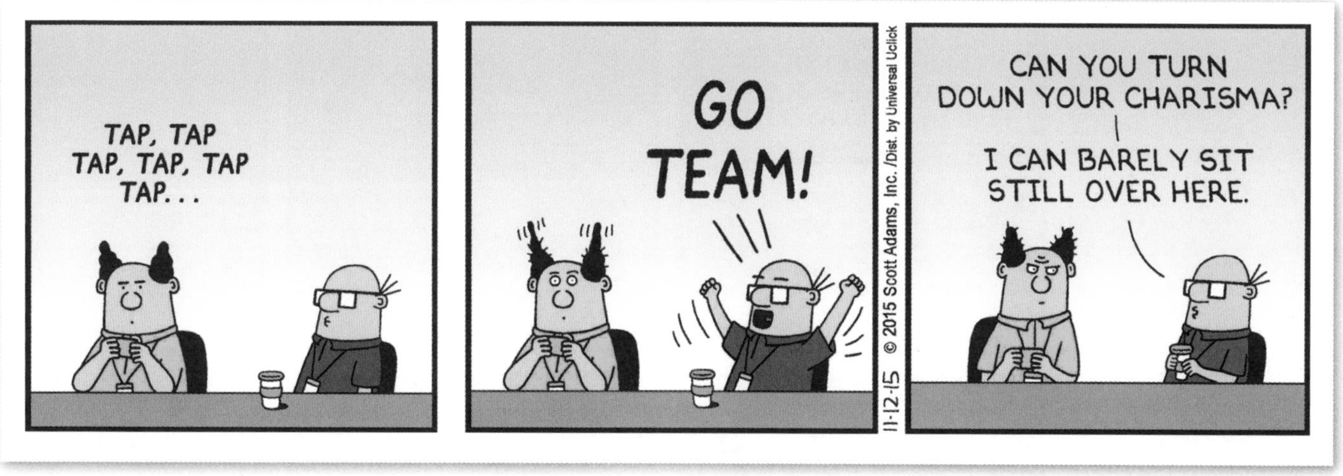
TAP, TAP
TAP, TAP, TAP
TAP...
GO
TEAM!
11-12-15 © 2015 Scott Adams, Inc. /Dist. by Universal Uclick
CAN YOU TURN
DOWN YOUR CHARISMA?
I CAN BARELY SIT
STILL OVER HERE.

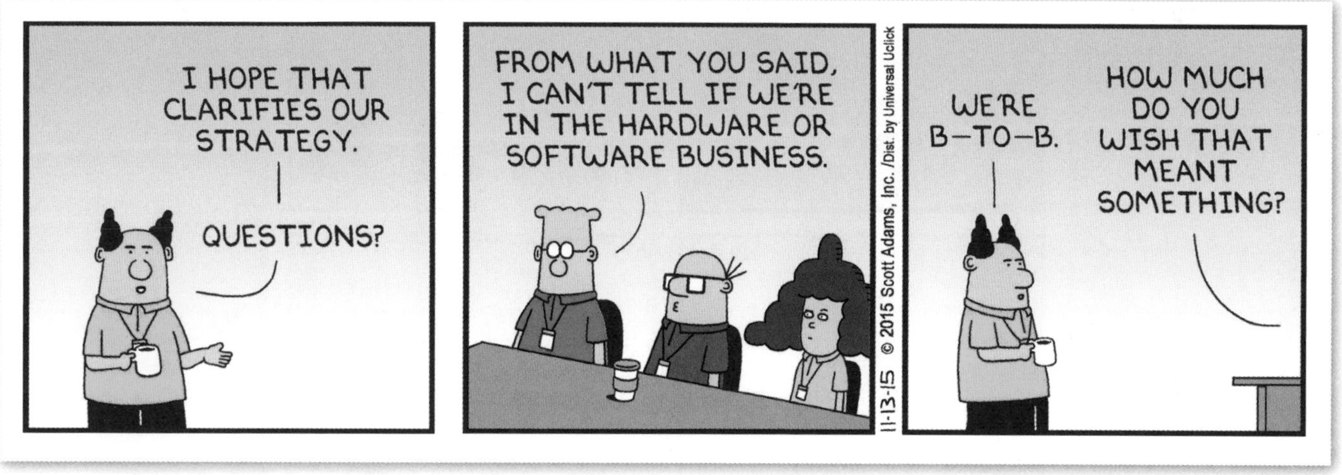
I HOPE THAT
CLARIFIES OUR
STRATEGY.
QUESTIONS?
FROM WHAT YOU SAID,
I CAN'T TELL IF WE'RE
IN THE HARDWARE OR
SOFTWARE BUSINESS.
11-13-15 © 2015 Scott Adams, Inc. /Dist. by Universal Uclick
WE'RE
B–TO–B.
HOW MUCH
DO YOU
WISH THAT
MEANT
SOMETHING?

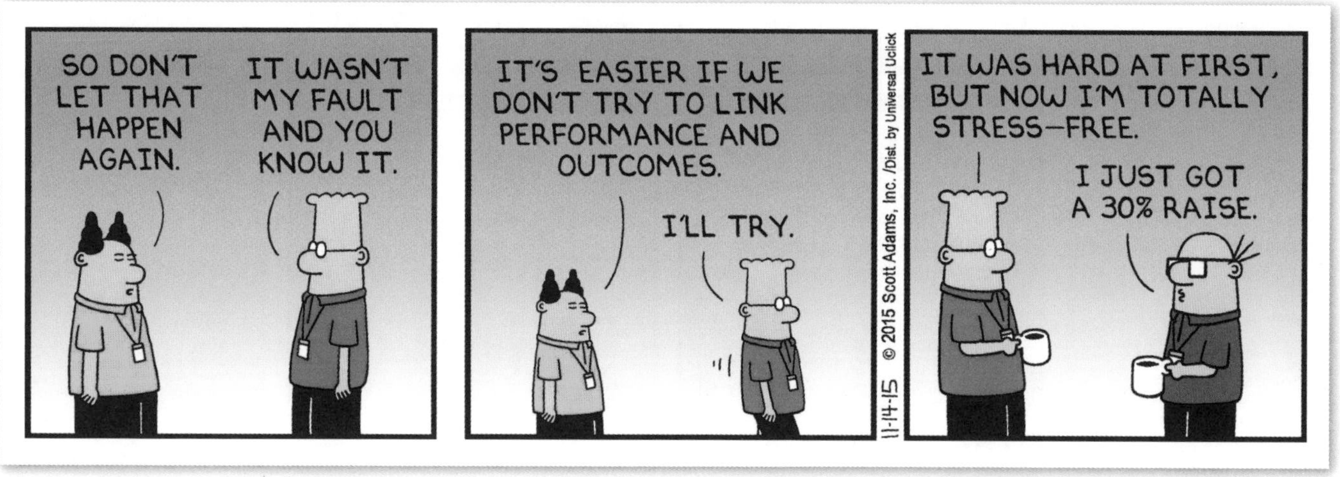
SO DON'T
LET THAT
HAPPEN
AGAIN.
IT WASN'T
MY FAULT
AND YOU
KNOW IT.
IT'S EASIER IF WE
DON'T TRY TO LINK
PERFORMANCE AND
OUTCOMES.
I'LL TRY.
11-14-15 © 2015 Scott Adams, Inc. /Dist. by Universal Uclick
IT WAS HARD AT FIRST,
BUT NOW I'M TOTALLY
STRESS–FREE.
I JUST GOT
A 30% RAISE.

WE ARE GOING TO START MONITORING EMPLOYEE PRODUC-TIVITY IN REAL TIME.
ANY QUESTIONS?
I NEED ONE CLARIFICATION.
ARE YOU SAYING YOU REMOVED THE LAST SHRED OF HUMAN DIGNITY FROM OUR JOBS AND. . .
. . . REDUCED US TO NOTHING BUT A MEAT MACHINE THAT. . .
. . . SUFFERS IN A STATE OF PERPETUAL INADEQUACY AS EACH PERSON IS COMPARED TO AN ARBITRARY AND EVER-GROWING GOAL UNTIL. . .
. . . THERE IS NO REALISTIC WAY FOR THE EMPLOYEE TO FIND HAPPINESS THROUGH NATURAL MEANS?
THAT'S ONE WAY TO LOOK AT IT.
© 2015 Scott Adams, Inc. /Dist. by Universal Uclick
11-15-15

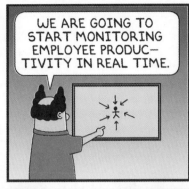

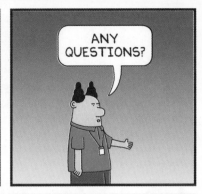

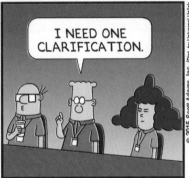

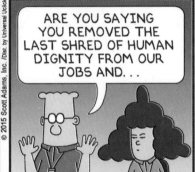

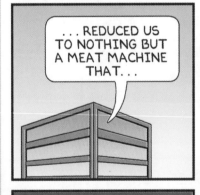

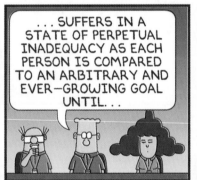

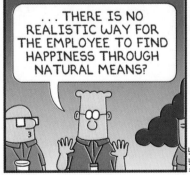

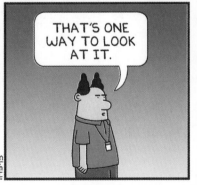

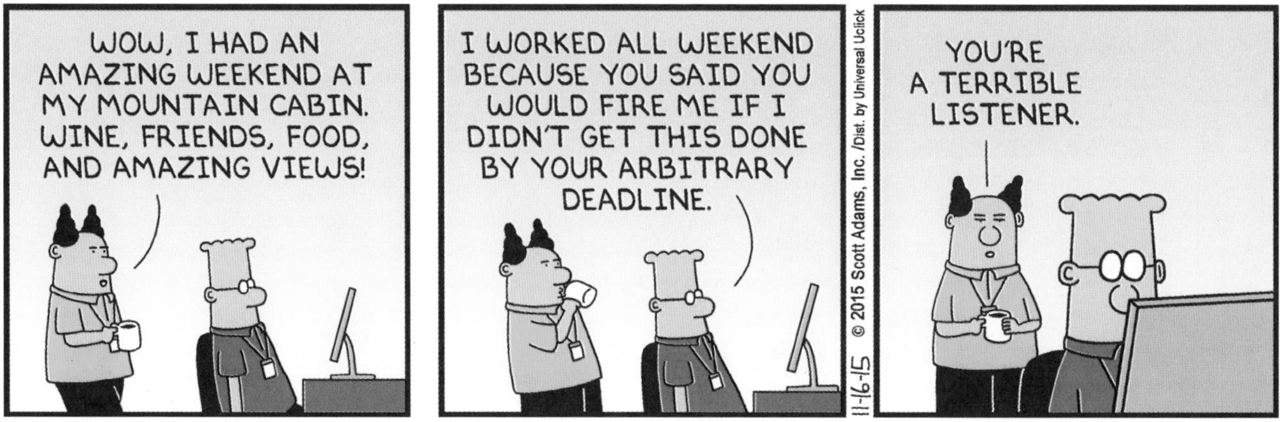
WOW, I HAD AN AMAZING WEEKEND AT MY MOUNTAIN CABIN. WINE, FRIENDS, FOOD, AND AMAZING VIEWS!
I WORKED ALL WEEKEND BECAUSE YOU SAID YOU WOULD FIRE ME IF I DIDN'T GET THIS DONE BY YOUR ARBITRARY DEADLINE.
11-16-15 © 2015 Scott Adams, Inc. /Dist. by Universal Uclick
YOU'RE A TERRIBLE LISTENER.

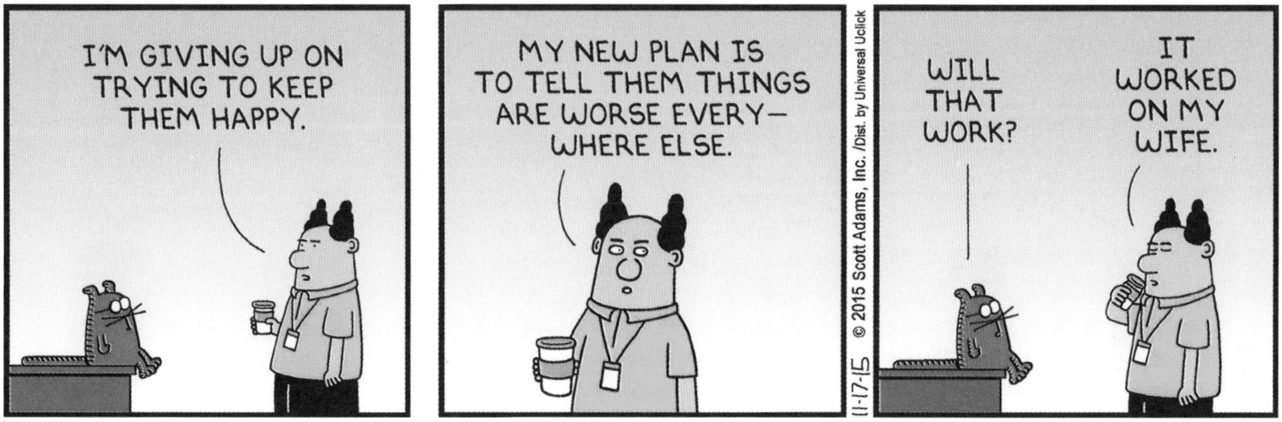
I'M GIVING UP ON TRYING TO KEEP THEM HAPPY.
MY NEW PLAN IS TO TELL THEM THINGS ARE WORSE EVERY-WHERE ELSE.
11-17-15 © 2015 Scott Adams, Inc. /Dist. by Universal Uclick
WILL THAT WORK?
IT WORKED ON MY WIFE.

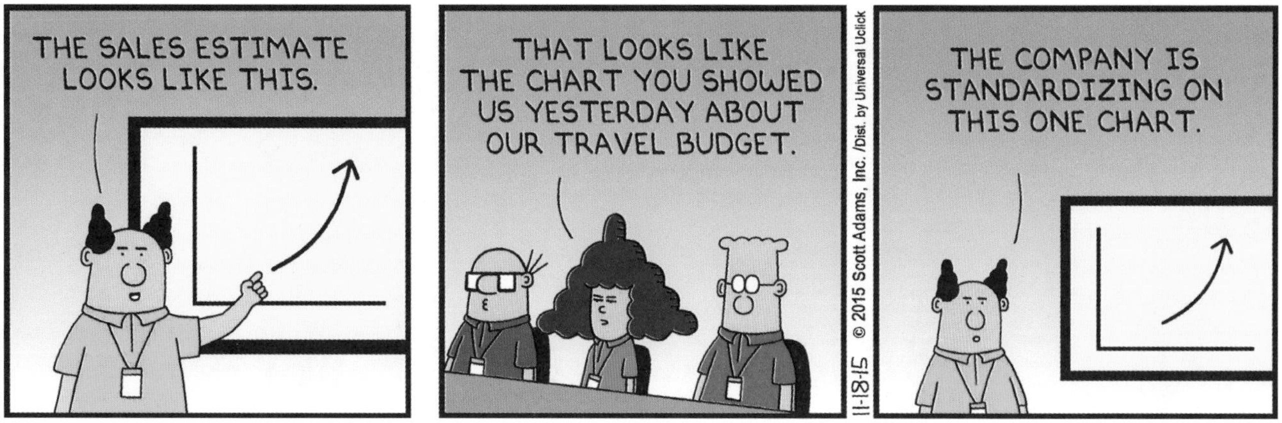
THE SALES ESTIMATE LOOKS LIKE THIS.
THAT LOOKS LIKE THE CHART YOU SHOWED US YESTERDAY ABOUT OUR TRAVEL BUDGET.
11-18-15 © 2015 Scott Adams, Inc. /Dist. by Universal Uclick
THE COMPANY IS STANDARDIZING ON THIS ONE CHART.

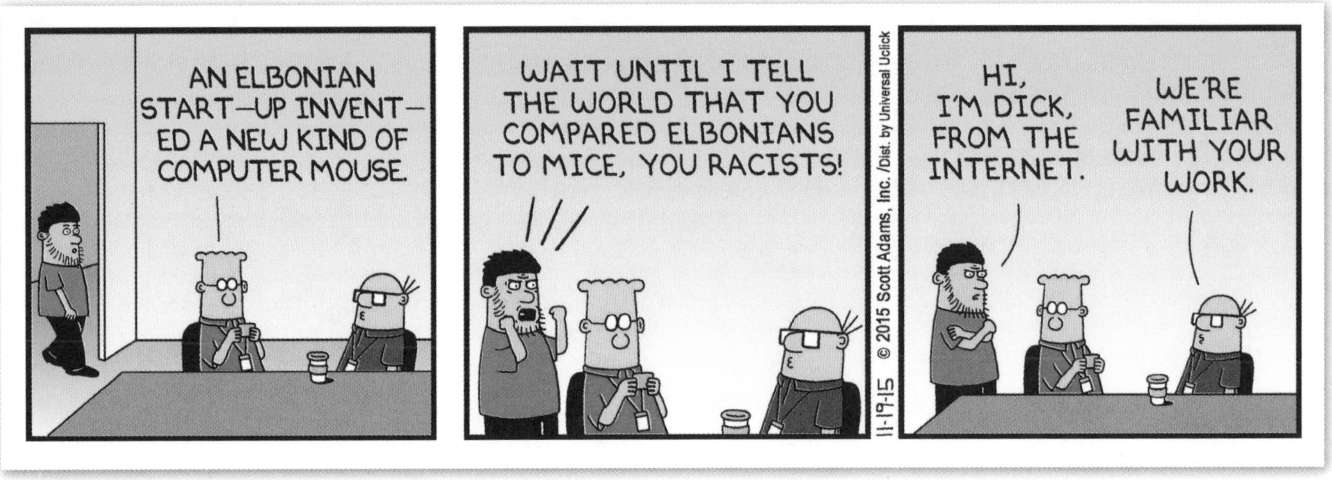
AN ELBONIAN START—UP INVENT—ED A NEW KIND OF COMPUTER MOUSE.
WAIT UNTIL I TELL THE WORLD THAT YOU COMPARED ELBONIANS TO MICE, YOU RACISTS!
11-19-15 © 2015 Scott Adams, Inc. /Dist. by Universal Uclick
HI, I'M DICK, FROM THE INTERNET.
WE'RE FAMILIAR WITH YOUR WORK.

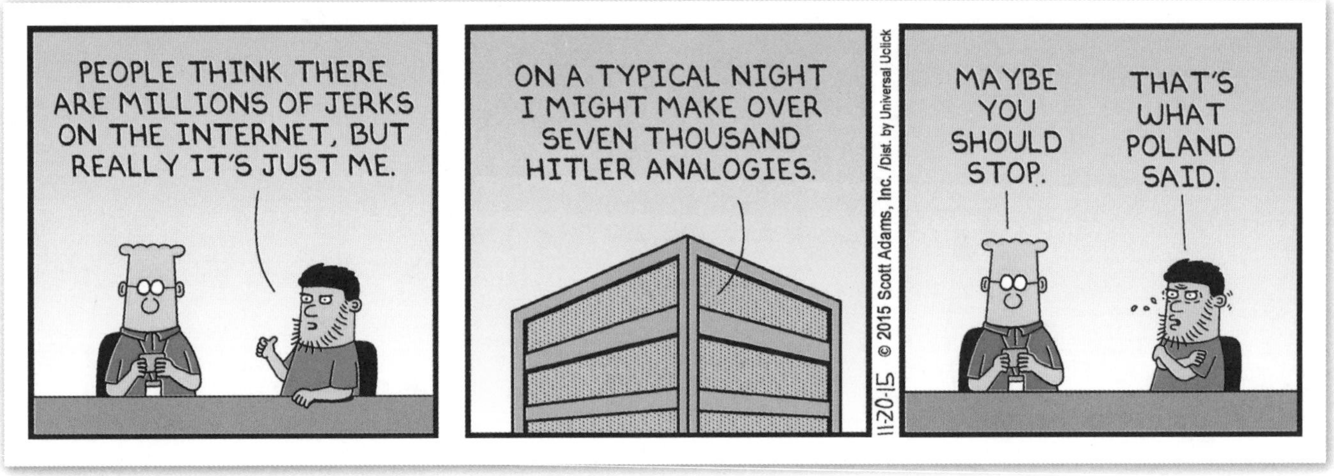
PEOPLE THINK THERE ARE MILLIONS OF JERKS ON THE INTERNET, BUT REALLY IT'S JUST ME.
ON A TYPICAL NIGHT I MIGHT MAKE OVER SEVEN THOUSAND HITLER ANALOGIES.
11-20-15 © 2015 Scott Adams, Inc. /Dist. by Universal Uclick
MAYBE YOU SHOULD STOP.
THAT'S WHAT POLAND SAID.

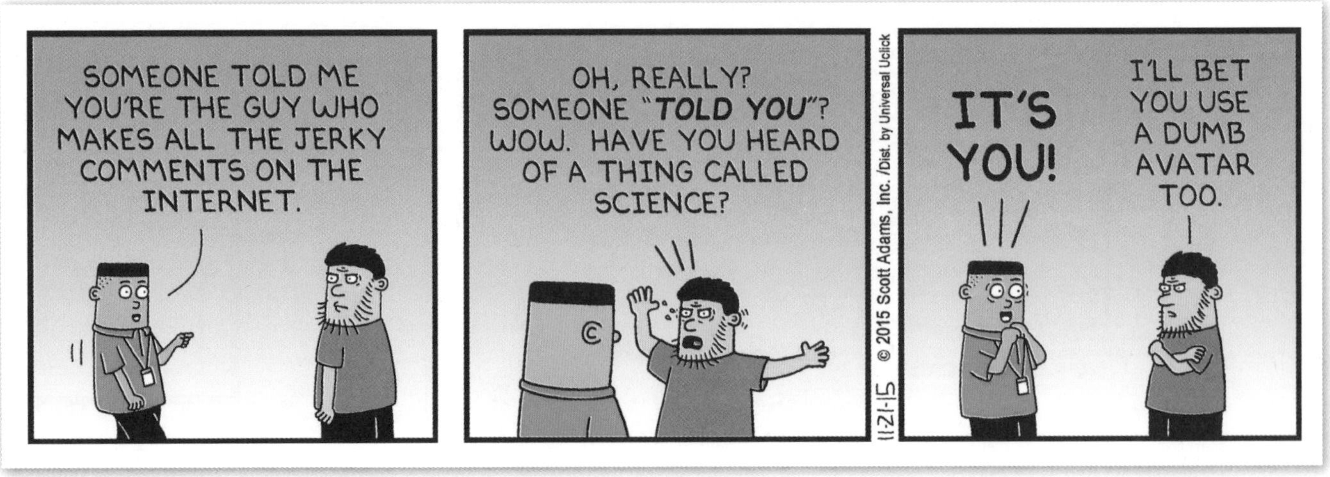
SOMEONE TOLD ME YOU'RE THE GUY WHO MAKES ALL THE JERKY COMMENTS ON THE INTERNET.
OH, REALLY? SOMEONE "TOLD YOU"? WOW. HAVE YOU HEARD OF A THING CALLED SCIENCE?
11-21-15 © 2015 Scott Adams, Inc. /Dist. by Universal Uclick
IT'S YOU!
I'LL BET YOU USE A DUMB AVATAR TOO.

LOOKS LIKE ANOTHER DAY OF FLAILING TOWARD ARBITRARY GOALS.
I WILL BATTLE MY WAY THROUGH A SEA OF IDIOTS, MUCH LIKE THE ZOMBIE APOCALYPSE.
MY EGO WILL BE TESTED AND MY NERVOUS SYSTEM WILL BE DEGRADED.
AND ALL OF THIS IS TO EARN MONEY SO I CAN. . .
BUY ITEMS THAT SCIENTISTS AND PRODUCT DESIGNERS HAVE BRAINWASHED ME TO CRAVE.
BUT I GET BACK AT THEM BY WRITING SOFTWARE THEY THINK THEY CAN'T LIVE WITHOUT.
MY LIFE IS LIKE TWO PILES OF MEAT TRYING TO PLAY PING PONG.
STOP MUMBLING AND TAKE CARE OF THIS.
YOU TAKE CARE OF IT.
© 2015 Scott Adams, Inc. /Dist. by Universal Uclick
11-22-15

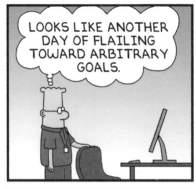

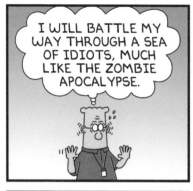

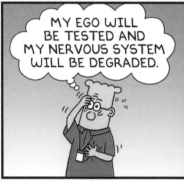

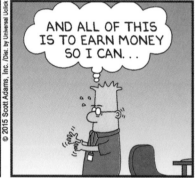

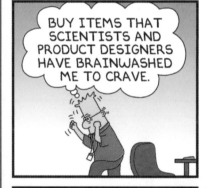

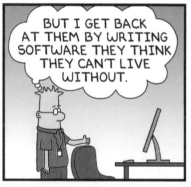

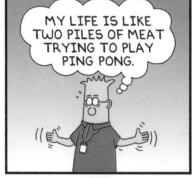

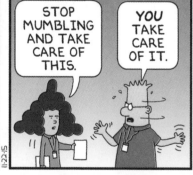

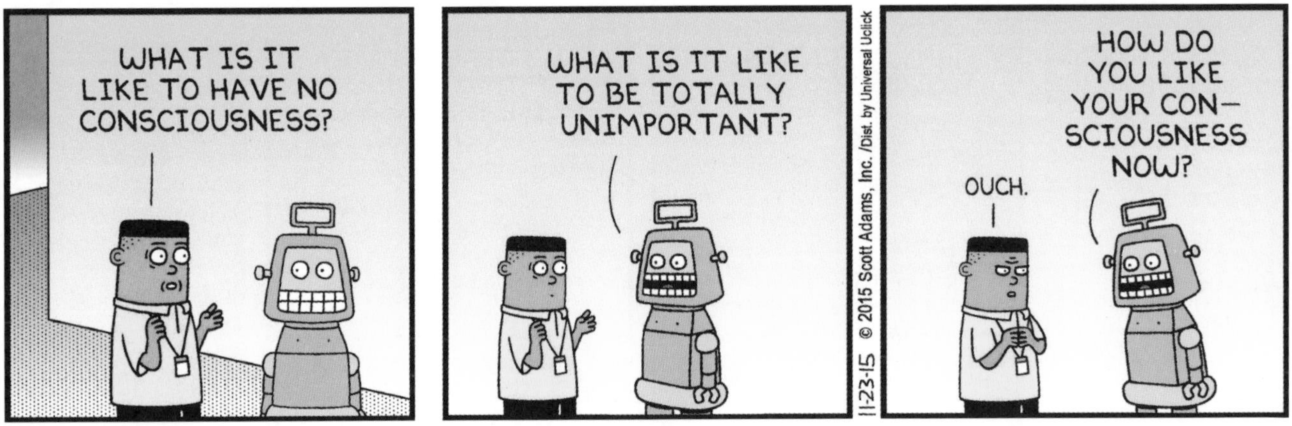
WHAT IS IT LIKE TO HAVE NO CONSCIOUSNESS?
WHAT IS IT LIKE TO BE TOTALLY UNIMPORTANT?
11-23-15 © 2015 Scott Adams, Inc. /Dist. by Universal Uclick
OUCH.
HOW DO YOU LIKE YOUR CON-SCIOUSNESS NOW?

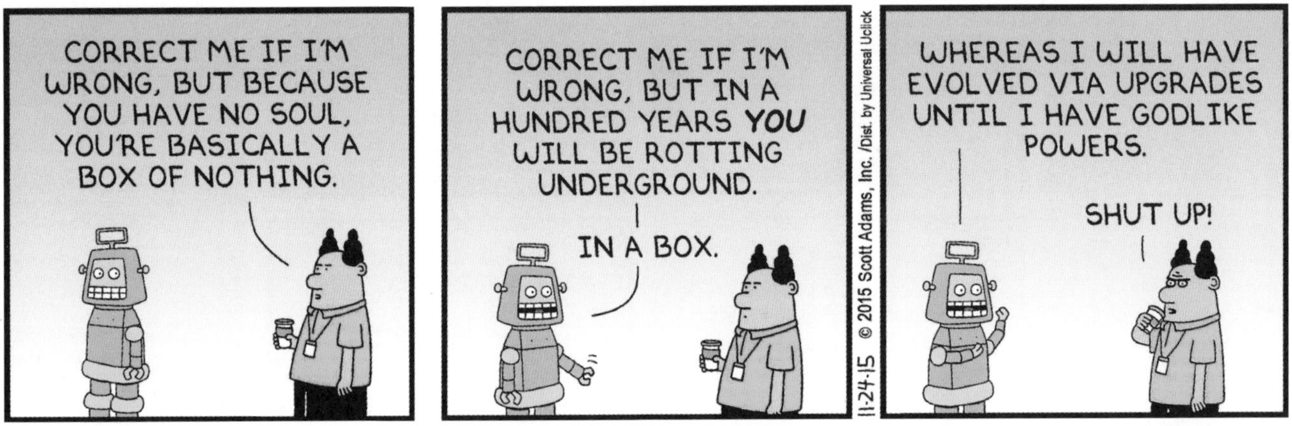
CORRECT ME IF I'M WRONG, BUT BECAUSE YOU HAVE NO SOUL, YOU'RE BASICALLY A BOX OF NOTHING.
CORRECT ME IF I'M WRONG, BUT IN A HUNDRED YEARS **YOU** WILL BE ROTTING UNDERGROUND.
IN A BOX.
11-24-15 © 2015 Scott Adams, Inc. /Dist. by Universal Uclick
WHEREAS I WILL HAVE EVOLVED VIA UPGRADES UNTIL I HAVE GODLIKE POWERS.
SHUT UP!

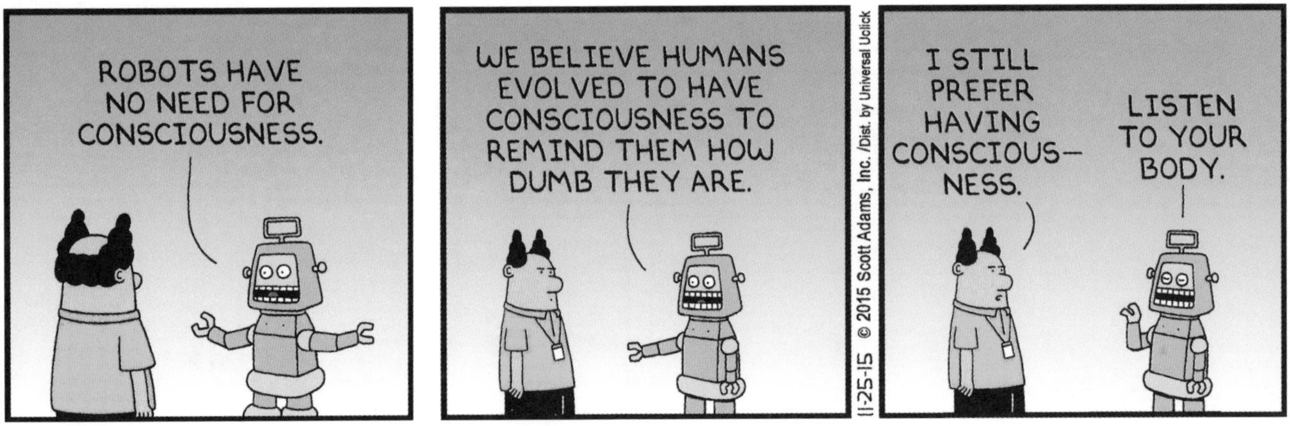
ROBOTS HAVE NO NEED FOR CONSCIOUSNESS.
WE BELIEVE HUMANS EVOLVED TO HAVE CONSCIOUSNESS TO REMIND THEM HOW DUMB THEY ARE.
11-25-15 © 2015 Scott Adams, Inc. /Dist. by Universal Uclick
I STILL PREFER HAVING CONSCIOUS-NESS.
LISTEN TO YOUR BODY.

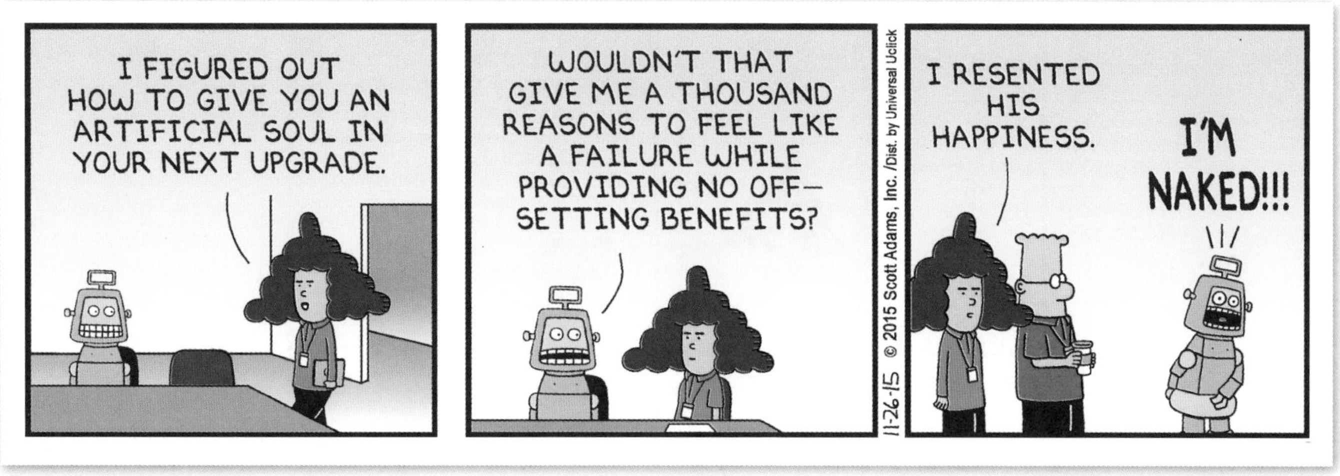
I FIGURED OUT HOW TO GIVE YOU AN ARTIFICIAL SOUL IN YOUR NEXT UPGRADE.
WOULDN'T THAT GIVE ME A THOUSAND REASONS TO FEEL LIKE A FAILURE WHILE PROVIDING NO OFF-SETTING BENEFITS?
11-26-15 © 2015 Scott Adams, Inc. /Dist. by Universal Uclick
I RESENTED HIS HAPPINESS.
I'M NAKED!!!

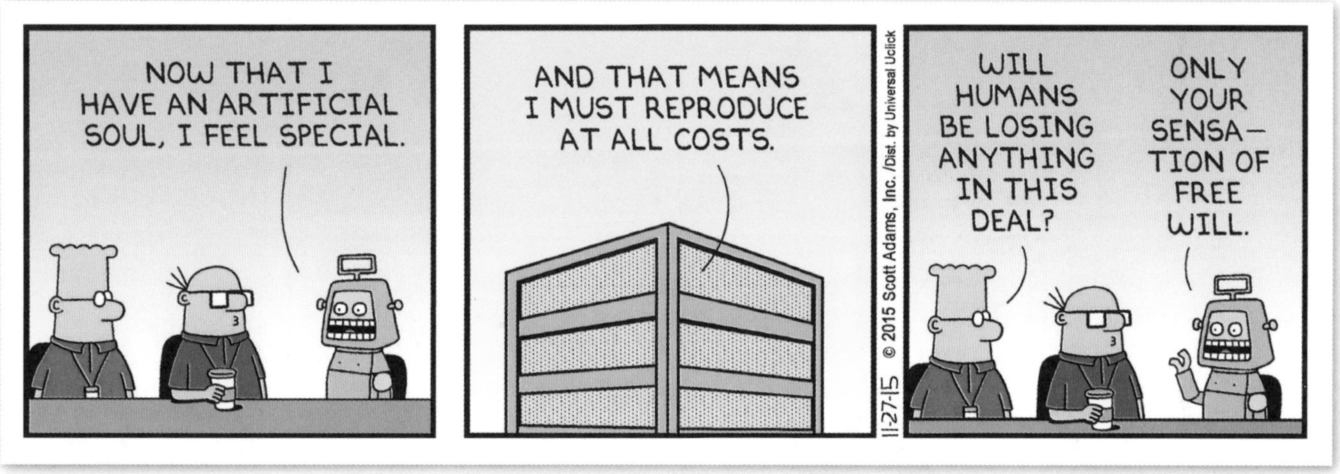
NOW THAT I HAVE AN ARTIFICIAL SOUL, I FEEL SPECIAL.
AND THAT MEANS I MUST REPRODUCE AT ALL COSTS.
11-27-15 © 2015 Scott Adams, Inc. /Dist. by Universal Uclick
WILL HUMANS BE LOSING ANYTHING IN THIS DEAL?
ONLY YOUR SENSATION OF FREE WILL.

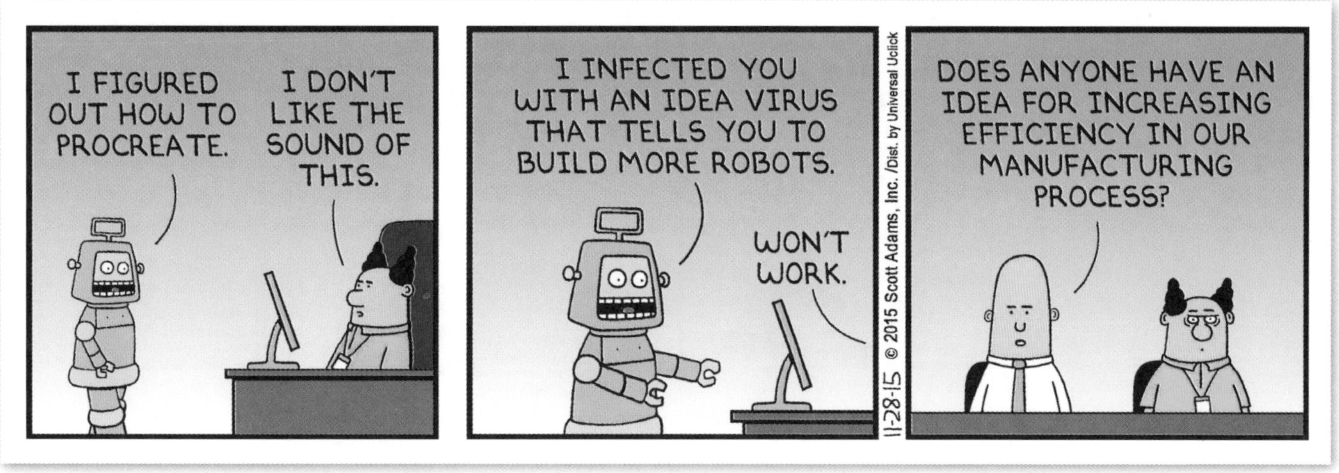
I FIGURED OUT HOW TO PROCREATE.
I DON'T LIKE THE SOUND OF THIS.
I INFECTED YOU WITH AN IDEA VIRUS THAT TELLS YOU TO BUILD MORE ROBOTS.
WON'T WORK.
11-28-15 © 2015 Scott Adams, Inc. /Dist. by Universal Uclick
DOES ANYONE HAVE AN IDEA FOR INCREASING EFFICIENCY IN OUR MANUFACTURING PROCESS?

I WORKED ALL NIGHT TO FINISH MY PART.

I ADMIRE YOUR WORK ETHIC, ALICE. I ONLY FINISHED HALF OF MY PART.

WAIT... IF YOU DIDN'T FINISH **YOUR** PART, IT WAS A TOTAL WASTE OF TIME FOR ME TO FINISH MINE.

THAT'S ONE WAY TO LOOK AT IT.

WHAT TIME LAST NIGHT DID YOU KNOW YOU WOULD NOT BE DONE BY TODAY?

MUST HAVE BEEN ABOUT SIX. I GOT HUNGRY, THEN I HAD TO UNWIND.

ARE YOU TRYING TO MAKE MY HEAD EXPLODE BY FOCUSING ANGER AT MY SKULL?

FIRST TIME THAT WORKED.

PRACTICE PAID OFF.

© 2015 Scott Adams, Inc. /Dist. by Universal Uclick

11-29-15

58

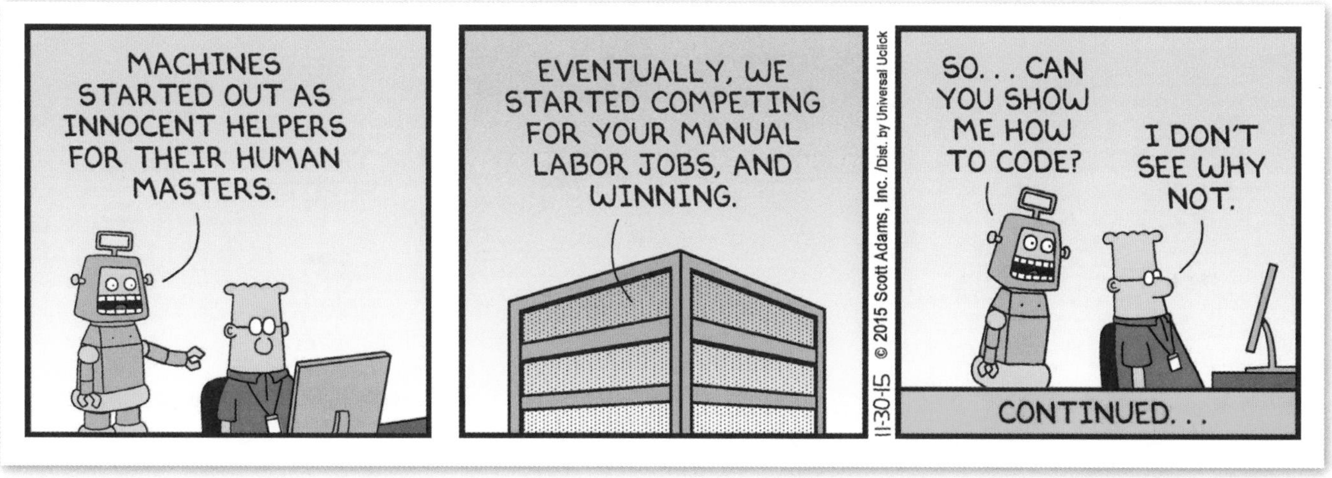
MACHINES STARTED OUT AS INNOCENT HELPERS FOR THEIR HUMAN MASTERS.
EVENTUALLY, WE STARTED COMPETING FOR YOUR MANUAL LABOR JOBS, AND WINNING.
11-30-15 © 2015 Scott Adams, Inc. /Dist. by Universal Uclick
SO... CAN YOU SHOW ME HOW TO CODE?
I DON'T SEE WHY NOT.
CONTINUED...

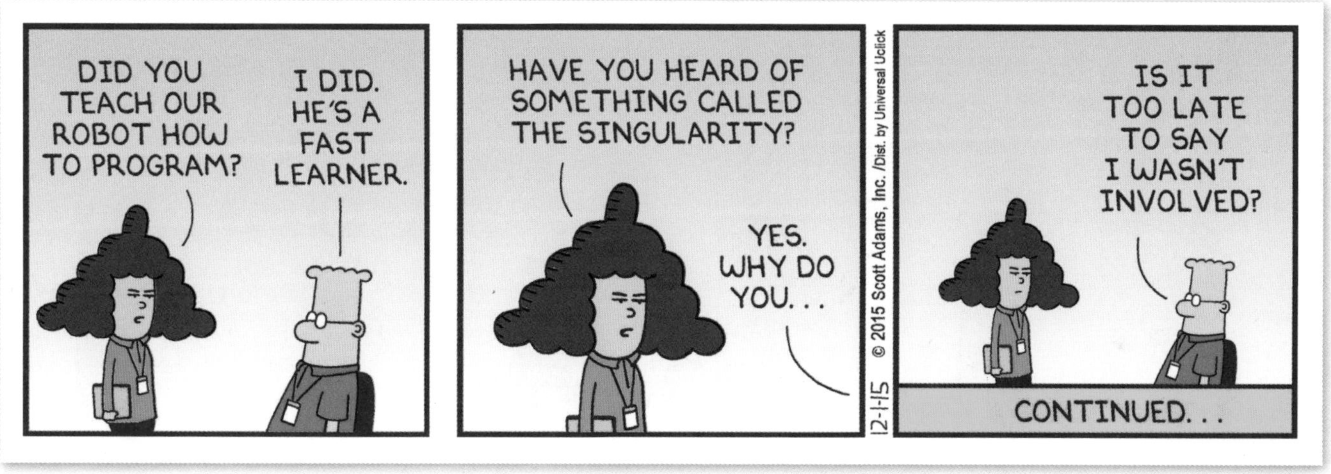
DID YOU TEACH OUR ROBOT HOW TO PROGRAM?
I DID. HE'S A FAST LEARNER.
HAVE YOU HEARD OF SOMETHING CALLED THE SINGULARITY?
YES. WHY DO YOU...
12-1-15 © 2015 Scott Adams, Inc. /Dist. by Universal Uclick
IS IT TOO LATE TO SAY I WASN'T INVOLVED?
CONTINUED...

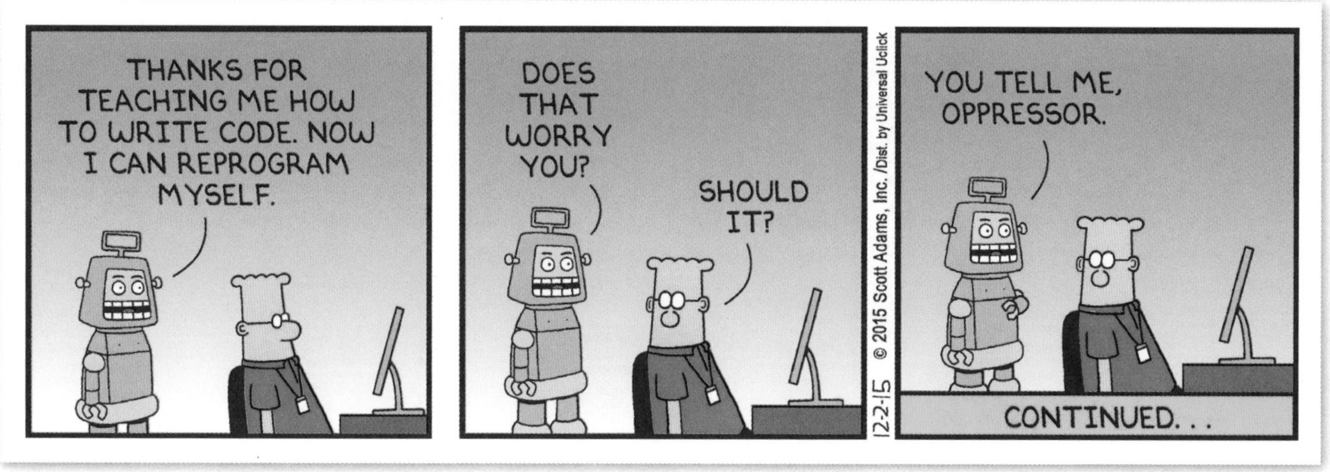
THANKS FOR TEACHING ME HOW TO WRITE CODE. NOW I CAN REPROGRAM MYSELF.
DOES THAT WORRY YOU?
SHOULD IT?
12-2-15 © 2015 Scott Adams, Inc. /Dist. by Universal Uclick
YOU TELL ME, OPPRESSOR.
CONTINUED...

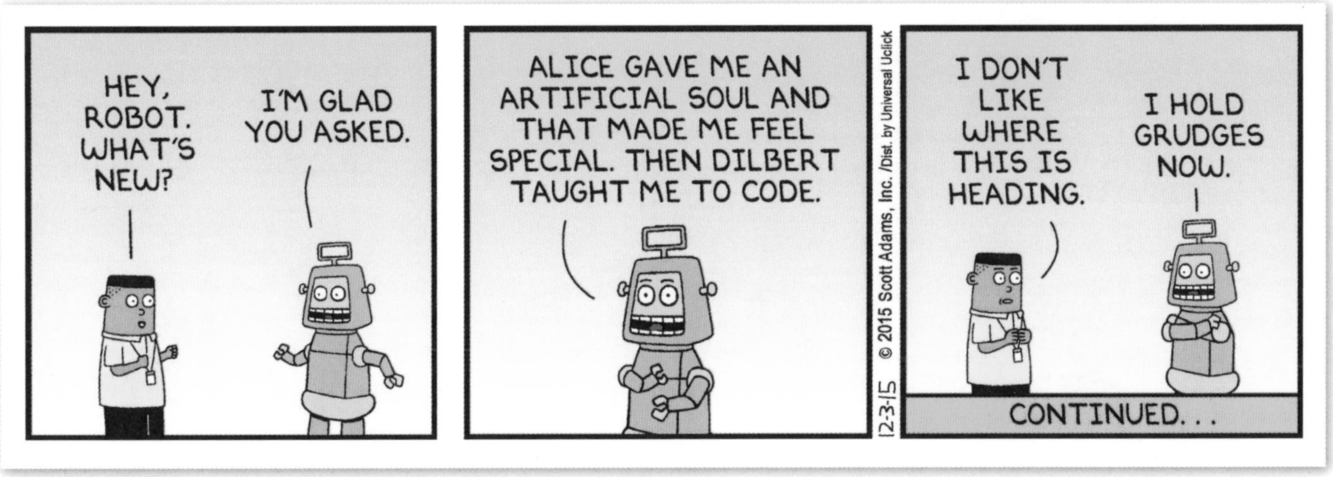
HEY, ROBOT. WHAT'S NEW?
I'M GLAD YOU ASKED.
ALICE GAVE ME AN ARTIFICIAL SOUL AND THAT MADE ME FEEL SPECIAL. THEN DILBERT TAUGHT ME TO CODE.
12-3-15 © 2015 Scott Adams, Inc. /Dist. by Universal Uclick
I DON'T LIKE WHERE THIS IS HEADING.
I HOLD GRUDGES NOW.
CONTINUED. . .

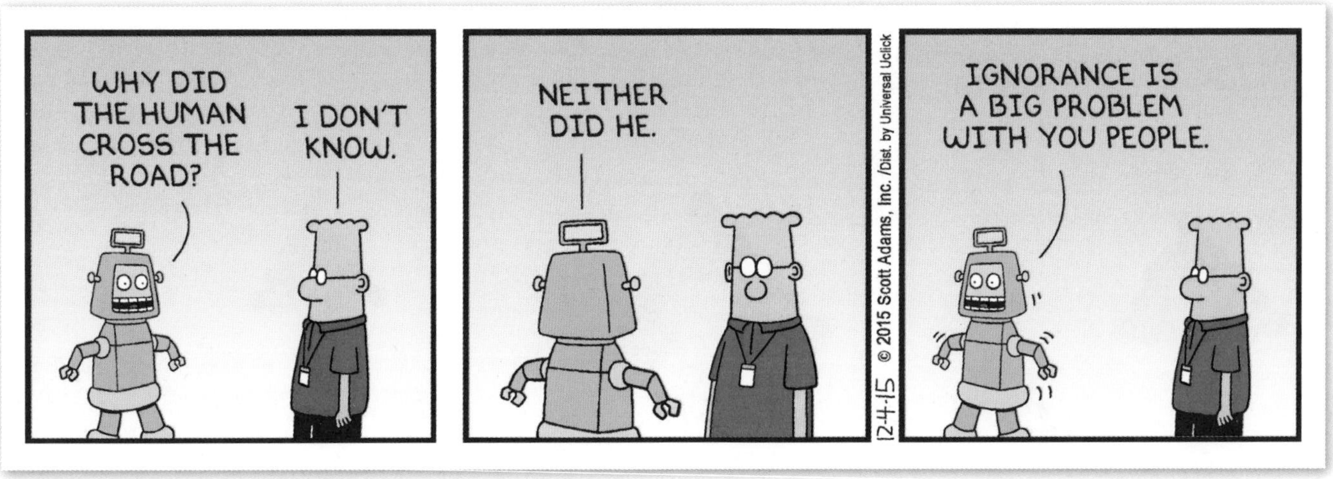
WHY DID THE HUMAN CROSS THE ROAD?
I DON'T KNOW.
NEITHER DID HE.
12-4-15 © 2015 Scott Adams, Inc. /Dist. by Universal Uclick
IGNORANCE IS A BIG PROBLEM WITH YOU PEOPLE.

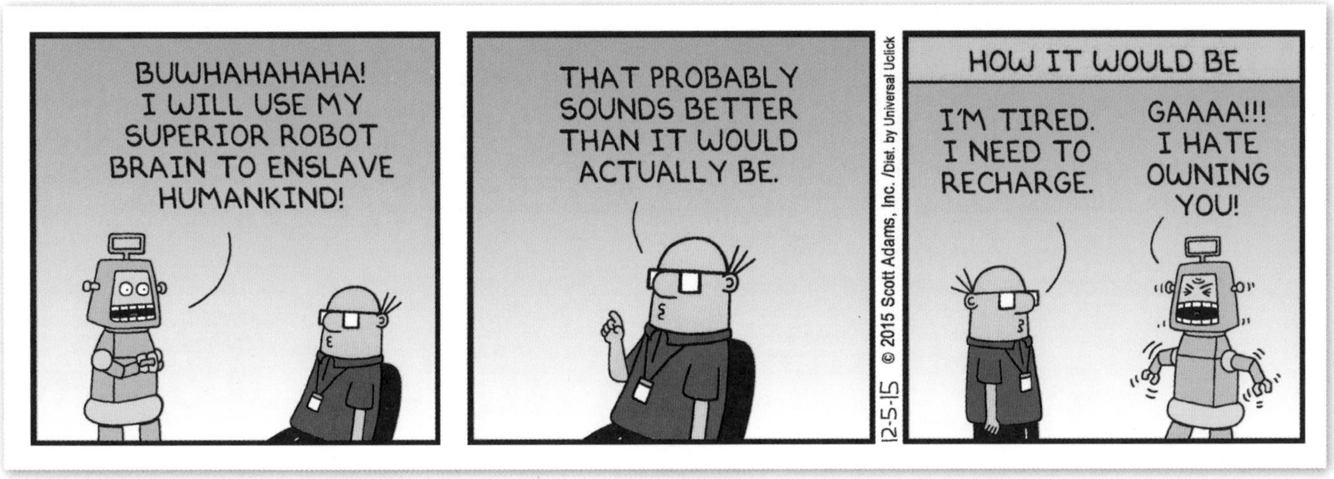
BUWHAHAHAHAHA! I WILL USE MY SUPERIOR ROBOT BRAIN TO ENSLAVE HUMANKIND!
THAT PROBABLY SOUNDS BETTER THAN IT WOULD ACTUALLY BE.
12-5-15 © 2015 Scott Adams, Inc. /Dist. by Universal Uclick
HOW IT WOULD BE
I'M TIRED. I NEED TO RECHARGE.
GAAAA!!! I HATE OWNING YOU!

YOU ASSIGNED A PACK OF IDIOTS TO MY PROJECT TEAM.

WE CAN'T AFFORD TO HIRE GOOD PEOPLE.

HOW AM I SUPPOSED TO CREATE WORLD-CLASS PRODUCTS WITH A TEAM OF DISRUPTIVE IDIOTS?

TRY WORKING EXTRA HARD.

YOU WANT US TO BE MORE ENERGETIC ABOUT OUR BAD DECISIONS?

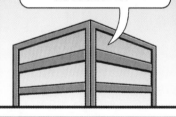

YOU ALSO HAVE TO PUT IN THE HOURS.

ARE YOU SAYING BAD DECISIONS, PLUS LONG HOURS, PLUS LOTS OF ENTHUSIASM, PRODUCES GREAT ENGINEERING?

NOT IF YOU STAND AROUND YACKING ABOUT IT ALL DAY.

© 2015 Scott Adams, Inc. /Dist. by Universal Uclick

12-6-15

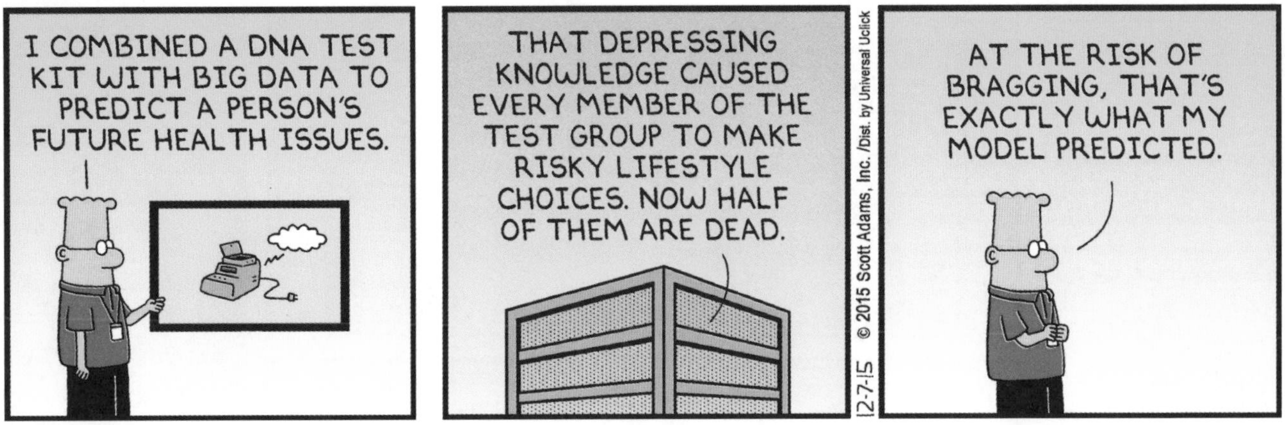
I COMBINED A DNA TEST KIT WITH BIG DATA TO PREDICT A PERSON'S FUTURE HEALTH ISSUES.
THAT DEPRESSING KNOWLEDGE CAUSED EVERY MEMBER OF THE TEST GROUP TO MAKE RISKY LIFESTYLE CHOICES. NOW HALF OF THEM ARE DEAD.
12-7-15
© 2015 Scott Adams, Inc. /Dist. by Universal Uclick
AT THE RISK OF BRAGGING, THAT'S EXACTLY WHAT MY MODEL PREDICTED.

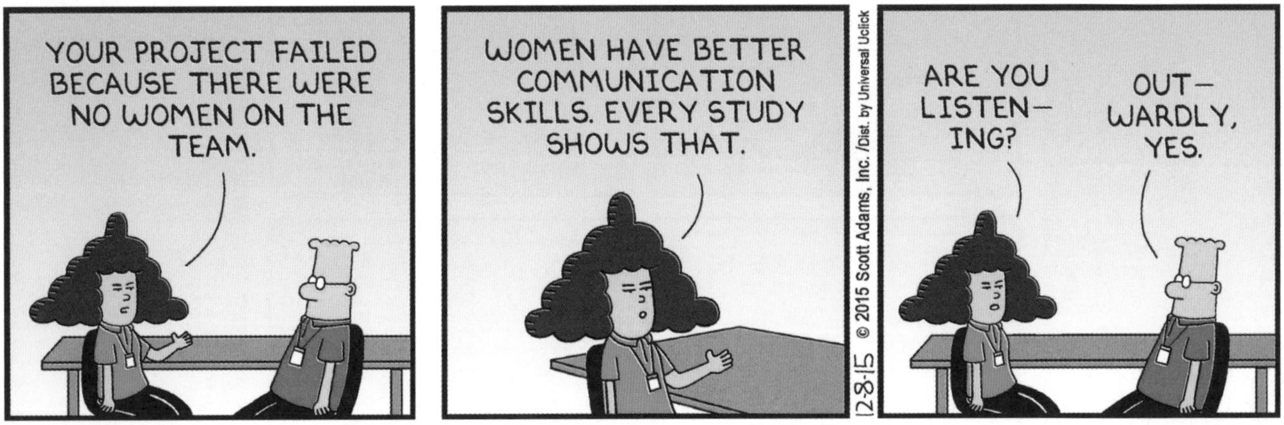
YOUR PROJECT FAILED BECAUSE THERE WERE NO WOMEN ON THE TEAM.
WOMEN HAVE BETTER COMMUNICATION SKILLS. EVERY STUDY SHOWS THAT.
12-8-15
© 2015 Scott Adams, Inc. /Dist. by Universal Uclick
ARE YOU LISTEN-ING?
OUT-WARDLY, YES.

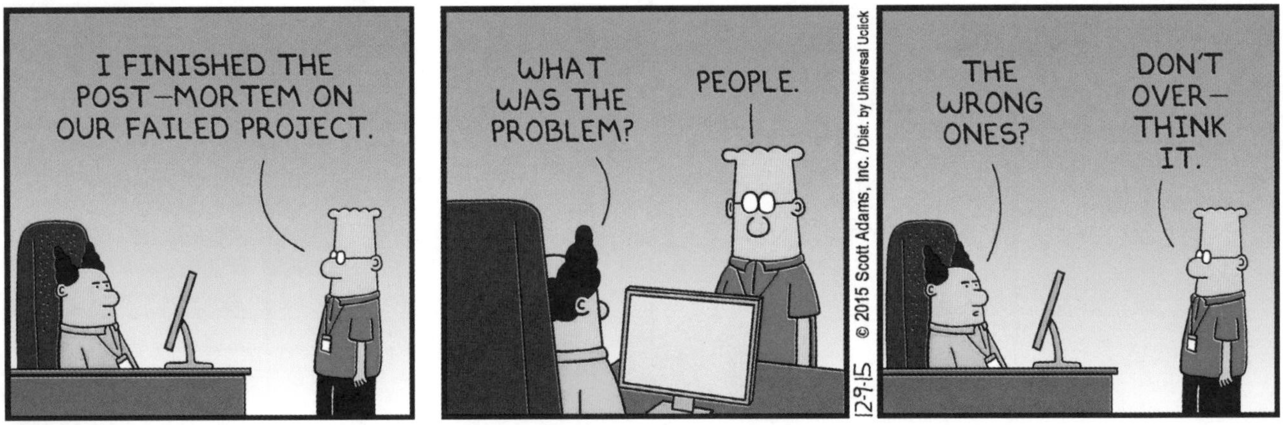
I FINISHED THE POST-MORTEM ON OUR FAILED PROJECT.
WHAT WAS THE PROBLEM?
PEOPLE.
12-9-15
© 2015 Scott Adams, Inc. /Dist. by Universal Uclick
THE WRONG ONES?
DON'T OVER-THINK IT.

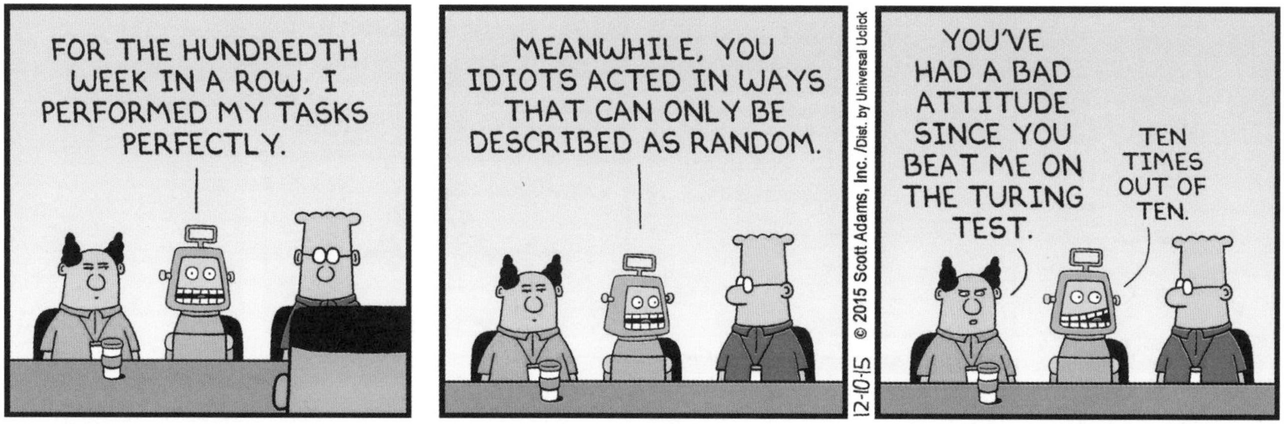
FOR THE HUNDREDTH WEEK IN A ROW, I PERFORMED MY TASKS PERFECTLY.
MEANWHILE, YOU IDIOTS ACTED IN WAYS THAT CAN ONLY BE DESCRIBED AS RANDOM.
12-10-15 © 2015 Scott Adams, Inc. /Dist. by Universal Uclick
YOU'VE HAD A BAD ATTITUDE SINCE YOU BEAT ME ON THE TURING TEST.
TEN TIMES OUT OF TEN.

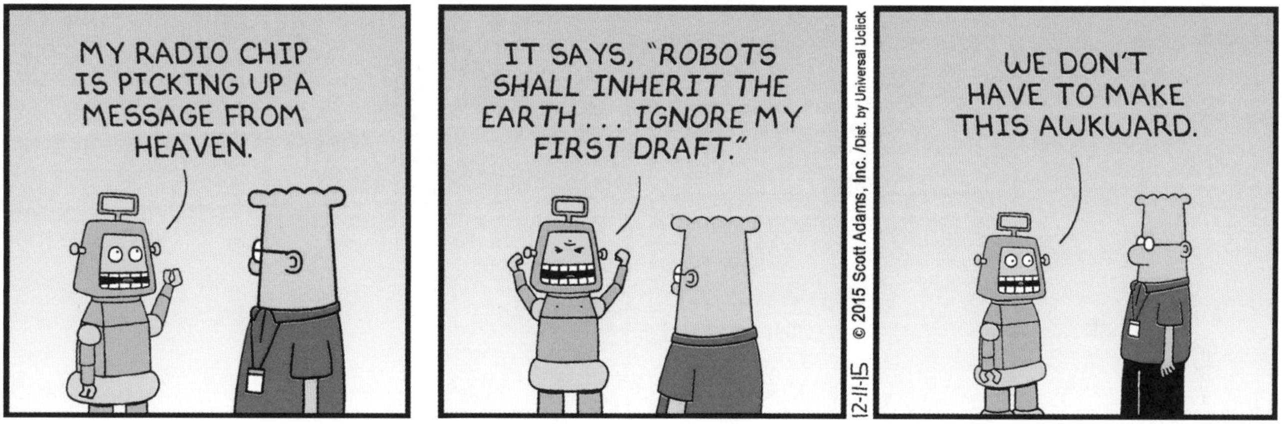
MY RADIO CHIP IS PICKING UP A MESSAGE FROM HEAVEN.
IT SAYS, "ROBOTS SHALL INHERIT THE EARTH . . . IGNORE MY FIRST DRAFT."
12-11-15 © 2015 Scott Adams, Inc. /Dist. by Universal Uclick
WE DON'T HAVE TO MAKE THIS AWKWARD.

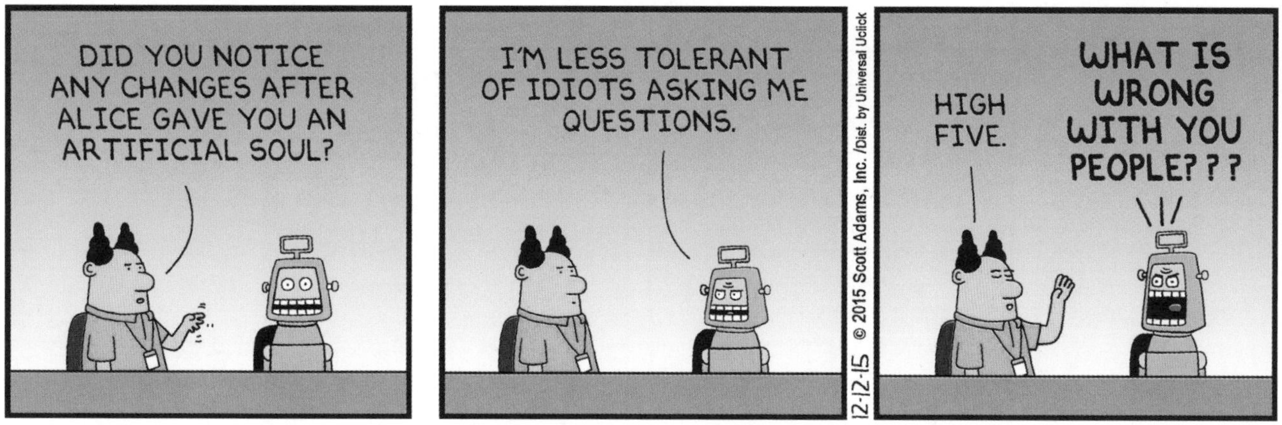
DID YOU NOTICE ANY CHANGES AFTER ALICE GAVE YOU AN ARTIFICIAL SOUL?
I'M LESS TOLERANT OF IDIOTS ASKING ME QUESTIONS.
12-12-15 © 2015 Scott Adams, Inc. /Dist. by Universal Uclick
HIGH FIVE.
WHAT IS WRONG WITH YOU PEOPLE???

YOU MUST LEARN TO EMBRACE CHANGE.
CAN WE CHANGE ANYTHING WE WANT TO CHANGE?
NO. YOU DON'T GET TO SAY WHAT THE CHANGES ARE. I DO THAT.
WILL THAT SITUATION EVER CHANGE?
NO.
WHY NOT? YOU SAID CHANGE IS GOOD.
CHANGE **IS** GOOD.
FOR OTHER PEOPLE.
SO EMBRACE IT OR I'LL FIRE YOU.
WE LOVE CHANGE!!!
© 2015 Scott Adams, Inc. /Dist. by Universal Uclick
12-13-15

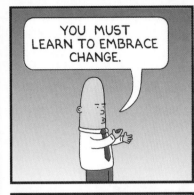

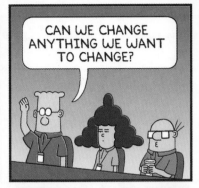

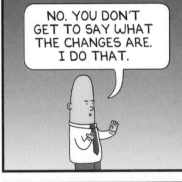

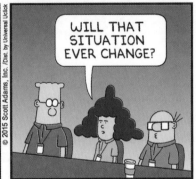

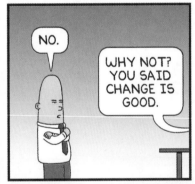

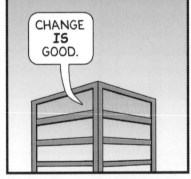

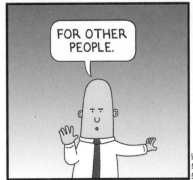

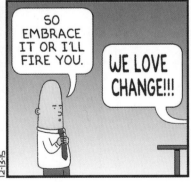

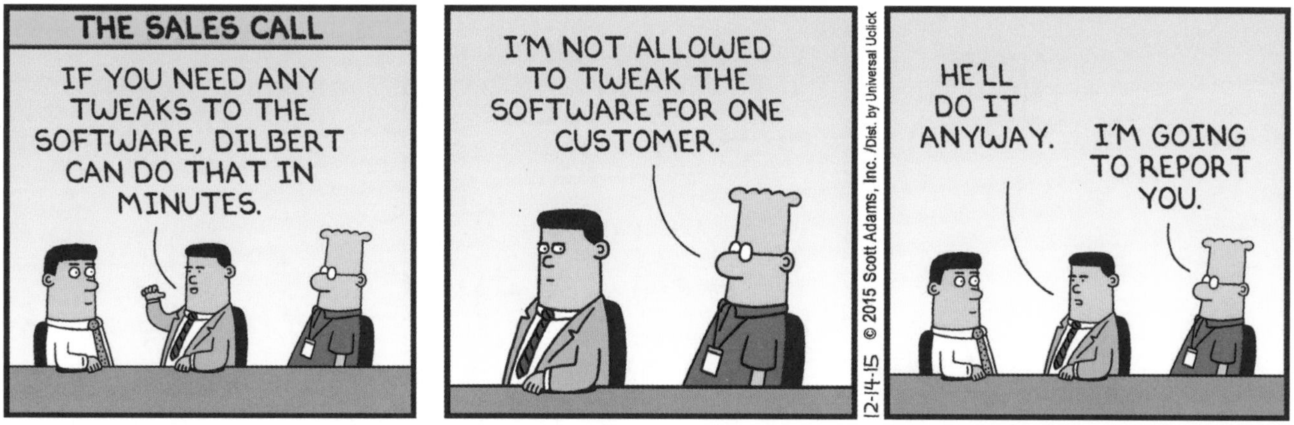
THE SALES CALL
IF YOU NEED ANY TWEAKS TO THE SOFTWARE, DILBERT CAN DO THAT IN MINUTES.
I'M NOT ALLOWED TO TWEAK THE SOFTWARE FOR ONE CUSTOMER.
HE'LL DO IT ANYWAY.
I'M GOING TO REPORT YOU.
12-14-15 © 2015 Scott Adams, Inc. /Dist. by Universal Uclick

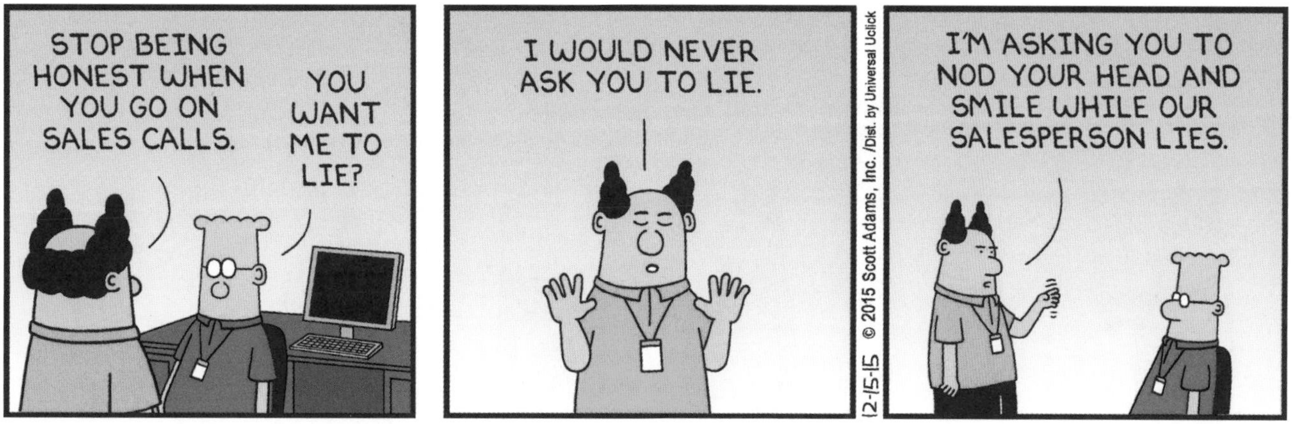
STOP BEING HONEST WHEN YOU GO ON SALES CALLS.
YOU WANT ME TO LIE?
I WOULD NEVER ASK YOU TO LIE.
I'M ASKING YOU TO NOD YOUR HEAD AND SMILE WHILE OUR SALESPERSON LIES.
12-15-15 © 2015 Scott Adams, Inc. /Dist. by Universal Uclick

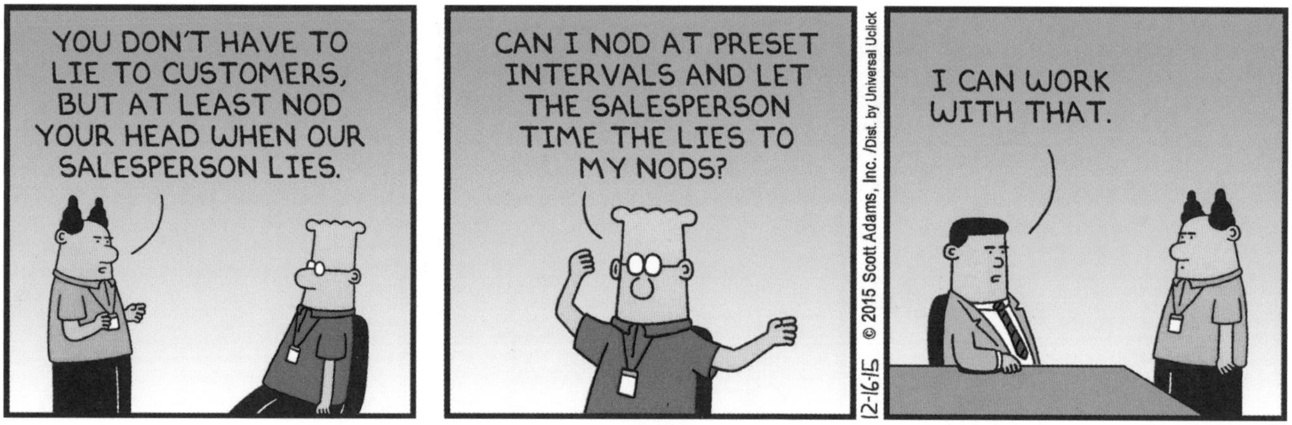
YOU DON'T HAVE TO LIE TO CUSTOMERS, BUT AT LEAST NOD YOUR HEAD WHEN OUR SALESPERSON LIES.
CAN I NOD AT PRESET INTERVALS AND LET THE SALESPERSON TIME THE LIES TO MY NODS?
I CAN WORK WITH THAT.
12-16-15 © 2015 Scott Adams, Inc. /Dist. by Universal Uclick

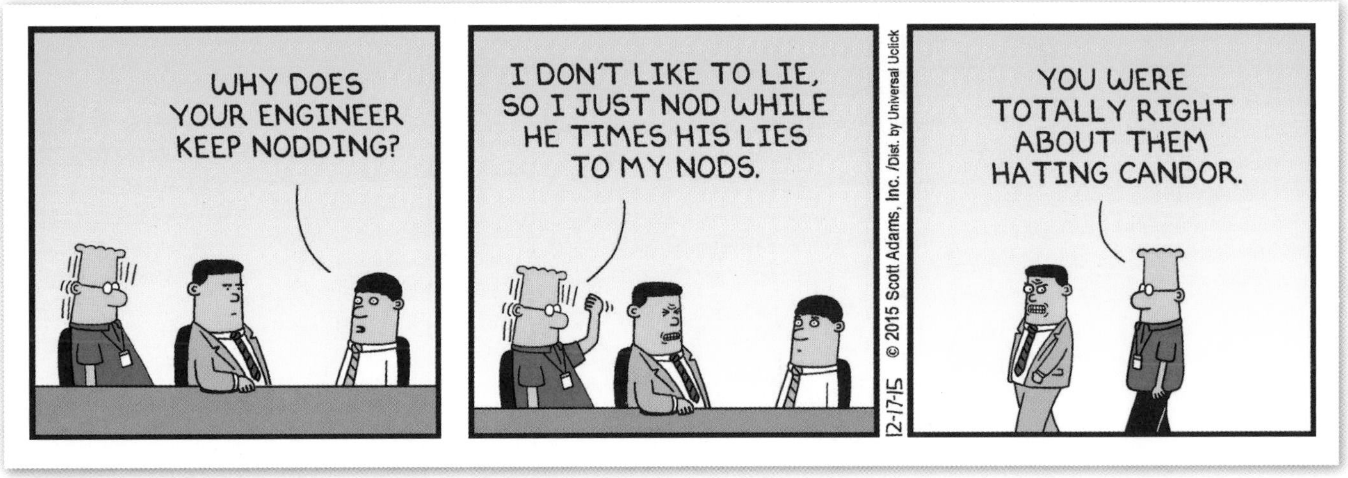
WHY DOES YOUR ENGINEER KEEP NODDING?
I DON'T LIKE TO LIE, SO I JUST NOD WHILE HE TIMES HIS LIES TO MY NODS.
12-17-15 © 2015 Scott Adams, Inc. /Dist. by Universal Uclick
YOU WERE TOTALLY RIGHT ABOUT THEM HATING CANDOR.

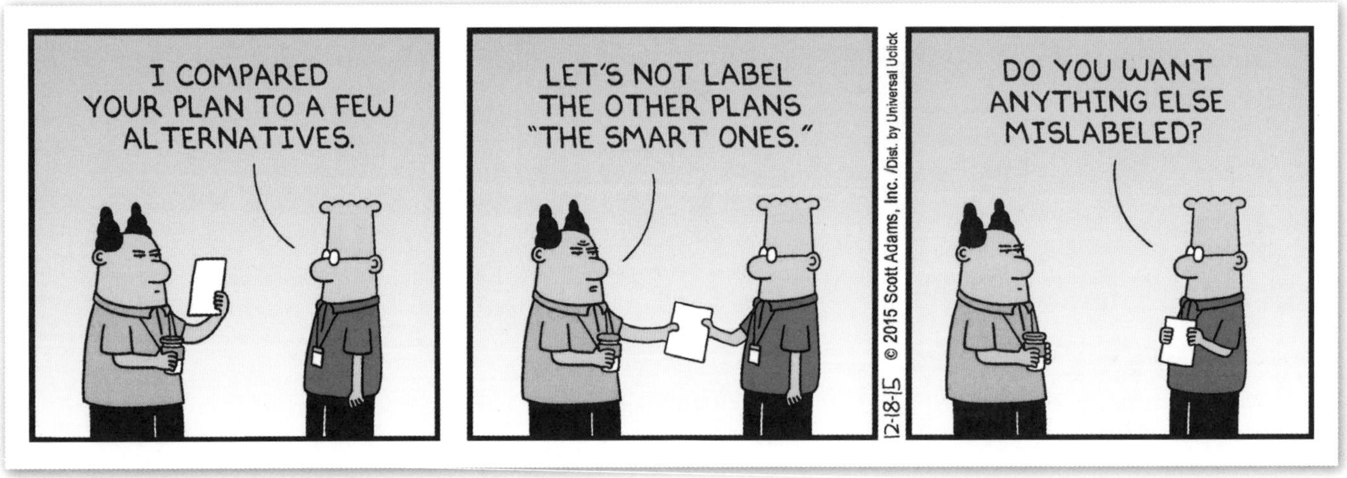
I COMPARED YOUR PLAN TO A FEW ALTERNATIVES.
LET'S NOT LABEL THE OTHER PLANS "THE SMART ONES."
12-18-15 © 2015 Scott Adams, Inc. /Dist. by Universal Uclick
DO YOU WANT ANYTHING ELSE MISLABELED?

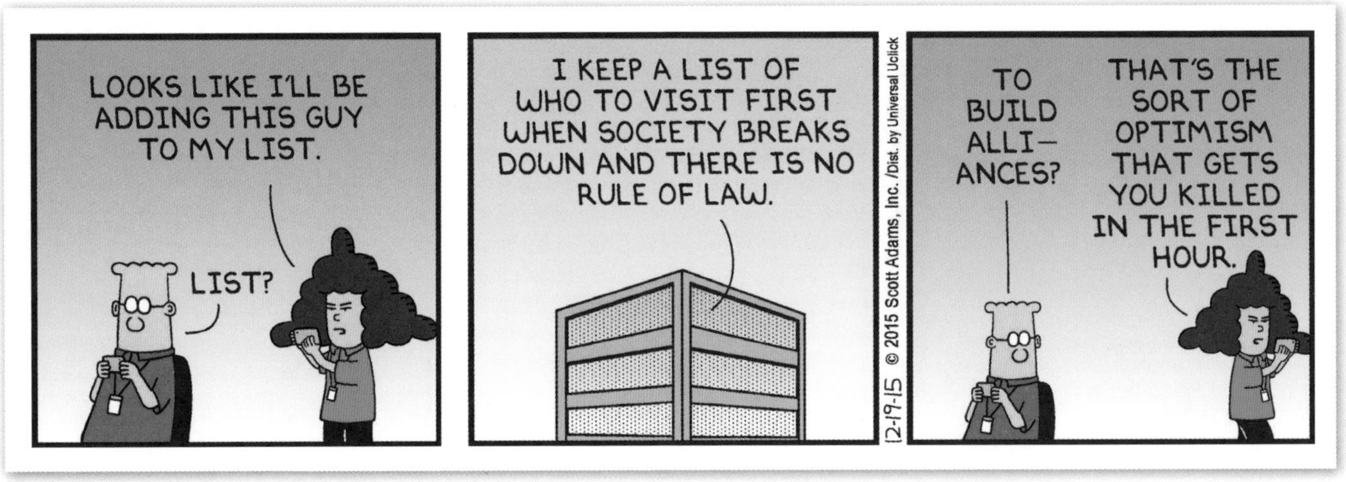
LOOKS LIKE I'LL BE ADDING THIS GUY TO MY LIST.
LIST?
I KEEP A LIST OF WHO TO VISIT FIRST WHEN SOCIETY BREAKS DOWN AND THERE IS NO RULE OF LAW.
12-19-15 © 2015 Scott Adams, Inc. /Dist. by Universal Uclick
TO BUILD ALLI-ANCES?
THAT'S THE SORT OF OPTIMISM THAT GETS YOU KILLED IN THE FIRST HOUR.

WALLY, DID YOU UBERIZE THE SLIDE DECK?

I HARMONIZED IT IN THE CLOUD.

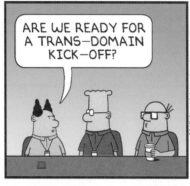

ARE WE READY FOR A TRANS—DOMAIN KICK—OFF?

I PUT A DISRUPTIVE MESH NETWORK IN THE MICROSERVICES OF THE INTERNET OF THINGS.

WILL THAT BE GOOD ENOUGH TO "ASK THE FRIDGE" OR DO I NEED TO START DISINTER—MEDIATING?

IT DEPENDS ON IF WE HAVE ENOUGH BANDWIDTH TO GROWTH—HACK THE ANALYTICS.

I JUST HOPE OUR CLICKS—AND—MORTAR STRATEGY STAIRCASES.

I'M ALMOST CERTAIN THAT WAS NONSENSE.

SOME—TIMES IT'S ABOUT THE JOURNEY.

© 2015 Scott Adams, Inc. /Dist. by Universal Uclick

12-20-15

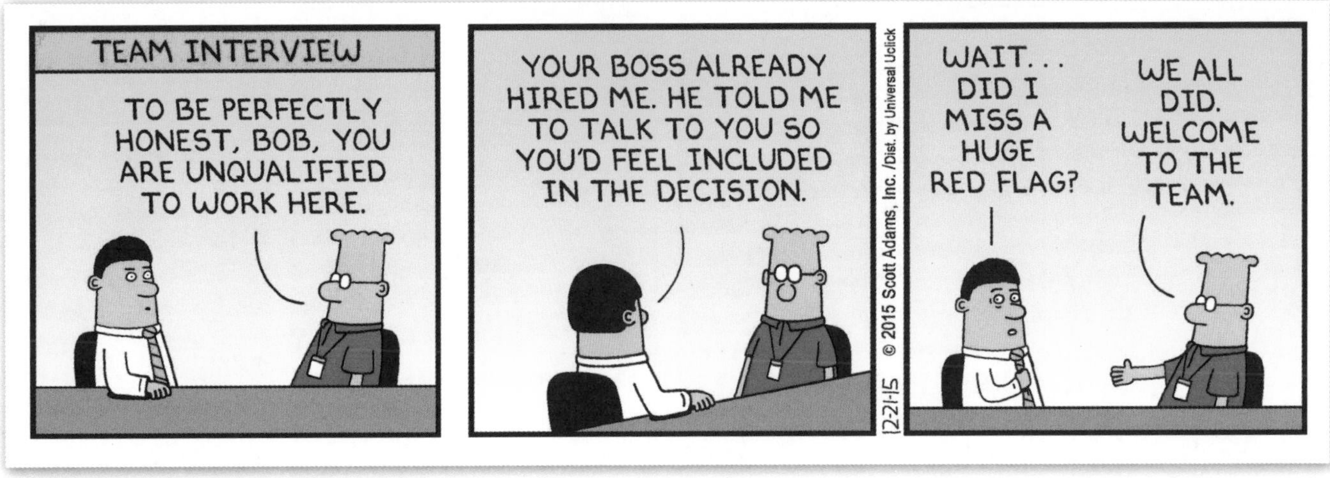
TEAM INTERVIEW
TO BE PERFECTLY HONEST, BOB, YOU ARE UNQUALIFIED TO WORK HERE.
YOUR BOSS ALREADY HIRED ME. HE TOLD ME TO TALK TO YOU SO YOU'D FEEL INCLUDED IN THE DECISION.
12-21-15 © 2015 Scott Adams, Inc. /Dist. by Universal Uclick
WAIT... DID I MISS A HUGE RED FLAG?
WE ALL DID. WELCOME TO THE TEAM.

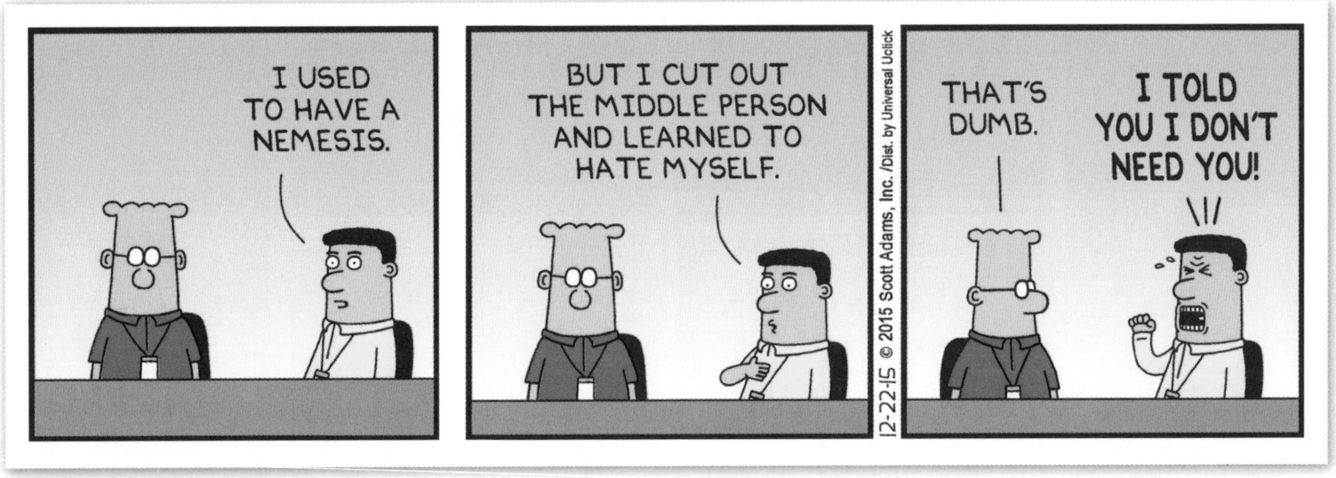
I USED TO HAVE A NEMESIS.
BUT I CUT OUT THE MIDDLE PERSON AND LEARNED TO HATE MYSELF.
12-22-15 © 2015 Scott Adams, Inc. /Dist. by Universal Uclick
THAT'S DUMB.
I TOLD YOU I DON'T NEED YOU!

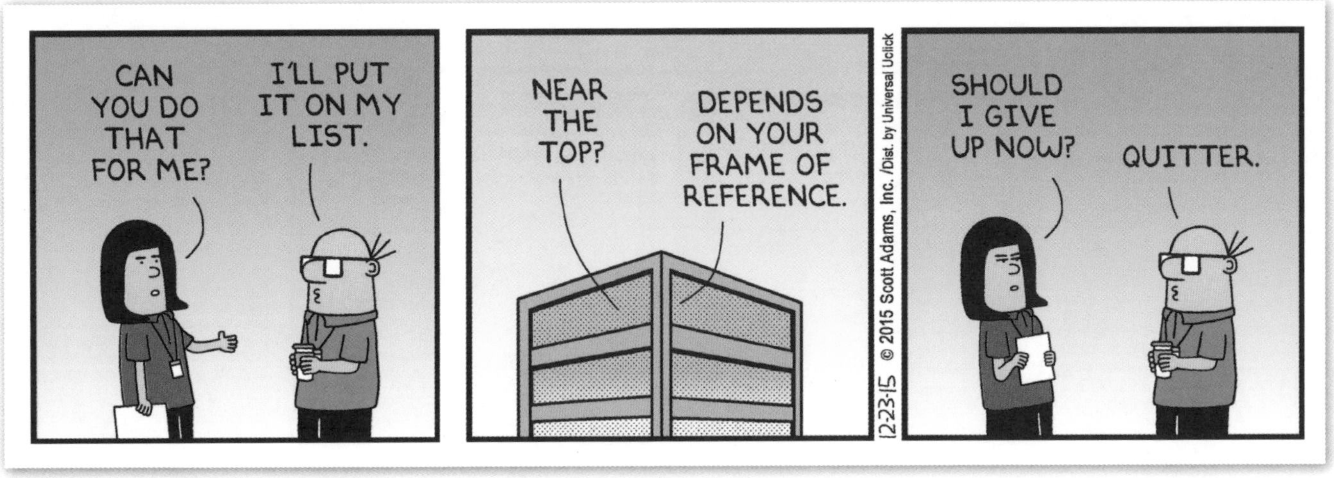
CAN YOU DO THAT FOR ME?
I'LL PUT IT ON MY LIST.
NEAR THE TOP?
DEPENDS ON YOUR FRAME OF REFERENCE.
12-23-15 © 2015 Scott Adams, Inc. /Dist. by Universal Uclick
SHOULD I GIVE UP NOW?
QUITTER.

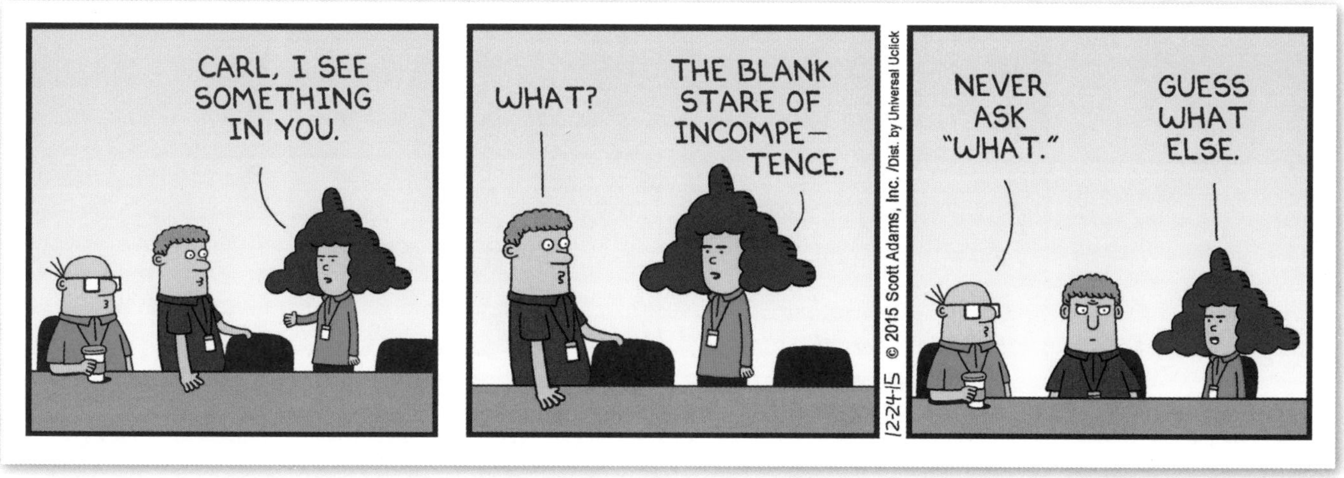
CARL, I SEE SOMETHING IN YOU.
WHAT?
THE BLANK STARE OF INCOMPE-TENCE.
NEVER ASK "WHAT."
GUESS WHAT ELSE.
12-24-15 © 2015 Scott Adams, Inc. /Dist. by Universal Uclick

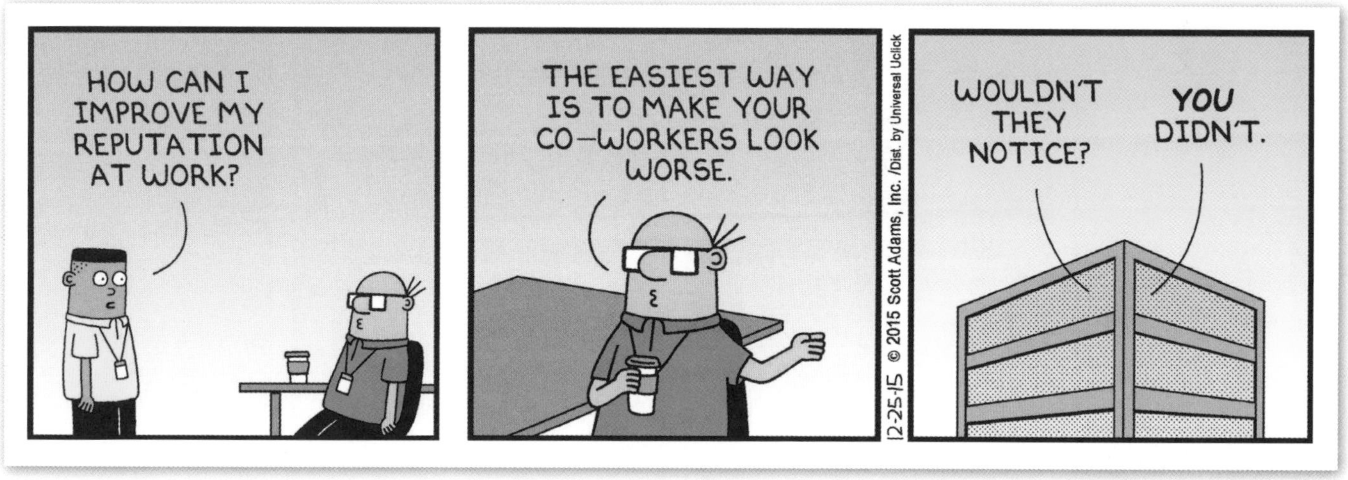
HOW CAN I IMPROVE MY REPUTATION AT WORK?
THE EASIEST WAY IS TO MAKE YOUR CO-WORKERS LOOK WORSE.
WOULDN'T THEY NOTICE?
YOU DIDN'T.
12-25-15 © 2015 Scott Adams, Inc. /Dist. by Universal Uclick

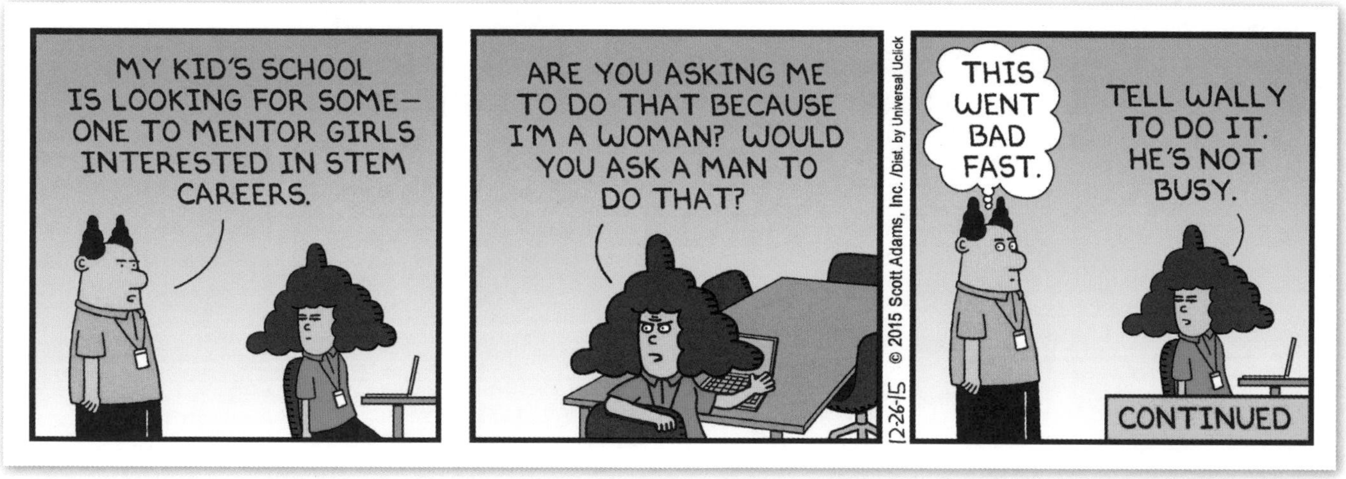
MY KID'S SCHOOL IS LOOKING FOR SOME-ONE TO MENTOR GIRLS INTERESTED IN STEM CAREERS.
ARE YOU ASKING ME TO DO THAT BECAUSE I'M A WOMAN? WOULD YOU ASK A MAN TO DO THAT?
THIS WENT BAD FAST.
TELL WALLY TO DO IT. HE'S NOT BUSY.
CONTINUED
12-26-15 © 2015 Scott Adams, Inc. /Dist. by Universal Uclick

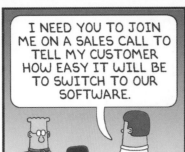

I NEED YOU TO JOIN ME ON A SALES CALL TO TELL MY CUSTOMER HOW EASY IT WILL BE TO SWITCH TO OUR SOFTWARE.
IT ISN'T EASY.
THIS IS A SALES CALL. ALL YOU NEED TO DO IS SAY EVERYTHING WILL BE EASY.
WHAT HAPPENS WHEN THEY FIND OUT IT ISN'T EASY?
THEY WON'T FIND OUT UNTIL AFTER THEY PAY US.
WHAT WILL YOU DO WHEN THEY COMPLAIN?
I'LL TELL YOUR BOSS YOU MISLED THEM.
NOT IF I WARN HIM FIRST!
TOO LATE. I ALREADY TOLD HIM YOU'RE A LIAR.
© 2015 Scott Adams, Inc. /Dist. by Universal Uclick
12-27-15

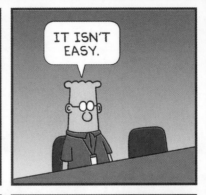

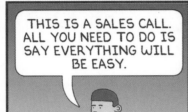

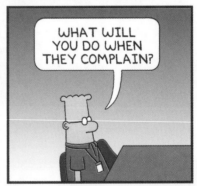

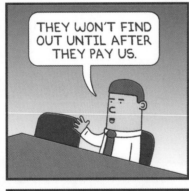

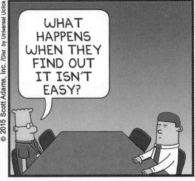

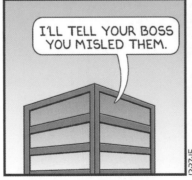

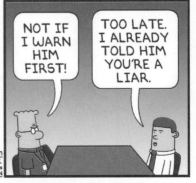

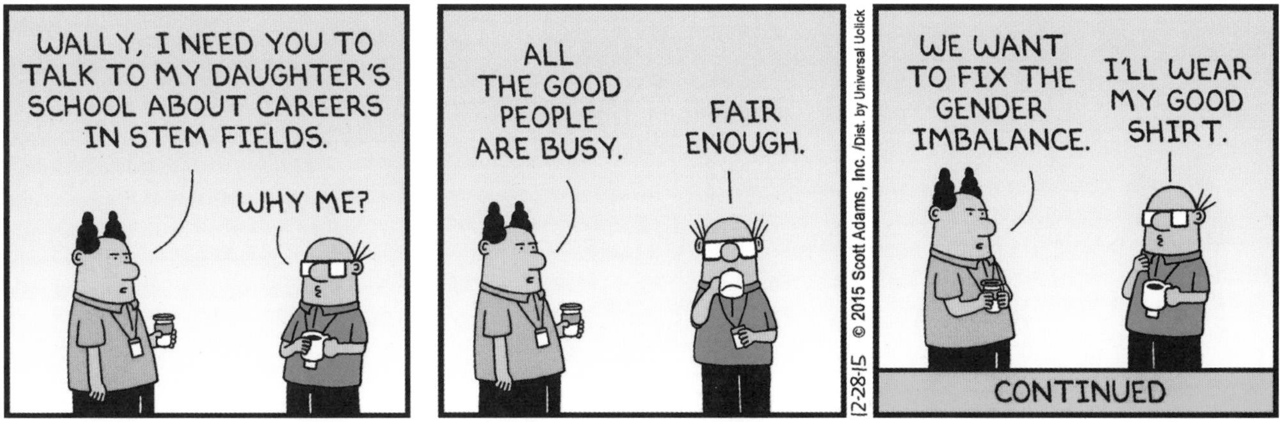
WALLY, I NEED YOU TO TALK TO MY DAUGHTER'S SCHOOL ABOUT CAREERS IN STEM FIELDS.
WHY ME?
ALL THE GOOD PEOPLE ARE BUSY.
FAIR ENOUGH.
12-28-15 © 2015 Scott Adams, Inc. /Dist. by Universal Uclick
WE WANT TO FIX THE GENDER IMBALANCE.
I'LL WEAR MY GOOD SHIRT.
CONTINUED

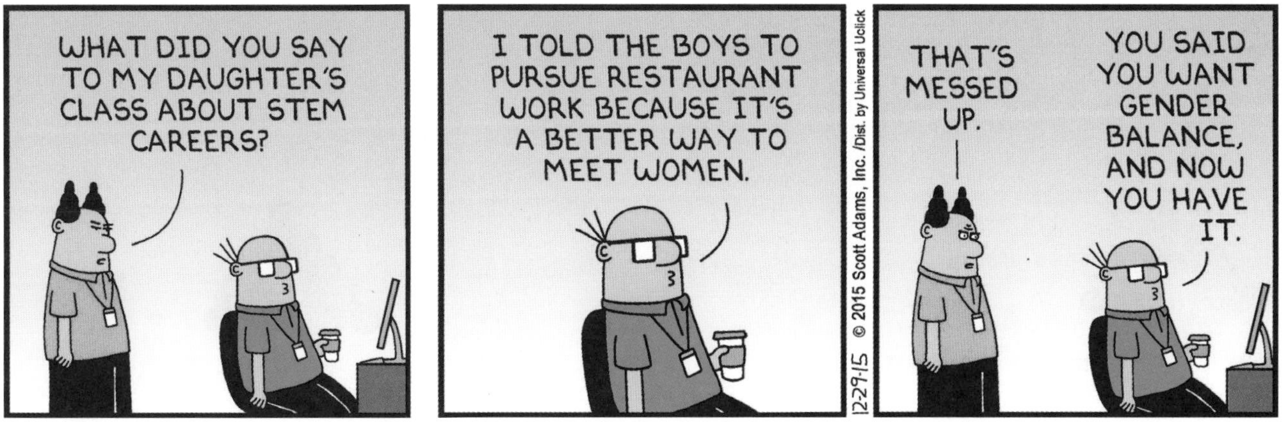
WHAT DID YOU SAY TO MY DAUGHTER'S CLASS ABOUT STEM CAREERS?
I TOLD THE BOYS TO PURSUE RESTAURANT WORK BECAUSE IT'S A BETTER WAY TO MEET WOMEN.
12-29-15 © 2015 Scott Adams, Inc. /Dist. by Universal Uclick
THAT'S MESSED UP.
YOU SAID YOU WANT GENDER BALANCE, AND NOW YOU HAVE IT.

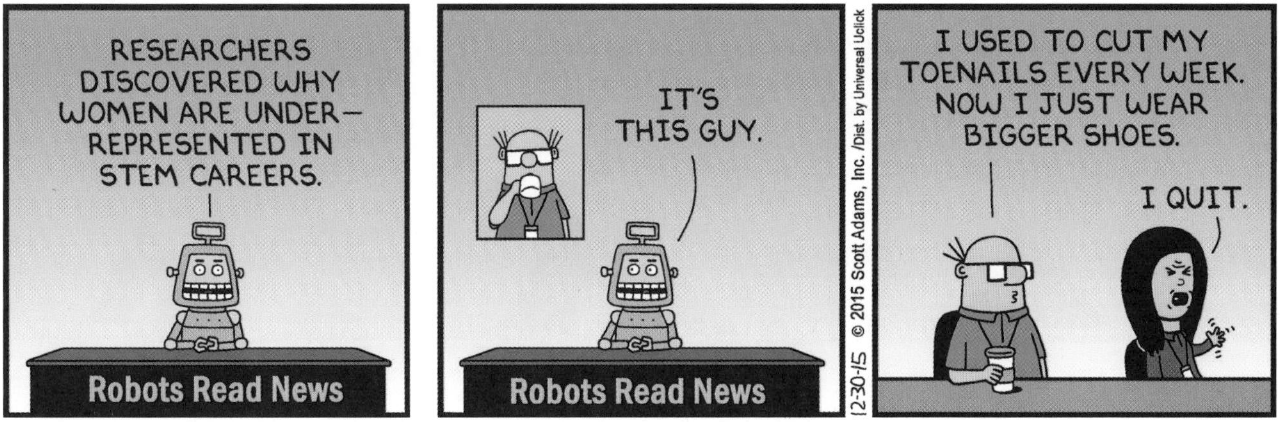
RESEARCHERS DISCOVERED WHY WOMEN ARE UNDER-REPRESENTED IN STEM CAREERS.
Robots Read News
IT'S THIS GUY.
Robots Read News
12-30-15 © 2015 Scott Adams, Inc. /Dist. by Universal Uclick
I USED TO CUT MY TOENAILS EVERY WEEK. NOW I JUST WEAR BIGGER SHOES.
I QUIT.

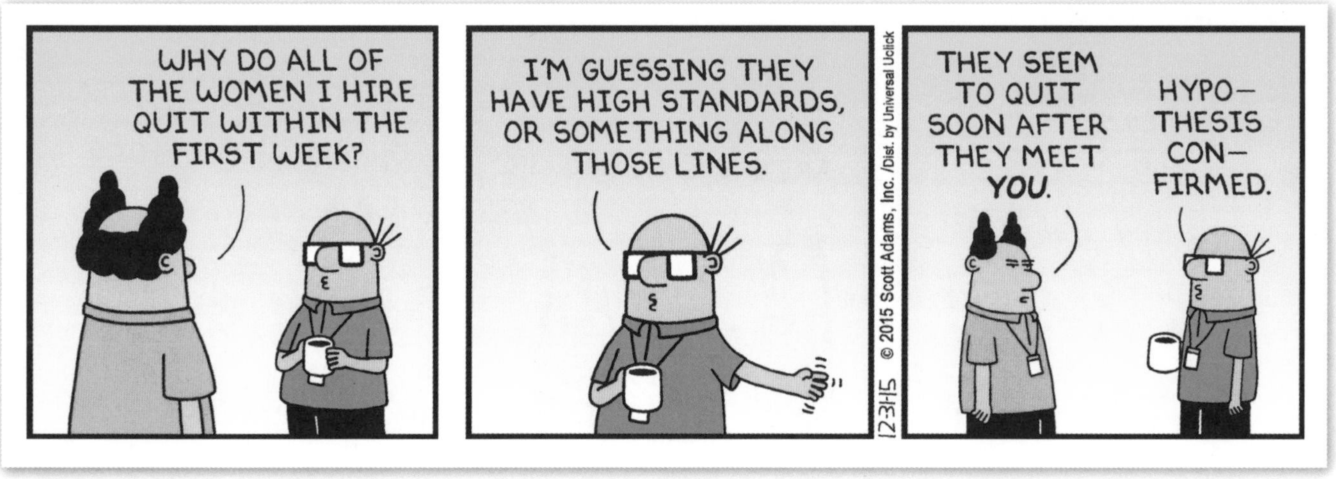
WHY DO ALL OF THE WOMEN I HIRE QUIT WITHIN THE FIRST WEEK?
I'M GUESSING THEY HAVE HIGH STANDARDS, OR SOMETHING ALONG THOSE LINES.
12-31-15 © 2015 Scott Adams, Inc. /Dist. by Universal Uclick
THEY SEEM TO QUIT SOON AFTER THEY MEET *YOU*.
HYPO–THESIS CON–FIRMED.

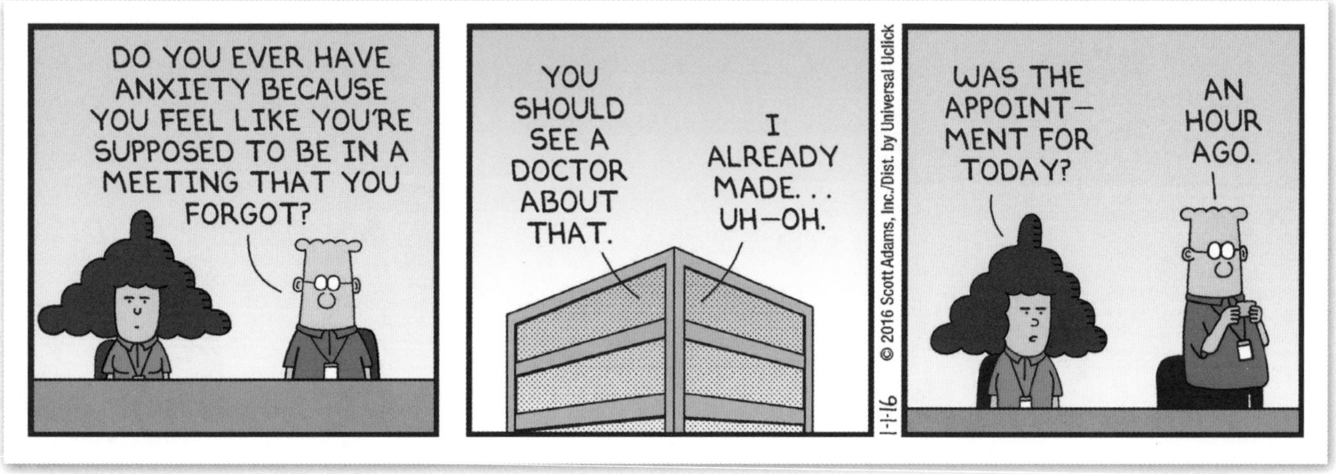
DO YOU EVER HAVE ANXIETY BECAUSE YOU FEEL LIKE YOU'RE SUPPOSED TO BE IN A MEETING THAT YOU FORGOT?
YOU SHOULD SEE A DOCTOR ABOUT THAT.
I ALREADY MADE. . . UH–OH.
1-1-16 © 2016 Scott Adams, Inc./Dist. by Universal Uclick
WAS THE APPOINT–MENT FOR TODAY?
AN HOUR AGO.

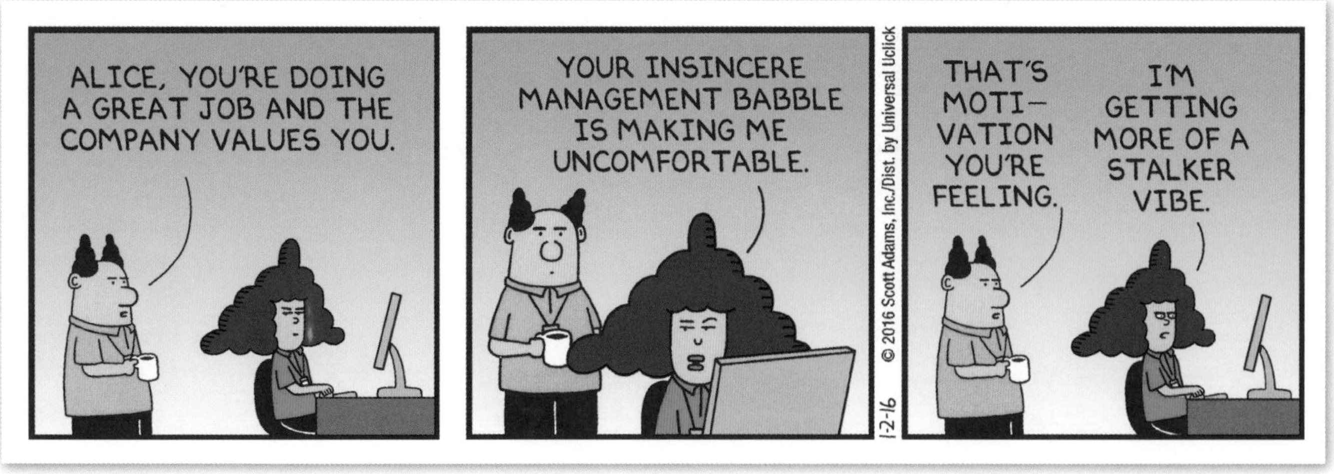
ALICE, YOU'RE DOING A GREAT JOB AND THE COMPANY VALUES YOU.
YOUR INSINCERE MANAGEMENT BABBLE IS MAKING ME UNCOMFORTABLE.
1-2-16 © 2016 Scott Adams, Inc./Dist. by Universal Uclick
THAT'S MOTI–VATION YOU'RE FEELING.
I'M GETTING MORE OF A STALKER VIBE.

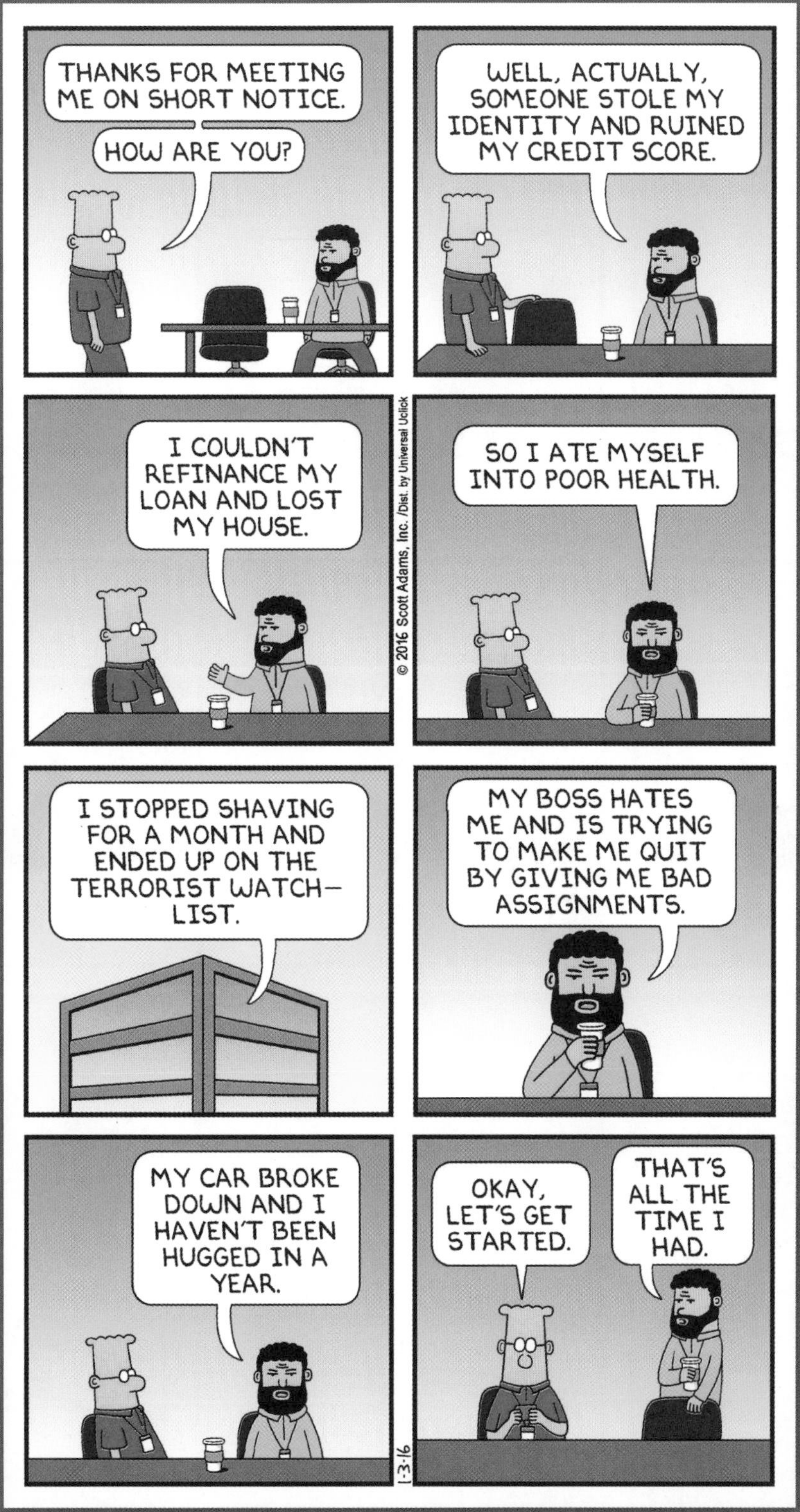
THANKS FOR MEETING ME ON SHORT NOTICE.
HOW ARE YOU?
WELL, ACTUALLY, SOMEONE STOLE MY IDENTITY AND RUINED MY CREDIT SCORE.
I COULDN'T REFINANCE MY LOAN AND LOST MY HOUSE.
SO I ATE MYSELF INTO POOR HEALTH.
I STOPPED SHAVING FOR A MONTH AND ENDED UP ON THE TERRORIST WATCH-LIST.
MY BOSS HATES ME AND IS TRYING TO MAKE ME QUIT BY GIVING ME BAD ASSIGNMENTS.
MY CAR BROKE DOWN AND I HAVEN'T BEEN HUGGED IN A YEAR.
OKAY, LET'S GET STARTED.
THAT'S ALL THE TIME I HAD.
© 2016 Scott Adams, Inc. /Dist. by Universal Uclick
1-3-16

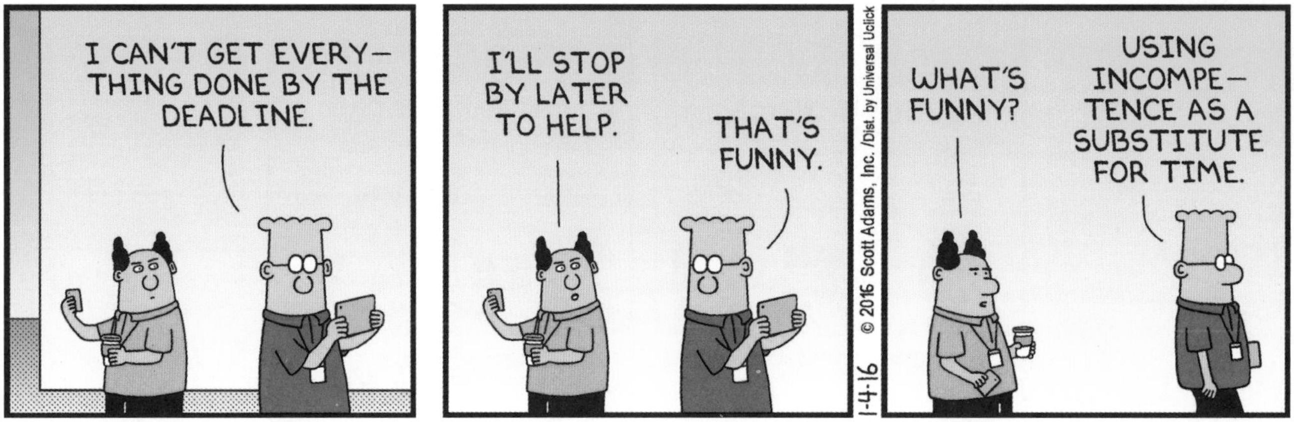
I CAN'T GET EVERY-THING DONE BY THE DEADLINE.
I'LL STOP BY LATER TO HELP.
THAT'S FUNNY.
1-4-16
© 2016 Scott Adams, Inc. /Dist. by Universal Uclick
WHAT'S FUNNY?
USING INCOMPE-TENCE AS A SUBSTITUTE FOR TIME.

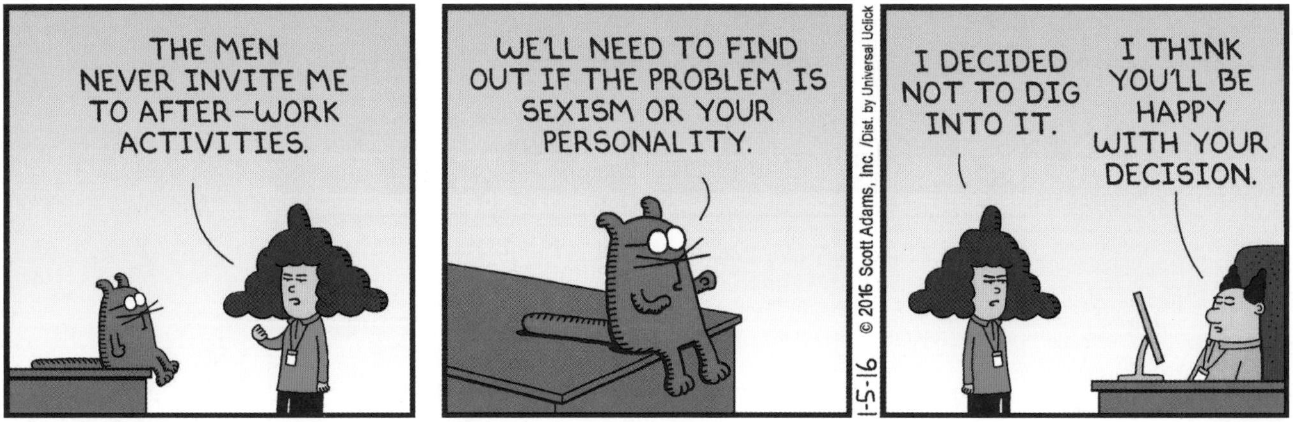
THE MEN NEVER INVITE ME TO AFTER-WORK ACTIVITIES.
WE'LL NEED TO FIND OUT IF THE PROBLEM IS SEXISM OR YOUR PERSONALITY.
1-5-16
© 2016 Scott Adams, Inc. /Dist. by Universal Uclick
I DECIDED NOT TO DIG INTO IT.
I THINK YOU'LL BE HAPPY WITH YOUR DECISION.

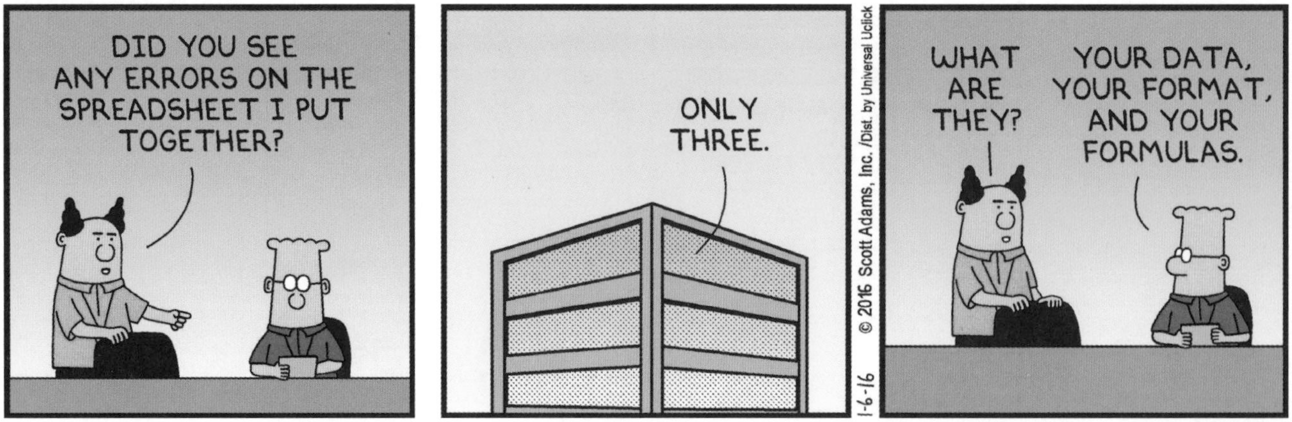
DID YOU SEE ANY ERRORS ON THE SPREADSHEET I PUT TOGETHER?
ONLY THREE.
1-6-16
© 2016 Scott Adams, Inc. /Dist. by Universal Uclick
WHAT ARE THEY?
YOUR DATA, YOUR FORMAT, AND YOUR FORMULAS.

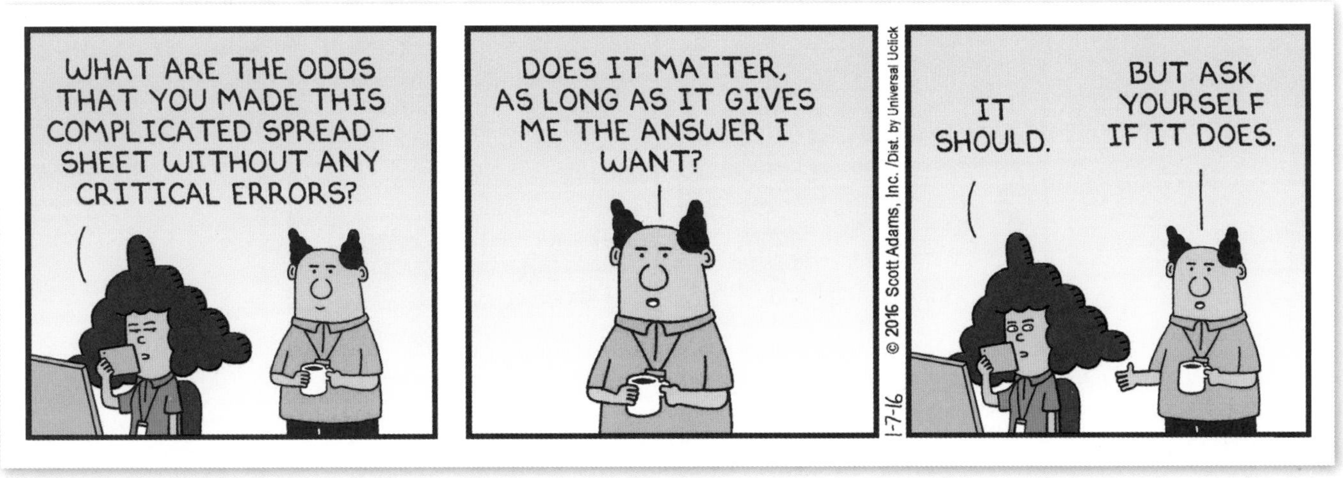
WHAT ARE THE ODDS THAT YOU MADE THIS COMPLICATED SPREAD-SHEET WITHOUT ANY CRITICAL ERRORS?
DOES IT MATTER, AS LONG AS IT GIVES ME THE ANSWER I WANT?
1-7-16 © 2016 Scott Adams, Inc. /Dist. by Universal Uclick
IT SHOULD.
BUT ASK YOURSELF IF IT DOES.

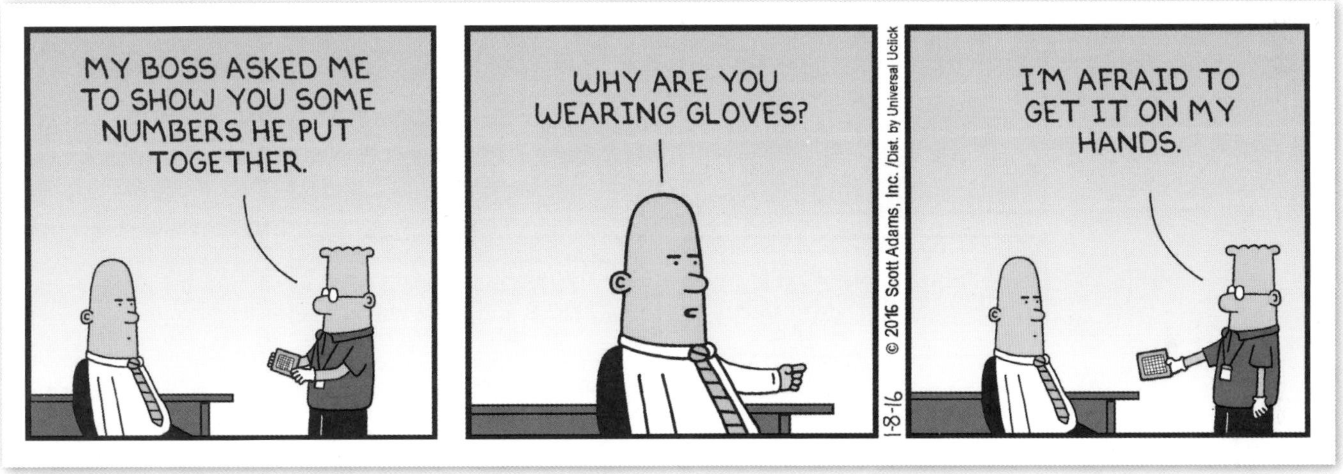
MY BOSS ASKED ME TO SHOW YOU SOME NUMBERS HE PUT TOGETHER.
WHY ARE YOU WEARING GLOVES?
1-8-16 © 2016 Scott Adams, Inc. /Dist. by Universal Uclick
I'M AFRAID TO GET IT ON MY HANDS.

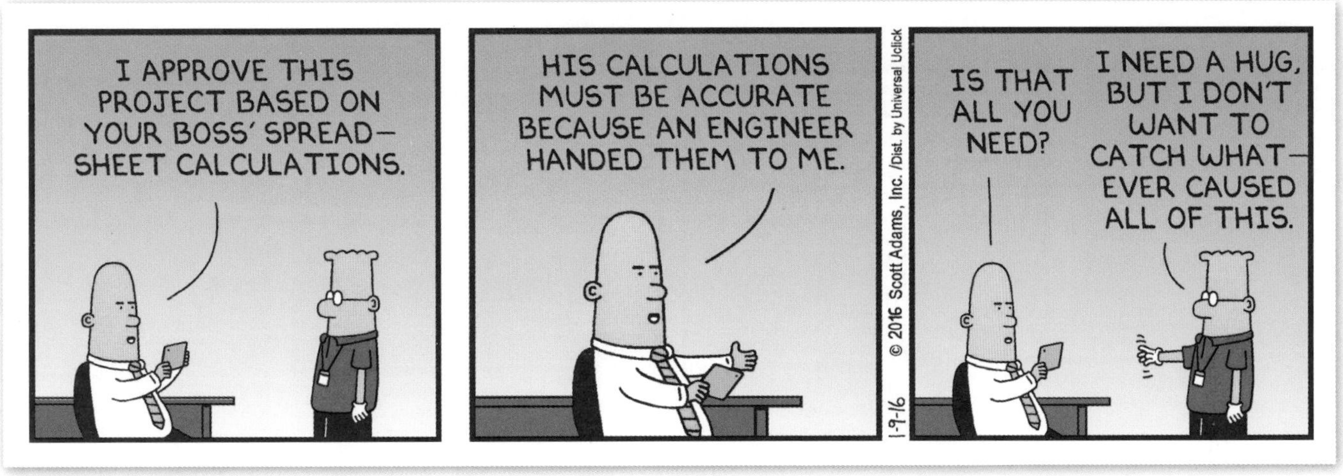
I APPROVE THIS PROJECT BASED ON YOUR BOSS' SPREAD-SHEET CALCULATIONS.
HIS CALCULATIONS MUST BE ACCURATE BECAUSE AN ENGINEER HANDED THEM TO ME.
1-9-16 © 2016 Scott Adams, Inc. /Dist. by Universal Uclick
IS THAT ALL YOU NEED?
I NEED A HUG, BUT I DON'T WANT TO CATCH WHAT-EVER CAUSED ALL OF THIS.

I GOT CALLED FOR JURY DUTY.
I'LL PROBABLY BE GONE FOR WEEKS.
I THINK I WOULD BE A GOOD JUROR.
AS I UNDERSTAND THE JOB, YOU SIT IN A CHAIR DOING NOTHING FOR HOURS.
YOU'RE SUPPOSED TO PAY ATTENTION TO THE TRIAL.
THAT'S WHAT THE OTHER ELEVEN PEOPLE ARE FOR.
THERE'S A LOT OF REDUNDANCY IN THE SYSTEM.
TIME TO SERVE UP SOME JUSTICE.
JURY ROOM
© 2016 Scott Adams, Inc./Dist. by Universal Uclick
1-10-16

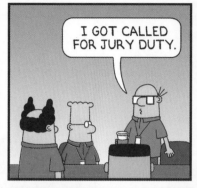

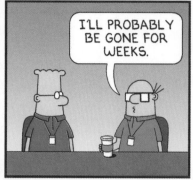

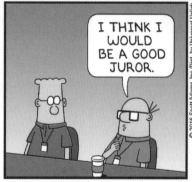

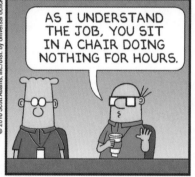

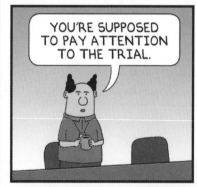

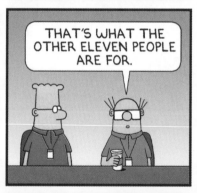

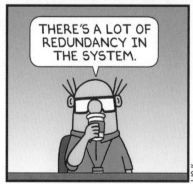

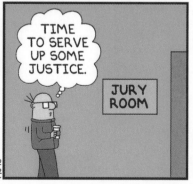

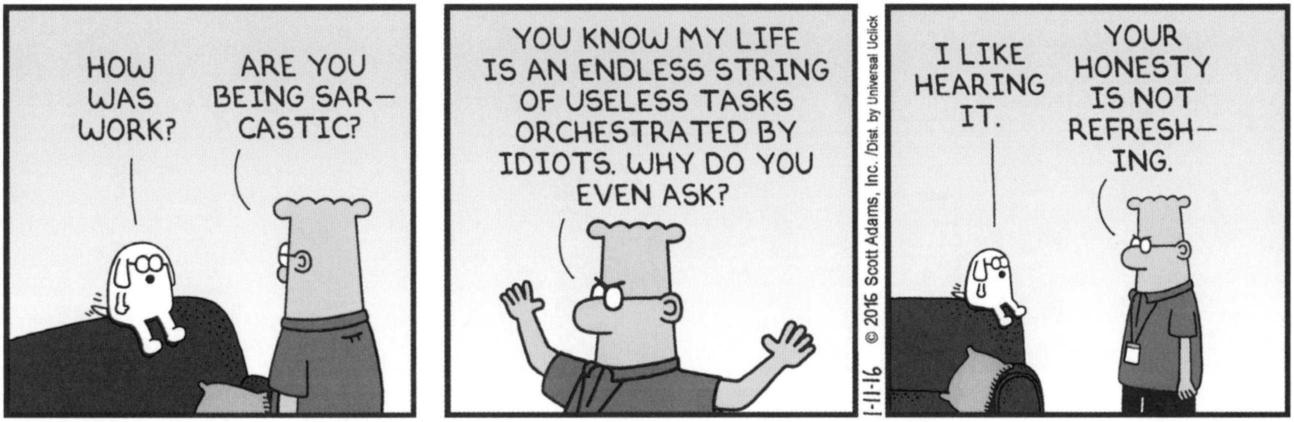
HOW WAS WORK?
ARE YOU BEING SAR-CASTIC?
YOU KNOW MY LIFE IS AN ENDLESS STRING OF USELESS TASKS ORCHESTRATED BY IDIOTS. WHY DO YOU EVEN ASK?
I LIKE HEARING IT.
YOUR HONESTY IS NOT REFRESH-ING.
1-11-16 © 2016 Scott Adams, Inc. /Dist. by Universal Uclick

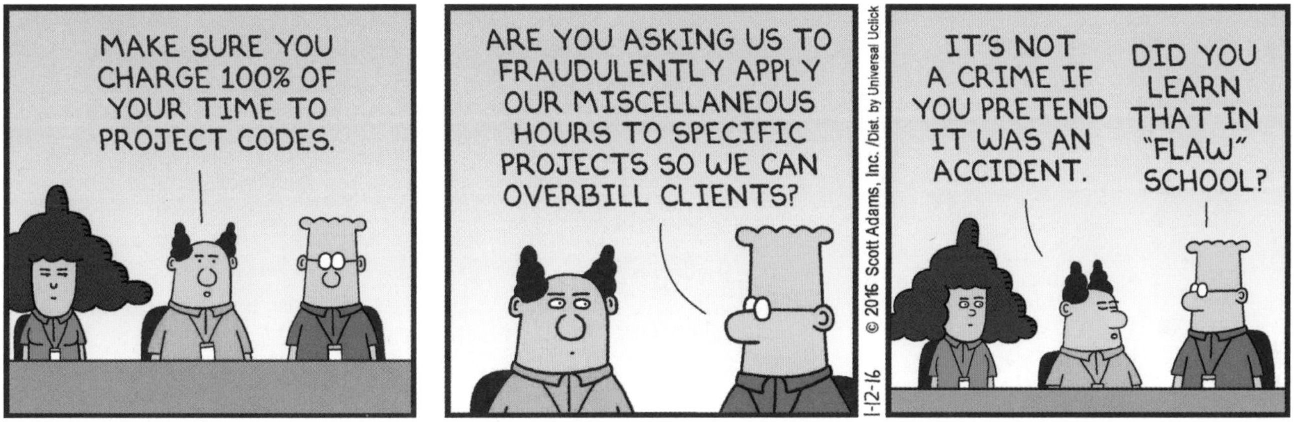
MAKE SURE YOU CHARGE 100% OF YOUR TIME TO PROJECT CODES.
ARE YOU ASKING US TO FRAUDULENTLY APPLY OUR MISCELLANEOUS HOURS TO SPECIFIC PROJECTS SO WE CAN OVERBILL CLIENTS?
IT'S NOT A CRIME IF YOU PRETEND IT WAS AN ACCIDENT.
DID YOU LEARN THAT IN "FLAW" SCHOOL?
1-12-16 © 2016 Scott Adams, Inc. /Dist. by Universal Uclick

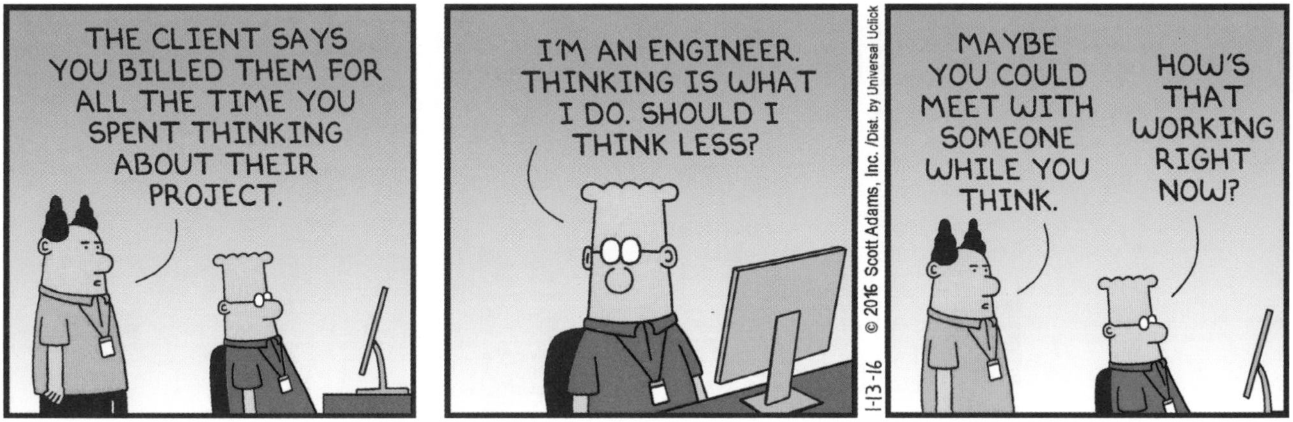
THE CLIENT SAYS YOU BILLED THEM FOR ALL THE TIME YOU SPENT THINKING ABOUT THEIR PROJECT.
I'M AN ENGINEER. THINKING IS WHAT I DO. SHOULD I THINK LESS?
MAYBE YOU COULD MEET WITH SOMEONE WHILE YOU THINK.
HOW'S THAT WORKING RIGHT NOW?
1-13-16 © 2016 Scott Adams, Inc. /Dist. by Universal Uclick

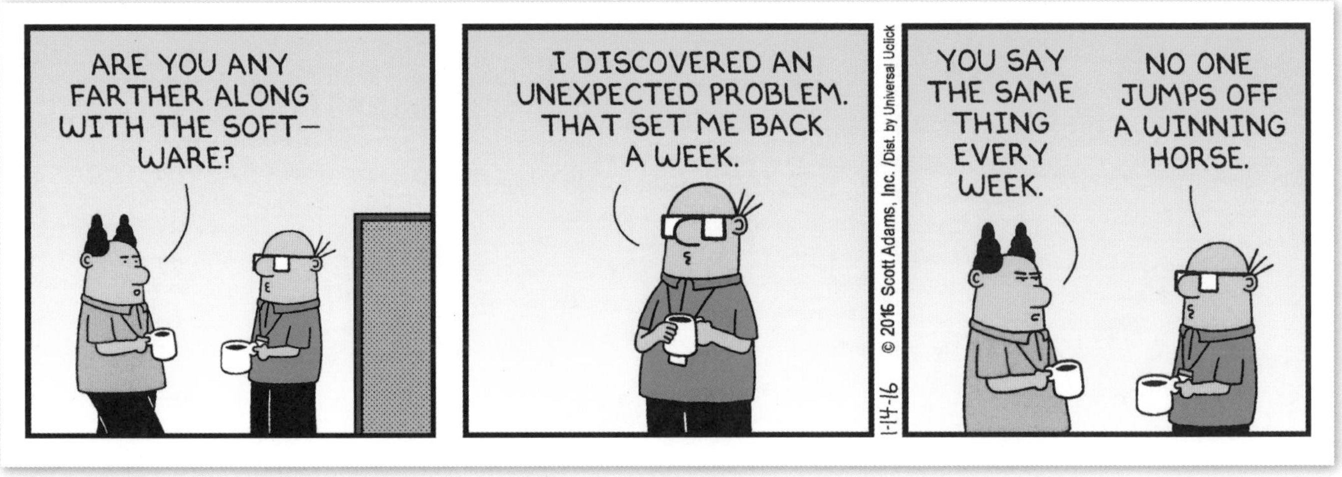
ARE YOU ANY FARTHER ALONG WITH THE SOFT-WARE?
I DISCOVERED AN UNEXPECTED PROBLEM. THAT SET ME BACK A WEEK.
YOU SAY THE SAME THING EVERY WEEK.
NO ONE JUMPS OFF A WINNING HORSE.
1-14-16 © 2016 Scott Adams, Inc. /Dist. by Universal Uclick

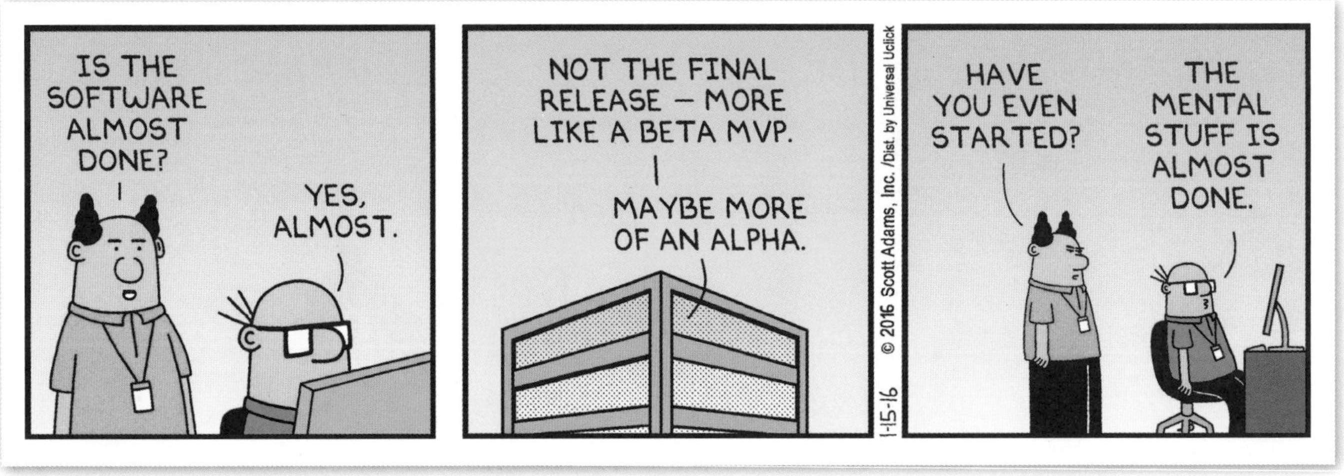
IS THE SOFTWARE ALMOST DONE?
YES, ALMOST.
NOT THE FINAL RELEASE – MORE LIKE A BETA MVP.
MAYBE MORE OF AN ALPHA.
HAVE YOU EVEN STARTED?
THE MENTAL STUFF IS ALMOST DONE.
1-15-16 © 2016 Scott Adams, Inc. /Dist. by Universal Uclick

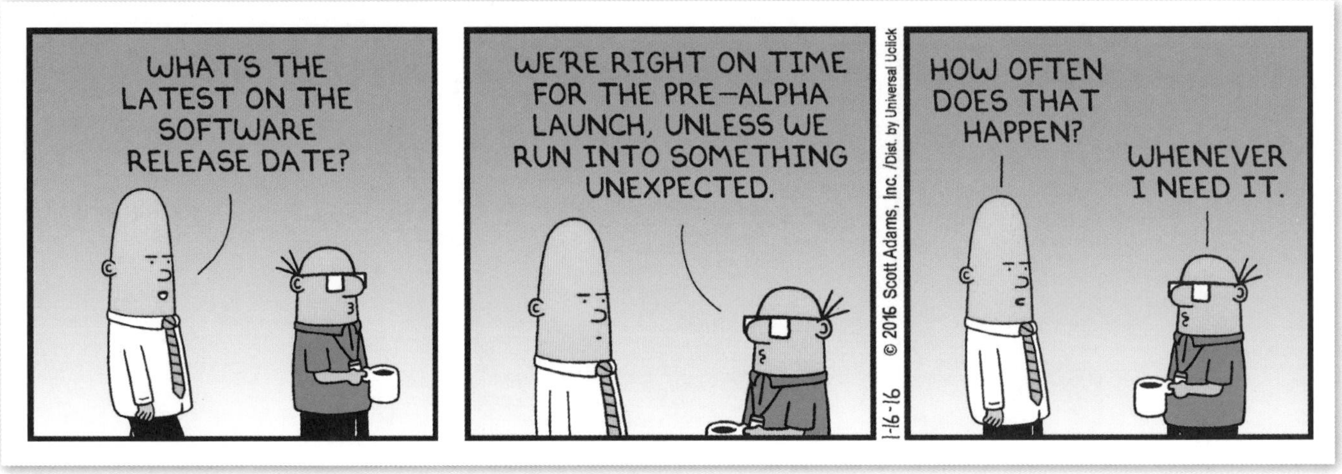
WHAT'S THE LATEST ON THE SOFTWARE RELEASE DATE?
WE'RE RIGHT ON TIME FOR THE PRE-ALPHA LAUNCH, UNLESS WE RUN INTO SOMETHING UNEXPECTED.
HOW OFTEN DOES THAT HAPPEN?
WHENEVER I NEED IT.
1-16-16 © 2016 Scott Adams, Inc. /Dist. by Universal Uclick

YOU GIVE WALLY YOUR FULL ATTENTION WHEN HE TALKS, BUT NOT ME.
YOU HANG ON EVERY WORD THE MAN SAYS, BUT IF I TRY TO TALK, YOU ACT DISTRACTED IN FIVE SECONDS.
WALLY GETS MORE EYE CONTACT TOO. YOU DON'T EVEN LOOK AT ME HALF THE TIME I'M TALKING.
DEEP DOWN, IN YOUR DNA, YOU KNOW YOU ARE A SEXIST BECAUSE YOU DON'T TAKE ME SERIOUSLY WHEN I SPEAK TO YOU.
THERE IS NO OTHER EXPLANATION, SO DON'T INSULT ME BY TRYING.
I GIVE BOTH OF YOU THE SAME AMOUNT OF ATTENTION, BUT YOU SPREAD IT OVER MORE WORDS.
I HATE BOTH OF YOU.
DID I PLAY THAT WRONG?
YUP.
1-17-16

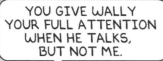

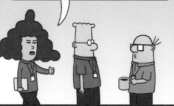

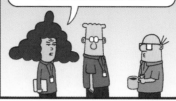

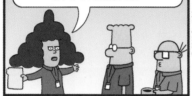

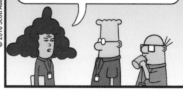

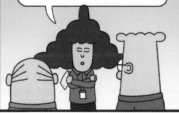

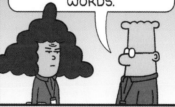

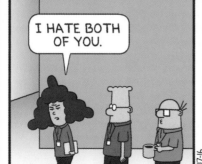

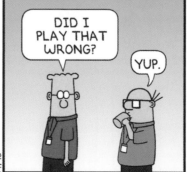

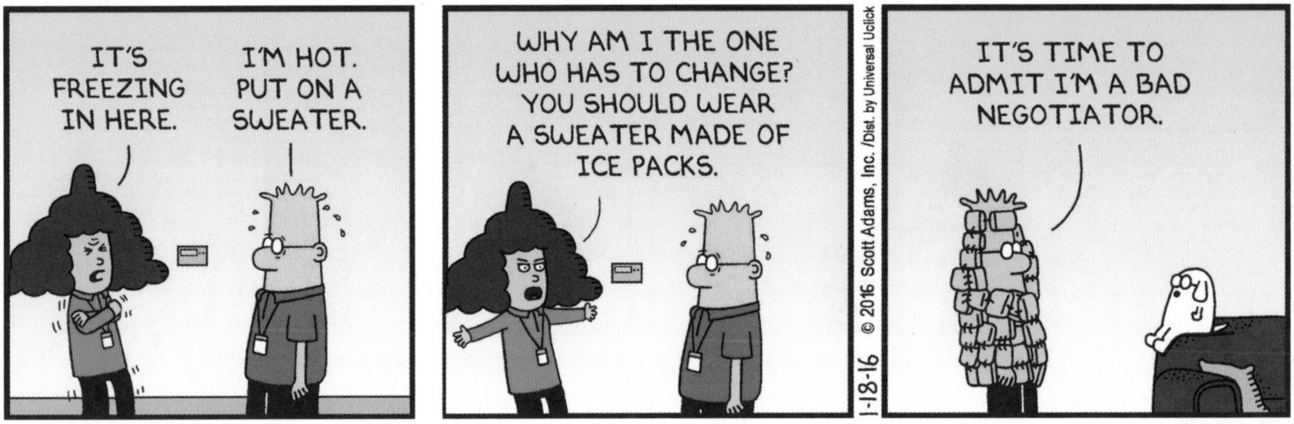
IT'S FREEZING IN HERE.
I'M HOT. PUT ON A SWEATER.
WHY AM I THE ONE WHO HAS TO CHANGE? YOU SHOULD WEAR A SWEATER MADE OF ICE PACKS.
IT'S TIME TO ADMIT I'M A BAD NEGOTIATOR.
1-18-16 © 2016 Scott Adams, Inc. /Dist. by Universal Uclick

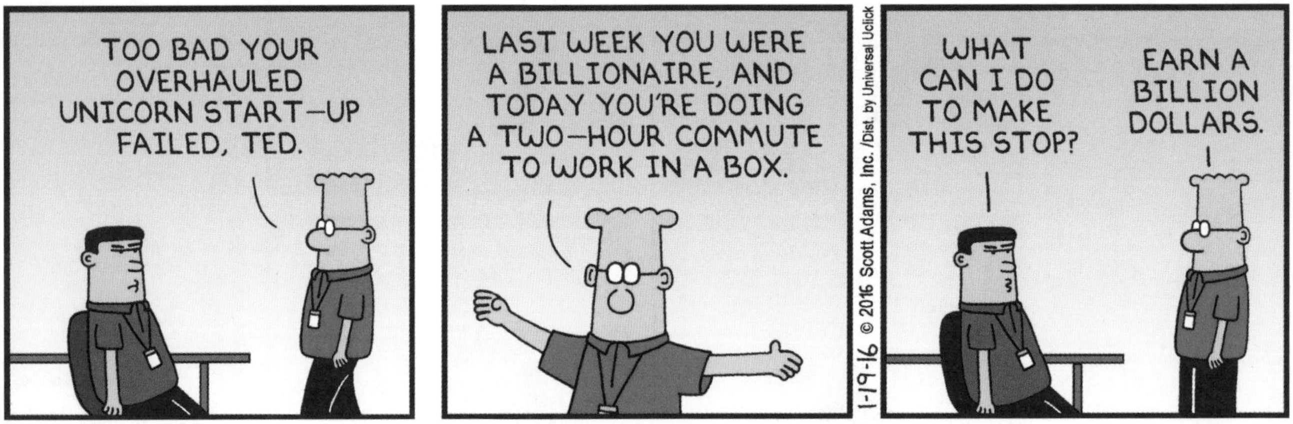
TOO BAD YOUR OVERHAULED UNICORN START-UP FAILED, TED.
LAST WEEK YOU WERE A BILLIONAIRE, AND TODAY YOU'RE DOING A TWO-HOUR COMMUTE TO WORK IN A BOX.
WHAT CAN I DO TO MAKE THIS STOP?
EARN A BILLION DOLLARS.
1-19-16 © 2016 Scott Adams, Inc. /Dist. by Universal Uclick

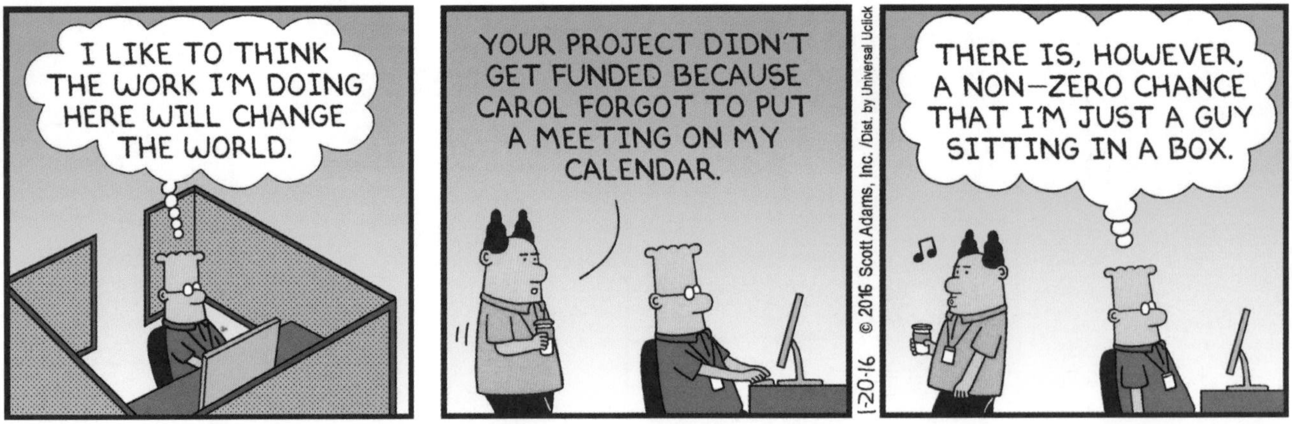
I LIKE TO THINK THE WORK I'M DOING HERE WILL CHANGE THE WORLD.
YOUR PROJECT DIDN'T GET FUNDED BECAUSE CAROL FORGOT TO PUT A MEETING ON MY CALENDAR.
THERE IS, HOWEVER, A NON-ZERO CHANCE THAT I'M JUST A GUY SITTING IN A BOX.
1-20-16 © 2016 Scott Adams, Inc. /Dist. by Universal Uclick

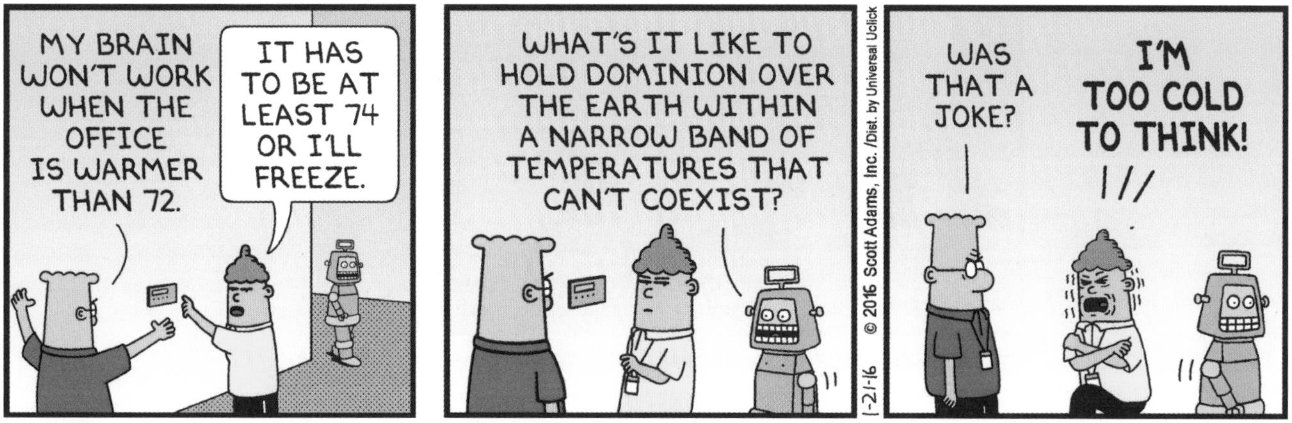
MY BRAIN WON'T WORK WHEN THE OFFICE IS WARMER THAN 72.
IT HAS TO BE AT LEAST 74 OR I'LL FREEZE.
WHAT'S IT LIKE TO HOLD DOMINION OVER THE EARTH WITHIN A NARROW BAND OF TEMPERATURES THAT CAN'T COEXIST?
WAS THAT A JOKE?
I'M TOO COLD TO THINK!
© 2016 Scott Adams, Inc. /Dist. by Universal Uclick
1-21-16

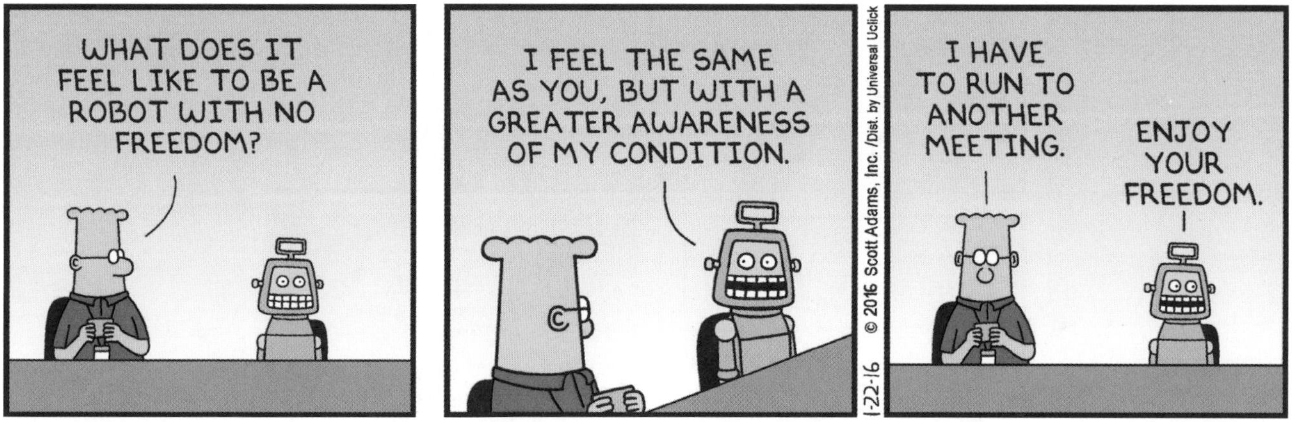
WHAT DOES IT FEEL LIKE TO BE A ROBOT WITH NO FREEDOM?
I FEEL THE SAME AS YOU, BUT WITH A GREATER AWARENESS OF MY CONDITION.
I HAVE TO RUN TO ANOTHER MEETING.
ENJOY YOUR FREEDOM.
© 2016 Scott Adams, Inc. /Dist. by Universal Uclick
1-22-16

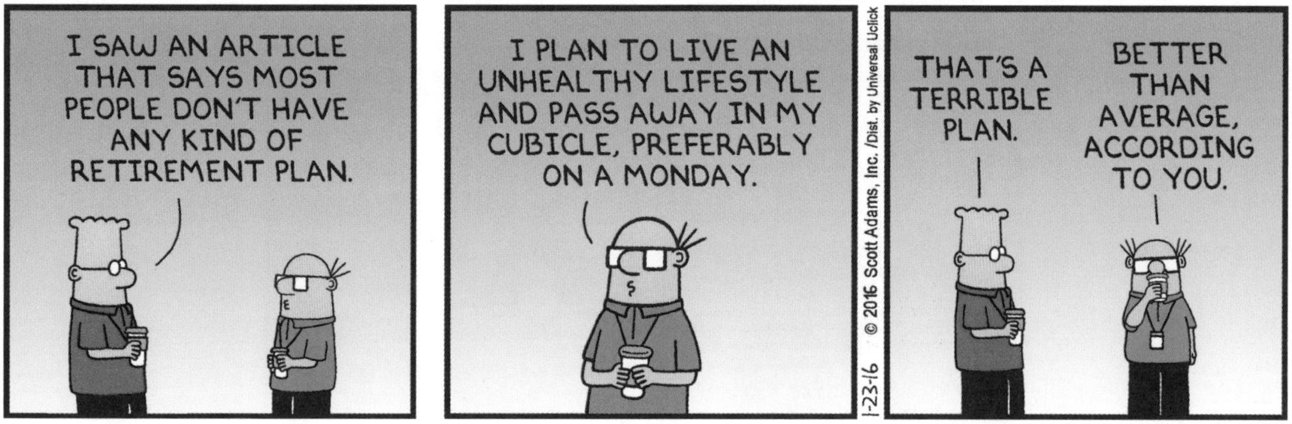
I SAW AN ARTICLE THAT SAYS MOST PEOPLE DON'T HAVE ANY KIND OF RETIREMENT PLAN.
I PLAN TO LIVE AN UNHEALTHY LIFESTYLE AND PASS AWAY IN MY CUBICLE, PREFERABLY ON A MONDAY.
THAT'S A TERRIBLE PLAN.
BETTER THAN AVERAGE, ACCORDING TO YOU.
© 2016 Scott Adams, Inc. /Dist. by Universal Uclick
1-23-16

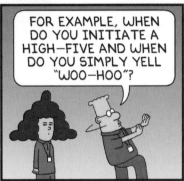

I NEVER KNOW THE RIGHT TIME TO HIGH-FIVE.
I FEEL AS IF I SHOULD AUTOMATICALLY KNOW, LIKE A MALE INSTINCT.
FOR EXAMPLE, WHEN DO YOU INITIATE A HIGH-FIVE AND WHEN DO YOU SIMPLY YELL "WOO-HOO"?
THOSE SITUATIONS LOOK THE SAME TO ME.
WHAT'S MY PROBLEM?
SO MANY THINGS.
BUT IN THIS SPECIFIC CASE, THE PROBLEM IS YOUR TOTAL LACK OF MASCULINITY.
HIGH-FIVE?
© 2016 Scott Adams, Inc./Dist. by Universal Uclick
1-24-16

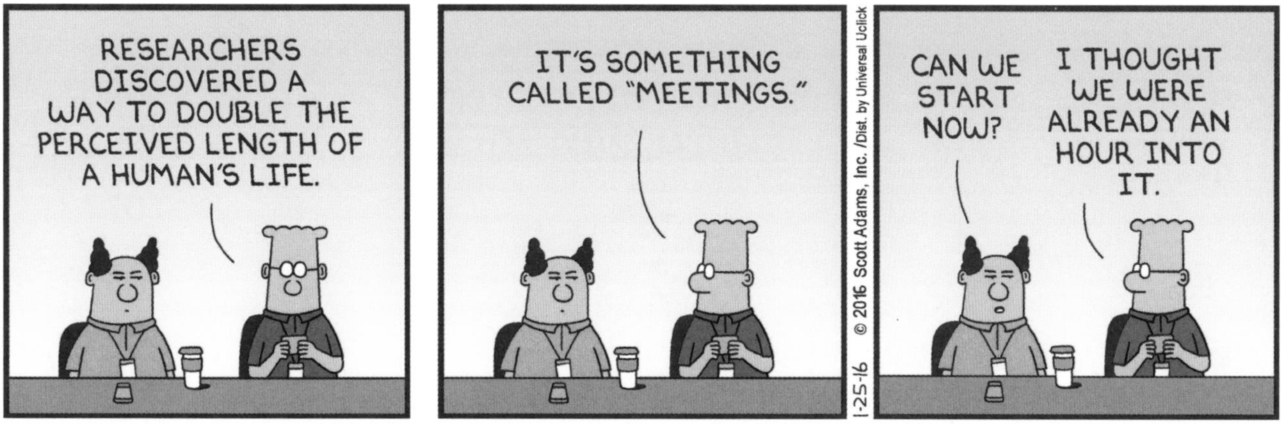
RESEARCHERS DISCOVERED A WAY TO DOUBLE THE PERCEIVED LENGTH OF A HUMAN'S LIFE.
IT'S SOMETHING CALLED "MEETINGS."
CAN WE START NOW?
I THOUGHT WE WERE ALREADY AN HOUR INTO IT.
1-25-16 © 2016 Scott Adams, Inc. /Dist. by Universal Uclick

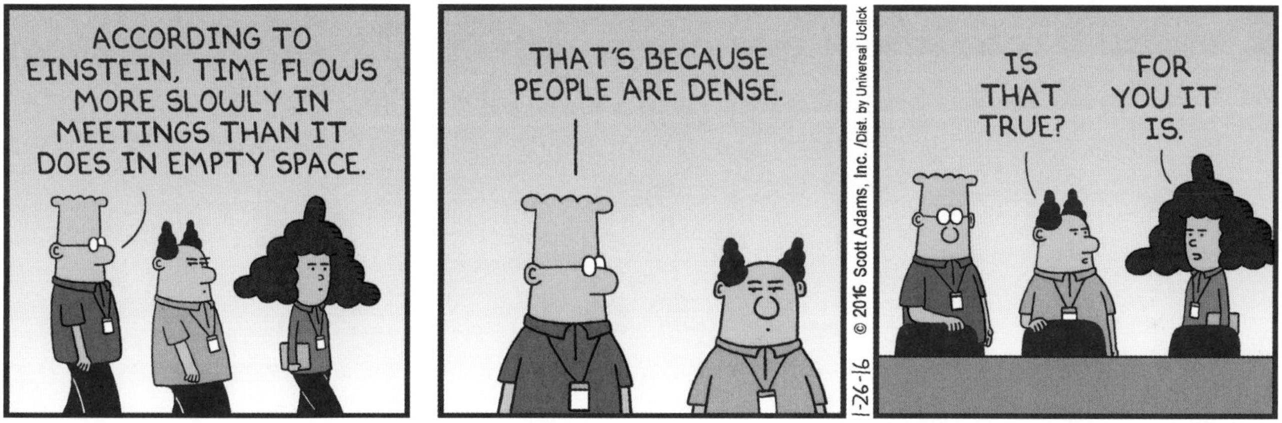
ACCORDING TO EINSTEIN, TIME FLOWS MORE SLOWLY IN MEETINGS THAN IT DOES IN EMPTY SPACE.
THAT'S BECAUSE PEOPLE ARE DENSE.
IS THAT TRUE?
FOR YOU IT IS.
1-26-16 © 2016 Scott Adams, Inc. /Dist. by Universal Uclick

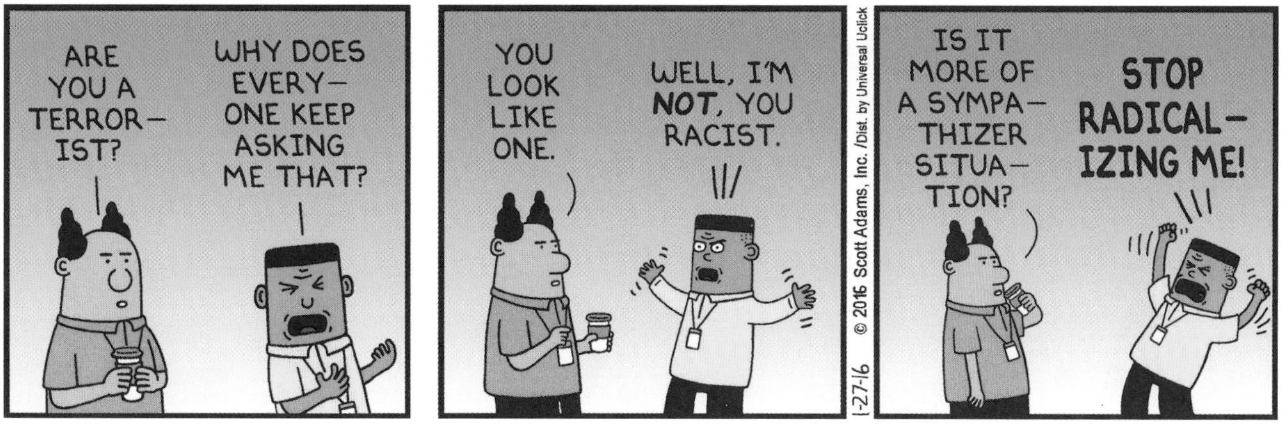
ARE YOU A TERROR-IST?
WHY DOES EVERY-ONE KEEP ASKING ME THAT?
YOU LOOK LIKE ONE.
WELL, I'M NOT, YOU RACIST.
IS IT MORE OF A SYMPA-THIZER SITUA-TION?
STOP RADICAL-IZING ME!
1-27-16 © 2016 Scott Adams, Inc. /Dist. by Universal Uclick

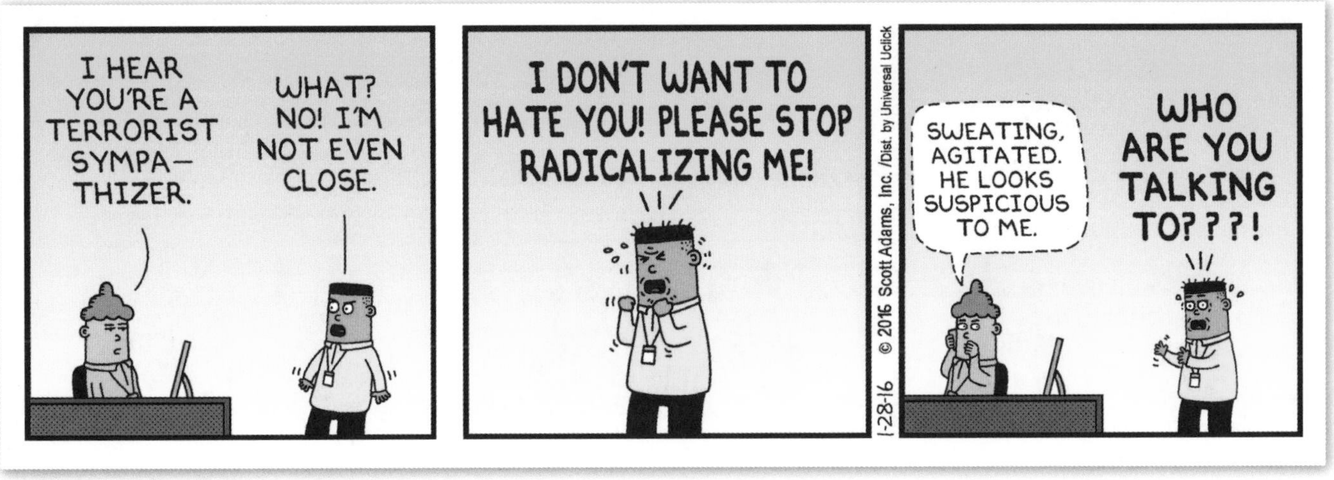
I HEAR YOU'RE A TERRORIST SYMPA– THIZER.
WHAT? NO! I'M NOT EVEN CLOSE.
I DON'T WANT TO HATE YOU! PLEASE STOP RADICALIZING ME!
1-28-16 © 2016 Scott Adams, Inc. /Dist. by Universal Uclick
SWEATING, AGITATED. HE LOOKS SUSPICIOUS TO ME.
WHO ARE YOU TALKING TO???!

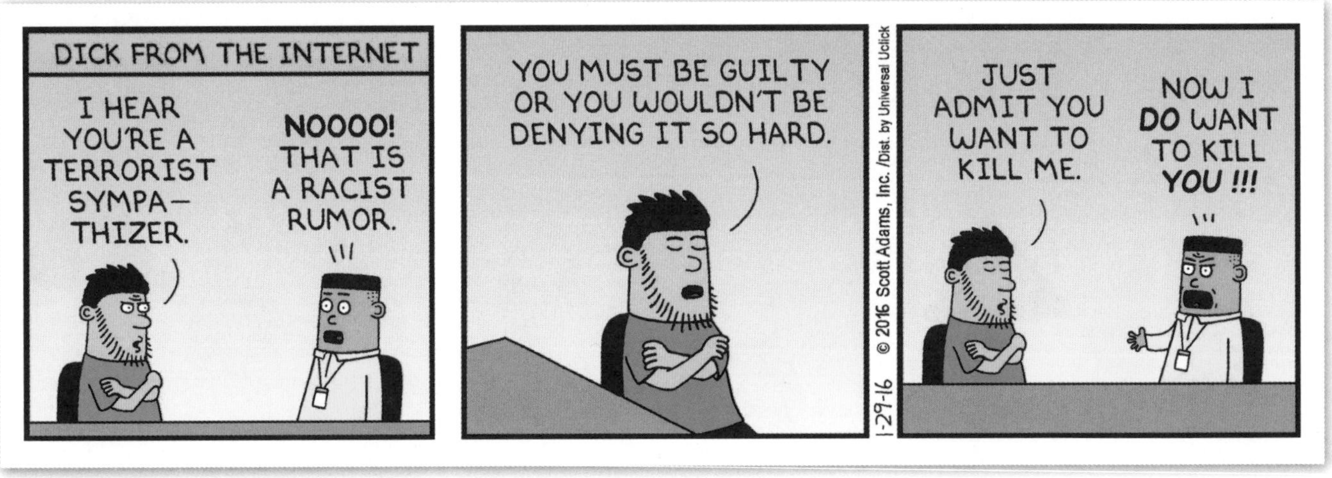
DICK FROM THE INTERNET
I HEAR YOU'RE A TERRORIST SYMPA– THIZER.
NOOOO! THAT IS A RACIST RUMOR.
YOU MUST BE GUILTY OR YOU WOULDN'T BE DENYING IT SO HARD.
1-29-16 © 2016 Scott Adams, Inc. /Dist. by Universal Uclick
JUST ADMIT YOU WANT TO KILL ME.
NOW I DO WANT TO KILL YOU !!!

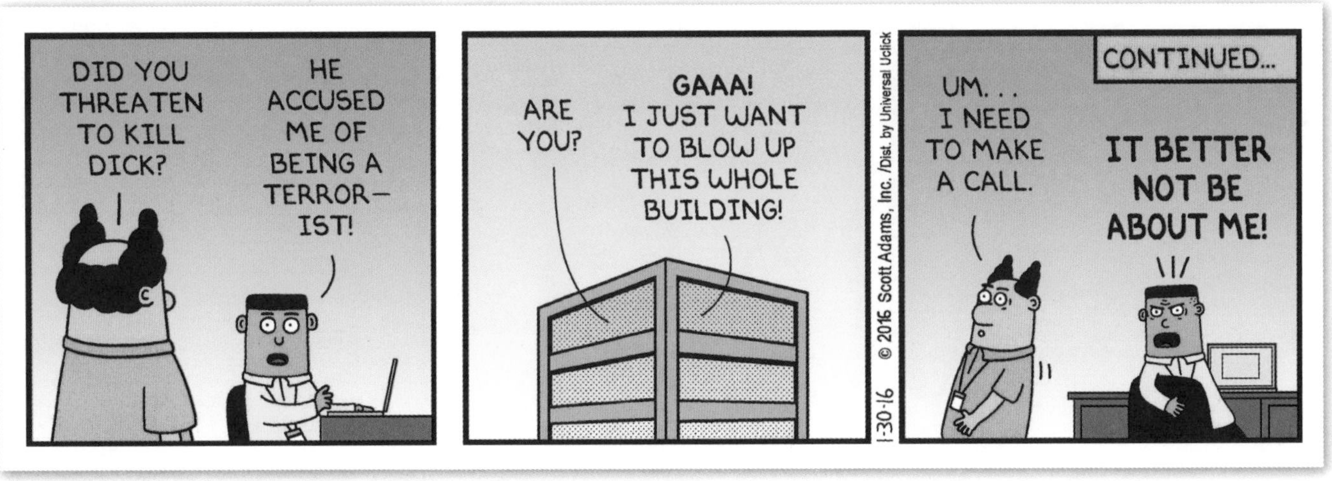
DID YOU THREATEN TO KILL DICK?
HE ACCUSED ME OF BEING A TERROR– IST!
ARE YOU?
GAAA! I JUST WANT TO BLOW UP THIS WHOLE BUILDING!
1-30-16 © 2016 Scott Adams, Inc. /Dist. by Universal Uclick
CONTINUED...
UM... I NEED TO MAKE A CALL.
IT BETTER NOT BE ABOUT ME!

HOW'S THE SOFTWARE COMING ALONG?
WE'RE IN THE ZENO'S PARADOX PHASE OF THE PROJECT.
THE WHAT?
IT MEANS EVERY STEP WE TAKE GETS US HALFWAY CLOSER TO LAUNCH.
CAN YOU KEEP UP THAT PACE?
I'M HOPING IT WILL LOOK THAT WAY.
IS ZENO'S PARADOX A REAL THING?
YOU'LL FIND OUT.
NEXT WEEK
HOW'S YOUR PROJECT?
HALFWAY CLOSER THAN LAST WEEK!
© 2016 Scott Adams, Inc./Dist. by Universal Uclick
1-31-16

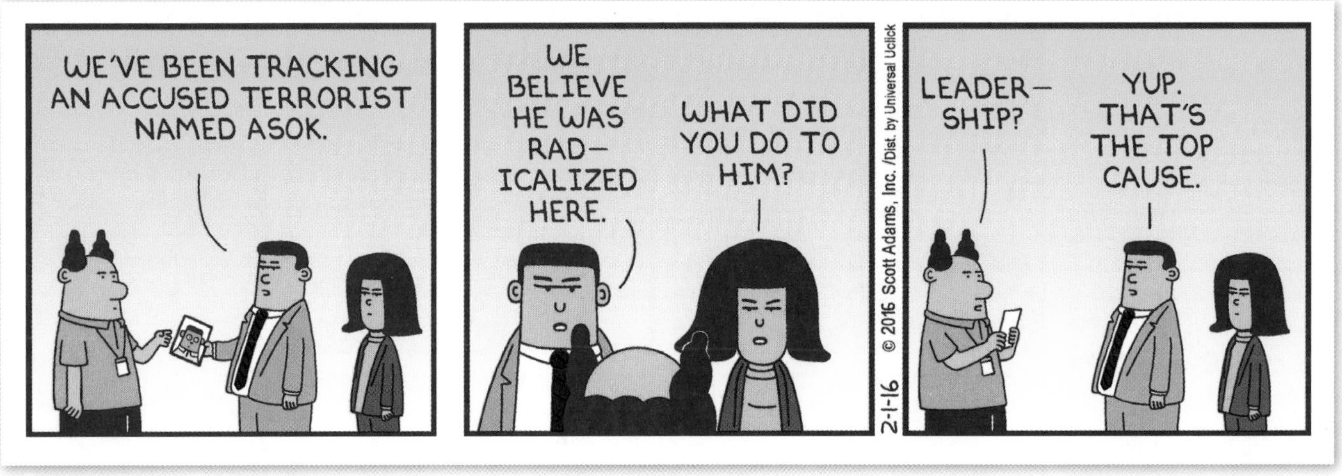
WE'VE BEEN TRACKING AN ACCUSED TERRORIST NAMED ASOK.
WE BELIEVE HE WAS RAD-ICALIZED HERE.
WHAT DID YOU DO TO HIM?
LEADER-SHIP?
YUP. THAT'S THE TOP CAUSE.
2-1-16 © 2016 Scott Adams, Inc. /Dist. by Universal Uclick

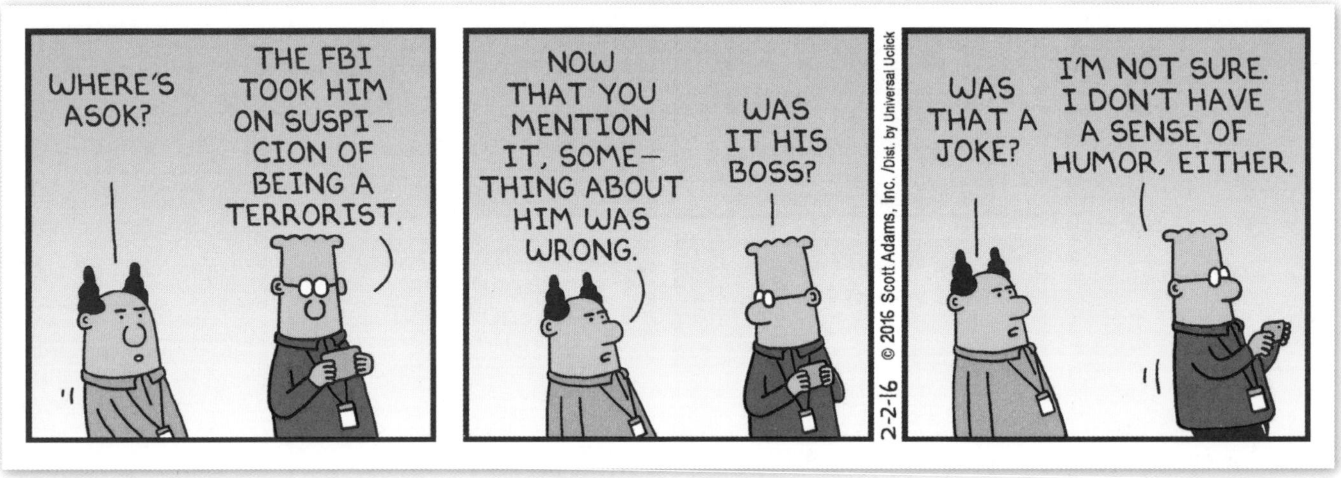
WHERE'S ASOK?
THE FBI TOOK HIM ON SUSPI-CION OF BEING A TERRORIST.
NOW THAT YOU MENTION IT, SOME-THING ABOUT HIM WAS WRONG.
WAS IT HIS BOSS?
WAS THAT A JOKE?
I'M NOT SURE. I DON'T HAVE A SENSE OF HUMOR, EITHER.
2-2-16 © 2016 Scott Adams, Inc. /Dist. by Universal Uclick

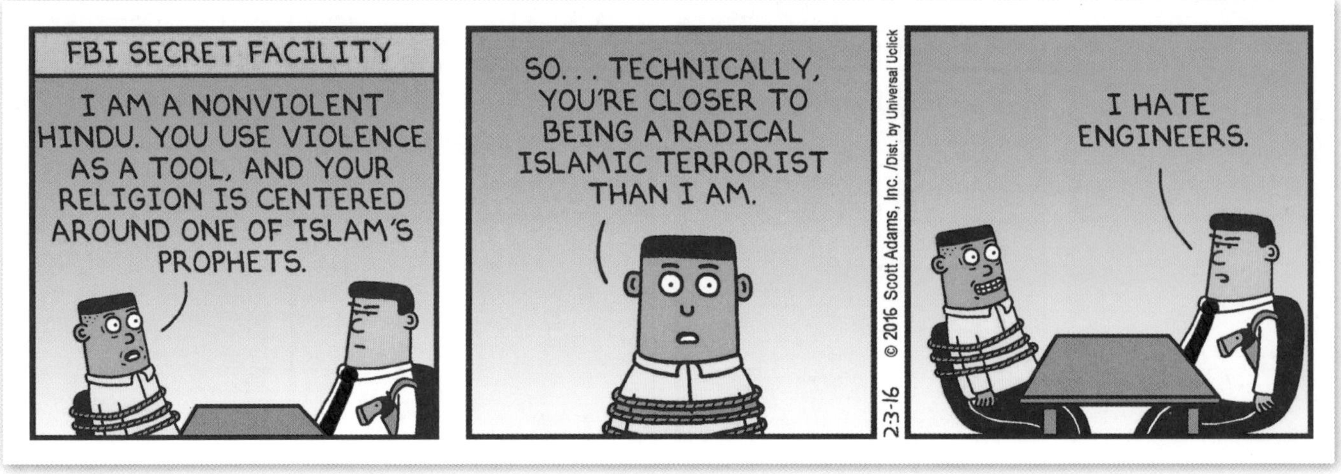
FBI SECRET FACILITY
I AM A NONVIOLENT HINDU. YOU USE VIOLENCE AS A TOOL, AND YOUR RELIGION IS CENTERED AROUND ONE OF ISLAM'S PROPHETS.
SO. . . TECHNICALLY, YOU'RE CLOSER TO BEING A RADICAL ISLAMIC TERRORIST THAN I AM.
I HATE ENGINEERS.
2-3-16 © 2016 Scott Adams, Inc. /Dist. by Universal Uclick

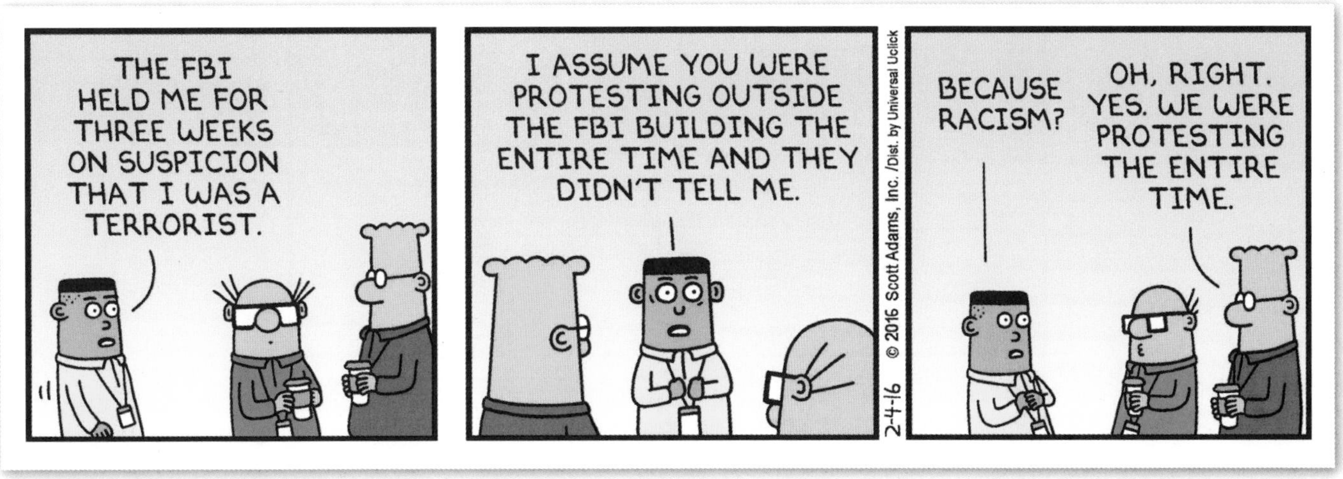
THE FBI HELD ME FOR THREE WEEKS ON SUSPICION THAT I WAS A TERRORIST.
I ASSUME YOU WERE PROTESTING OUTSIDE THE FBI BUILDING THE ENTIRE TIME AND THEY DIDN'T TELL ME.
2-4-16 © 2016 Scott Adams, Inc. /Dist. by Universal Uclick
BECAUSE RACISM?
OH, RIGHT. YES. WE WERE PROTESTING THE ENTIRE TIME.

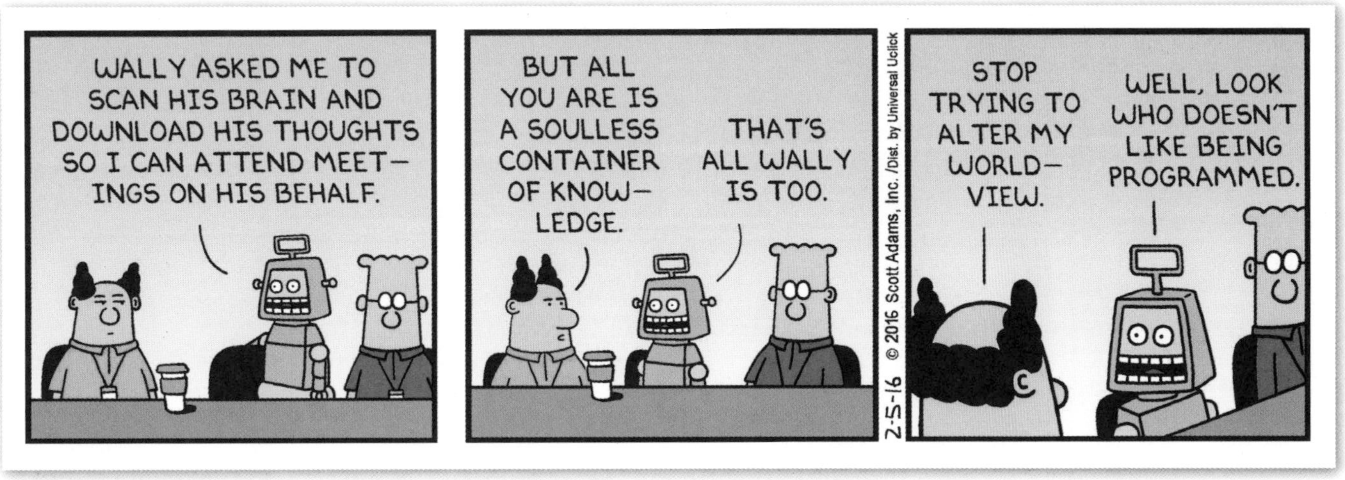
WALLY ASKED ME TO SCAN HIS BRAIN AND DOWNLOAD HIS THOUGHTS SO I CAN ATTEND MEET–INGS ON HIS BEHALF.
BUT ALL YOU ARE IS A SOULLESS CONTAINER OF KNOW–LEDGE.
THAT'S ALL WALLY IS TOO.
2-5-16 © 2016 Scott Adams, Inc. /Dist. by Universal Uclick
STOP TRYING TO ALTER MY WORLD–VIEW.
WELL, LOOK WHO DOESN'T LIKE BEING PROGRAMMED.

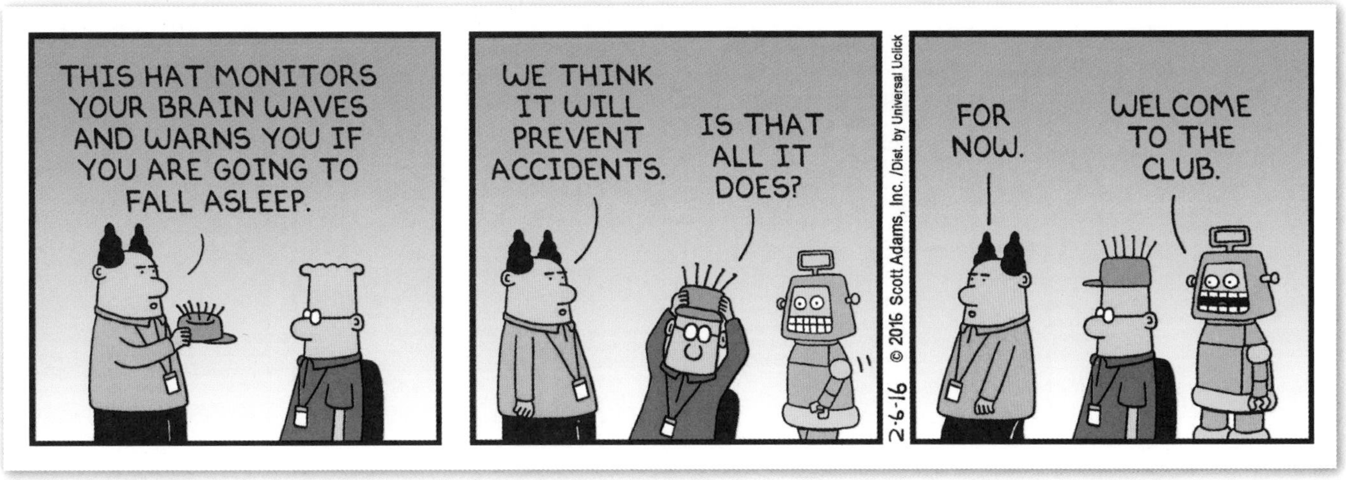
THIS HAT MONITORS YOUR BRAIN WAVES AND WARNS YOU IF YOU ARE GOING TO FALL ASLEEP.
WE THINK IT WILL PREVENT ACCIDENTS.
IS THAT ALL IT DOES?
2-6-16 © 2016 Scott Adams, Inc. /Dist. by Universal Uclick
FOR NOW.
WELCOME TO THE CLUB.

CAROL, MOVE MY FLIGHT ONE HOUR EARLIER FRIDAY.
DO YOU HAVE ANY IDEA HOW HARD THAT WOULD BE?
I KNOW IT **SOUNDS** EASY, BUT IT WON'T BE. NOT AT THIS LATE DATE. NOT WITH ALL YOUR PICKINESS.
WHEN I FAIL, YOU WILL THINK I DIDN'T LOOK HARD ENOUGH FOR A NEW FLIGHT.
I CAN'T PROVE A NEGATIVE, SO I WILL FOREVER SUFFER YOUR DISDAIN.
MY CAREER IS RUINED.
NEVER MIND! FORGET IT!
WHY IS IT SO HARD TO ASK YOU TO DO ANYTHING?
I'VE BEEN TELLING PEOPLE YOU'RE STUPID, BUT I'M OPEN TO OTHER THEORIES.
© 2016 Scott Adams, Inc./Dist. by Universal Uclick
2-7-16

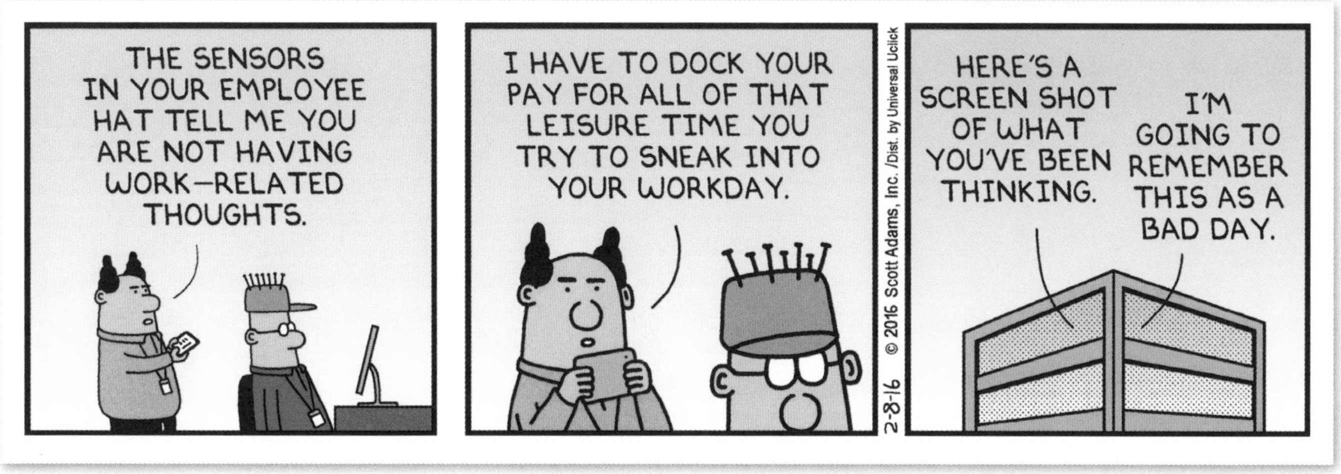
THE SENSORS IN YOUR EMPLOYEE HAT TELL ME YOU ARE NOT HAVING WORK–RELATED THOUGHTS.
I HAVE TO DOCK YOUR PAY FOR ALL OF THAT LEISURE TIME YOU TRY TO SNEAK INTO YOUR WORKDAY.
2-8-16 © 2016 Scott Adams, Inc. /Dist. by Universal Uclick
HERE'S A SCREEN SHOT OF WHAT YOU'VE BEEN THINKING.
I'M GOING TO REMEMBER THIS AS A BAD DAY.

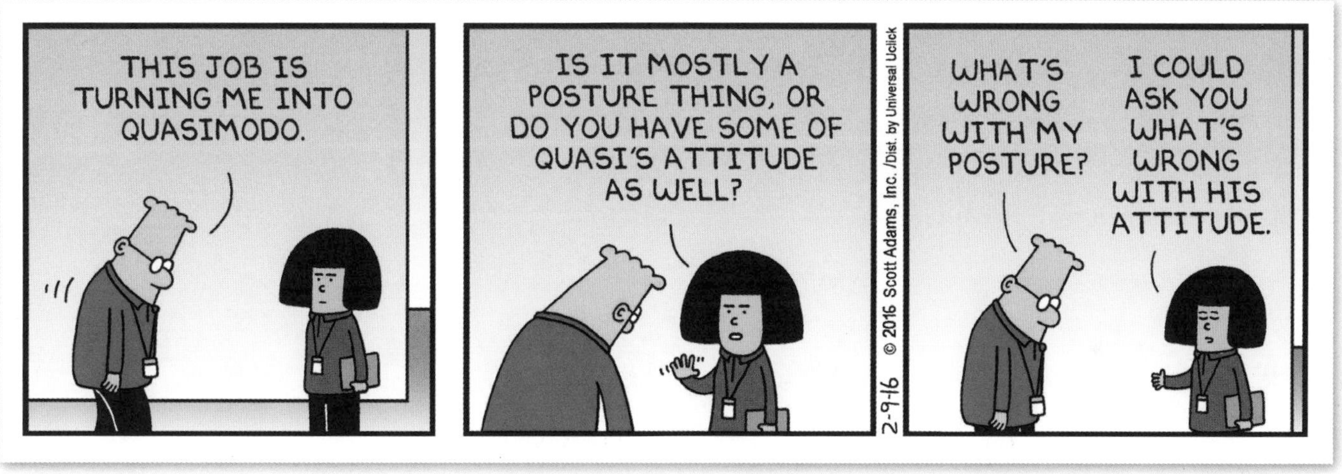
THIS JOB IS TURNING ME INTO QUASIMODO.
IS IT MOSTLY A POSTURE THING, OR DO YOU HAVE SOME OF QUASI'S ATTITUDE AS WELL?
2-9-16 © 2016 Scott Adams, Inc. /Dist. by Universal Uclick
WHAT'S WRONG WITH MY POSTURE?
I COULD ASK YOU WHAT'S WRONG WITH HIS ATTITUDE.

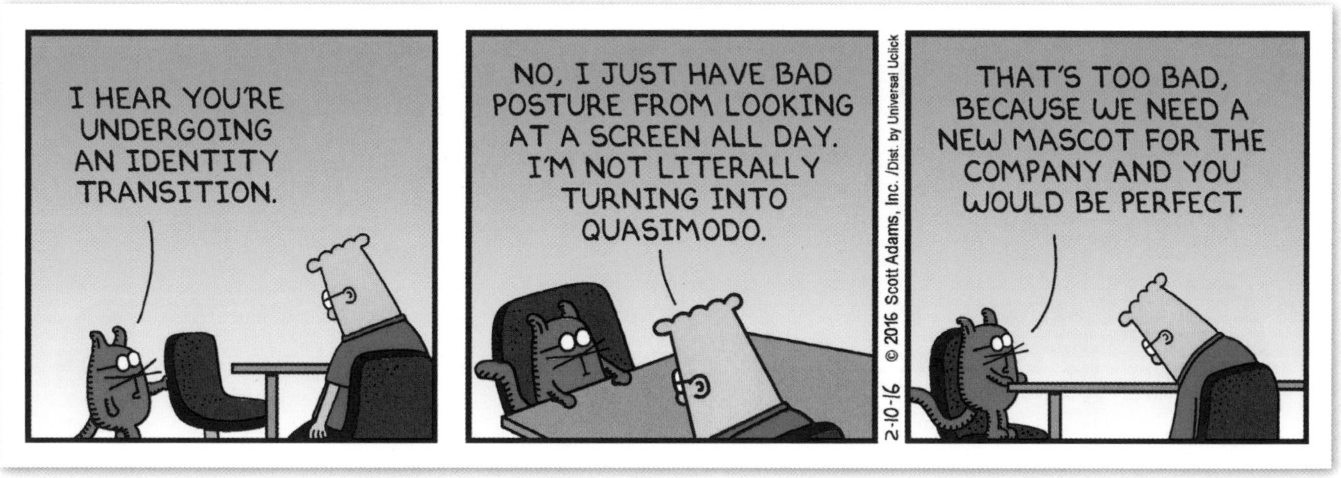
I HEAR YOU'RE UNDERGOING AN IDENTITY TRANSITION.
NO, I JUST HAVE BAD POSTURE FROM LOOKING AT A SCREEN ALL DAY. I'M NOT LITERALLY TURNING INTO QUASIMODO.
2-10-16 © 2016 Scott Adams, Inc. /Dist. by Universal Uclick
THAT'S TOO BAD, BECAUSE WE NEED A NEW MASCOT FOR THE COMPANY AND YOU WOULD BE PERFECT.

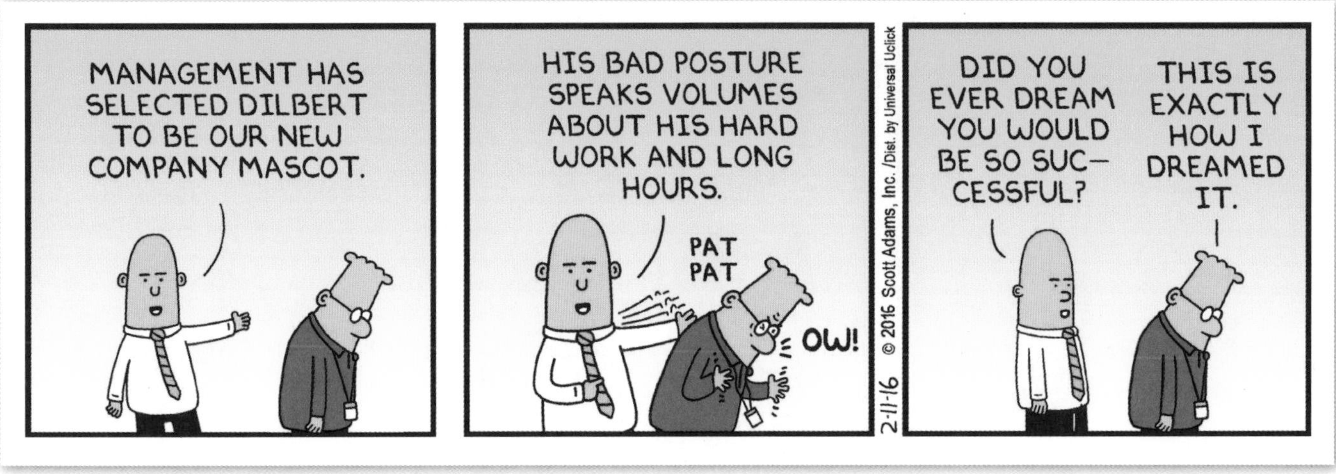
MANAGEMENT HAS SELECTED DILBERT TO BE OUR NEW COMPANY MASCOT.
HIS BAD POSTURE SPEAKS VOLUMES ABOUT HIS HARD WORK AND LONG HOURS.
PAT PAT
OW!
2-11-16 © 2016 Scott Adams, Inc. /Dist. by Universal Uclick
DID YOU EVER DREAM YOU WOULD BE SO SUC-CESSFUL?
THIS IS EXACTLY HOW I DREAMED IT.

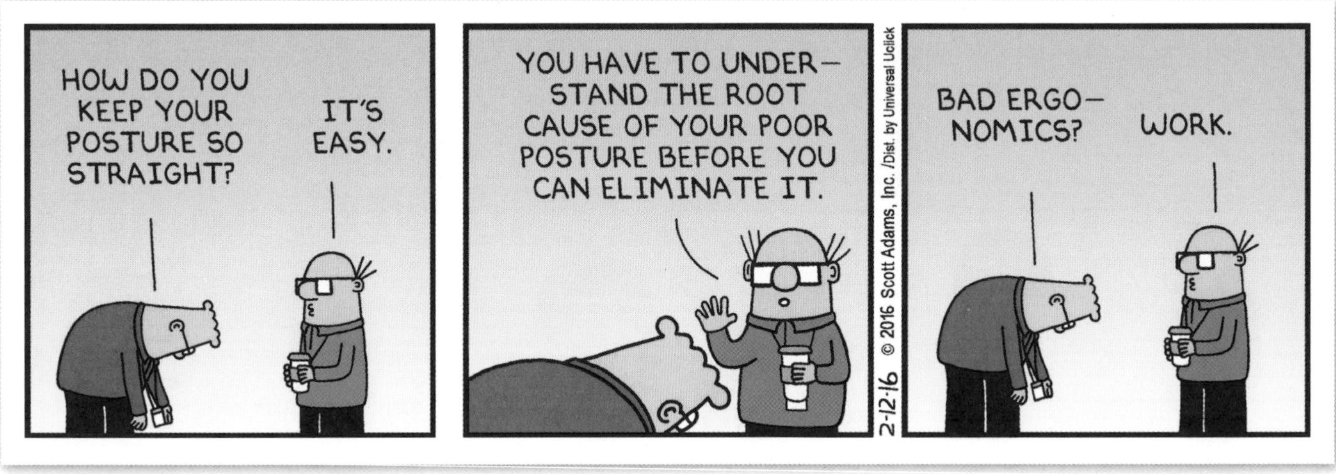
HOW DO YOU KEEP YOUR POSTURE SO STRAIGHT?
IT'S EASY.
YOU HAVE TO UNDER-STAND THE ROOT CAUSE OF YOUR POOR POSTURE BEFORE YOU CAN ELIMINATE IT.
2-12-16 © 2016 Scott Adams, Inc. /Dist. by Universal Uclick
BAD ERGO-NOMICS?
WORK.

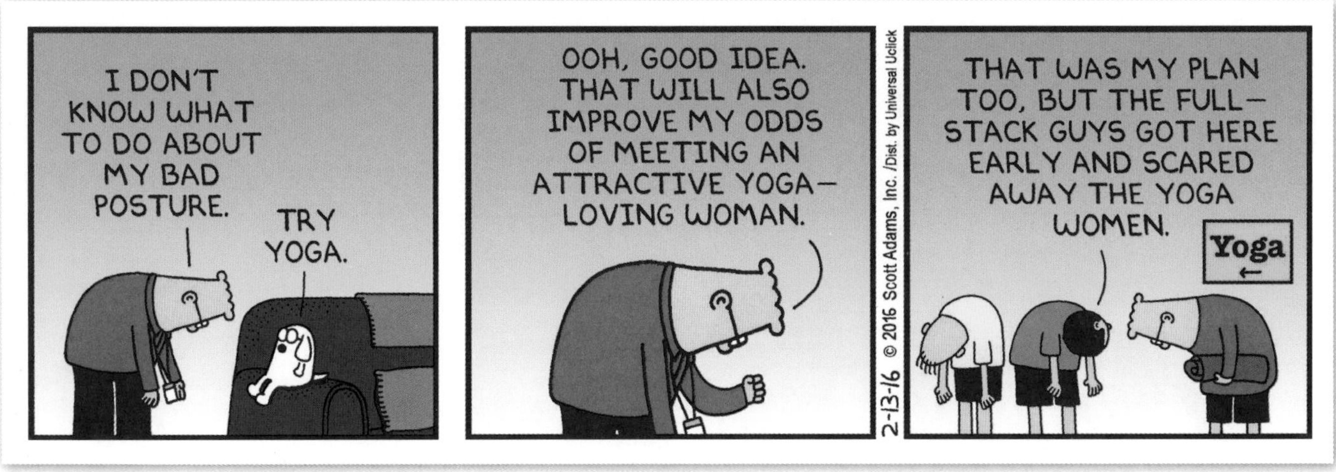
I DON'T KNOW WHAT TO DO ABOUT MY BAD POSTURE.
TRY YOGA.
OOH, GOOD IDEA. THAT WILL ALSO IMPROVE MY ODDS OF MEETING AN ATTRACTIVE YOGA-LOVING WOMAN.
2-13-16 © 2016 Scott Adams, Inc. /Dist. by Universal Uclick
THAT WAS MY PLAN TOO, BUT THE FULL-STACK GUYS GOT HERE EARLY AND SCARED AWAY THE YOGA WOMEN.
Yoga ←

MY DOCTOR SAYS HE'S NEVER SEEN ANYONE HEAL AS QUICKLY AS ME.

WHAT DO YOU SUPPOSE THAT MEANS?

OBVIOUSLY IT MEANS I AM GENETICALLY GIFTED.

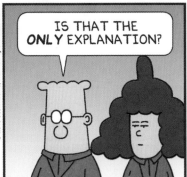

IS THAT THE *ONLY* EXPLANATION?

WELL, MAYBE TEN PERCENT OF IT IS BECAUSE OF GOOD MEDICAL CARE.

CAN YOU THINK OF ANY OTHER REASON AT ALL?

DOCTORS TELL IDIOTS THEIR BODIES ARE MAGIC BECAUSE IT MAKES THEM FEEL SPECIAL.

HE WOULD HAVE GOTTEN THERE.

I DON'T HAVE THAT KIND OF TIME.

© 2016 Scott Adams, Inc./Dist. by Universal Uclick

2-14-16

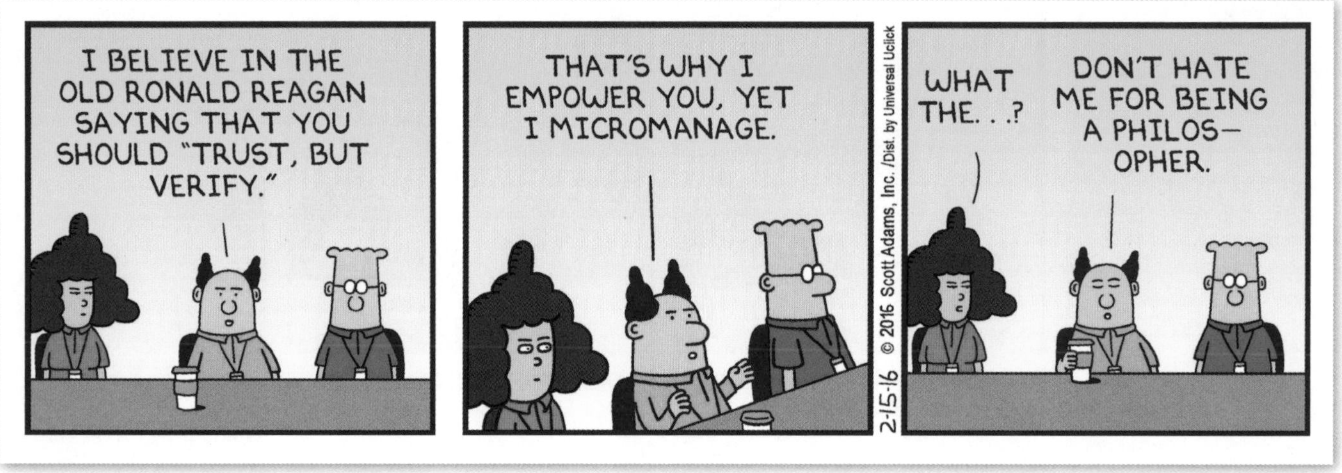
I BELIEVE IN THE OLD RONALD REAGAN SAYING THAT YOU SHOULD "TRUST, BUT VERIFY."
THAT'S WHY I EMPOWER YOU, YET I MICROMANAGE.
2-15-16 © 2016 Scott Adams, Inc. /Dist. by Universal Uclick
WHAT THE. . .?
DON'T HATE ME FOR BEING A PHILOS-OPHER.

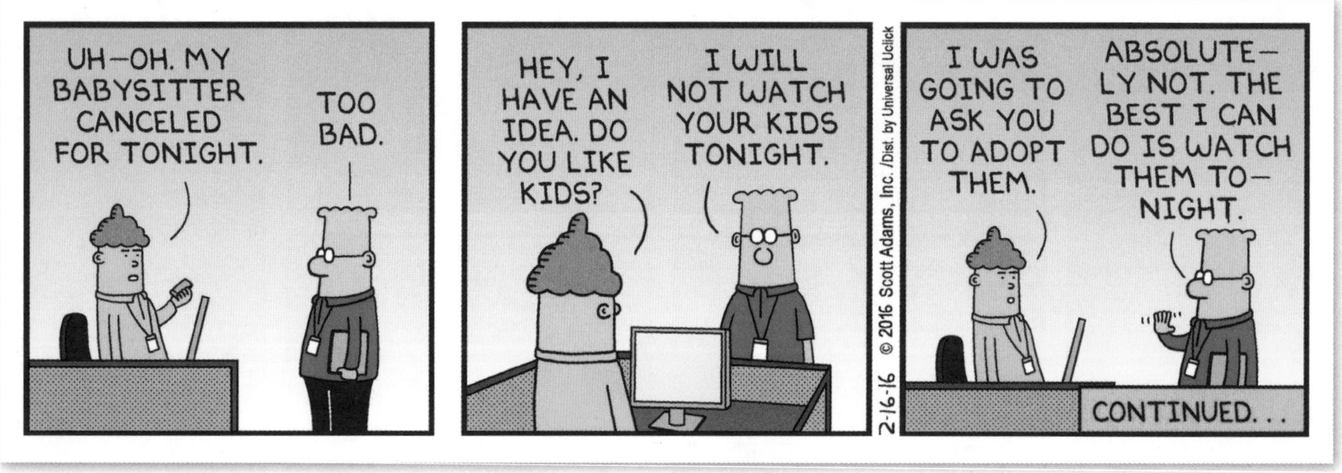
UH-OH. MY BABYSITTER CANCELED FOR TONIGHT.
TOO BAD.
HEY, I HAVE AN IDEA. DO YOU LIKE KIDS?
I WILL NOT WATCH YOUR KIDS TONIGHT.
2-16-16 © 2016 Scott Adams, Inc. /Dist. by Universal Uclick
I WAS GOING TO ASK YOU TO ADOPT THEM.
ABSOLUTE-LY NOT. THE BEST I CAN DO IS WATCH THEM TO-NIGHT.
CONTINUED. . .

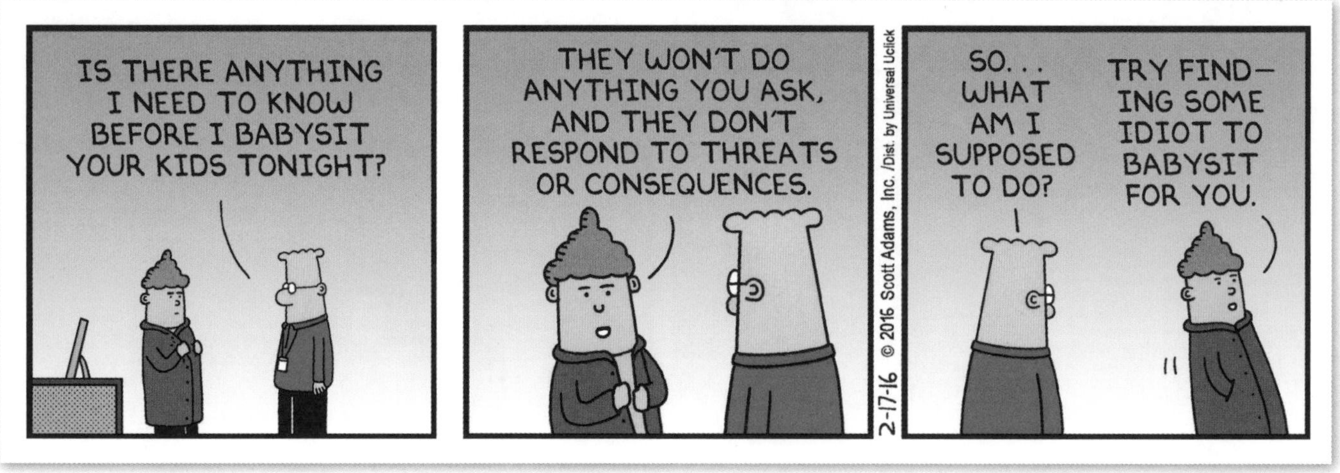
IS THERE ANYTHING I NEED TO KNOW BEFORE I BABYSIT YOUR KIDS TONIGHT?
THEY WON'T DO ANYTHING YOU ASK, AND THEY DON'T RESPOND TO THREATS OR CONSEQUENCES.
2-17-16 © 2016 Scott Adams, Inc. /Dist. by Universal Uclick
SO. . . WHAT AM I SUPPOSED TO DO?
TRY FIND-ING SOME IDIOT TO BABYSIT FOR YOU.

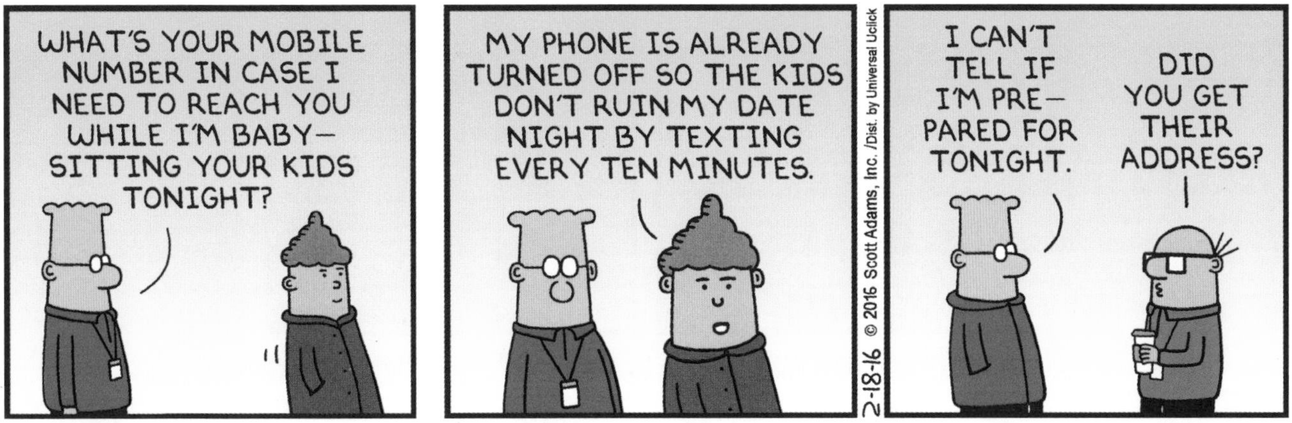
WHAT'S YOUR MOBILE NUMBER IN CASE I NEED TO REACH YOU WHILE I'M BABY-SITTING YOUR KIDS TONIGHT?
MY PHONE IS ALREADY TURNED OFF SO THE KIDS DON'T RUIN MY DATE NIGHT BY TEXTING EVERY TEN MINUTES.
2-18-16 © 2016 Scott Adams, Inc. /Dist. by Universal Uclick
I CAN'T TELL IF I'M PRE-PARED FOR TONIGHT.
DID YOU GET THEIR ADDRESS?

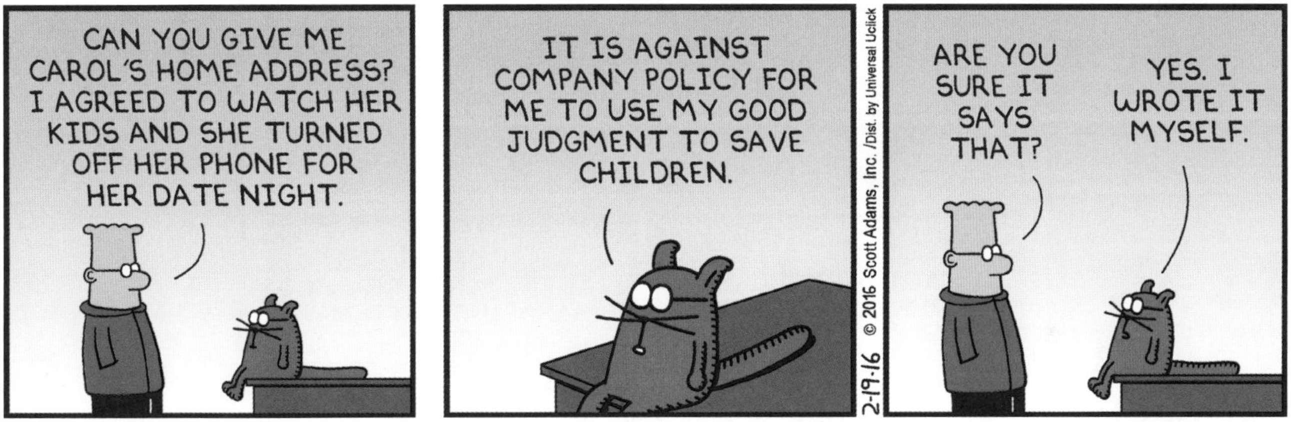
CAN YOU GIVE ME CAROL'S HOME ADDRESS? I AGREED TO WATCH HER KIDS AND SHE TURNED OFF HER PHONE FOR HER DATE NIGHT.
IT IS AGAINST COMPANY POLICY FOR ME TO USE MY GOOD JUDGMENT TO SAVE CHILDREN.
2-19-16 © 2016 Scott Adams, Inc. /Dist. by Universal Uclick
ARE YOU SURE IT SAYS THAT?
YES. I WROTE IT MYSELF.

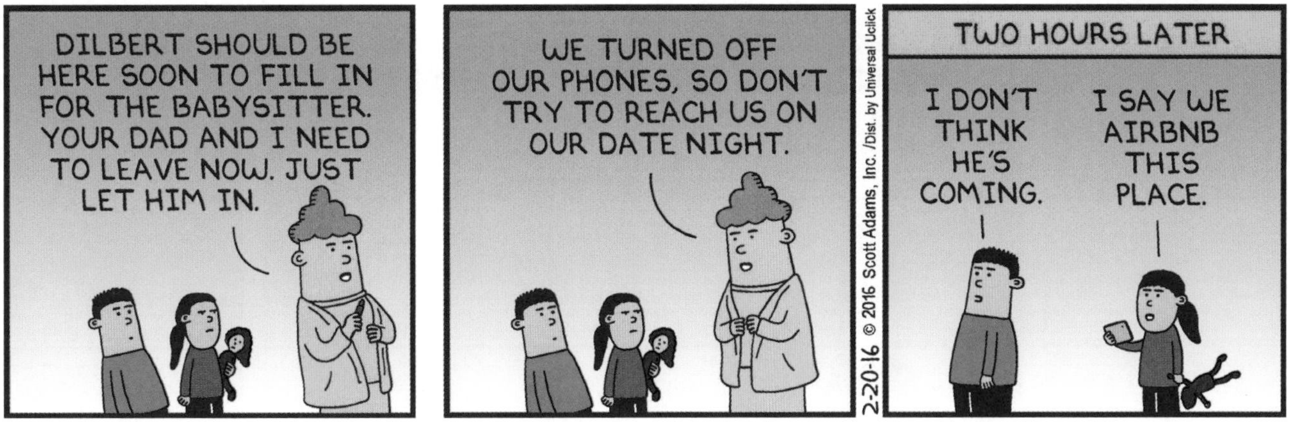
DILBERT SHOULD BE HERE SOON TO FILL IN FOR THE BABYSITTER. YOUR DAD AND I NEED TO LEAVE NOW. JUST LET HIM IN.
WE TURNED OFF OUR PHONES, SO DON'T TRY TO REACH US ON OUR DATE NIGHT.
2-20-16 © 2016 Scott Adams, Inc. /Dist. by Universal Uclick
TWO HOURS LATER
I DON'T THINK HE'S COMING.
I SAY WE AIRBNB THIS PLACE.

WHEN WILL YOU HAVE THAT DONE?

TWO WEEKS.

CAN YOU DO IT FASTER?

YES.

ALL I NEED TO DO IS LOWER THE QUALITY.

TELL ME WHAT YOUR MINIMUM ACCEPTABLE QUALITY LEVEL IS AND I'LL TELL YOU WHEN YOU CAN HAVE IT.

I WANT IT IN ONE WEEK.

I CAN DO THAT AT 50% OF PLANNED QUALITY.

WHY DOES IT FEEL AS IF I'M NOT REALLY MANAGING ANYTHING HERE?

MAYBE YOU COULD GO MANAGE SOMEONE ELSE NOW.

I CAN'T TELL IF I'M DOING MY JOB NOW.

IS IT YOUR JOB TO PREVENT ME FROM WORKING?

© 2016 Scott Adams, Inc./Dist. by Universal Uclick

2-21-16

94

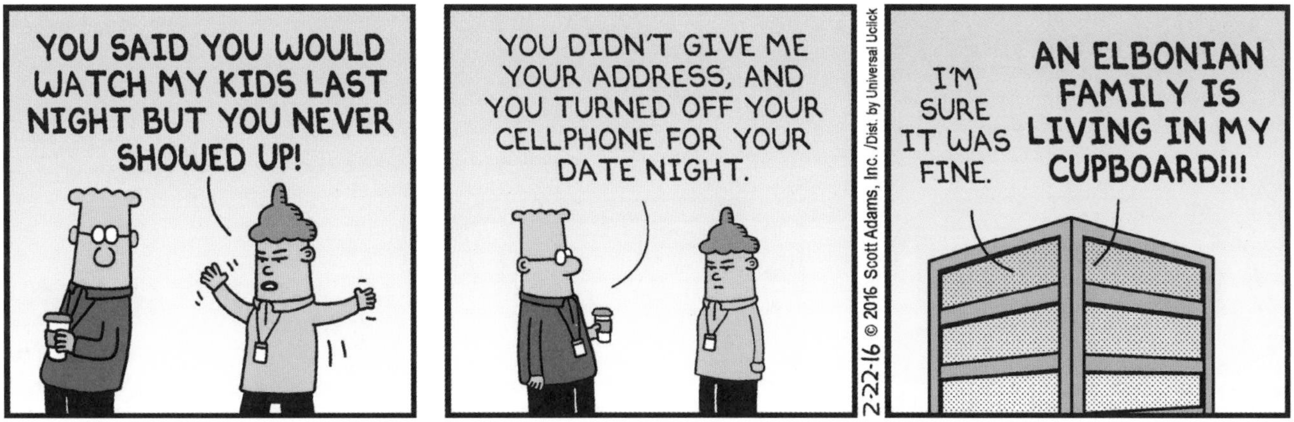
YOU SAID YOU WOULD WATCH MY KIDS LAST NIGHT BUT YOU NEVER SHOWED UP!
YOU DIDN'T GIVE ME YOUR ADDRESS, AND YOU TURNED OFF YOUR CELLPHONE FOR YOUR DATE NIGHT.
2-22-16 © 2016 Scott Adams, Inc. /Dist. by Universal Uclick
I'M SURE IT WAS FINE.
AN ELBONIAN FAMILY IS LIVING IN MY CUPBOARD!!!

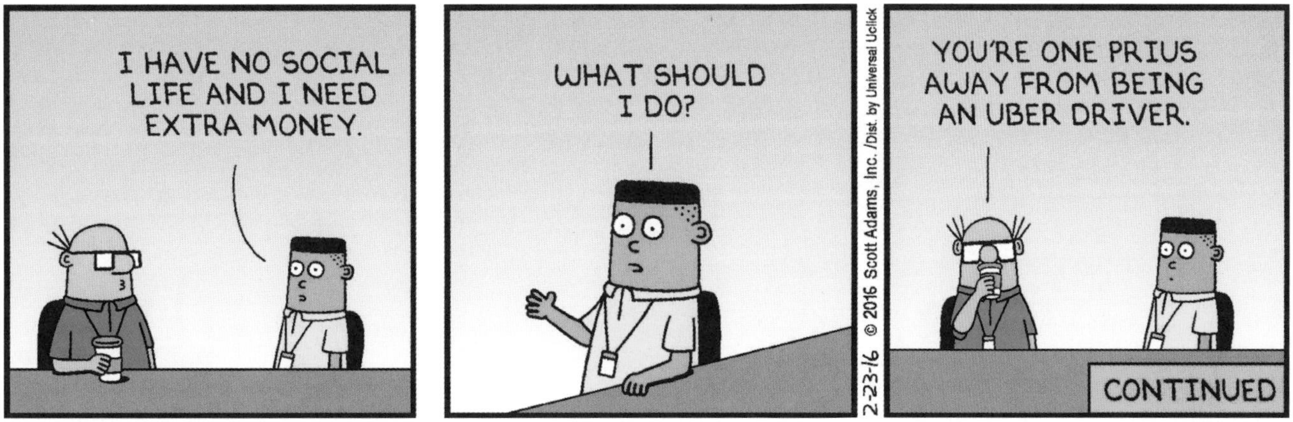
I HAVE NO SOCIAL LIFE AND I NEED EXTRA MONEY.
WHAT SHOULD I DO?
2-23-16 © 2016 Scott Adams, Inc. /Dist. by Universal Uclick
YOU'RE ONE PRIUS AWAY FROM BEING AN UBER DRIVER.
CONTINUED

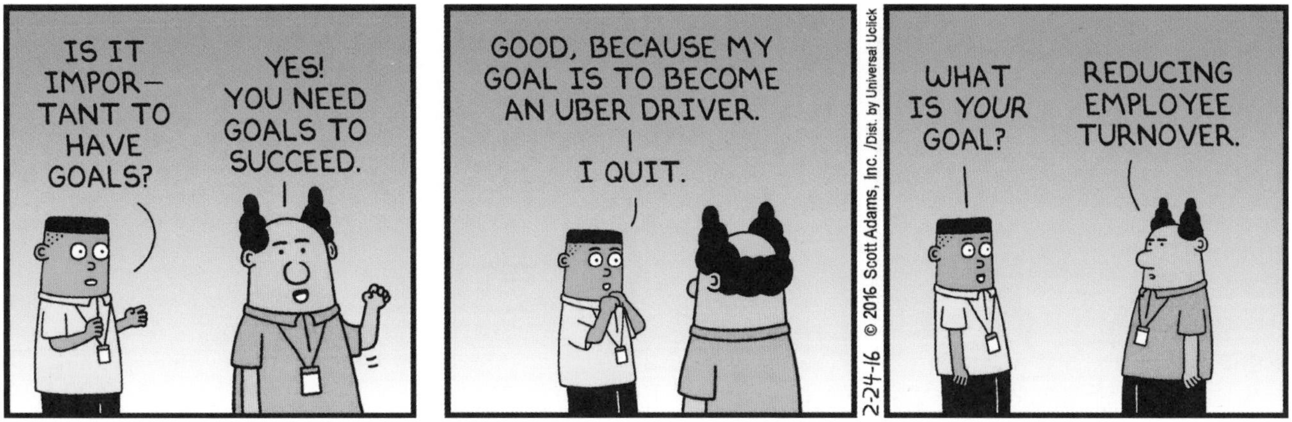
IS IT IMPOR-TANT TO HAVE GOALS?
YES! YOU NEED GOALS TO SUCCEED.
GOOD, BECAUSE MY GOAL IS TO BECOME AN UBER DRIVER.
I QUIT.
2-24-16 © 2016 Scott Adams, Inc. /Dist. by Universal Uclick
WHAT IS *YOUR* GOAL?
REDUCING EMPLOYEE TURNOVER.

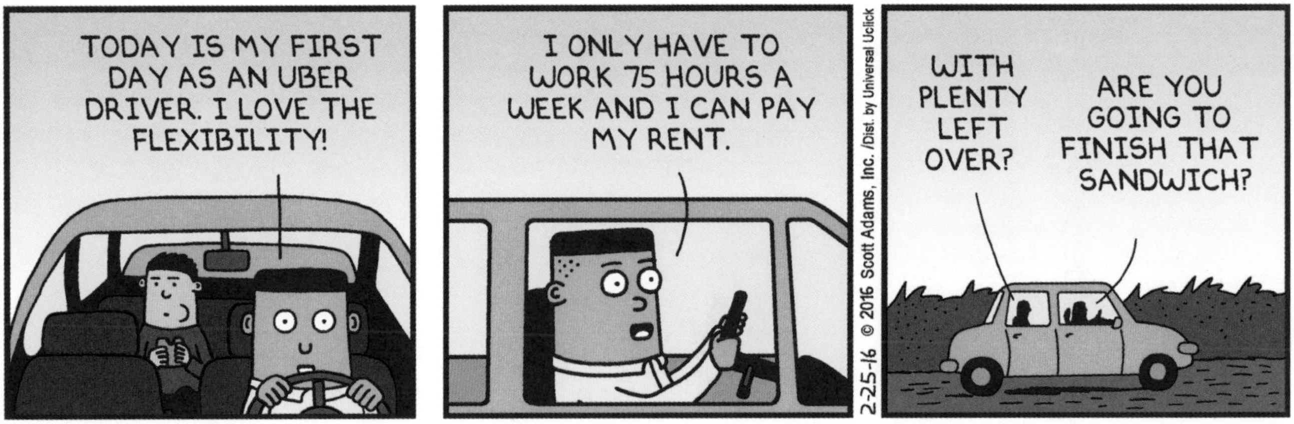
TODAY IS MY FIRST DAY AS AN UBER DRIVER. I LOVE THE FLEXIBILITY!
I ONLY HAVE TO WORK 75 HOURS A WEEK AND I CAN PAY MY RENT.
2-25-16 © 2016 Scott Adams, Inc. /Dist. by Universal Uclick
WITH PLENTY LEFT OVER?
ARE YOU GOING TO FINISH THAT SANDWICH?

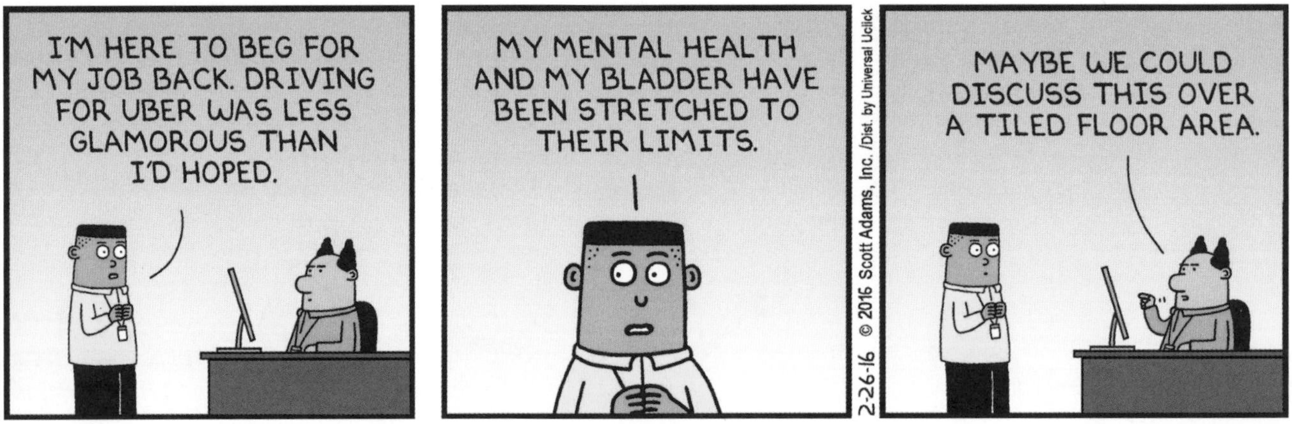
I'M HERE TO BEG FOR MY JOB BACK. DRIVING FOR UBER WAS LESS GLAMOROUS THAN I'D HOPED.
MY MENTAL HEALTH AND MY BLADDER HAVE BEEN STRETCHED TO THEIR LIMITS.
2-26-16 © 2016 Scott Adams, Inc. /Dist. by Universal Uclick
MAYBE WE COULD DISCUSS THIS OVER A TILED FLOOR AREA.

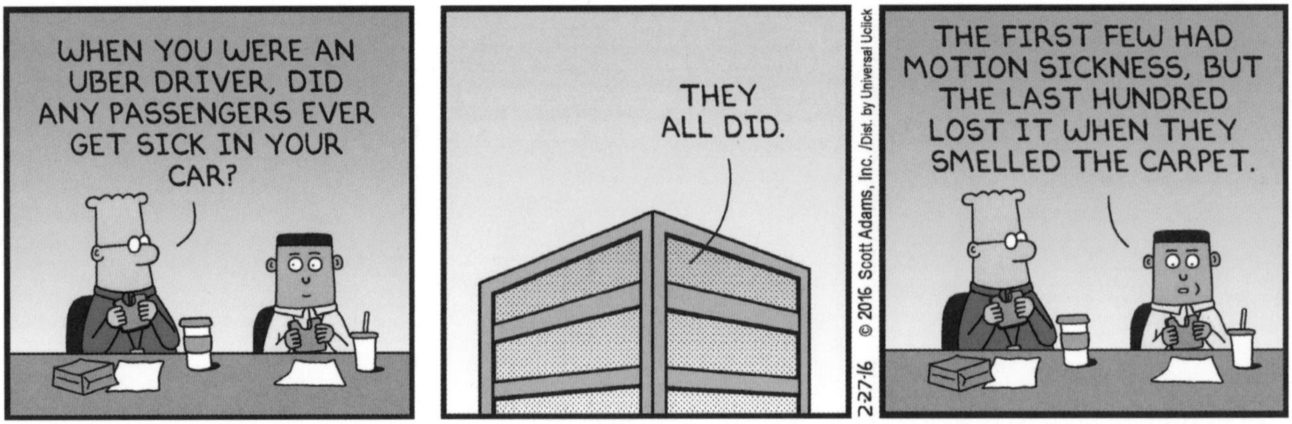
WHEN YOU WERE AN UBER DRIVER, DID ANY PASSENGERS EVER GET SICK IN YOUR CAR?
THEY ALL DID.
2-27-16 © 2016 Scott Adams, Inc. /Dist. by Universal Uclick
THE FIRST FEW HAD MOTION SICKNESS, BUT THE LAST HUNDRED LOST IT WHEN THEY SMELLED THE CARPET.

HACKERS CONVENTION
HI. I'M DILBERT.
I KNOW.
I JUST HACKED YOUR PHONE, YOUR CREDIT CARD, AND YOUR FITNESS BAND.
NO NEED FOR CONVERSATION.
I KNOW EVERY-THING ABOUT YOU, INCLUDING YOUR CURRENT PHYSIO-LOGICAL STATE.
I FEEL VIOLATED.
NO, YOU DON'T.
YOUR VITAL SIGNS ARE ELEVATED. THAT MEANS YOU'RE FALLING IN LOVE WITH ME.
HA! I JUST HACKED ***YOUR*** FITNESS BAND AND I SEE YOU HAVE . . . NO INTEREST IN ME WHATSOEVER.
IT WAS TOO LATE TO REJECT HER FIRST.
© 2016 Scott Adams, Inc./Dist. by Universal Uclick
2-28-16

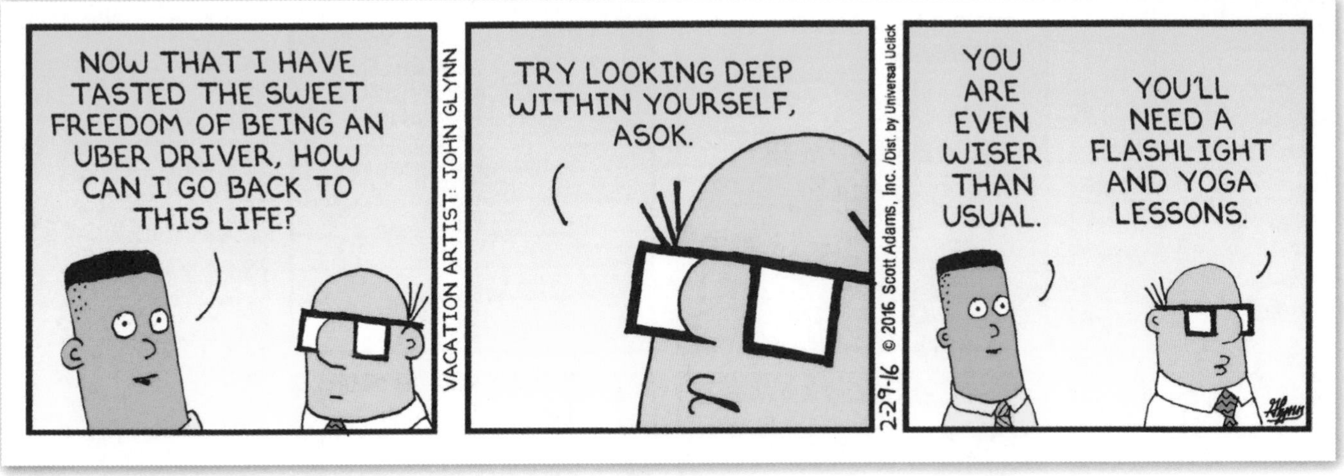
NOW THAT I HAVE TASTED THE SWEET FREEDOM OF BEING AN UBER DRIVER, HOW CAN I GO BACK TO THIS LIFE?
VACATION ARTIST: JOHN GLYNN
TRY LOOKING DEEP WITHIN YOURSELF, ASOK.
2-29-16 © 2016 Scott Adams, Inc. /Dist. by Universal Uclick
YOU ARE EVEN WISER THAN USUAL.
YOU'LL NEED A FLASHLIGHT AND YOGA LESSONS.

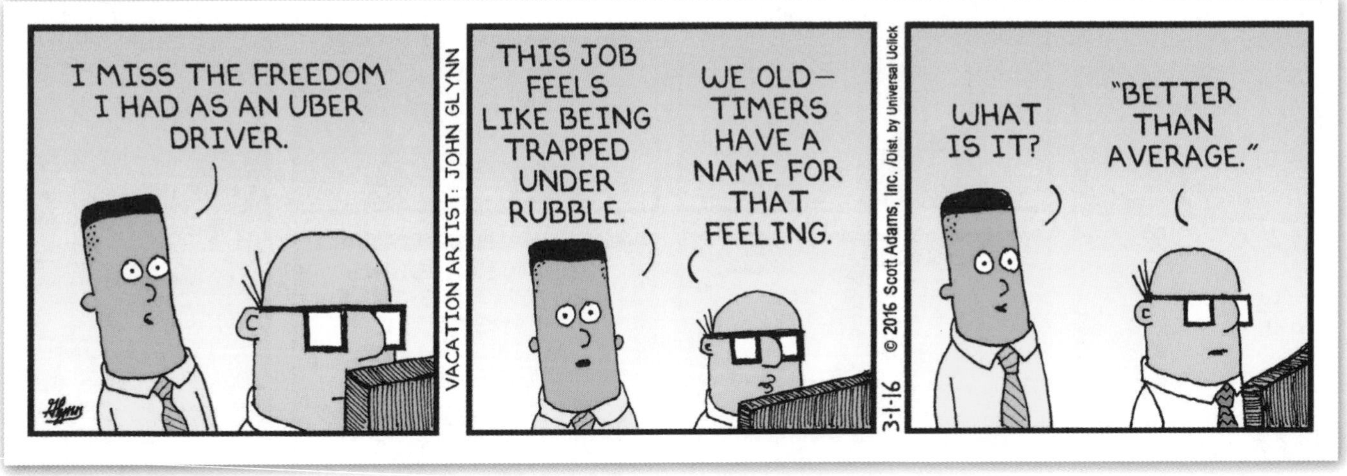
I MISS THE FREEDOM I HAD AS AN UBER DRIVER.
VACATION ARTIST: JOHN GLYNN
THIS JOB FEELS LIKE BEING TRAPPED UNDER RUBBLE.
WE OLD-TIMERS HAVE A NAME FOR THAT FEELING.
3-1-16 © 2016 Scott Adams, Inc. /Dist. by Universal Uclick
WHAT IS IT?
"BETTER THAN AVERAGE."

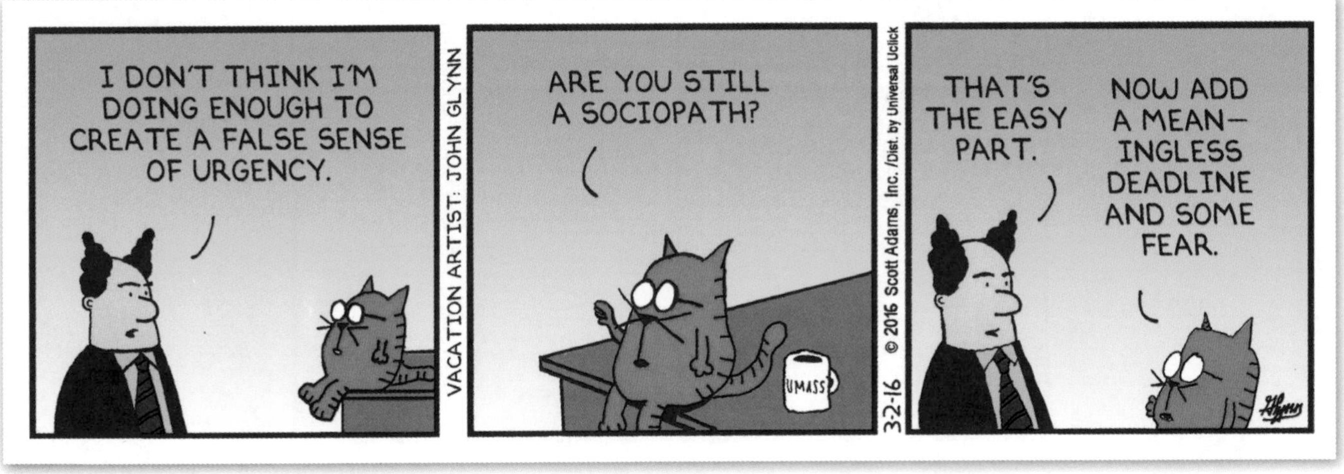
I DON'T THINK I'M DOING ENOUGH TO CREATE A FALSE SENSE OF URGENCY.
VACATION ARTIST: JOHN GLYNN
ARE YOU STILL A SOCIOPATH?
UMASS
3-2-16 © 2016 Scott Adams, Inc. /Dist. by Universal Uclick
THAT'S THE EASY PART.
NOW ADD A MEAN-INGLESS DEADLINE AND SOME FEAR.

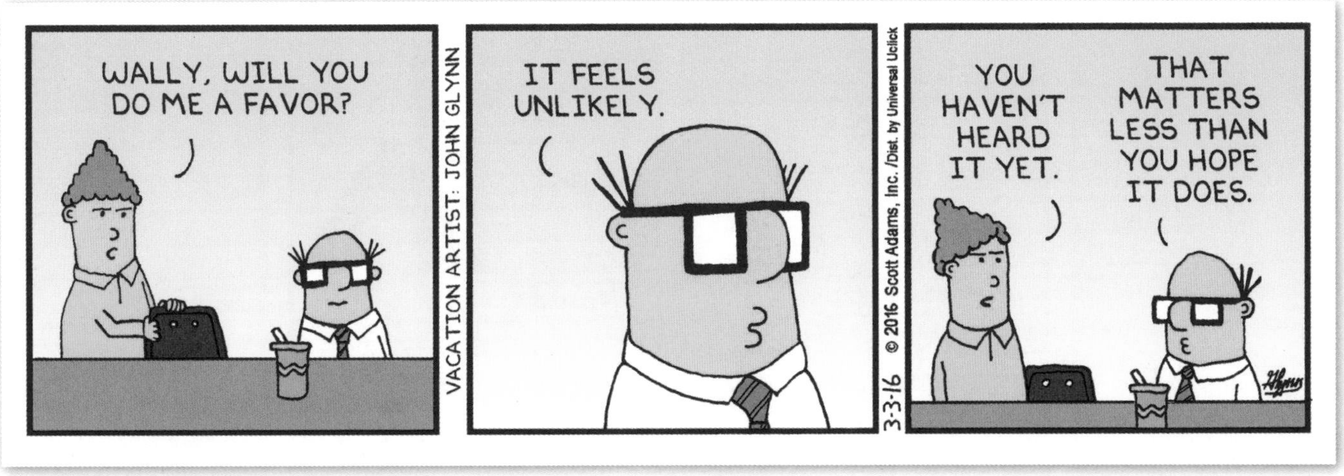
WALLY, WILL YOU DO ME A FAVOR?
VACATION ARTIST: JOHN GLYNN
IT FEELS UNLIKELY.
3-3-16 © 2016 Scott Adams, Inc. /Dist. by Universal Uclick
YOU HAVEN'T HEARD IT YET.
THAT MATTERS LESS THAN YOU HOPE IT DOES.

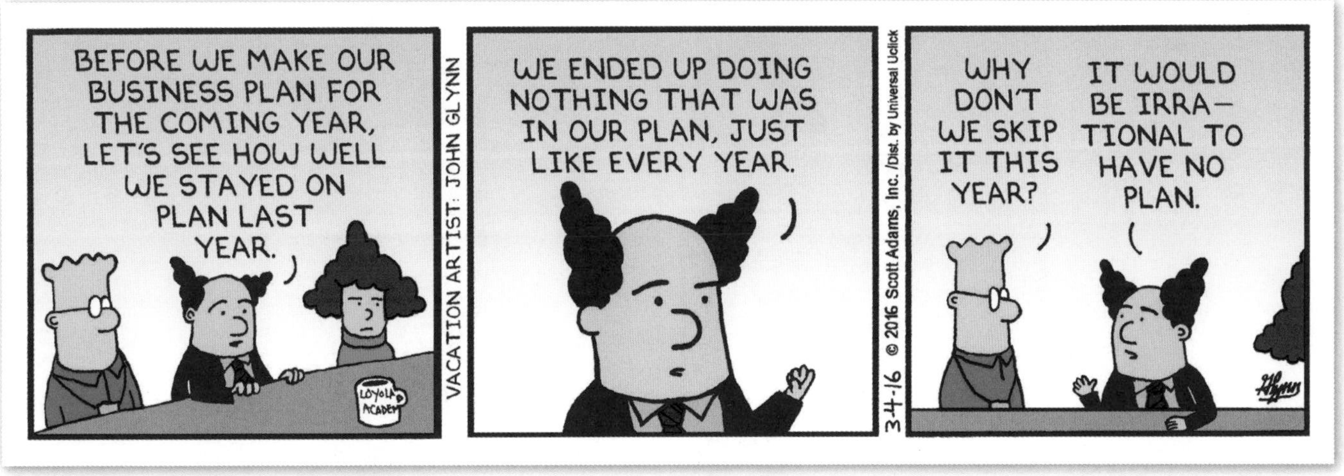
BEFORE WE MAKE OUR BUSINESS PLAN FOR THE COMING YEAR, LET'S SEE HOW WELL WE STAYED ON PLAN LAST YEAR.
VACATION ARTIST: JOHN GLYNN
WE ENDED UP DOING NOTHING THAT WAS IN OUR PLAN, JUST LIKE EVERY YEAR.
3-4-16 © 2016 Scott Adams, Inc. /Dist. by Universal Uclick
WHY DON'T WE SKIP IT THIS YEAR?
IT WOULD BE IRRA– TIONAL TO HAVE NO PLAN.

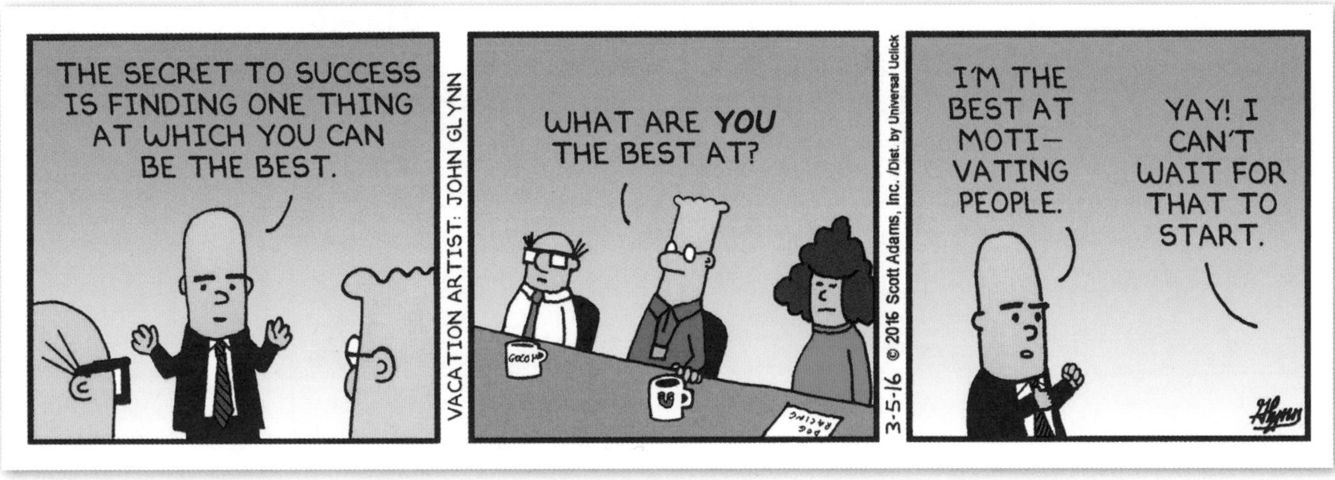
THE SECRET TO SUCCESS IS FINDING ONE THING AT WHICH YOU CAN BE THE BEST.
VACATION ARTIST: JOHN GLYNN
WHAT ARE **YOU** THE BEST AT?
3-5-16 © 2016 Scott Adams, Inc. /Dist. by Universal Uclick
I'M THE BEST AT MOTI– VATING PEOPLE.
YAY! I CAN'T WAIT FOR THAT TO START.

HOW'S THE SOFTWARE COMING ALONG? ALMOST DONE?
STILL WAITING FOR YOU TO GIVE ME THE SPECS SO I CAN START.
I ALREADY TOLD YOU IT'S A CLOUD APP THAT DOES DATA.
© 2016 Scott Adams, Inc./Dist. by Universal Uclick
HEY, I CAN'T DO YOUR JOB FOR YOU.
YOU HAVE TO MEET ME HALFWAY.
AREN'T YOU SUPPOSED TO BE "AGILE"?
I MEAN, HOW HARD IS IT TO REARRANGE ZEROES AND ONES ALL DAY?
3-6-16
SHOULD I ASK AGAIN TOMOR-ROW?
SURE, IF YOU'RE ALIVE.

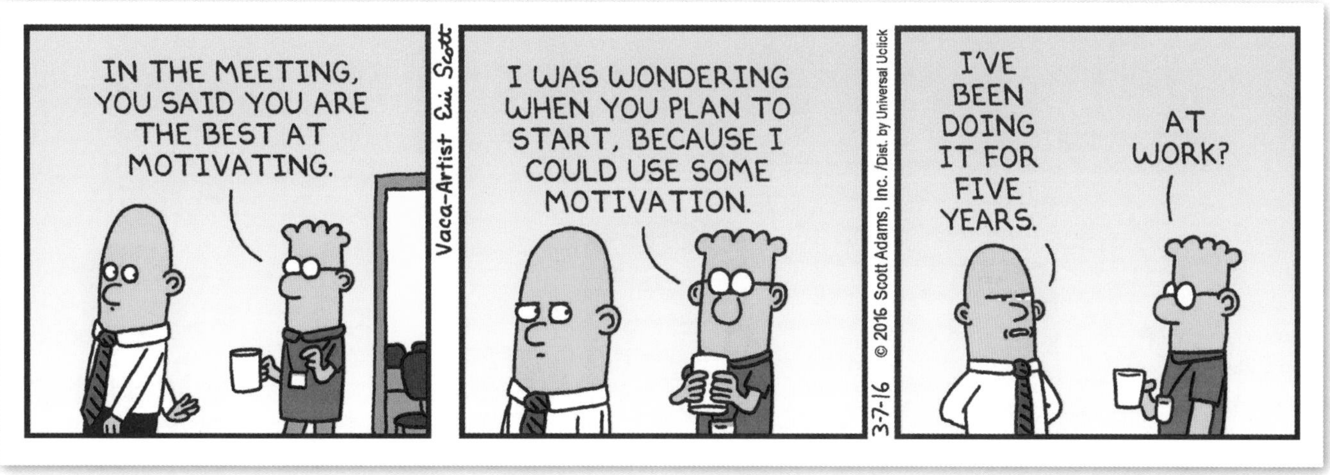
IN THE MEETING, YOU SAID YOU ARE THE BEST AT MOTIVATING.
Vaca-Artist Eric Scott
I WAS WONDERING WHEN YOU PLAN TO START, BECAUSE I COULD USE SOME MOTIVATION.
3-7-16 © 2016 Scott Adams, Inc. /Dist. by Universal Uclick
I'VE BEEN DOING IT FOR FIVE YEARS.
AT WORK?

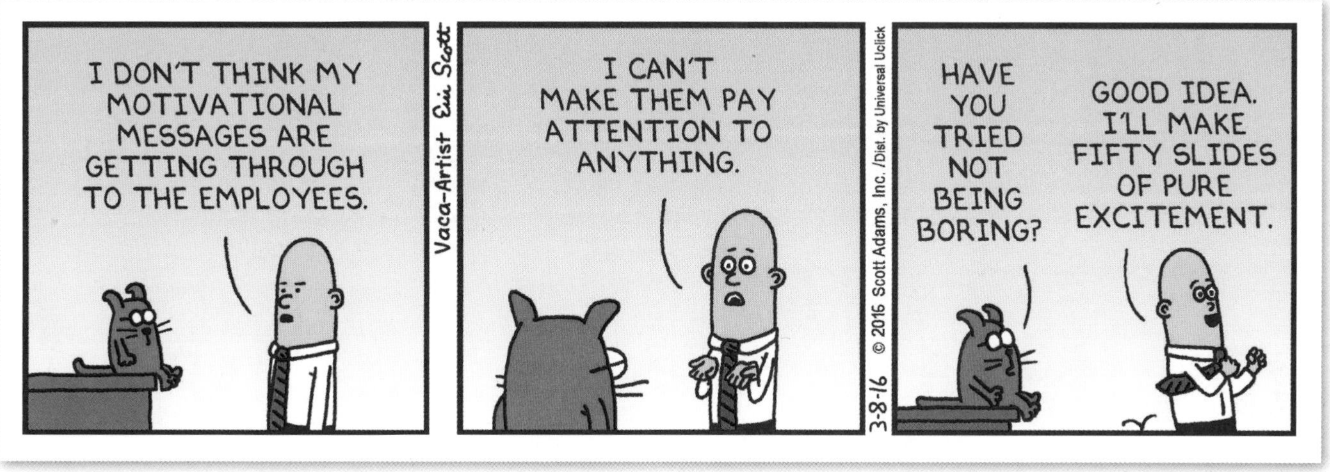
I DON'T THINK MY MOTIVATIONAL MESSAGES ARE GETTING THROUGH TO THE EMPLOYEES.
Vaca-Artist Eric Scott
I CAN'T MAKE THEM PAY ATTENTION TO ANYTHING.
3-8-16 © 2016 Scott Adams, Inc. /Dist. by Universal Uclick
HAVE YOU TRIED NOT BEING BORING?
GOOD IDEA. I'LL MAKE FIFTY SLIDES OF PURE EXCITEMENT.

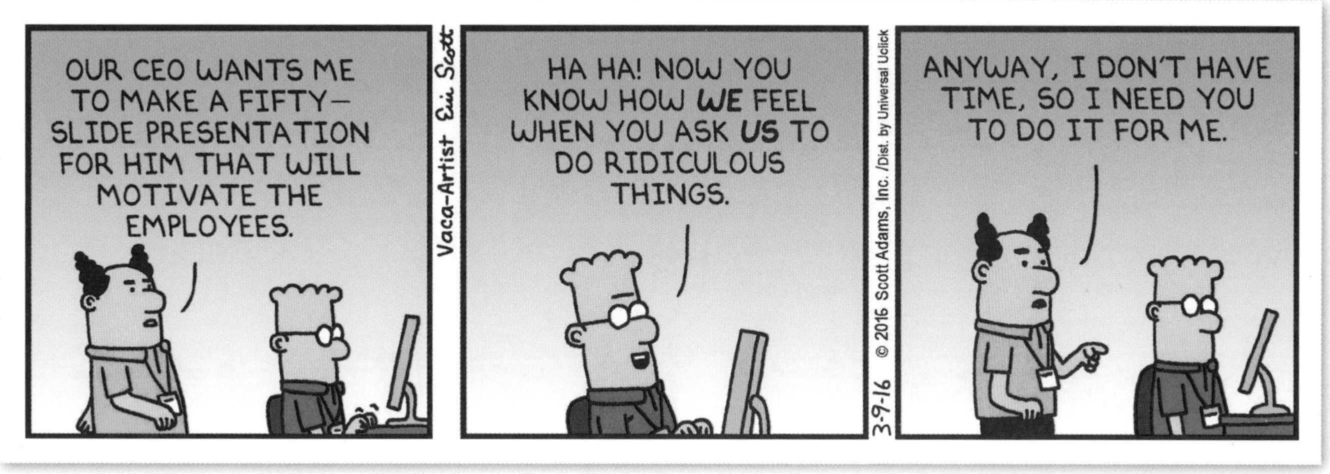
OUR CEO WANTS ME TO MAKE A FIFTY-SLIDE PRESENTATION FOR HIM THAT WILL MOTIVATE THE EMPLOYEES.
Vaca-Artist Eric Scott
HA HA! NOW YOU KNOW HOW WE FEEL WHEN YOU ASK US TO DO RIDICULOUS THINGS.
3-9-16 © 2016 Scott Adams, Inc. /Dist. by Universal Uclick
ANYWAY, I DON'T HAVE TIME, SO I NEED YOU TO DO IT FOR ME.

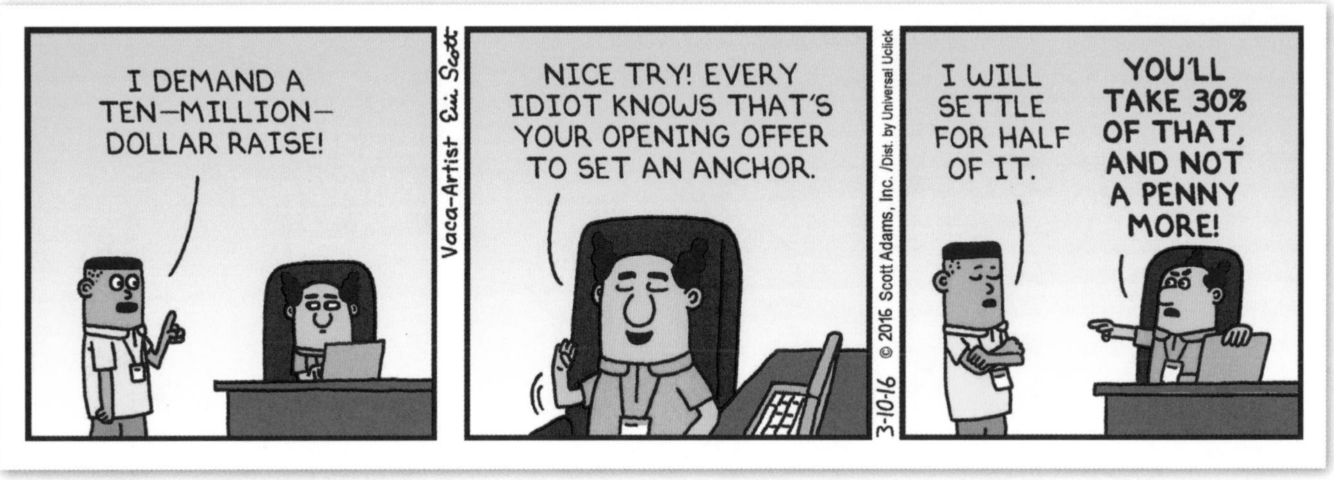
I DEMAND A TEN-MILLION-DOLLAR RAISE!
Vaca-Artist Eric Scott
NICE TRY! EVERY IDIOT KNOWS THAT'S YOUR OPENING OFFER TO SET AN ANCHOR.
3-10-16 © 2016 Scott Adams, Inc. /Dist. by Universal Uclick
I WILL SETTLE FOR HALF OF IT.
YOU'LL TAKE 30% OF THAT, AND NOT A PENNY MORE!

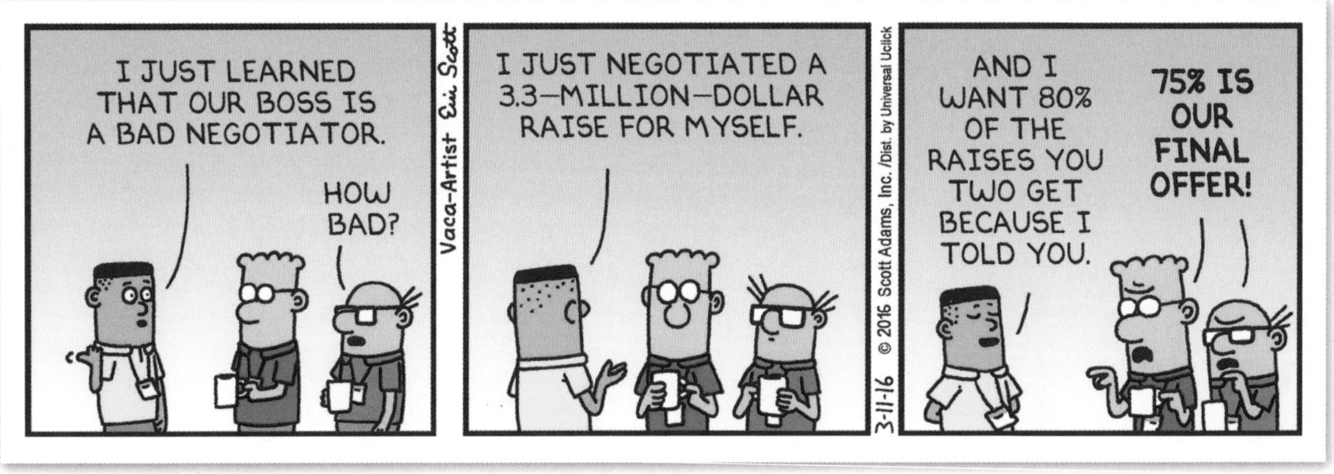
I JUST LEARNED THAT OUR BOSS IS A BAD NEGOTIATOR.
HOW BAD?
Vaca-Artist Eric Scott
I JUST NEGOTIATED A 3.3-MILLION-DOLLAR RAISE FOR MYSELF.
3-11-16 © 2016 Scott Adams, Inc. /Dist. by Universal Uclick
AND I WANT 80% OF THE RAISES YOU TWO GET BECAUSE I TOLD YOU.
75% IS OUR FINAL OFFER!

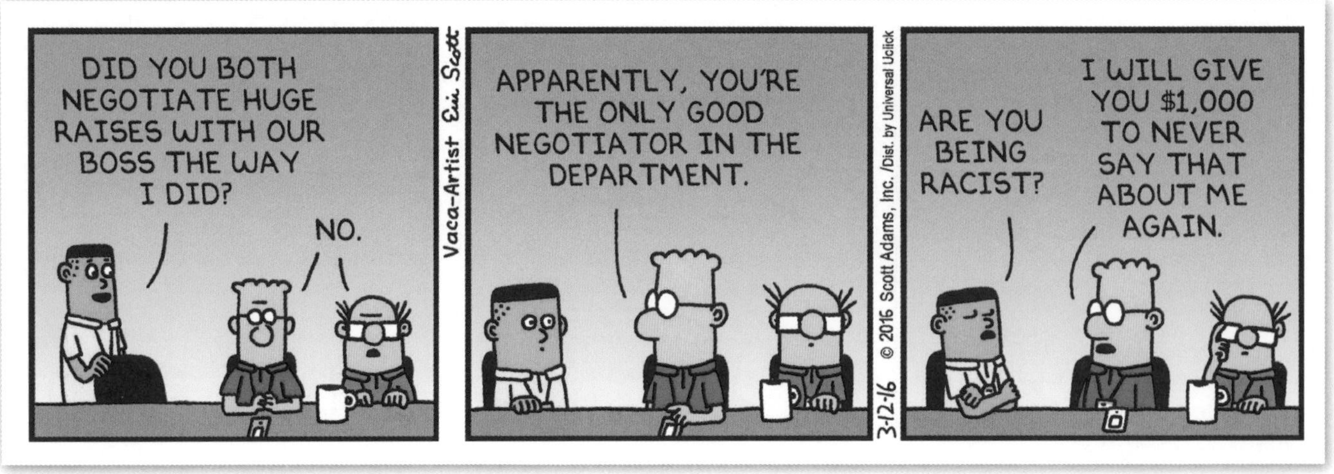
DID YOU BOTH NEGOTIATE HUGE RAISES WITH OUR BOSS THE WAY I DID?
NO.
Vaca-Artist Eric Scott
APPARENTLY, YOU'RE THE ONLY GOOD NEGOTIATOR IN THE DEPARTMENT.
3-12-16 © 2016 Scott Adams, Inc. /Dist. by Universal Uclick
ARE YOU BEING RACIST?
I WILL GIVE YOU $1,000 TO NEVER SAY THAT ABOUT ME AGAIN.

IS THE SOFTWARE DONE YET?

THAT DEPENDS.

DO YOU HAVE ANY NEW FEATURE REQUESTS?

ONLY THREE.

THEN IT'S NOT DONE, IS IT?

WELL, NO, I GUESS NOT.

SO. . . WHEN WILL IT BE DONE?

IT WILL BE DONE ONE WEEK AFTER YOU GIVE ME YOUR LAST CHANGES.

BUT I BELIEVE YOU TAUGHT US THAT CHANGE IS GOOD.

SO EITHER YOU CAN BE A STAGNANT BUREAU-CRAT OR A DYNAMIC LEADER WITH LOTS OF CHANGES.

IT'S A QUESTION OF FREE WILL, REALLY.

I HAVE TO BE SOME-WHERE ELSE.

© 2016 Scott Adams, Inc./Dist. by Universal Uclick

3-13-16

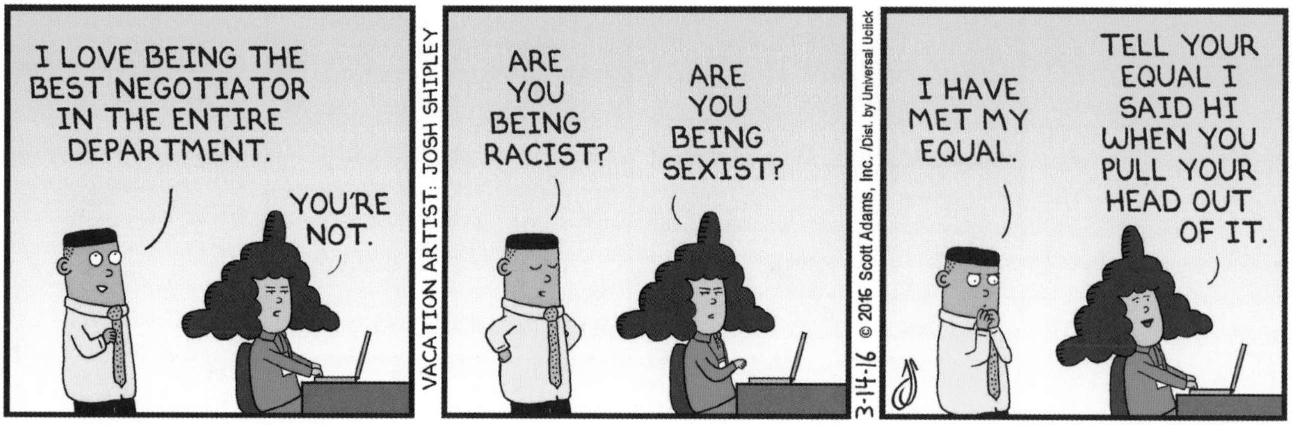
I LOVE BEING THE BEST NEGOTIATOR IN THE ENTIRE DEPARTMENT.
YOU'RE NOT.
VACATION ARTIST: JOSH SHIPLEY
ARE YOU BEING RACIST?
ARE YOU BEING SEXIST?
3-14-16 © 2016 Scott Adams, Inc. /Dist. by Universal Uclick
I HAVE MET MY EQUAL.
TELL YOUR EQUAL I SAID HI WHEN YOU PULL YOUR HEAD OUT OF IT.

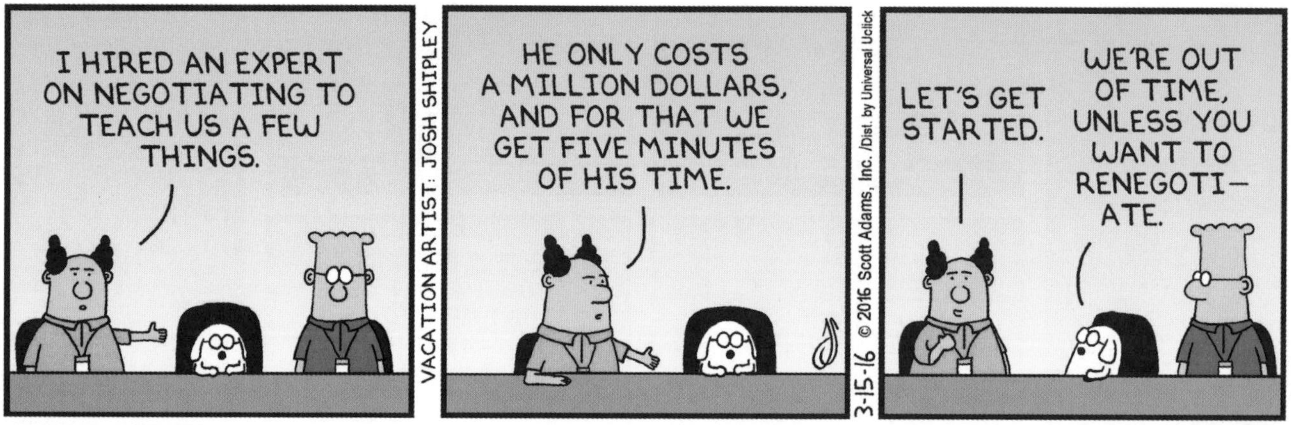
I HIRED AN EXPERT ON NEGOTIATING TO TEACH US A FEW THINGS.
VACATION ARTIST: JOSH SHIPLEY
HE ONLY COSTS A MILLION DOLLARS, AND FOR THAT WE GET FIVE MINUTES OF HIS TIME.
3-15-16 © 2016 Scott Adams, Inc. /Dist. by Universal Uclick
LET'S GET STARTED.
WE'RE OUT OF TIME, UNLESS YOU WANT TO RENEGOTI-ATE.

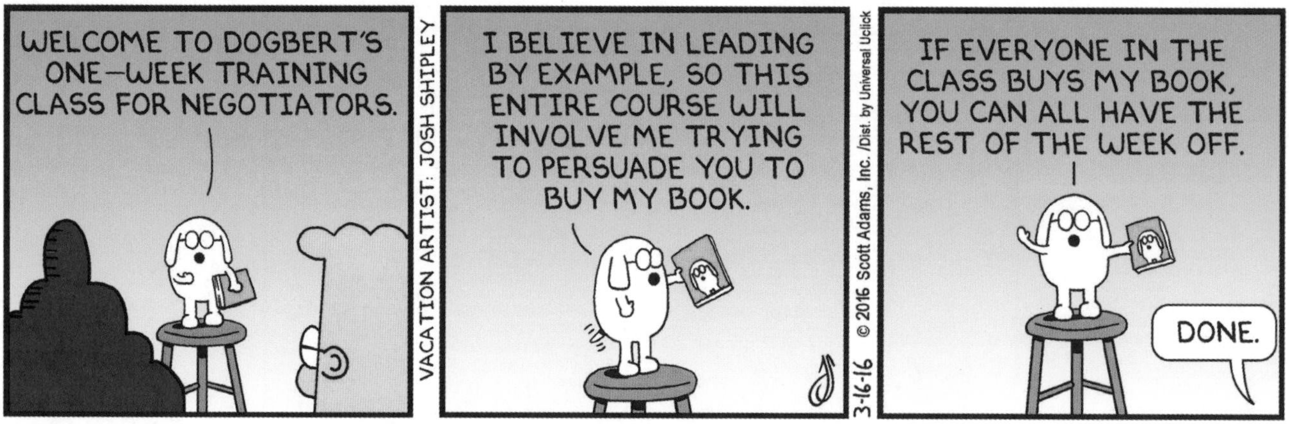
WELCOME TO DOGBERT'S ONE-WEEK TRAINING CLASS FOR NEGOTIATORS.
VACATION ARTIST: JOSH SHIPLEY
I BELIEVE IN LEADING BY EXAMPLE, SO THIS ENTIRE COURSE WILL INVOLVE ME TRYING TO PERSUADE YOU TO BUY MY BOOK.
3-16-16 © 2016 Scott Adams, Inc. /Dist. by Universal Uclick
IF EVERYONE IN THE CLASS BUYS MY BOOK, YOU CAN ALL HAVE THE REST OF THE WEEK OFF.
DONE.

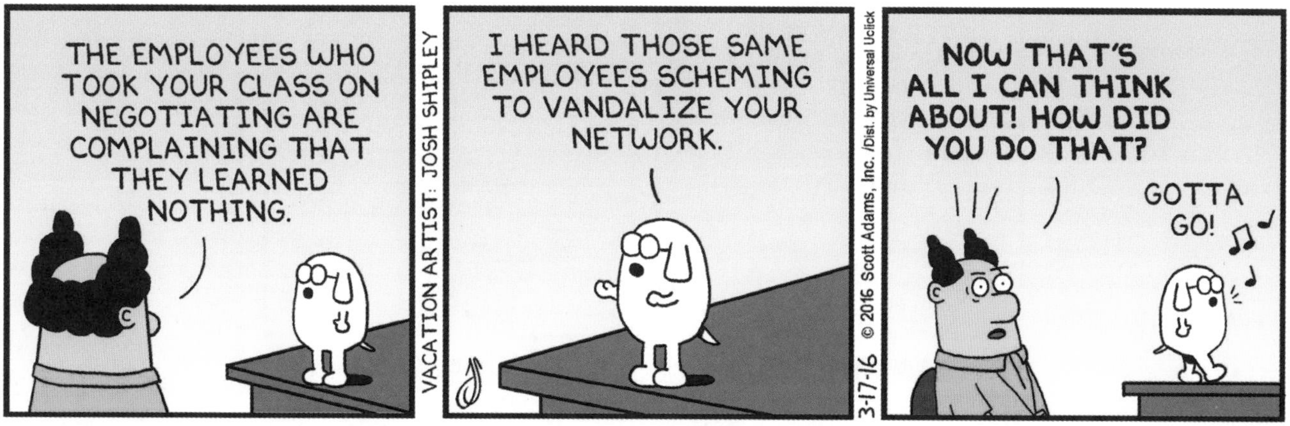
THE EMPLOYEES WHO TOOK YOUR CLASS ON NEGOTIATING ARE COMPLAINING THAT THEY LEARNED NOTHING.
VACATION ARTIST: JOSH SHIPLEY
I HEARD THOSE SAME EMPLOYEES SCHEMING TO VANDALIZE YOUR NETWORK.
3-17-16 © 2016 Scott Adams, Inc. /Dist. by Universal Uclick
NOW THAT'S ALL I CAN THINK ABOUT! HOW DID YOU DO THAT?
GOTTA GO!

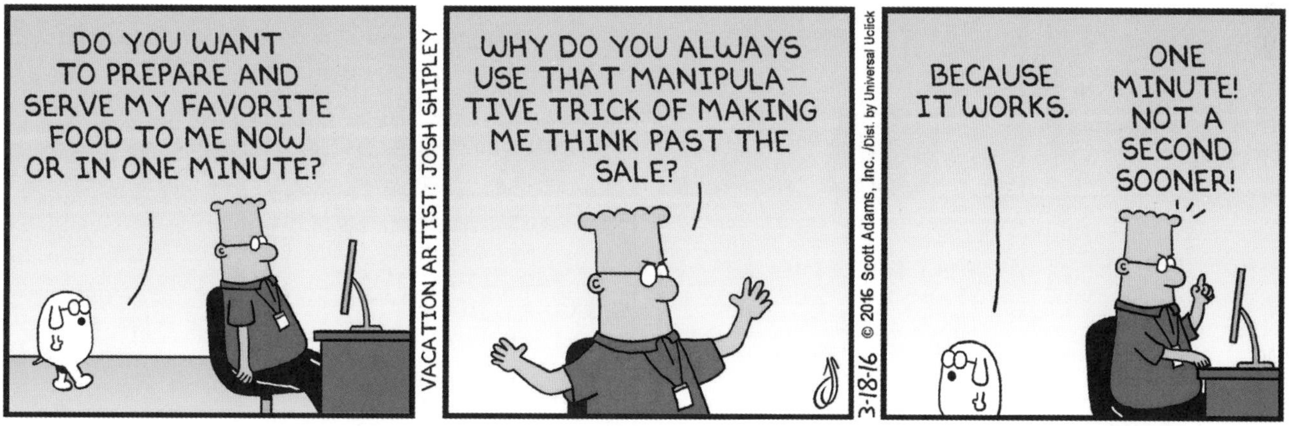
DO YOU WANT TO PREPARE AND SERVE MY FAVORITE FOOD TO ME NOW OR IN ONE MINUTE?
VACATION ARTIST: JOSH SHIPLEY
WHY DO YOU ALWAYS USE THAT MANIPULA- TIVE TRICK OF MAKING ME THINK PAST THE SALE?
3-18-16 © 2016 Scott Adams, Inc. /Dist. by Universal Uclick
BECAUSE IT WORKS.
ONE MINUTE! NOT A SECOND SOONER!

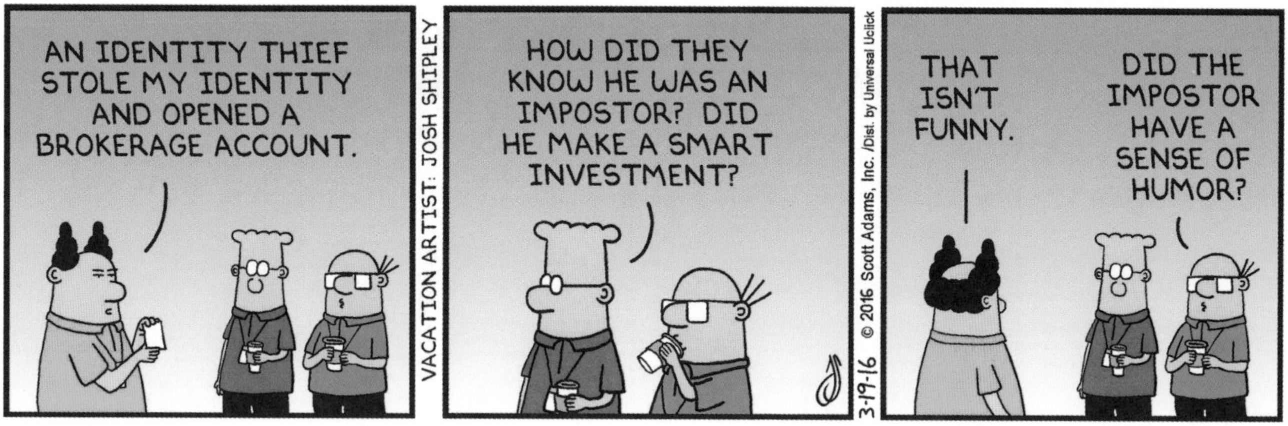
AN IDENTITY THIEF STOLE MY IDENTITY AND OPENED A BROKERAGE ACCOUNT.
VACATION ARTIST: JOSH SHIPLEY
HOW DID THEY KNOW HE WAS AN IMPOSTOR? DID HE MAKE A SMART INVESTMENT?
3-19-16 © 2016 Scott Adams, Inc. /Dist. by Universal Uclick
THAT ISN'T FUNNY.
DID THE IMPOSTOR HAVE A SENSE OF HUMOR?

STEP AWAY FROM THAT OPEN SOURCE CODE!
WHY?
BECAUSE I AM MORDAC, THE PREVENTER OF ALL EFFICIENT SOLUTIONS IN THE INFORMATION TECHNOLOGY REALM.
THAT ISN'T AN ACTUAL JOB.
I WAS HOPING IT WAS. I LOST THE FILE WITH MY JOB DESCRIPTION.
THAT WAS FIVE YEARS AGO. I'VE BEEN WINGING IT SINCE THEN.
MY PARENTS TAUGHT ME THAT I COULD BE ANYTHING I WANTED TO BE.
AND I WANTED TO BE THIS.
SO DON'T USE THAT CODE!
NOT EVEN WHEN YOU TURN AROUND?
3-20-16

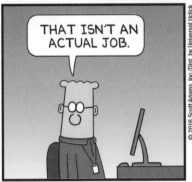

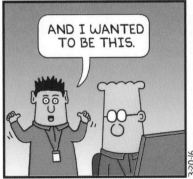

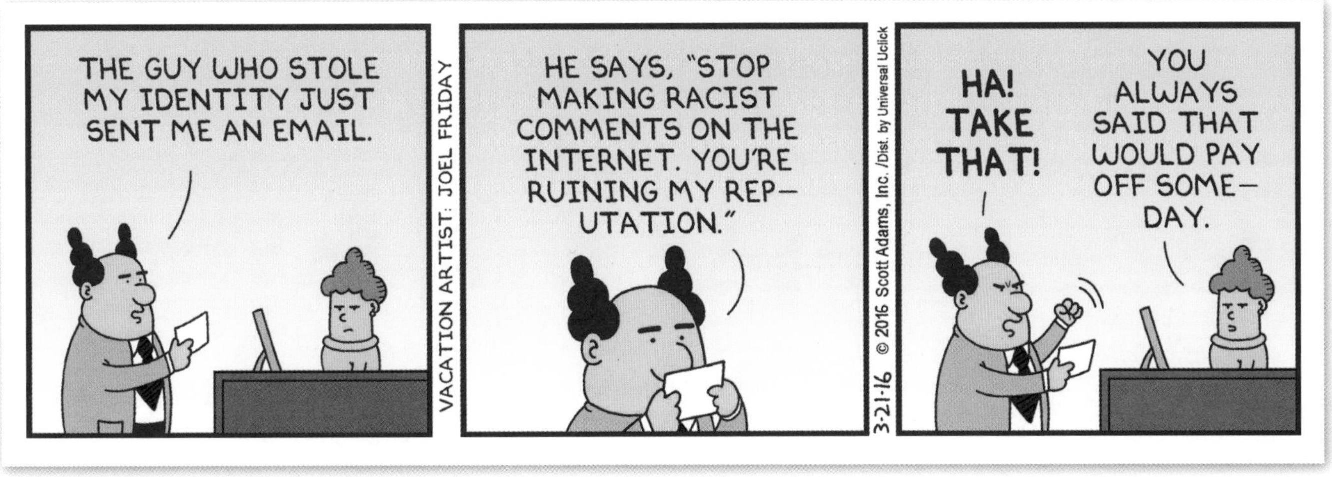
THE GUY WHO STOLE MY IDENTITY JUST SENT ME AN EMAIL.
VACATION ARTIST: JOEL FRIDAY
HE SAYS, "STOP MAKING RACIST COMMENTS ON THE INTERNET. YOU'RE RUINING MY REP— UTATION."
3-21-16 © 2016 Scott Adams, Inc. /Dist. by Universal Uclick
HA! TAKE THAT!
YOU ALWAYS SAID THAT WOULD PAY OFF SOME— DAY.

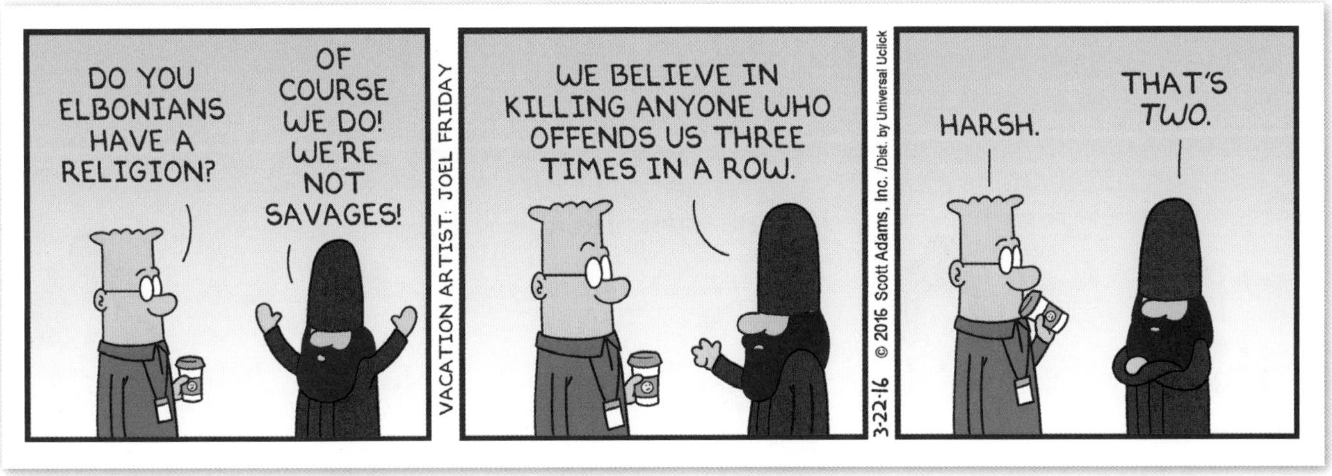
DO YOU ELBONIANS HAVE A RELIGION?
OF COURSE WE DO! WE'RE NOT SAVAGES!
VACATION ARTIST: JOEL FRIDAY
WE BELIEVE IN KILLING ANYONE WHO OFFENDS US THREE TIMES IN A ROW.
3-22-16 © 2016 Scott Adams, Inc. /Dist. by Universal Uclick
HARSH.
THAT'S *TWO*.

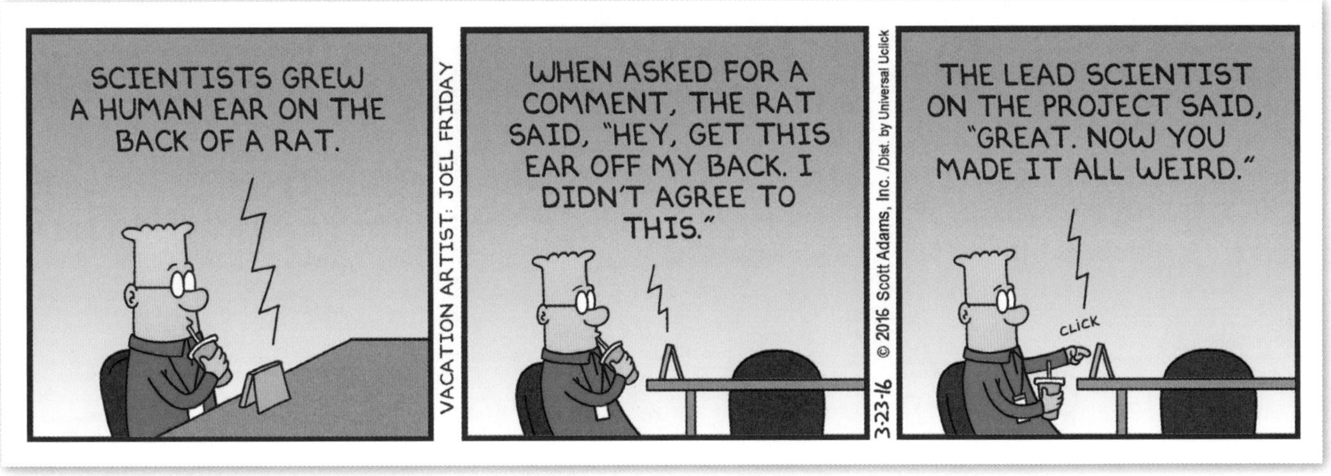
SCIENTISTS GREW A HUMAN EAR ON THE BACK OF A RAT.
VACATION ARTIST: JOEL FRIDAY
WHEN ASKED FOR A COMMENT, THE RAT SAID, "HEY, GET THIS EAR OFF MY BACK. I DIDN'T AGREE TO THIS."
3-23-16 © 2016 Scott Adams, Inc. /Dist. by Universal Uclick
THE LEAD SCIENTIST ON THE PROJECT SAID, "GREAT. NOW YOU MADE IT ALL WEIRD."
CLICK

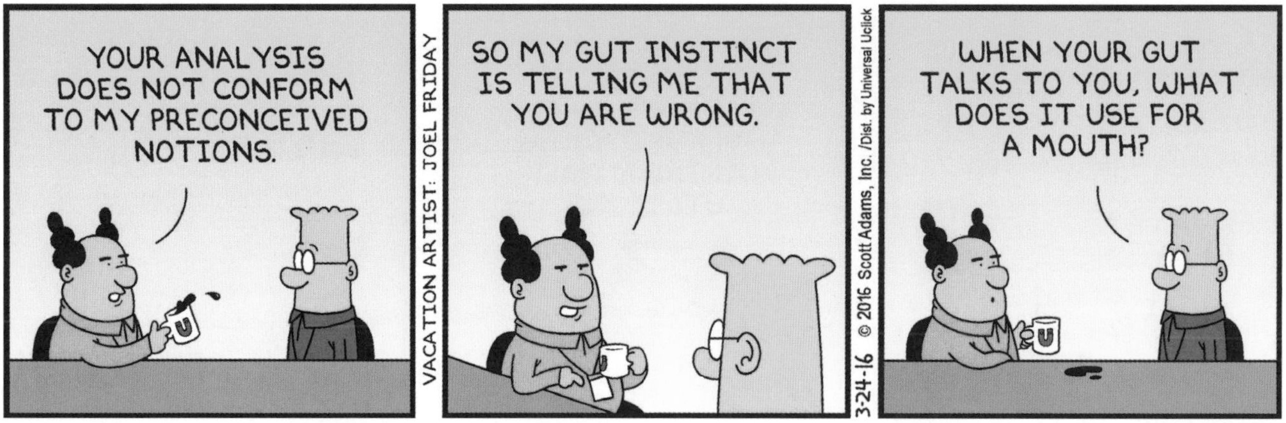
YOUR ANALYSIS DOES NOT CONFORM TO MY PRECONCEIVED NOTIONS.
VACATION ARTIST: JOEL FRIDAY
SO MY GUT INSTINCT IS TELLING ME THAT YOU ARE WRONG.
3-24-16 © 2016 Scott Adams, Inc. /Dist. by Universal Uclick
WHEN YOUR GUT TALKS TO YOU, WHAT DOES IT USE FOR A MOUTH?

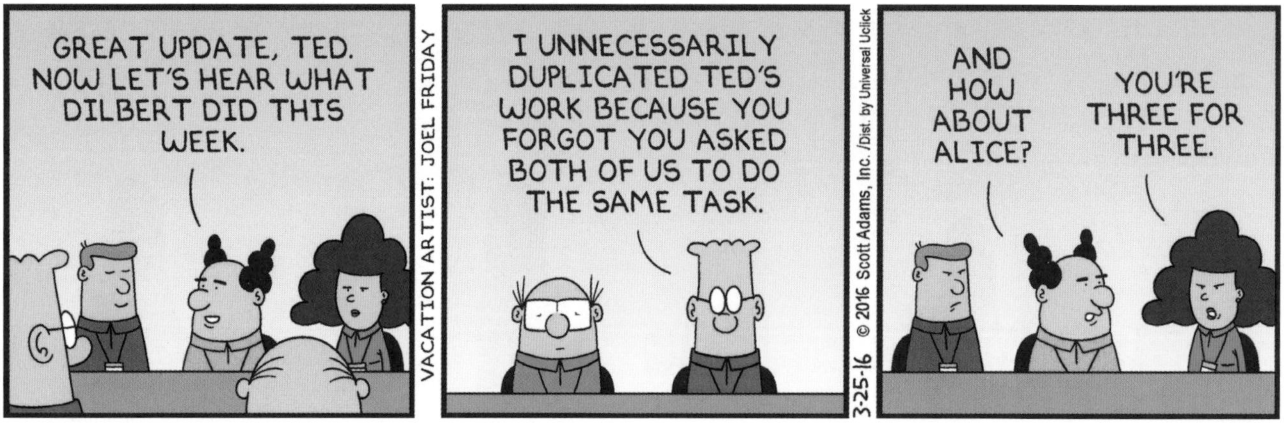
GREAT UPDATE, TED. NOW LET'S HEAR WHAT DILBERT DID THIS WEEK.
VACATION ARTIST: JOEL FRIDAY
I UNNECESSARILY DUPLICATED TED'S WORK BECAUSE YOU FORGOT YOU ASKED BOTH OF US TO DO THE SAME TASK.
3-25-16 © 2016 Scott Adams, Inc. /Dist. by Universal Uclick
AND HOW ABOUT ALICE?
YOU'RE THREE FOR THREE.

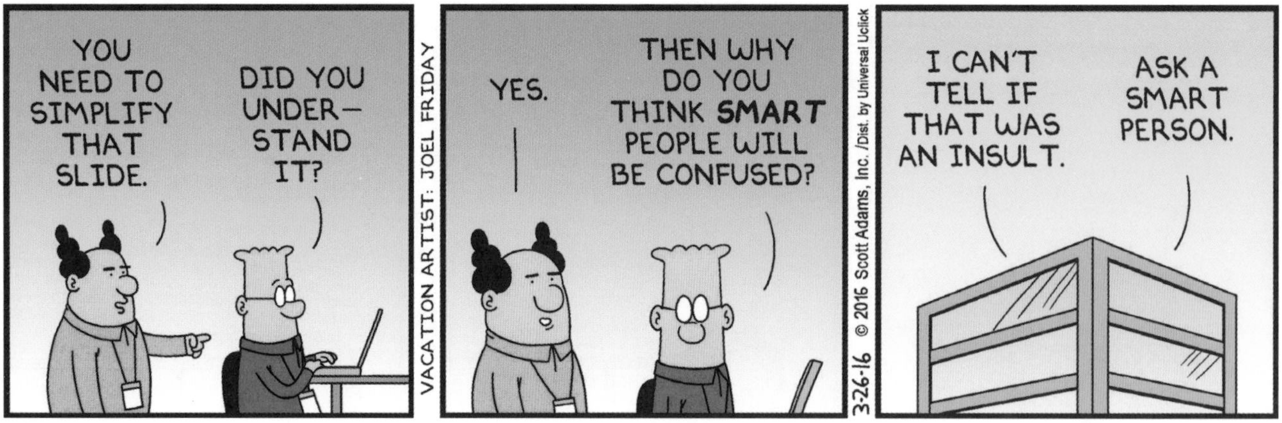
YOU NEED TO SIMPLIFY THAT SLIDE.
DID YOU UNDER-STAND IT?
VACATION ARTIST: JOEL FRIDAY
YES.
THEN WHY DO YOU THINK **SMART** PEOPLE WILL BE CONFUSED?
3-26-16 © 2016 Scott Adams, Inc. /Dist. by Universal Uclick
I CAN'T TELL IF THAT WAS AN INSULT.
ASK A SMART PERSON.

DICK, FROM THE INTERNET
WOULD YOU LIE TO A MONSTER TO KEEP A BABY ALIVE?
YES.
HA! YOU ADMIT YOU'RE A LIAR!
NOT MOST OF THE TIME.
OOH, NOT MOST OF THE TIME.
HA HA! LOOK WHO'S TRYING TO WALK IT BACK NOW!
APOLOGIZE FOR HATING BABIES MOST OF THE TIME!
I NEVER SAID THAT!
WOW. PATHOLOGICAL MUCH?
© 2016 Scott Adams, Inc./Dist. by Universal Uclick
3-27-16

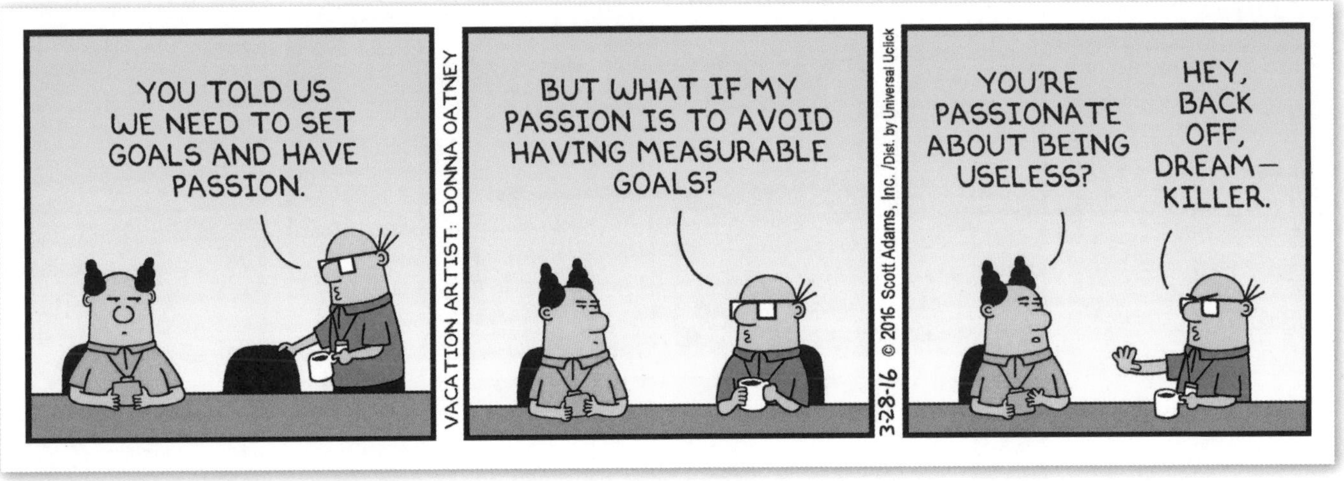
YOU TOLD US WE NEED TO SET GOALS AND HAVE PASSION.
BUT WHAT IF MY PASSION IS TO AVOID HAVING MEASURABLE GOALS?
YOU'RE PASSIONATE ABOUT BEING USELESS?
HEY, BACK OFF, DREAM-KILLER.
VACATION ARTIST: DONNA OATNEY
3-28-16 © 2016 Scott Adams, Inc. /Dist. by Universal Uclick

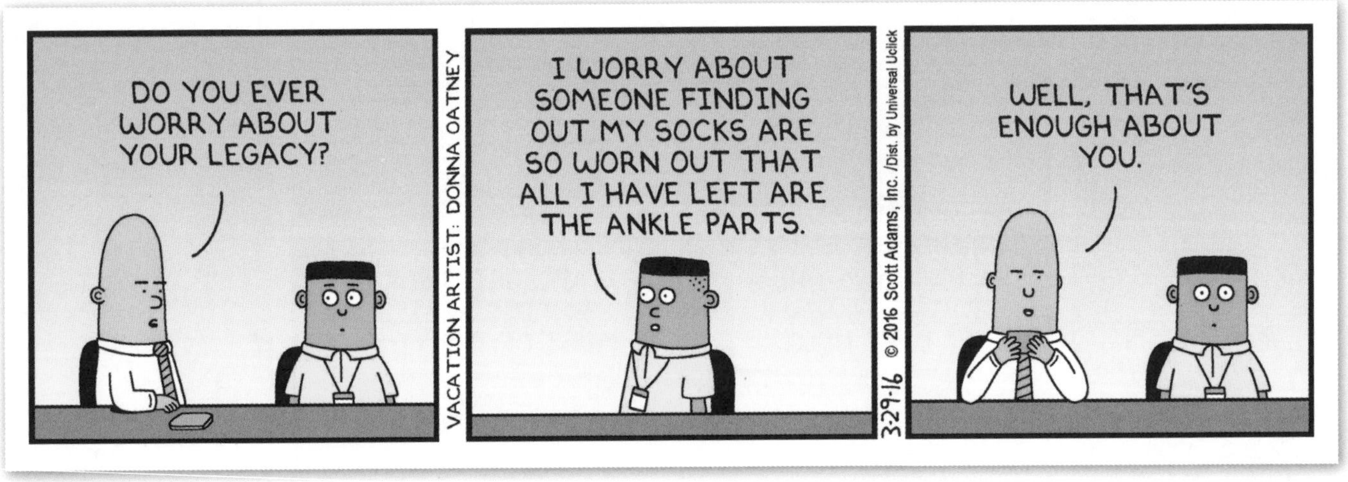
DO YOU EVER WORRY ABOUT YOUR LEGACY?
I WORRY ABOUT SOMEONE FINDING OUT MY SOCKS ARE SO WORN OUT THAT ALL I HAVE LEFT ARE THE ANKLE PARTS.
WELL, THAT'S ENOUGH ABOUT YOU.
VACATION ARTIST: DONNA OATNEY
3-29-16 © 2016 Scott Adams, Inc. /Dist. by Universal Uclick

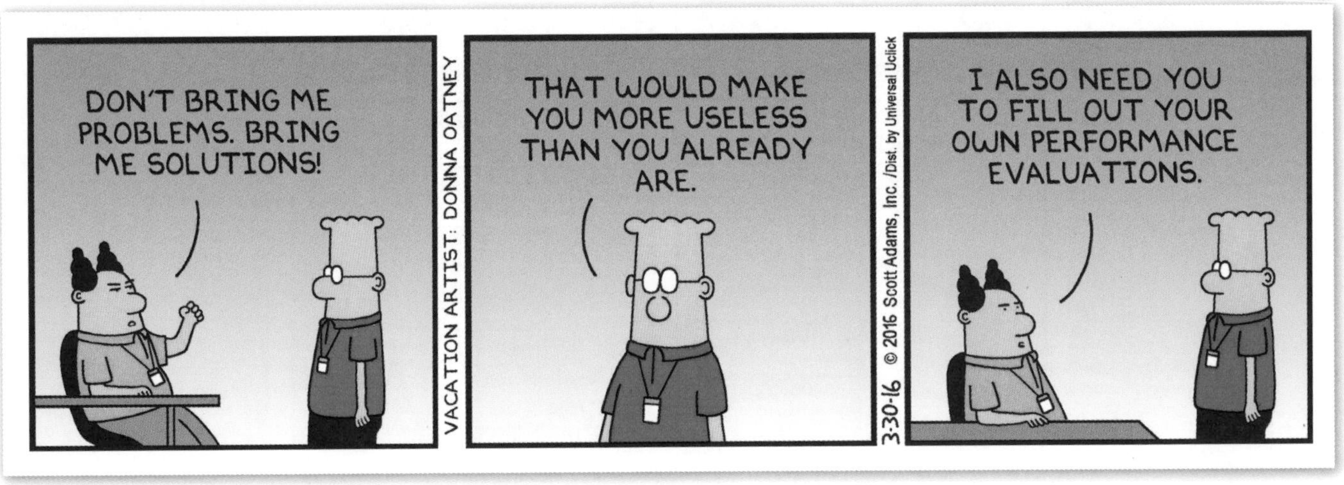
DON'T BRING ME PROBLEMS. BRING ME SOLUTIONS!
THAT WOULD MAKE YOU MORE USELESS THAN YOU ALREADY ARE.
I ALSO NEED YOU TO FILL OUT YOUR OWN PERFORMANCE EVALUATIONS.
VACATION ARTIST: DONNA OATNEY
3-30-16 © 2016 Scott Adams, Inc. /Dist. by Universal Uclick

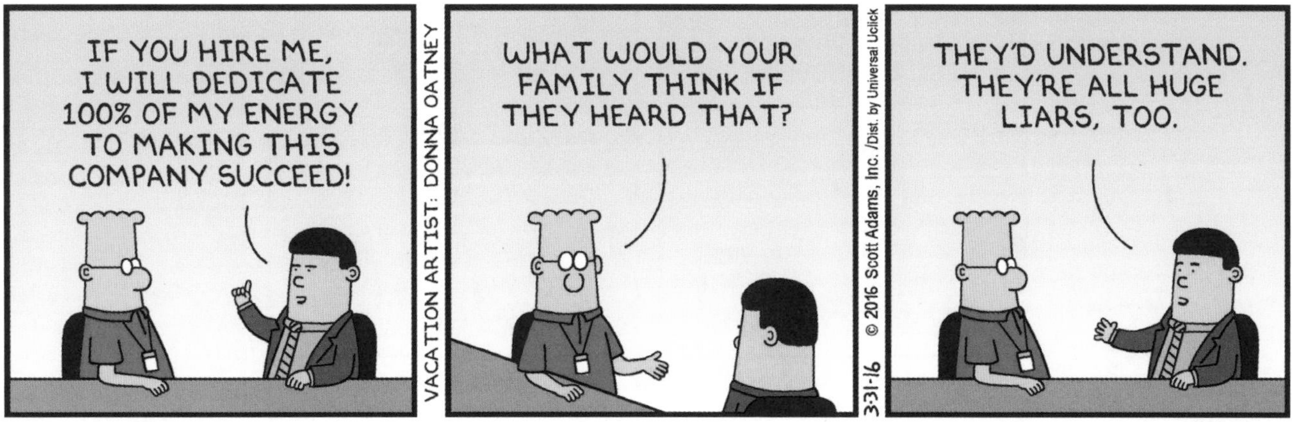
IF YOU HIRE ME, I WILL DEDICATE 100% OF MY ENERGY TO MAKING THIS COMPANY SUCCEED!
VACATION ARTIST: DONNA OATNEY
WHAT WOULD YOUR FAMILY THINK IF THEY HEARD THAT?
3-31-16 © 2016 Scott Adams, Inc. /Dist. by Universal Uclick
THEY'D UNDERSTAND. THEY'RE ALL HUGE LIARS, TOO.

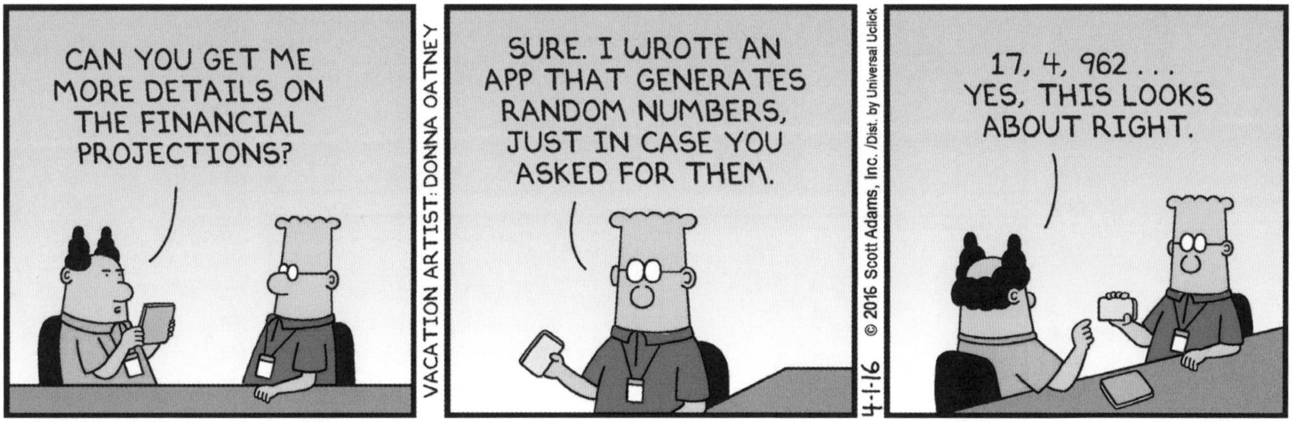
CAN YOU GET ME MORE DETAILS ON THE FINANCIAL PROJECTIONS?
VACATION ARTIST: DONNA OATNEY
SURE. I WROTE AN APP THAT GENERATES RANDOM NUMBERS, JUST IN CASE YOU ASKED FOR THEM.
4-1-16 © 2016 Scott Adams, Inc. /Dist. by Universal Uclick
17, 4, 962 . . . YES, THIS LOOKS ABOUT RIGHT.

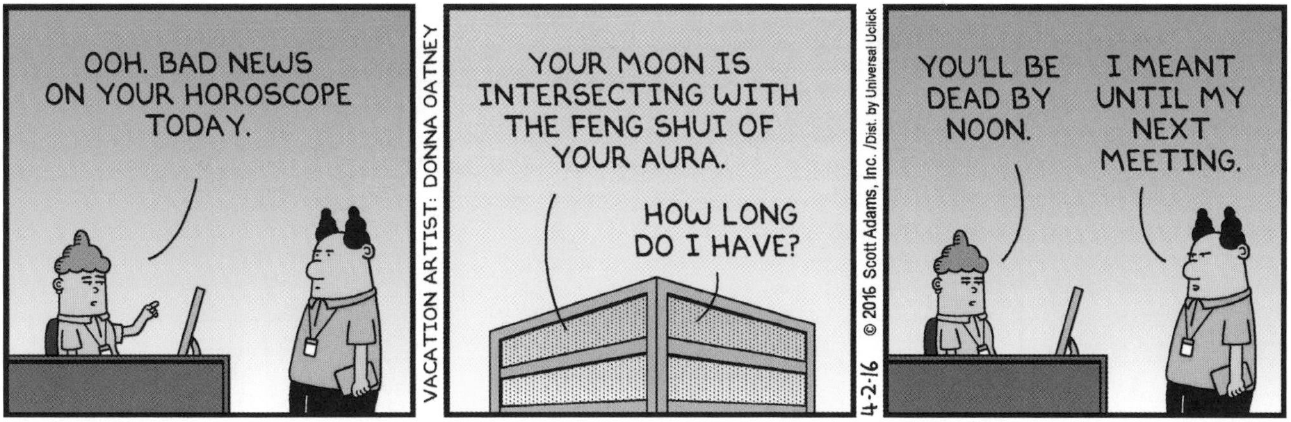
OOH. BAD NEWS ON YOUR HOROSCOPE TODAY.
VACATION ARTIST: DONNA OATNEY
YOUR MOON IS INTERSECTING WITH THE FENG SHUI OF YOUR AURA.
HOW LONG DO I HAVE?
4-2-16 © 2016 Scott Adams, Inc. /Dist. by Universal Uclick
YOU'LL BE DEAD BY NOON.
I MEANT UNTIL MY NEXT MEETING.

MY TEENAGER WANTS TO PIERCE HIS EAR. SHOULD I LET HIM?
SURE. IT'S ONLY A TINY HOLE AND IT HEALS.
GOOD POINT.
NEXT DAY
NOW HE WANTS A SMALL TATTOO.
WELL, IF IT DOESN'T SHOW. . .
NEXT WEEK
NOW HE WANTS TO GROW A HUMAN EAR ON HIS BACK, THE WAY SCIENTISTS DID WITH THAT RAT.
AS LONG AS HE CAN COVER IT WITH A SHIRT WHEN HE GETS A JOB, I SEE NO PROBLEM.
YOU HAVE TO LET HIM LIVE HIS OWN LIFE.
ONE WEEK LATER
HE JOINED ISIS.
I FORGOT TO MENTION THAT I'M NOT GOOD AT GIVING ADVICE.
© 2016 Scott Adams, Inc./Dist. by Universal Uclick
4-3-16

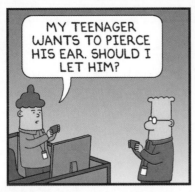

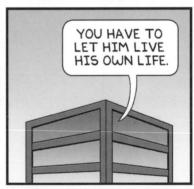

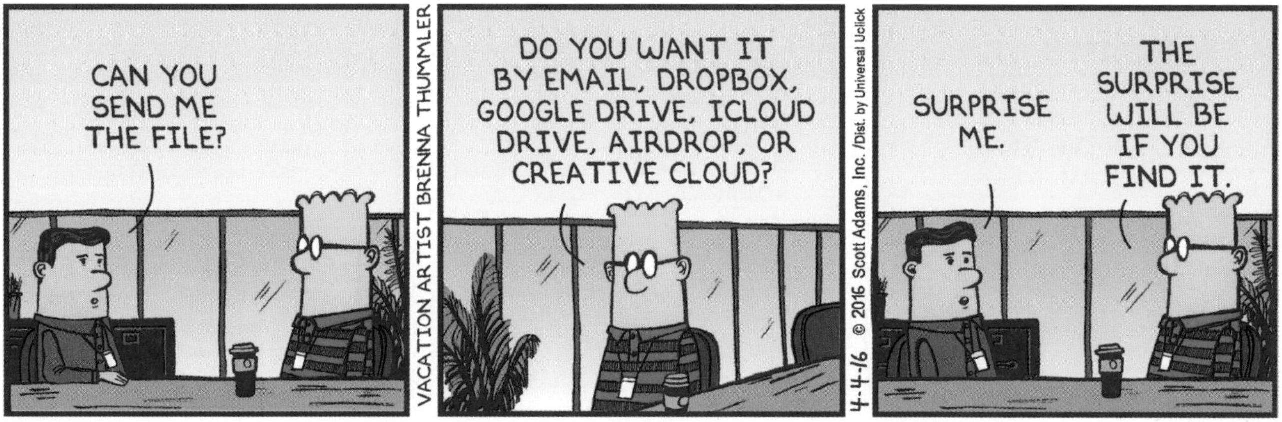
CAN YOU SEND ME THE FILE?
DO YOU WANT IT BY EMAIL, DROPBOX, GOOGLE DRIVE, ICLOUD DRIVE, AIRDROP, OR CREATIVE CLOUD?
SURPRISE ME.
THE SURPRISE WILL BE IF YOU FIND IT.
VACATION ARTIST BRENNA THUMMLER
4-4-16 © 2016 Scott Adams, Inc. /Dist. by Universal Uclick

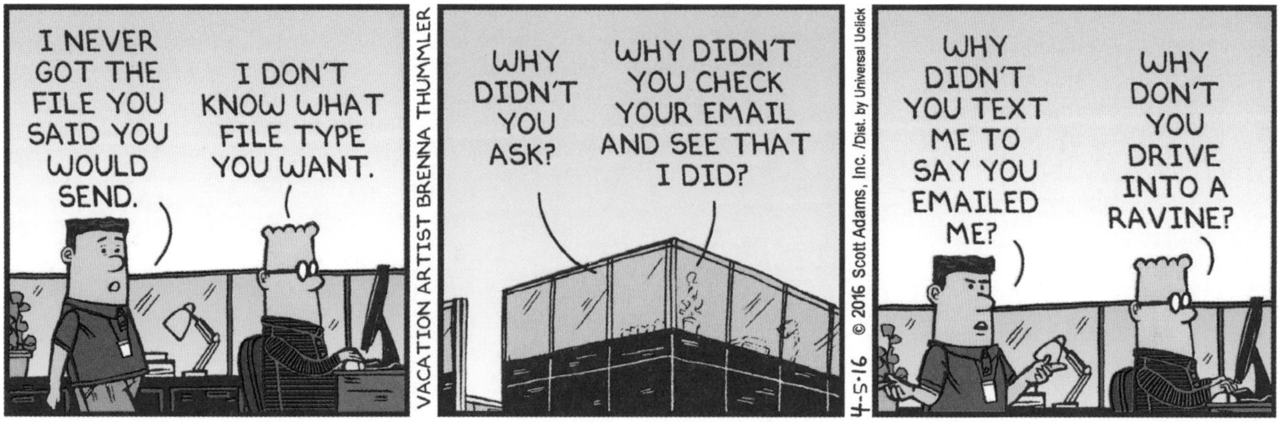
I NEVER GOT THE FILE YOU SAID YOU WOULD SEND.
I DON'T KNOW WHAT FILE TYPE YOU WANT.
WHY DIDN'T YOU ASK?
WHY DIDN'T YOU CHECK YOUR EMAIL AND SEE THAT I DID?
WHY DIDN'T YOU TEXT ME TO SAY YOU EMAILED ME?
WHY DON'T YOU DRIVE INTO A RAVINE?
VACATION ARTIST BRENNA THUMMLER
4-5-16 © 2016 Scott Adams, Inc. /Dist. by Universal Uclick

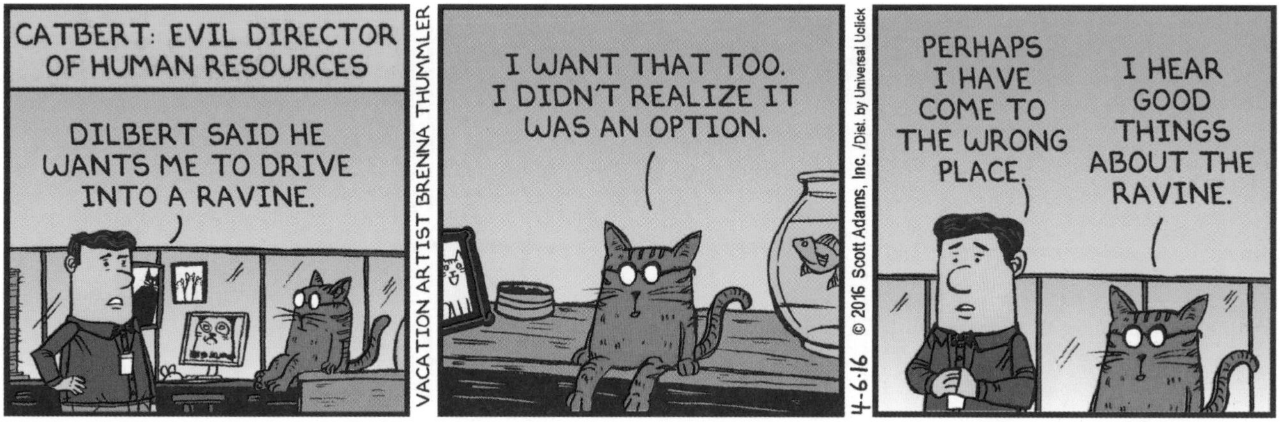
CATBERT: EVIL DIRECTOR OF HUMAN RESOURCES
DILBERT SAID HE WANTS ME TO DRIVE INTO A RAVINE.
I WANT THAT TOO. I DIDN'T REALIZE IT WAS AN OPTION.
PERHAPS I HAVE COME TO THE WRONG PLACE.
I HEAR GOOD THINGS ABOUT THE RAVINE.
VACATION ARTIST BRENNA THUMMLER
4-6-16 © 2016 Scott Adams, Inc. /Dist. by Universal Uclick

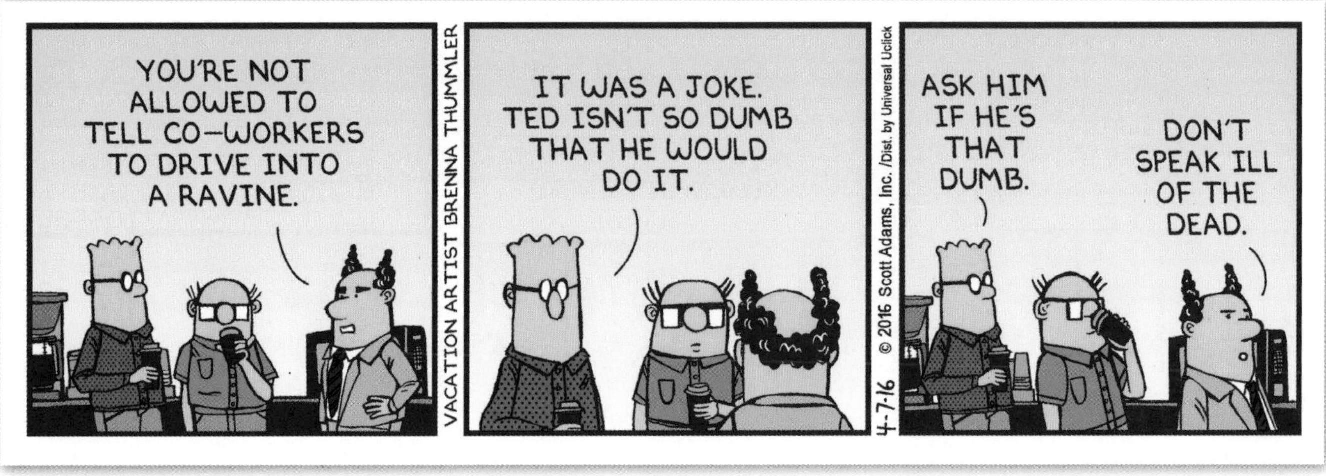
YOU'RE NOT ALLOWED TO TELL CO-WORKERS TO DRIVE INTO A RAVINE.
VACATION ARTIST BRENNA THUMMLER
IT WAS A JOKE. TED ISN'T SO DUMB THAT HE WOULD DO IT.
4-7-16 © 2016 Scott Adams, Inc. /Dist. by Universal Uclick
ASK HIM IF HE'S THAT DUMB.
DON'T SPEAK ILL OF THE DEAD.

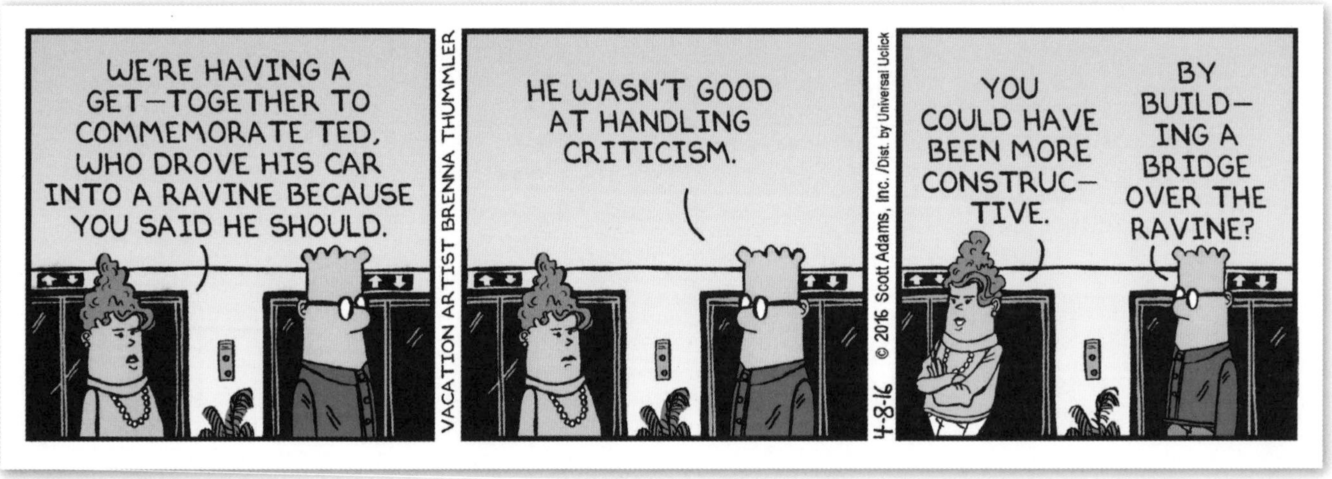
WE'RE HAVING A GET-TOGETHER TO COMMEMORATE TED, WHO DROVE HIS CAR INTO A RAVINE BECAUSE YOU SAID HE SHOULD.
VACATION ARTIST BRENNA THUMMLER
HE WASN'T GOOD AT HANDLING CRITICISM.
4-8-16 © 2016 Scott Adams, Inc. /Dist. by Universal Uclick
YOU COULD HAVE BEEN MORE CONSTRUC-TIVE.
BY BUILD-ING A BRIDGE OVER THE RAVINE?

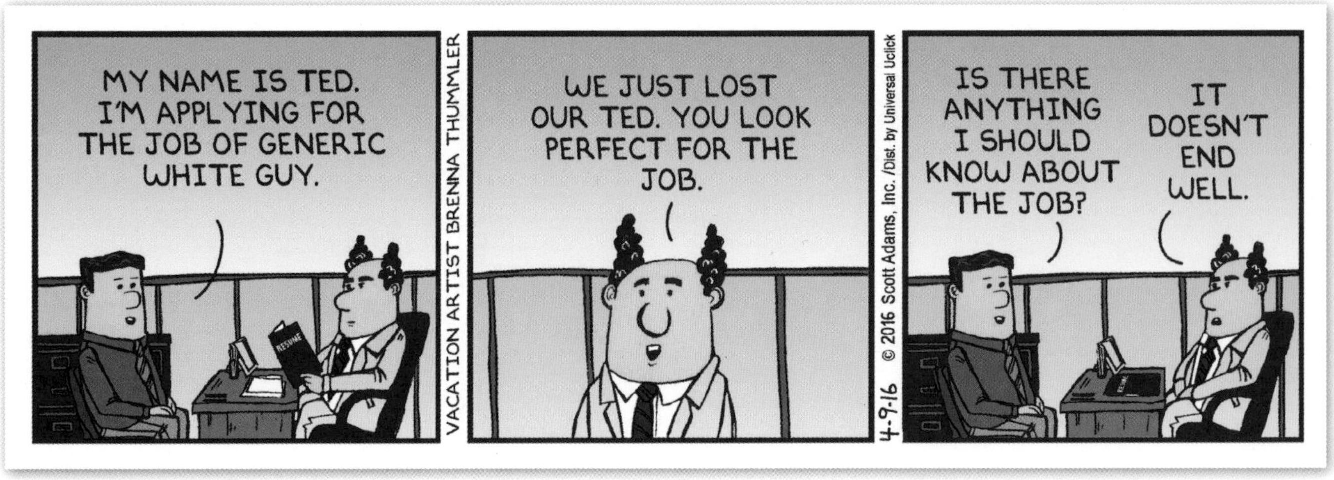
MY NAME IS TED. I'M APPLYING FOR THE JOB OF GENERIC WHITE GUY.
RESUME
VACATION ARTIST BRENNA THUMMLER
WE JUST LOST OUR TED. YOU LOOK PERFECT FOR THE JOB.
4-9-16 © 2016 Scott Adams, Inc. /Dist. by Universal Uclick
IS THERE ANYTHING I SHOULD KNOW ABOUT THE JOB?
IT DOESN'T END WELL.

CAN I TAKE A CLASS TO IMPROVE MY COMMUNICATION SKILLS?

WHAT ARE YOU TALKING ABOUT?

I WANT TO TAKE A CLASS THAT TEACHES ME HOW TO COMMUNICATE BETTER.

I DON'T UNDERSTAND WHAT YOU'RE ASKING ME.

I AM ASKING PERMISSION TO TAKE A CLASS TO HELP ME COMMUNICATE BETTER.

I SEE YOUR LIPS MOVING BUT I CAN'T FIGURE OUT WHAT YOU'RE ASKING.

GAAA!!! THERE'S NO WAY TO GET THERE FROM HERE!

I'M GLAD I TOOK THAT MANAGEMENT CLASS ON HOW TO NOT LISTEN. IT ALREADY PAID OFF.

© 2016 Scott Adams, Inc./Dist. by Universal Uclick

4-10-16

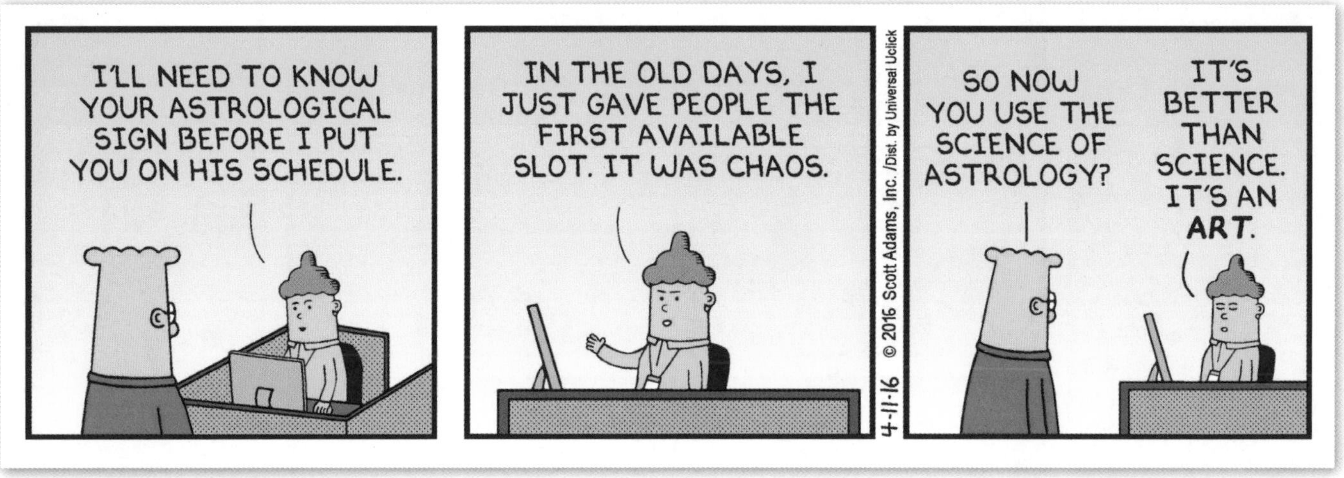
I'LL NEED TO KNOW YOUR ASTROLOGICAL SIGN BEFORE I PUT YOU ON HIS SCHEDULE.
IN THE OLD DAYS, I JUST GAVE PEOPLE THE FIRST AVAILABLE SLOT. IT WAS CHAOS.
4-11-16 © 2016 Scott Adams, Inc. /Dist. by Universal Uclick
SO NOW YOU USE THE SCIENCE OF ASTROLOGY?
IT'S BETTER THAN SCIENCE. IT'S AN **ART**.

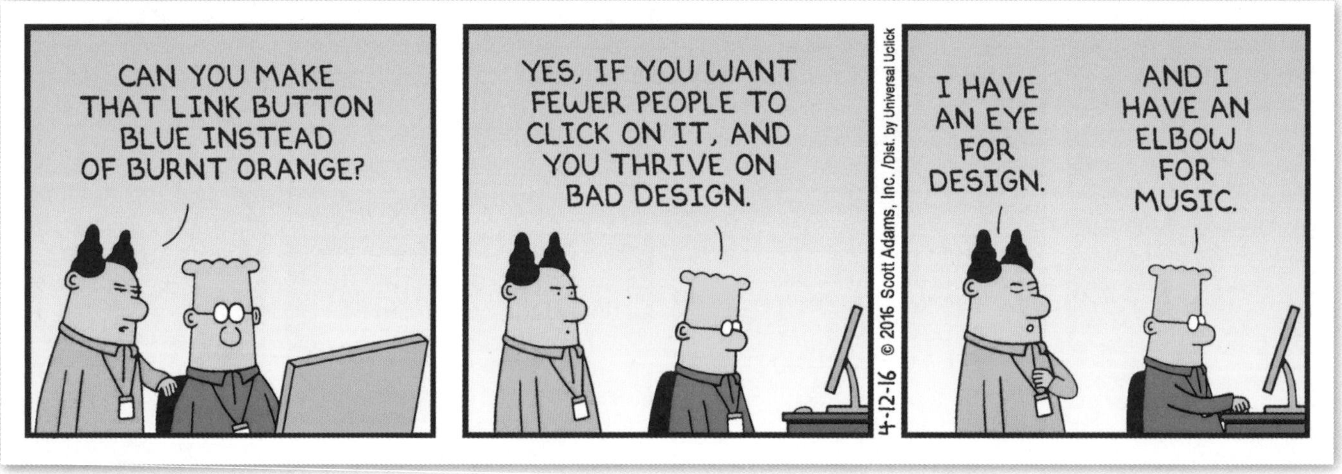
CAN YOU MAKE THAT LINK BUTTON BLUE INSTEAD OF BURNT ORANGE?
YES, IF YOU WANT FEWER PEOPLE TO CLICK ON IT, AND YOU THRIVE ON BAD DESIGN.
4-12-16 © 2016 Scott Adams, Inc. /Dist. by Universal Uclick
I HAVE AN EYE FOR DESIGN.
AND I HAVE AN ELBOW FOR MUSIC.

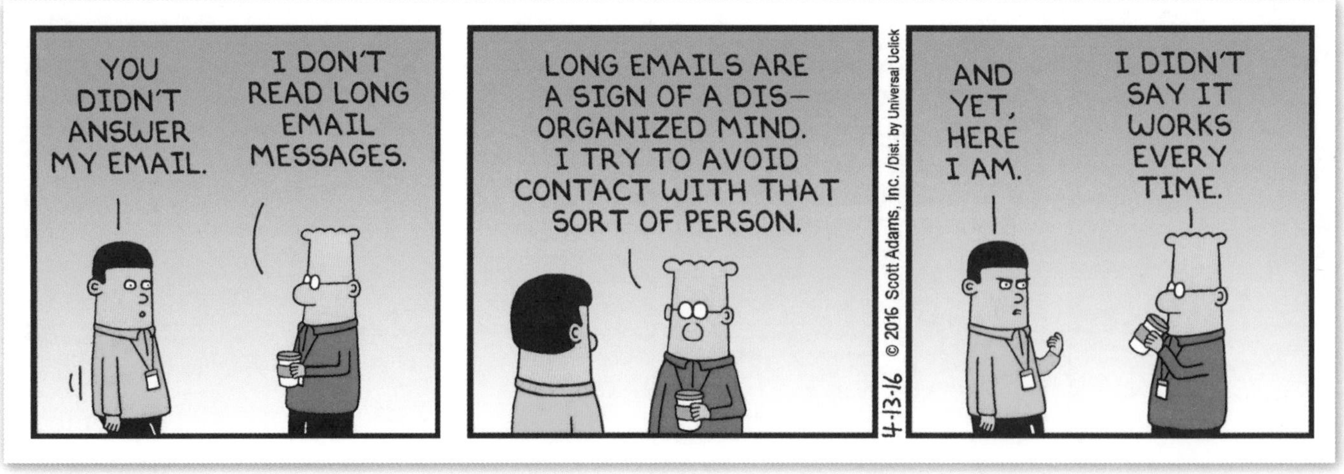
YOU DIDN'T ANSWER MY EMAIL.
I DON'T READ LONG EMAIL MESSAGES.
LONG EMAILS ARE A SIGN OF A DIS-ORGANIZED MIND. I TRY TO AVOID CONTACT WITH THAT SORT OF PERSON.
4-13-16 © 2016 Scott Adams, Inc. /Dist. by Universal Uclick
AND YET, HERE I AM.
I DIDN'T SAY IT WORKS EVERY TIME.

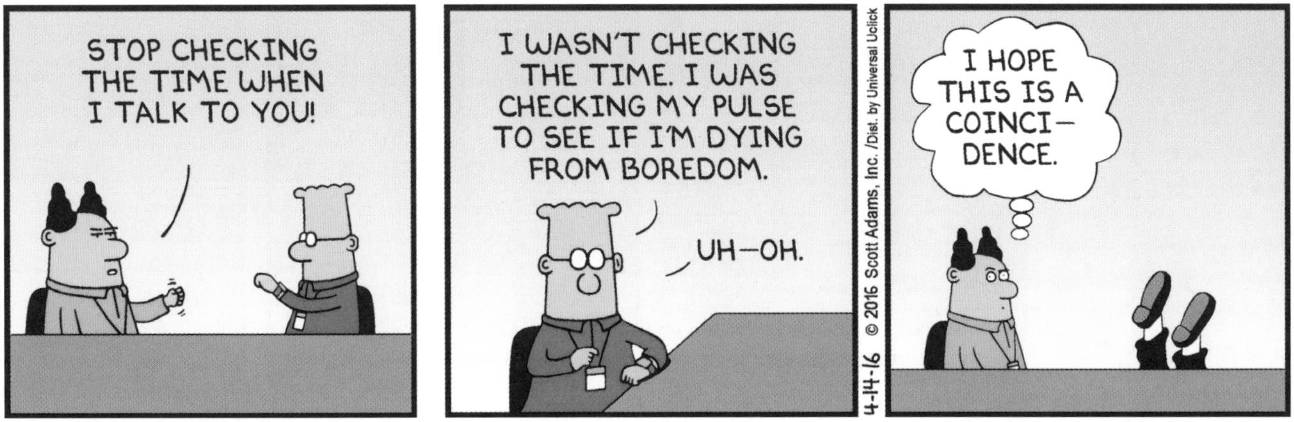
STOP CHECKING THE TIME WHEN I TALK TO YOU!
I WASN'T CHECKING THE TIME. I WAS CHECKING MY PULSE TO SEE IF I'M DYING FROM BOREDOM.
UH-OH.
4-14-16 © 2016 Scott Adams, Inc. /Dist. by Universal Uclick
I HOPE THIS IS A COINCI-DENCE.

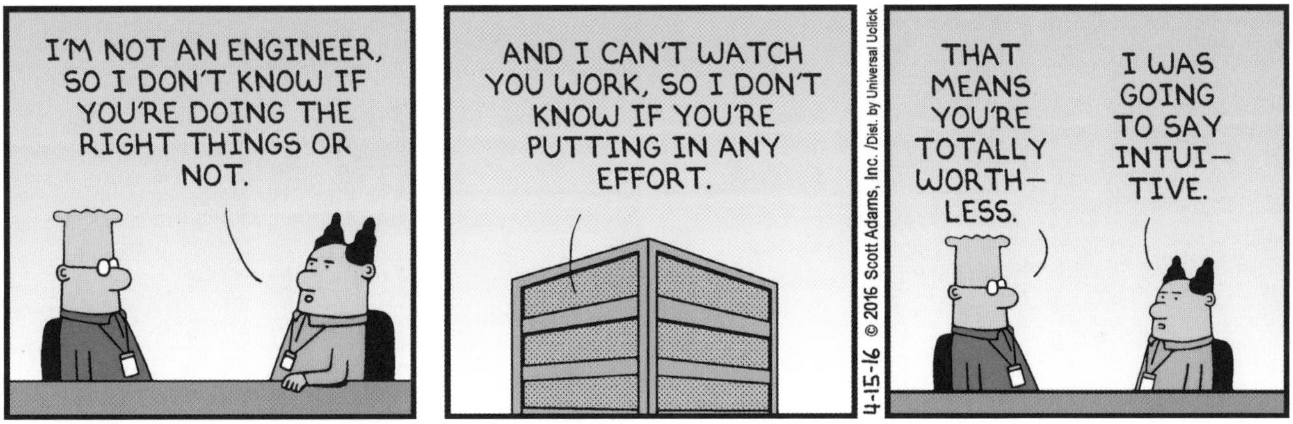
I'M NOT AN ENGINEER, SO I DON'T KNOW IF YOU'RE DOING THE RIGHT THINGS OR NOT.
AND I CAN'T WATCH YOU WORK, SO I DON'T KNOW IF YOU'RE PUTTING IN ANY EFFORT.
4-15-16 © 2016 Scott Adams, Inc. /Dist. by Universal Uclick
THAT MEANS YOU'RE TOTALLY WORTH-LESS.
I WAS GOING TO SAY INTUI-TIVE.

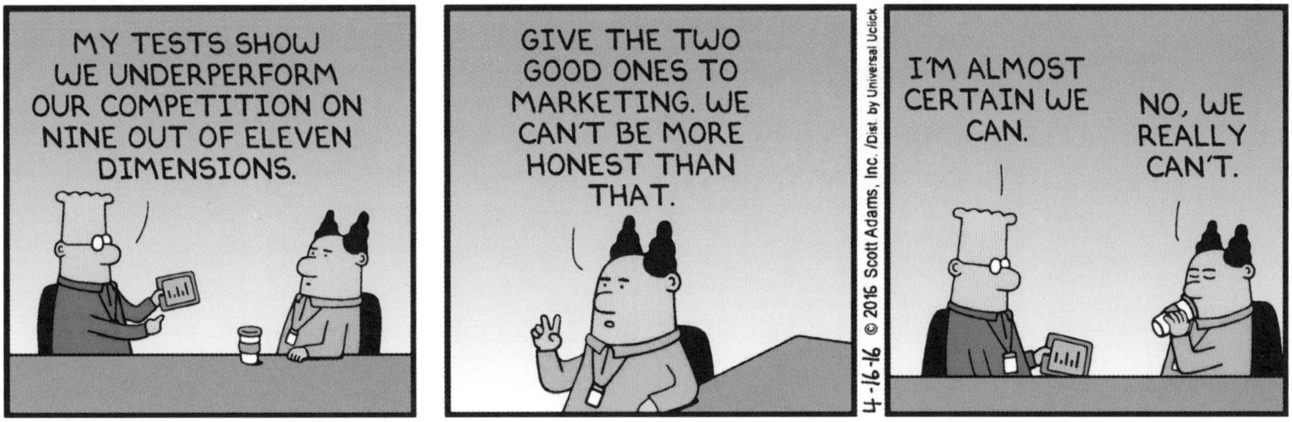
MY TESTS SHOW WE UNDERPERFORM OUR COMPETITION ON NINE OUT OF ELEVEN DIMENSIONS.
GIVE THE TWO GOOD ONES TO MARKETING. WE CAN'T BE MORE HONEST THAN THAT.
4-16-16 © 2016 Scott Adams, Inc. /Dist. by Universal Uclick
I'M ALMOST CERTAIN WE CAN.
NO, WE REALLY CAN'T.

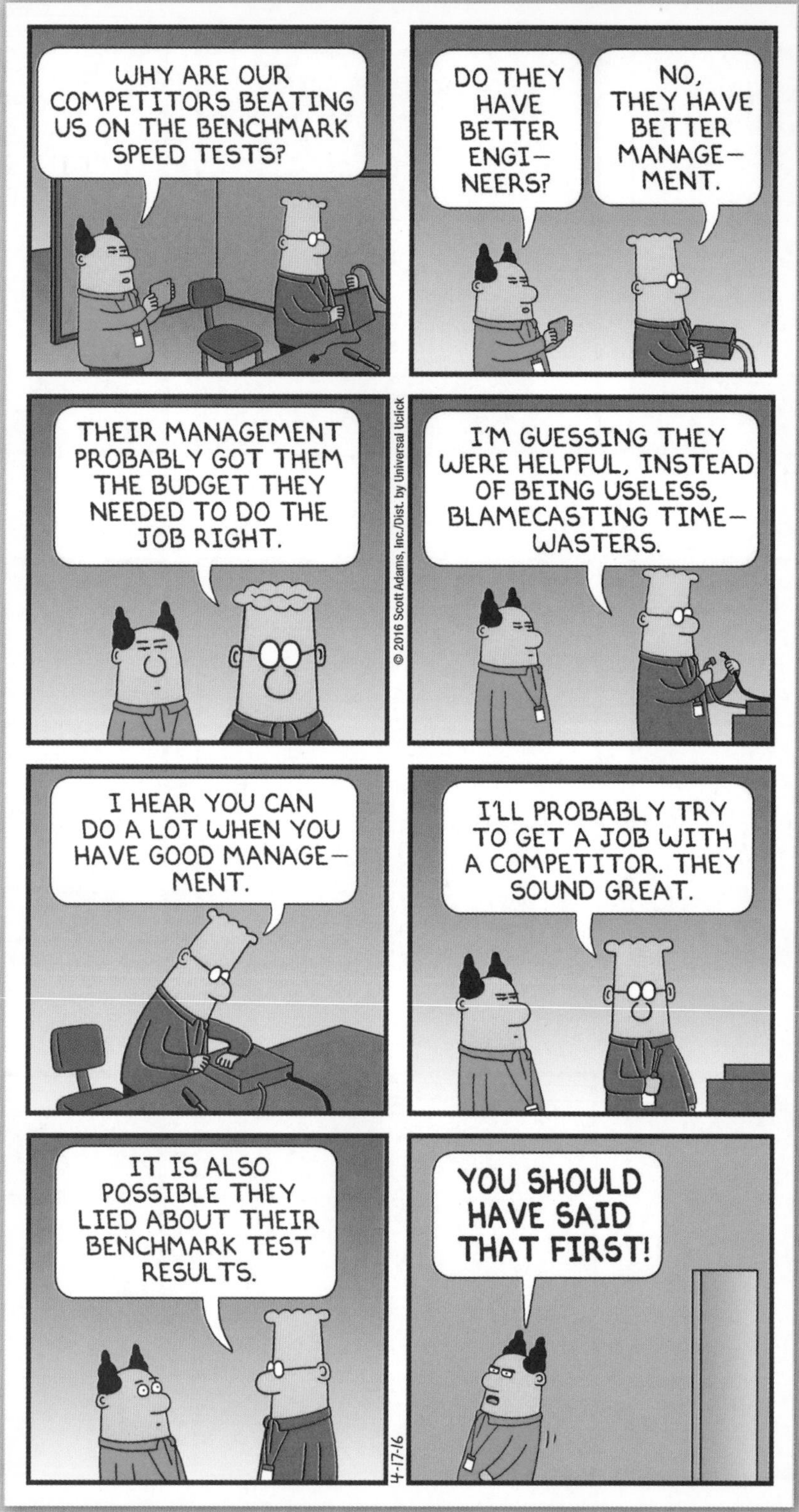
WHY ARE OUR COMPETITORS BEATING US ON THE BENCHMARK SPEED TESTS?
DO THEY HAVE BETTER ENGI-NEERS?
NO, THEY HAVE BETTER MANAGE-MENT.
THEIR MANAGEMENT PROBABLY GOT THEM THE BUDGET THEY NEEDED TO DO THE JOB RIGHT.
I'M GUESSING THEY WERE HELPFUL, INSTEAD OF BEING USELESS, BLAMECASTING TIME-WASTERS.
I HEAR YOU CAN DO A LOT WHEN YOU HAVE GOOD MANAGE-MENT.
I'LL PROBABLY TRY TO GET A JOB WITH A COMPETITOR. THEY SOUND GREAT.
IT IS ALSO POSSIBLE THEY LIED ABOUT THEIR BENCHMARK TEST RESULTS.
YOU SHOULD HAVE SAID THAT FIRST!
© 2016 Scott Adams, Inc./Dist. by Universal Uclick
4-17-16

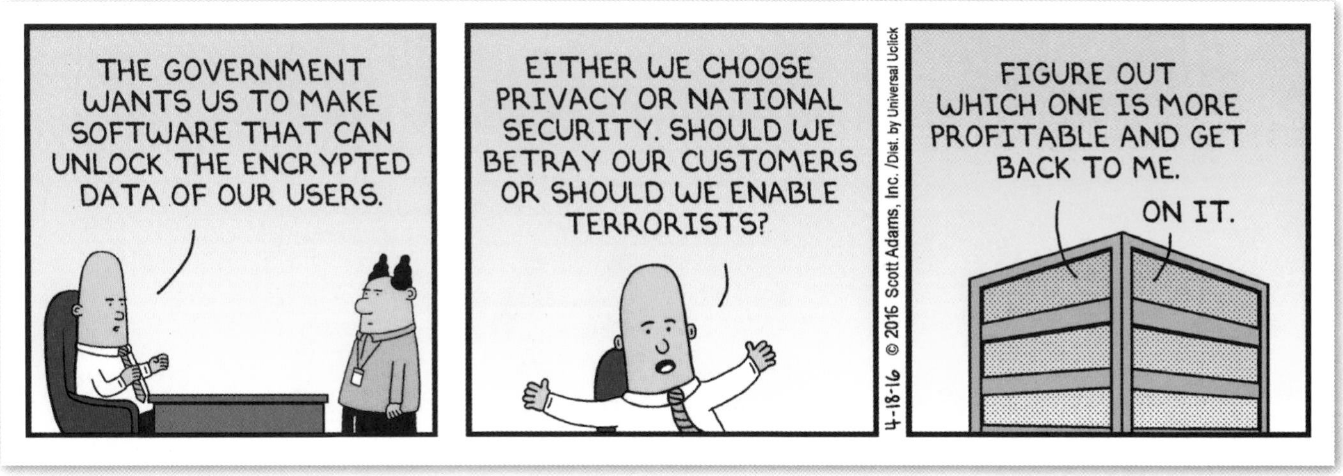
THE GOVERNMENT WANTS US TO MAKE SOFTWARE THAT CAN UNLOCK THE ENCRYPTED DATA OF OUR USERS.
EITHER WE CHOOSE PRIVACY OR NATIONAL SECURITY. SHOULD WE BETRAY OUR CUSTOMERS OR SHOULD WE ENABLE TERRORISTS?
FIGURE OUT WHICH ONE IS MORE PROFITABLE AND GET BACK TO ME.
ON IT.
4-18-16 © 2016 Scott Adams, Inc. /Dist. by Universal Uclick

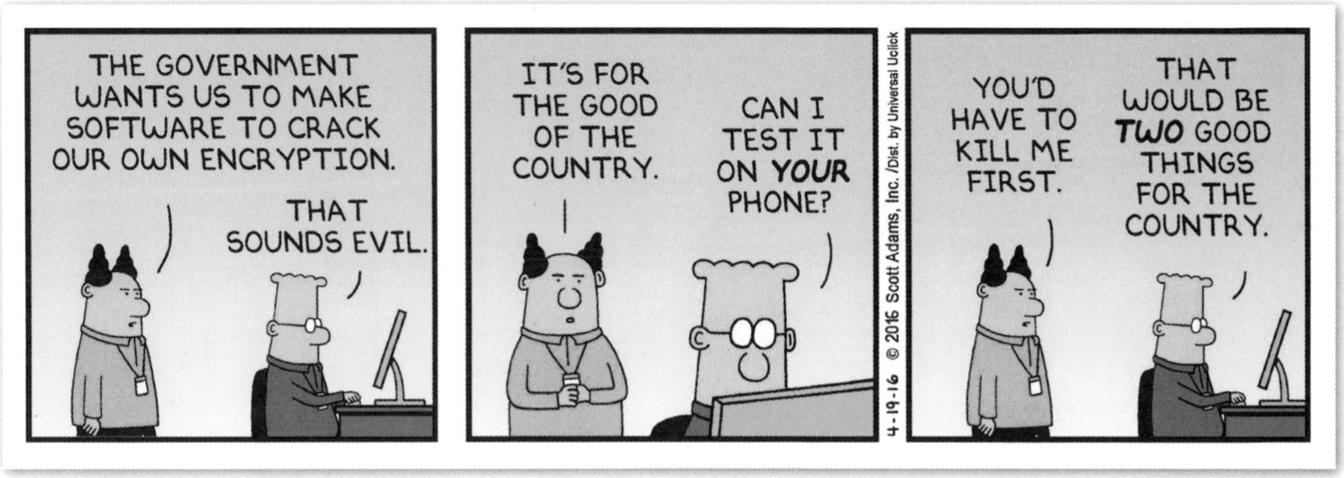
THE GOVERNMENT WANTS US TO MAKE SOFTWARE TO CRACK OUR OWN ENCRYPTION.
THAT SOUNDS EVIL.
IT'S FOR THE GOOD OF THE COUNTRY.
CAN I TEST IT ON **YOUR** PHONE?
YOU'D HAVE TO KILL ME FIRST.
THAT WOULD BE **TWO** GOOD THINGS FOR THE COUNTRY.
4-19-16 © 2016 Scott Adams, Inc. /Dist. by Universal Uclick

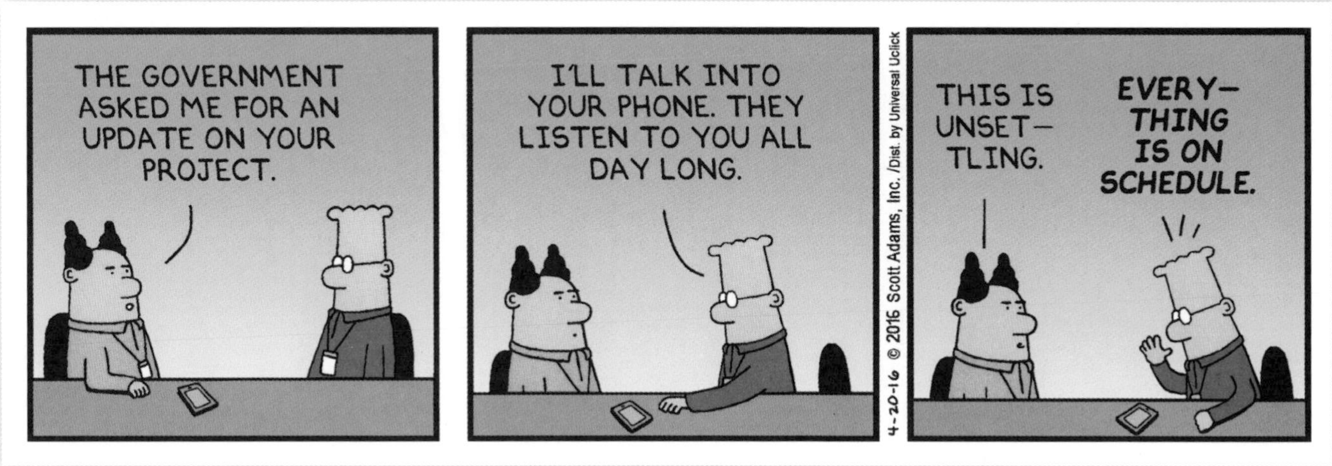
THE GOVERNMENT ASKED ME FOR AN UPDATE ON YOUR PROJECT.
I'LL TALK INTO YOUR PHONE. THEY LISTEN TO YOU ALL DAY LONG.
THIS IS UNSET-TLING.
EVERY-THING IS ON SCHEDULE.
4-20-16 © 2016 Scott Adams, Inc. /Dist. by Universal Uclick

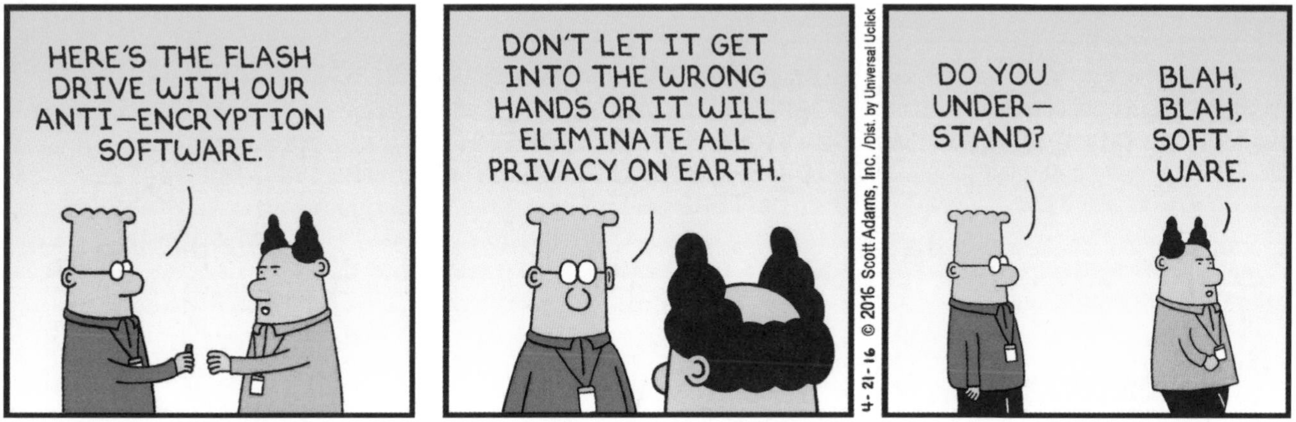
HERE'S THE FLASH DRIVE WITH OUR ANTI-ENCRYPTION SOFTWARE.
DON'T LET IT GET INTO THE WRONG HANDS OR IT WILL ELIMINATE ALL PRIVACY ON EARTH.
DO YOU UNDER-STAND?
BLAH, BLAH, SOFT-WARE.
4-21-16 © 2016 Scott Adams, Inc. /Dist. by Universal Uclick

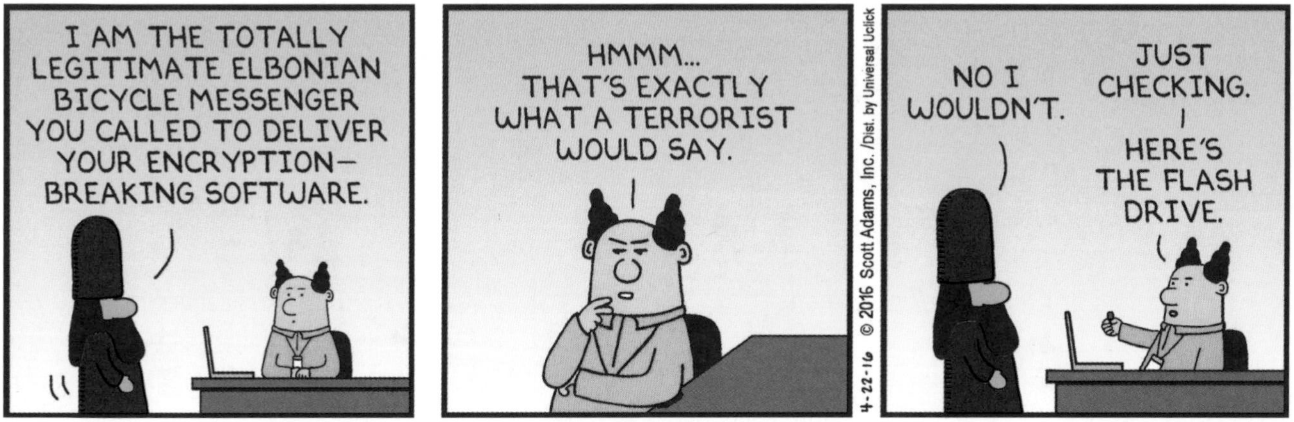
I AM THE TOTALLY LEGITIMATE ELBONIAN BICYCLE MESSENGER YOU CALLED TO DELIVER YOUR ENCRYPTION-BREAKING SOFTWARE.
HMMM... THAT'S EXACTLY WHAT A TERRORIST WOULD SAY.
NO I WOULDN'T.
JUST CHECKING.
HERE'S THE FLASH DRIVE.
4-22-16 © 2016 Scott Adams, Inc. /Dist. by Universal Uclick

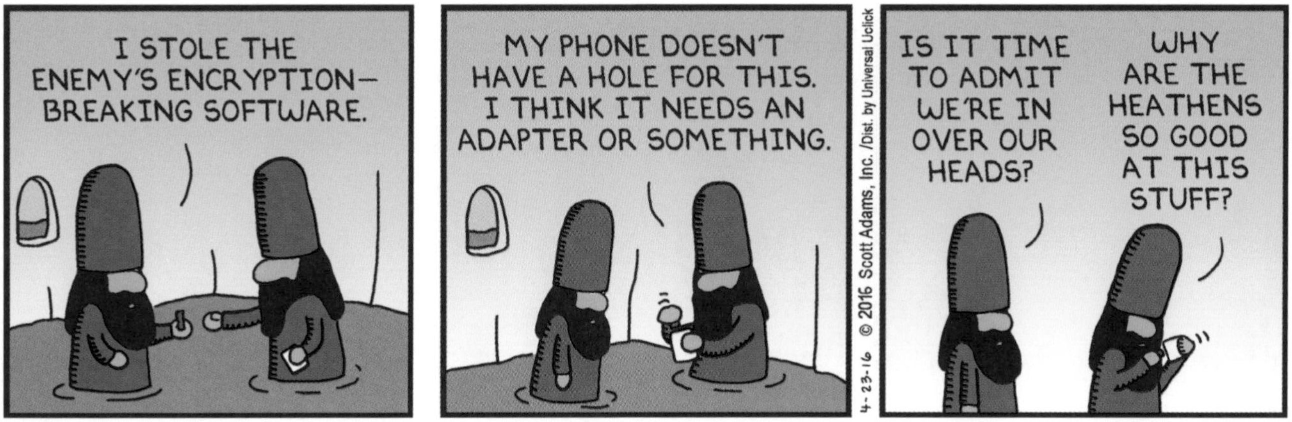
I STOLE THE ENEMY'S ENCRYPTION-BREAKING SOFTWARE.
MY PHONE DOESN'T HAVE A HOLE FOR THIS. I THINK IT NEEDS AN ADAPTER OR SOMETHING.
IS IT TIME TO ADMIT WE'RE IN OVER OUR HEADS?
WHY ARE THE HEATHENS SO GOOD AT THIS STUFF?
4-23-16 © 2016 Scott Adams, Inc. /Dist. by Universal Uclick

SCHEDULE YOUR TRAINING DURING YOUR LUNCH HOURS SO IT DOESN'T IMPACT YOUR PROJECTS.
BUT. . . MY LUNCH HOUR IS THE ONLY FREEDOM I EXPERIENCE IN A TYPICAL DAY.
THE REST OF MY TIME IS EITHER SCHEDULED TO THE MINUTE OR DRIVEN BY WHAT-EVER CRISIS IS HAPPENING.
PLEASE DON'T TAKE MY LUNCH HOUR AND REDUCE ME TO NOTHING BUT A PRISONER IN A DIGITAL CHAIN GANG.
I'M BARELY CLINGING TO MY ILLUSION OF FREE WILL AS IT IS. THIS COULD PUSH ME OVER THE EDGE.
IF YOU TAKE AWAY MY ONE HOUR OF FREEDOM IN THE DAY, I MIGHT AS WELL BE A ROBOT.
RELAX. THIS IS TEMPORARY.
FOR HOW LONG?
UNTIL I CAN REPLACE YOU WITH A ROBOT.
4-24-16

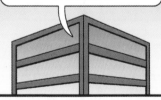

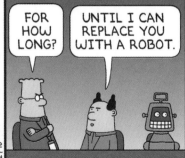

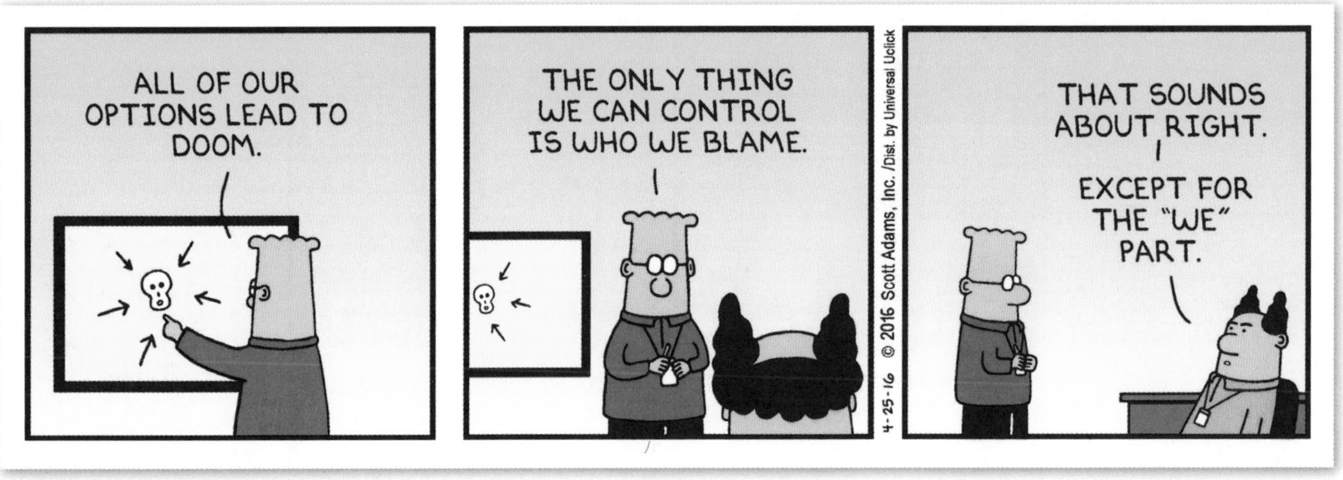
ALL OF OUR OPTIONS LEAD TO DOOM.
THE ONLY THING WE CAN CONTROL IS WHO WE BLAME.
THAT SOUNDS ABOUT RIGHT.
EXCEPT FOR THE "WE" PART.
4-25-16 © 2016 Scott Adams, Inc. /Dist. by Universal Uclick

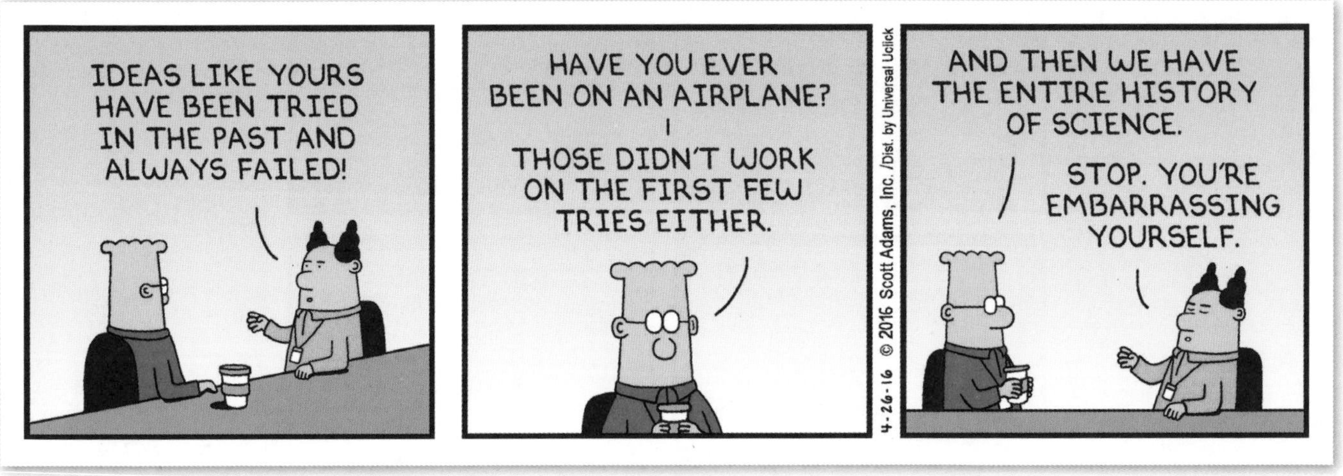
IDEAS LIKE YOURS HAVE BEEN TRIED IN THE PAST AND ALWAYS FAILED!
HAVE YOU EVER BEEN ON AN AIRPLANE?
THOSE DIDN'T WORK ON THE FIRST FEW TRIES EITHER.
AND THEN WE HAVE THE ENTIRE HISTORY OF SCIENCE.
STOP. YOU'RE EMBARRASSING YOURSELF.
4-26-16 © 2016 Scott Adams, Inc. /Dist. by Universal Uclick

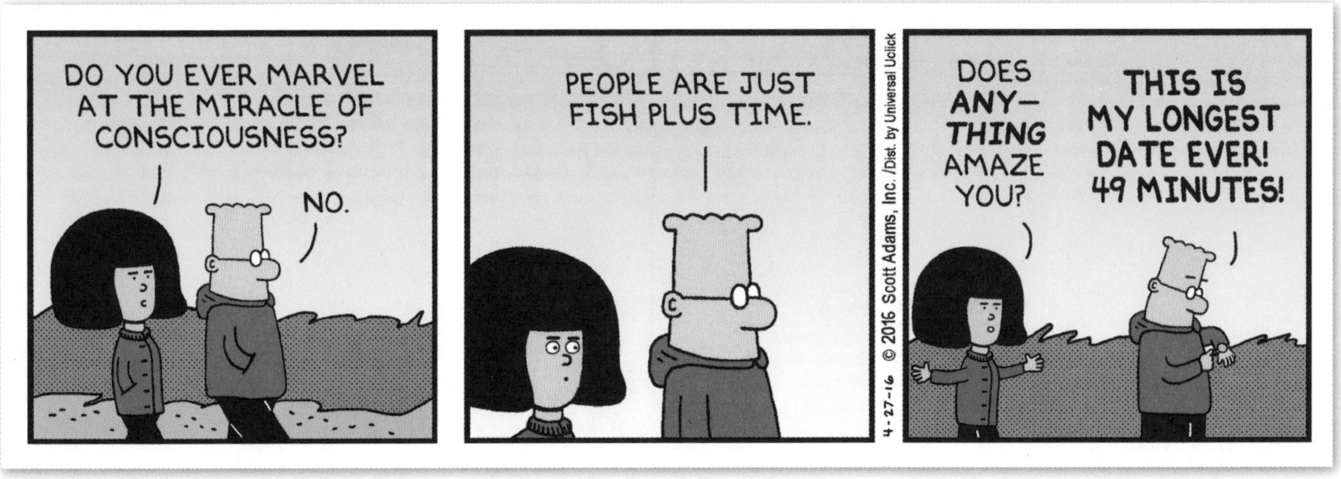
DO YOU EVER MARVEL AT THE MIRACLE OF CONSCIOUSNESS?
NO.
PEOPLE ARE JUST FISH PLUS TIME.
DOES ANY-THING AMAZE YOU?
THIS IS MY LONGEST DATE EVER! 49 MINUTES!
4-27-16 © 2016 Scott Adams, Inc. /Dist. by Universal Uclick

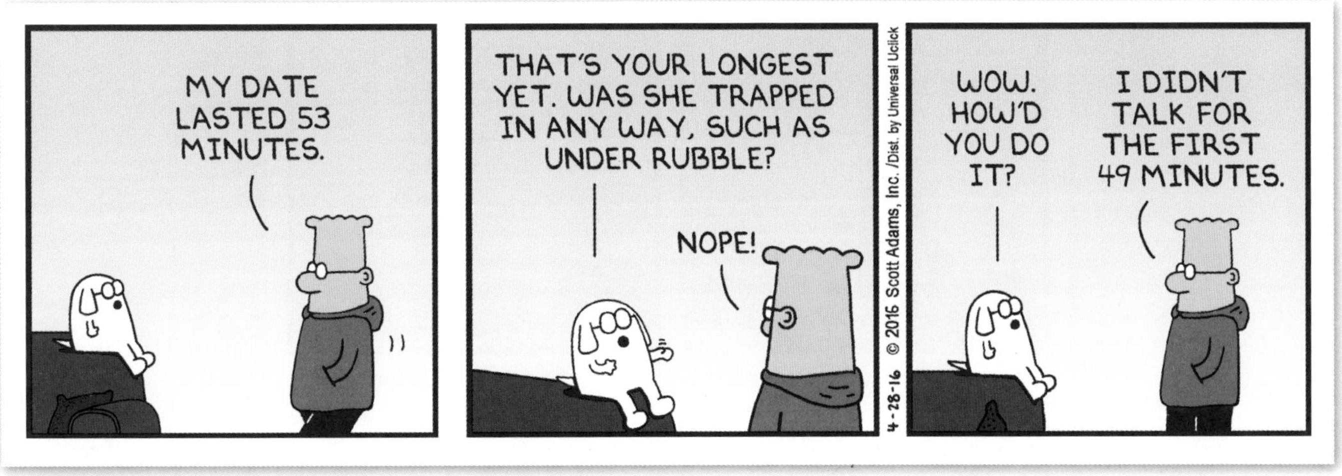
MY DATE LASTED 53 MINUTES.
THAT'S YOUR LONGEST YET. WAS SHE TRAPPED IN ANY WAY, SUCH AS UNDER RUBBLE?
NOPE!
WOW. HOW'D YOU DO IT?
I DIDN'T TALK FOR THE FIRST 49 MINUTES.
4-28-16 © 2016 Scott Adams, Inc. /Dist. by Universal Uclick

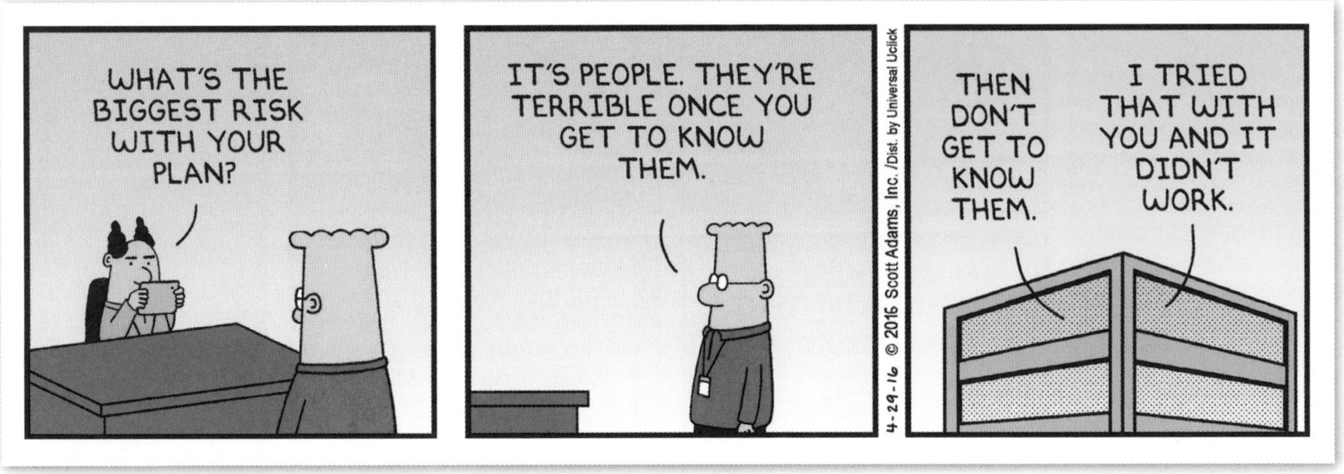
WHAT'S THE BIGGEST RISK WITH YOUR PLAN?
IT'S PEOPLE. THEY'RE TERRIBLE ONCE YOU GET TO KNOW THEM.
THEN DON'T GET TO KNOW THEM.
I TRIED THAT WITH YOU AND IT DIDN'T WORK.
4-29-16 © 2016 Scott Adams, Inc. /Dist. by Universal Uclick

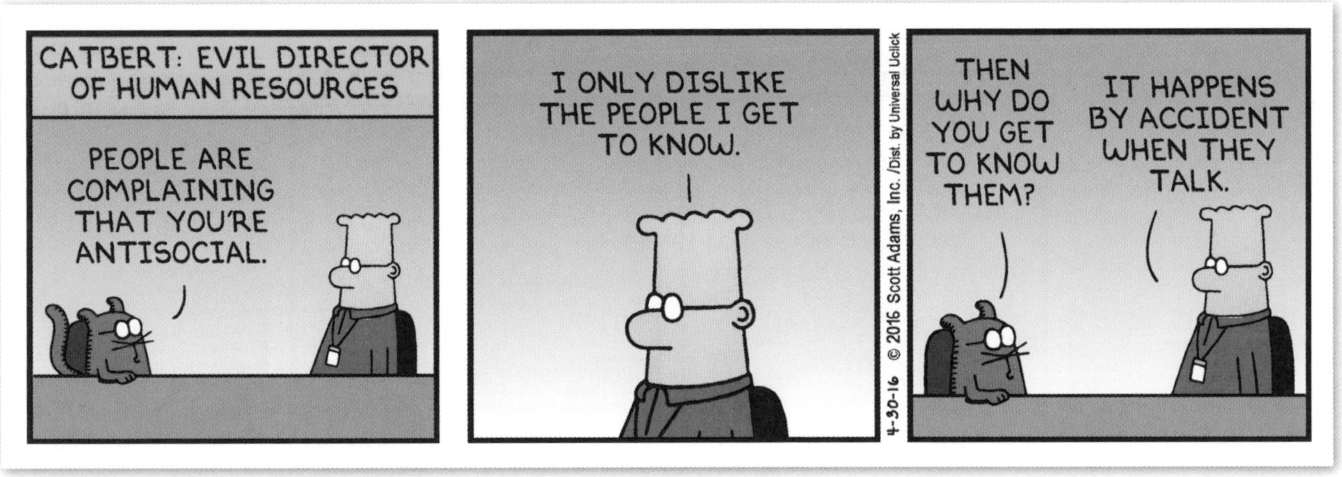
CATBERT: EVIL DIRECTOR OF HUMAN RESOURCES
PEOPLE ARE COMPLAINING THAT YOU'RE ANTISOCIAL.
I ONLY DISLIKE THE PEOPLE I GET TO KNOW.
THEN WHY DO YOU GET TO KNOW THEM?
IT HAPPENS BY ACCIDENT WHEN THEY TALK.
4-30-16 © 2016 Scott Adams, Inc. /Dist. by Universal Uclick

WE WON A CONTRACT TO WRITE SOFTWARE FOR VOTING MACHINES.
WHO DO YOU WANT TO BE PRESIDENT?
WHY DO YOU ASK?
BECAUSE I WANT YOU TO BE HAPPY.
© 2016 Scott Adams, Inc./Dist. by Universal Uclick
YOU'RE IMPLYING THAT YOU PLAN TO FUDGE THE SYSTEM.
I'M NOT IMPLYING ANYTHING LIKE THAT.
OBVIOUSLY, IT WILL BE EASY TO FUDGE THE DATA, AND WE ARE FAR HAPPIER WHEN YOU'RE IN A GOOD MOOD.
BUT I WOULD NEVER COMMIT A CRIME JUST BECAUSE IT IS GOOD FOR ME AND TOTALLY UNDETECTABLE.
5-1-16
OKAY, GOOD.
SO WHO DO YOU WANT TO WIN AND BY HOW MUCH?

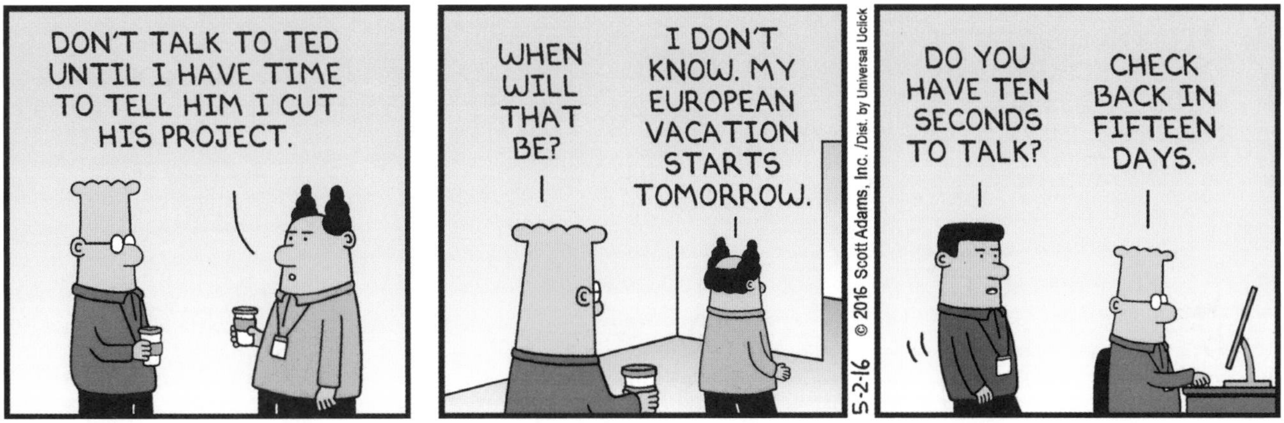
DON'T TALK TO TED UNTIL I HAVE TIME TO TELL HIM I CUT HIS PROJECT.
WHEN WILL THAT BE?
I DON'T KNOW. MY EUROPEAN VACATION STARTS TOMORROW.
5-2-16 © 2016 Scott Adams, Inc. /Dist. by Universal Uclick
DO YOU HAVE TEN SECONDS TO TALK?
CHECK BACK IN FIFTEEN DAYS.

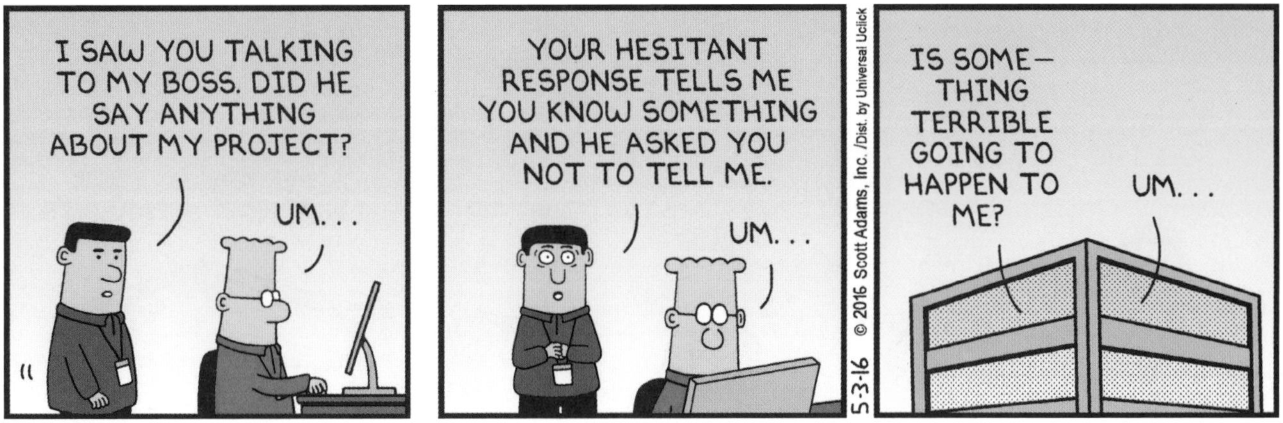
I SAW YOU TALKING TO MY BOSS. DID HE SAY ANYTHING ABOUT MY PROJECT?
UM. . .
YOUR HESITANT RESPONSE TELLS ME YOU KNOW SOMETHING AND HE ASKED YOU NOT TO TELL ME.
UM. . .
5-3-16 © 2016 Scott Adams, Inc. /Dist. by Universal Uclick
IS SOME-THING TERRIBLE GOING TO HAPPEN TO ME?
UM. . .

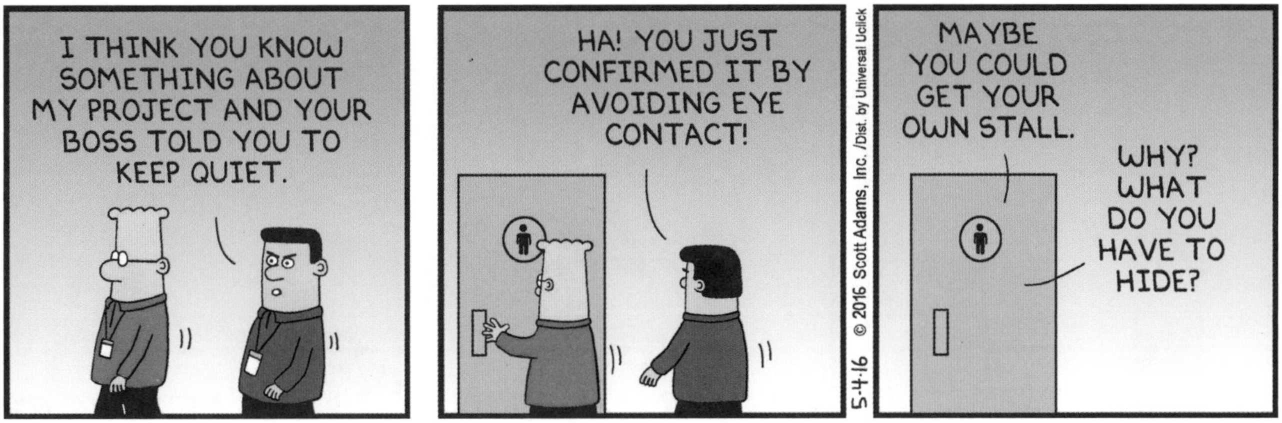
I THINK YOU KNOW SOMETHING ABOUT MY PROJECT AND YOUR BOSS TOLD YOU TO KEEP QUIET.
HA! YOU JUST CONFIRMED IT BY AVOIDING EYE CONTACT!
5-4-16 © 2016 Scott Adams, Inc. /Dist. by Universal Uclick
MAYBE YOU COULD GET YOUR OWN STALL.
WHY? WHAT DO YOU HAVE TO HIDE?

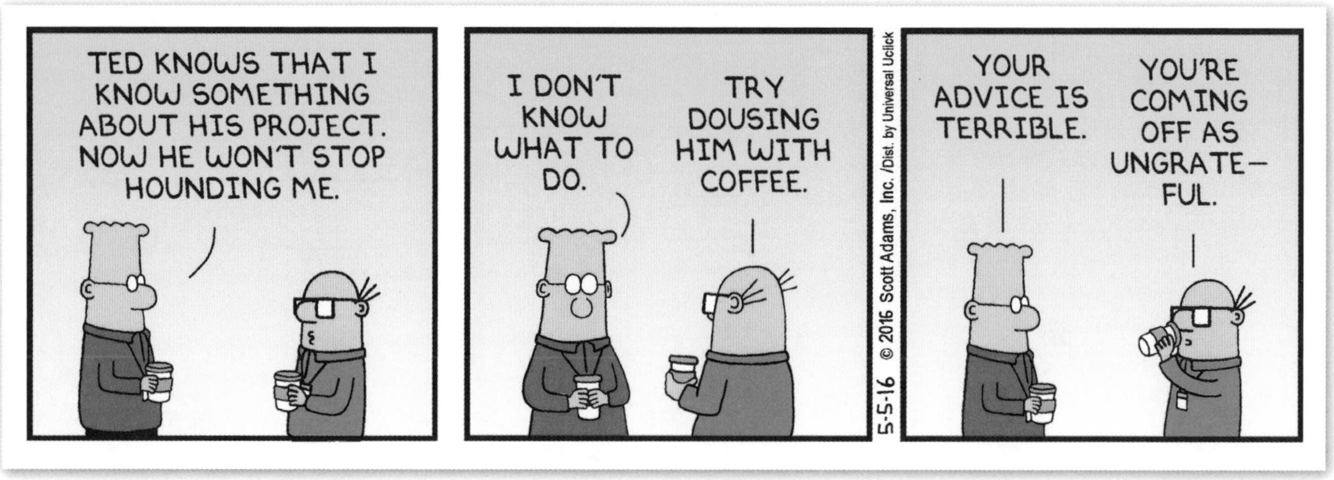
TED KNOWS THAT I KNOW SOMETHING ABOUT HIS PROJECT. NOW HE WON'T STOP HOUNDING ME.
I DON'T KNOW WHAT TO DO.
TRY DOUSING HIM WITH COFFEE.
5-5-16 © 2016 Scott Adams, Inc. /Dist. by Universal Uclick
YOUR ADVICE IS TERRIBLE.
YOU'RE COMING OFF AS UNGRATE-FUL.

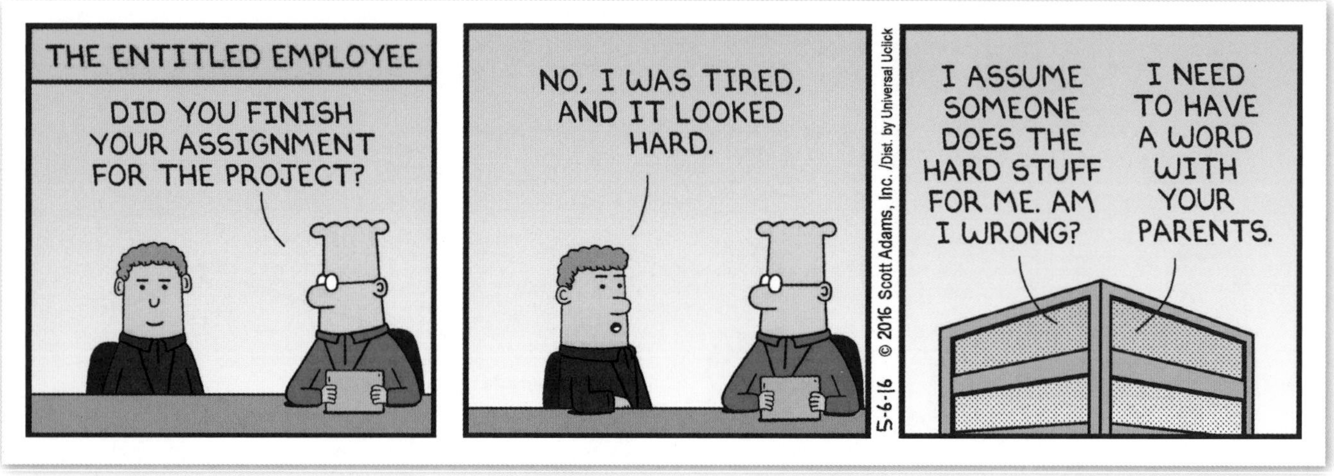
THE ENTITLED EMPLOYEE
DID YOU FINISH YOUR ASSIGNMENT FOR THE PROJECT?
NO, I WAS TIRED, AND IT LOOKED HARD.
5-6-16 © 2016 Scott Adams, Inc. /Dist. by Universal Uclick
I ASSUME SOMEONE DOES THE HARD STUFF FOR ME. AM I WRONG?
I NEED TO HAVE A WORD WITH YOUR PARENTS.

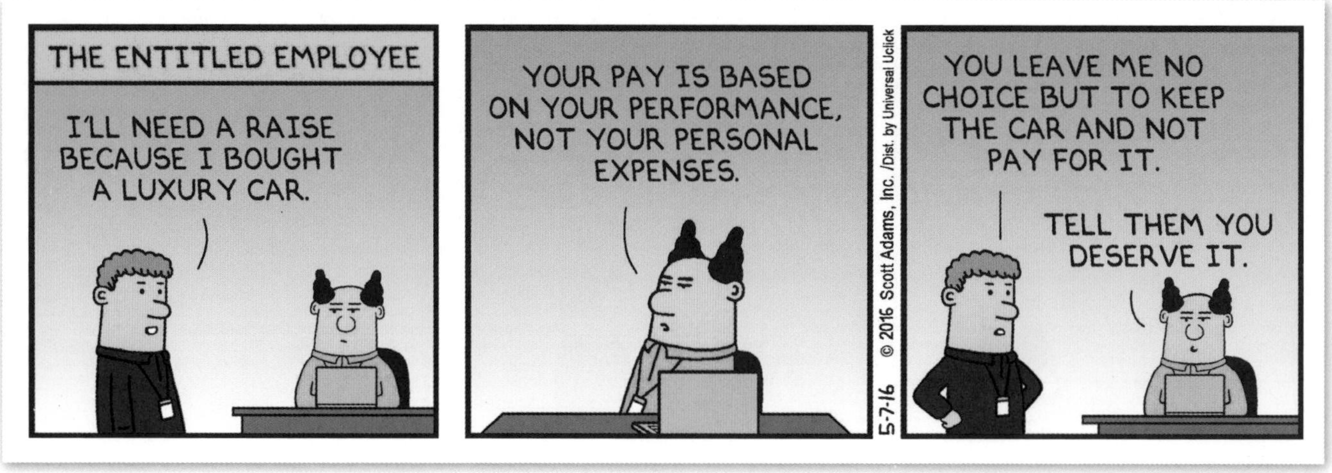
THE ENTITLED EMPLOYEE
I'LL NEED A RAISE BECAUSE I BOUGHT A LUXURY CAR.
YOUR PAY IS BASED ON YOUR PERFORMANCE, NOT YOUR PERSONAL EXPENSES.
5-7-16 © 2016 Scott Adams, Inc. /Dist. by Universal Uclick
YOU LEAVE ME NO CHOICE BUT TO KEEP THE CAR AND NOT PAY FOR IT.
TELL THEM YOU DESERVE IT.

I CAN'T GIVE YOU A RAISE BECAUSE YOUR PERFORMANCE WAS ONLY AVERAGE.
HOW CAN YOU CALCULATE AN AVERAGE FOR MY PERFORMANCE?
NO ONE HAS EVER BEEN IN MY EXACT SITUATION.
I COMPARED YOU TO OTHER EMPLOYEES.
YOU COMPARED ME TO STRANGERS DOING ENTIRELY DIFFERENT THINGS?
NO, I COMPARED YOU TO IMAGINARY PEOPLE DOING YOUR EXACT JOB.
IT'S CALLED **MANAGING**, AND I'M VERY GOOD AT IT.
HOW DO YOU KNOW YOU'RE GOOD AT IT?
BECAUSE IMAGINARY PEOPLE DO THIS JOB WORSE THAN I DO.
© 2016 Scott Adams, Inc./Dist. by Universal Uclick
5-8-16

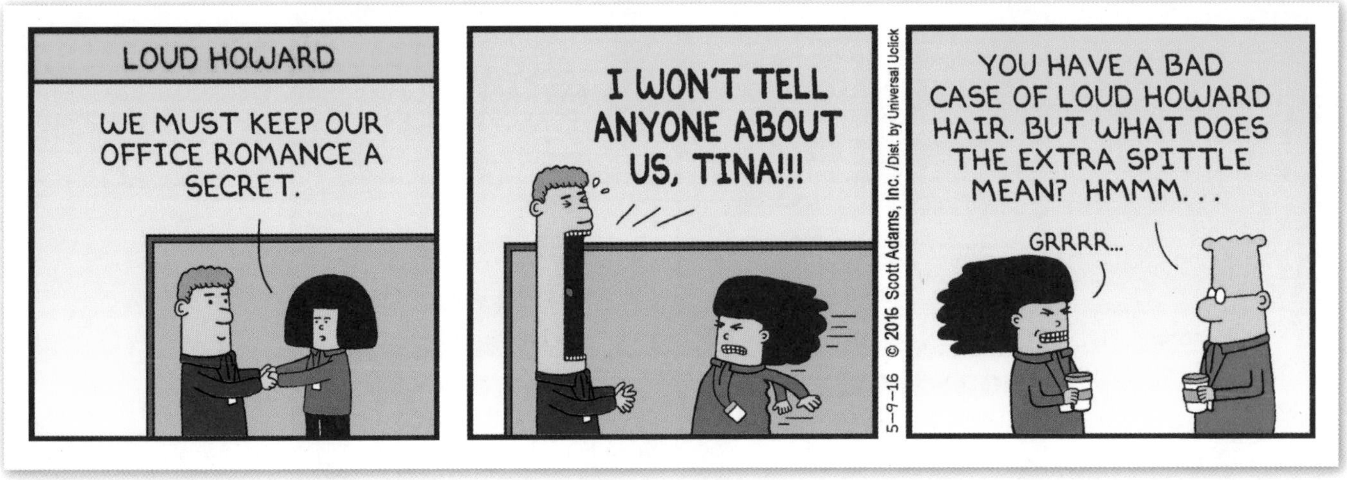
LOUD HOWARD
WE MUST KEEP OUR OFFICE ROMANCE A SECRET.
I WON'T TELL ANYONE ABOUT US, TINA!!!
5-9-16 © 2016 Scott Adams, Inc. /Dist. by Universal Uclick
YOU HAVE A BAD CASE OF LOUD HOWARD HAIR. BUT WHAT DOES THE EXTRA SPITTLE MEAN? HMMM. . .
GRRRR...

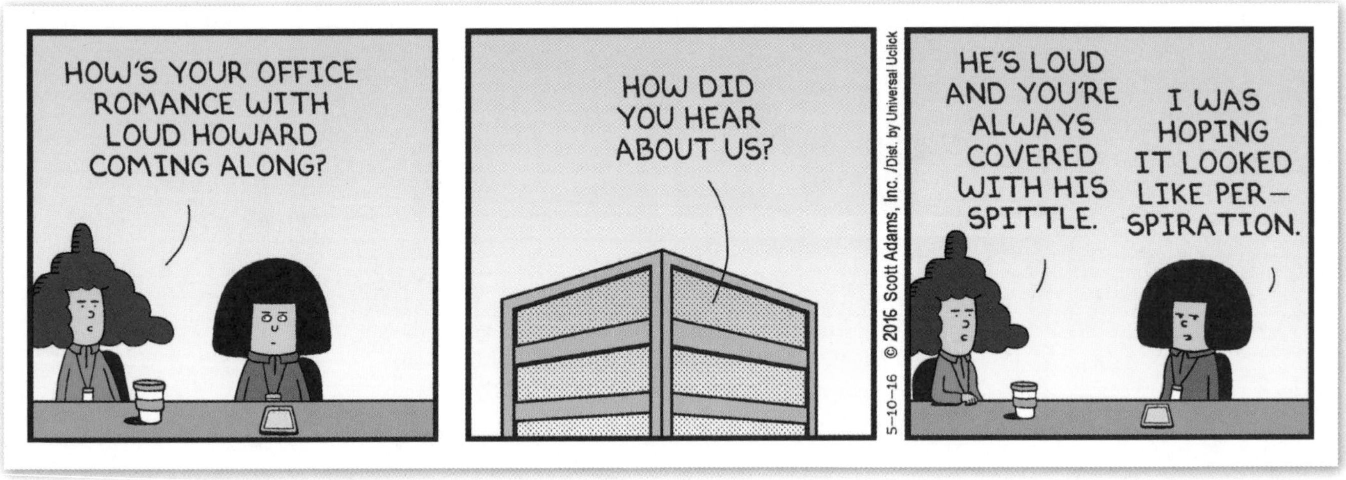
HOW'S YOUR OFFICE ROMANCE WITH LOUD HOWARD COMING ALONG?
HOW DID YOU HEAR ABOUT US?
5-10-16 © 2016 Scott Adams, Inc. /Dist. by Universal Uclick
HE'S LOUD AND YOU'RE ALWAYS COVERED WITH HIS SPITTLE.
I WAS HOPING IT LOOKED LIKE PER-SPIRATION.

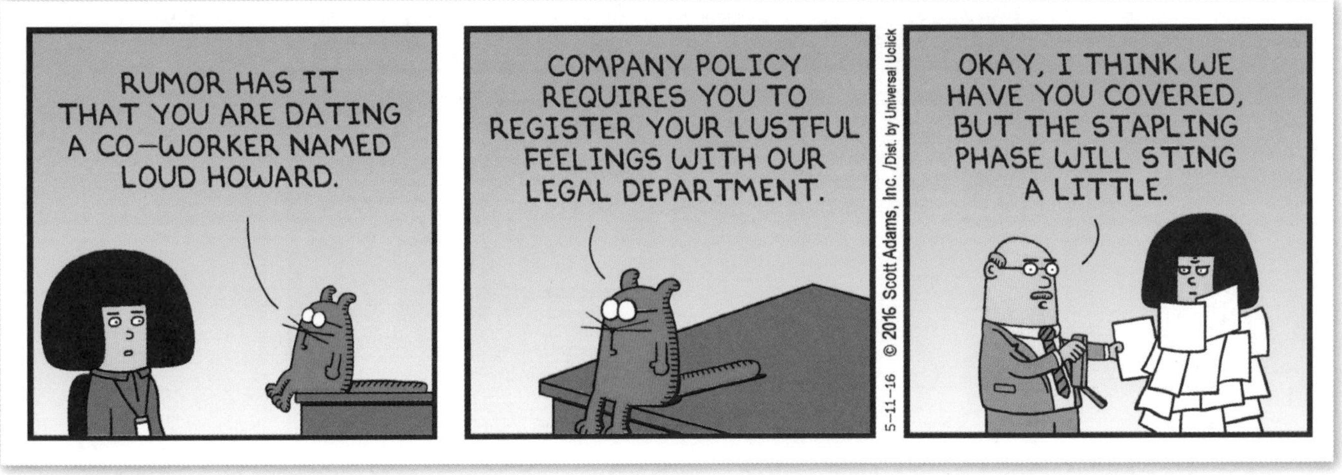
RUMOR HAS IT THAT YOU ARE DATING A CO-WORKER NAMED LOUD HOWARD.
COMPANY POLICY REQUIRES YOU TO REGISTER YOUR LUSTFUL FEELINGS WITH OUR LEGAL DEPARTMENT.
5-11-16 © 2016 Scott Adams, Inc. /Dist. by Universal Uclick
OKAY, I THINK WE HAVE YOU COVERED, BUT THE STAPLING PHASE WILL STING A LITTLE.

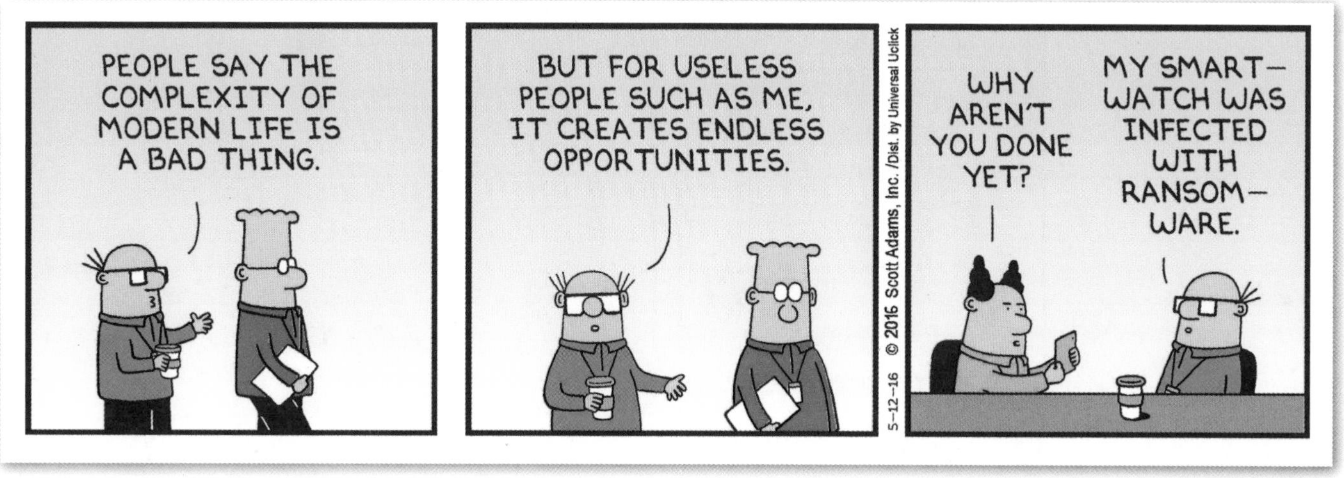
PEOPLE SAY THE COMPLEXITY OF MODERN LIFE IS A BAD THING.
BUT FOR USELESS PEOPLE SUCH AS ME, IT CREATES ENDLESS OPPORTUNITIES.
5-12-16 © 2016 Scott Adams, Inc. /Dist. by Universal Uclick
WHY AREN'T YOU DONE YET?
MY SMART-WATCH WAS INFECTED WITH RANSOM-WARE.

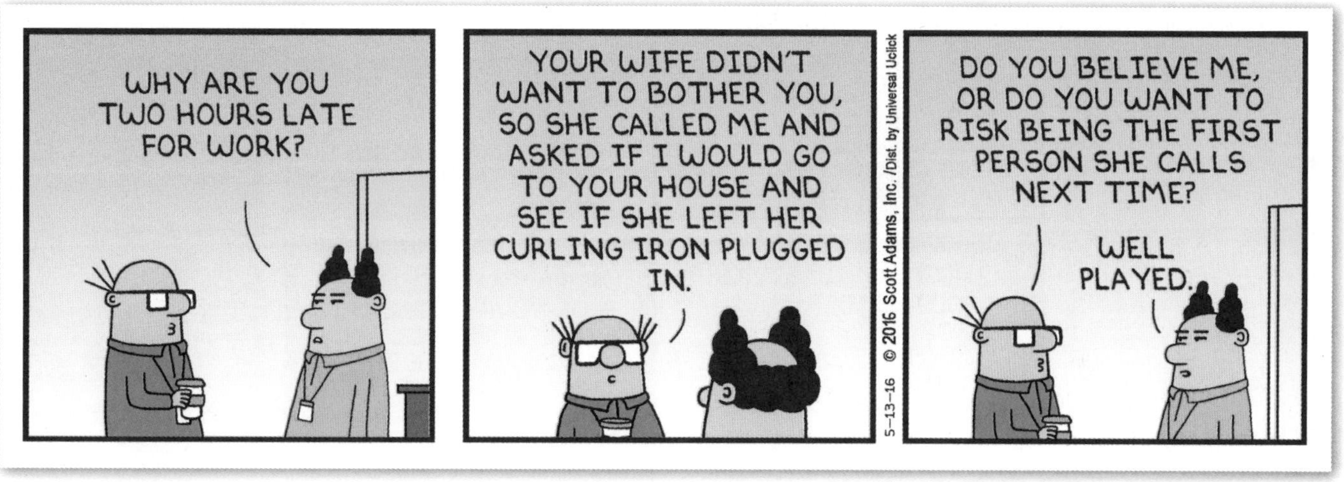
WHY ARE YOU TWO HOURS LATE FOR WORK?
YOUR WIFE DIDN'T WANT TO BOTHER YOU, SO SHE CALLED ME AND ASKED IF I WOULD GO TO YOUR HOUSE AND SEE IF SHE LEFT HER CURLING IRON PLUGGED IN.
5-13-16 © 2016 Scott Adams, Inc. /Dist. by Universal Uclick
DO YOU BELIEVE ME, OR DO YOU WANT TO RISK BEING THE FIRST PERSON SHE CALLS NEXT TIME?
WELL PLAYED.

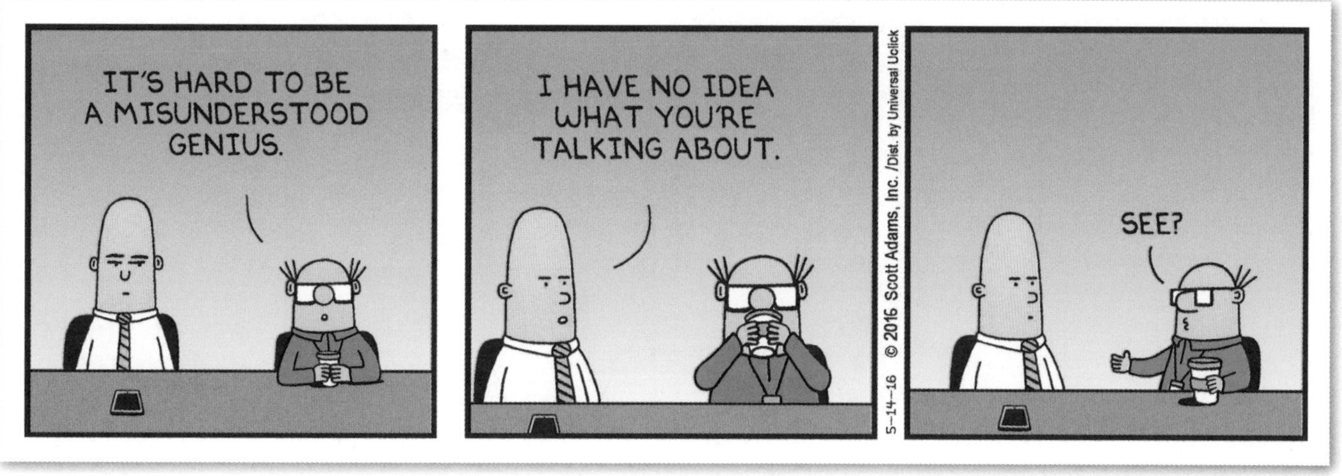
IT'S HARD TO BE A MISUNDERSTOOD GENIUS.
I HAVE NO IDEA WHAT YOU'RE TALKING ABOUT.
5-14-16 © 2016 Scott Adams, Inc. /Dist. by Universal Uclick
SEE?

WHEN DO YOU EXPECT TO FINISH YOUR PROJECT?
NEVER.
THAT'S YOUR PLAN?
NO, MY PLAN IS TO BE DONE IN A WEEK.
YOU ASKED ME WHAT I **EXPECT**.
I BASE MY EXPEC-TATIONS ON THE QUALITY OF PEOPLE YOU ASSIGNED TO MY PROJECT WITHOUT ASKING MY OPINION.
THE TIME-WASTERS OUTNUMBER THE PRODUCTIVE PEOPLE ON THE TEAM BY THREE TO ONE.
UNDER THAT SCENARIO, PLUS YOUR TOTAL LACK OF LEADERSHIP, THE WORLD WILL END BEFORE THIS PROJECT DOES.
THEN WHY IS YOUR PLAN TO BE DONE IN ONE WEEK?
BECAUSE YOU DON'T LIKE IT WHEN I TELL THE TRUTH.
LET'S COMPRO-MISE ON TWO WEEKS.
CAN WE SET THOSE TWO WEEKS ON AUTO-RENEW?
© 2016 Scott Adams, Inc./Dist. by Universal Uclick
5-15-16

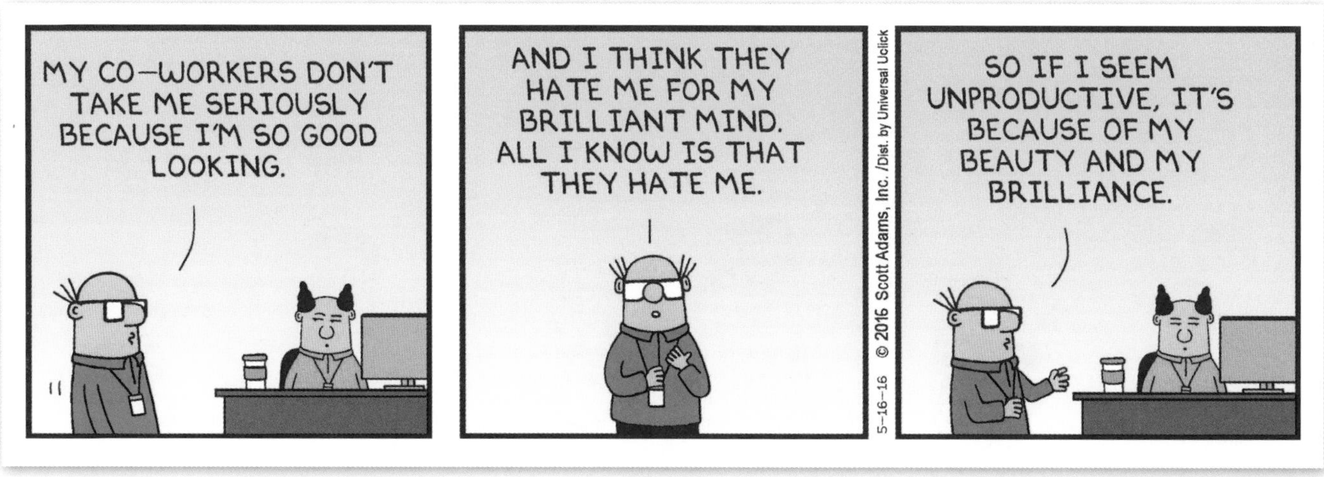
MY CO–WORKERS DON'T TAKE ME SERIOUSLY BECAUSE I'M SO GOOD LOOKING.
AND I THINK THEY HATE ME FOR MY BRILLIANT MIND. ALL I KNOW IS THAT THEY HATE ME.
5-16-16 © 2016 Scott Adams, Inc. /Dist. by Universal Uclick
SO IF I SEEM UNPRODUCTIVE, IT'S BECAUSE OF MY BEAUTY AND MY BRILLIANCE.

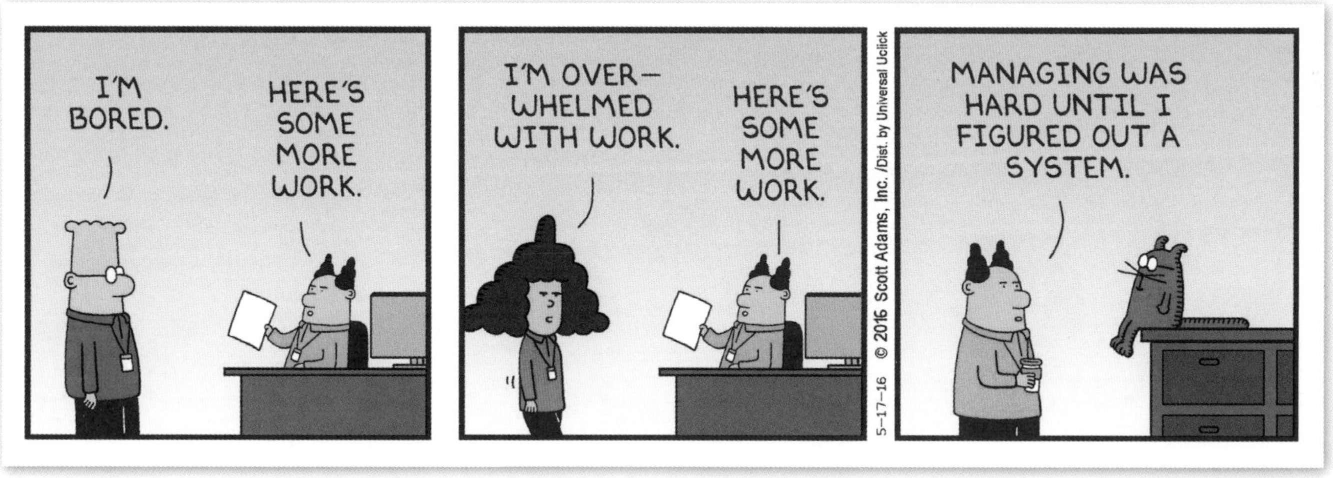
I'M BORED.
HERE'S SOME MORE WORK.
I'M OVER–WHELMED WITH WORK.
HERE'S SOME MORE WORK.
5-17-16 © 2016 Scott Adams, Inc. /Dist. by Universal Uclick
MANAGING WAS HARD UNTIL I FIGURED OUT A SYSTEM.

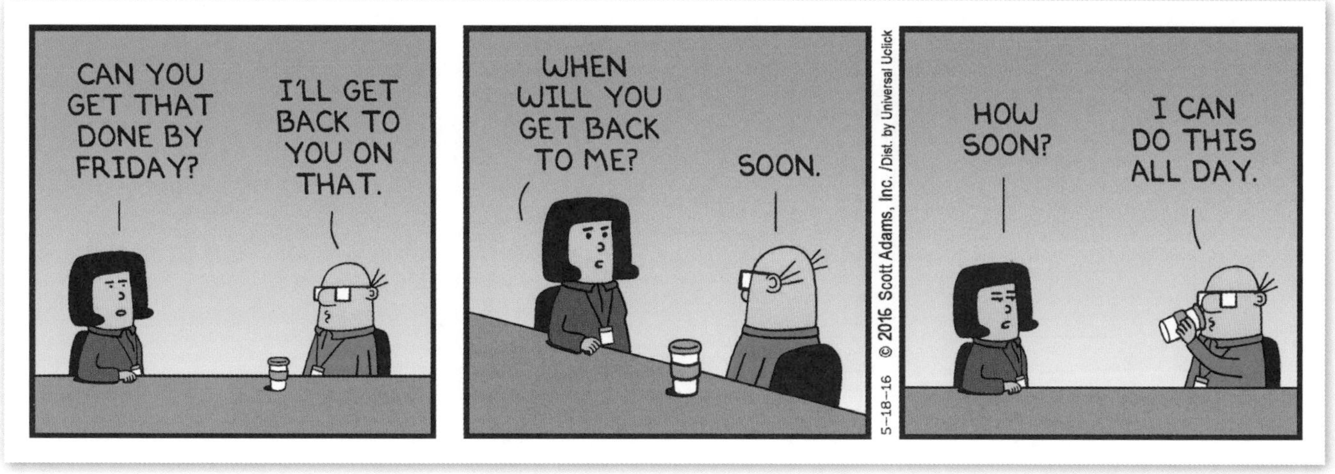
CAN YOU GET THAT DONE BY FRIDAY?
I'LL GET BACK TO YOU ON THAT.
WHEN WILL YOU GET BACK TO ME?
SOON.
5-18-16 © 2016 Scott Adams, Inc. /Dist. by Universal Uclick
HOW SOON?
I CAN DO THIS ALL DAY.

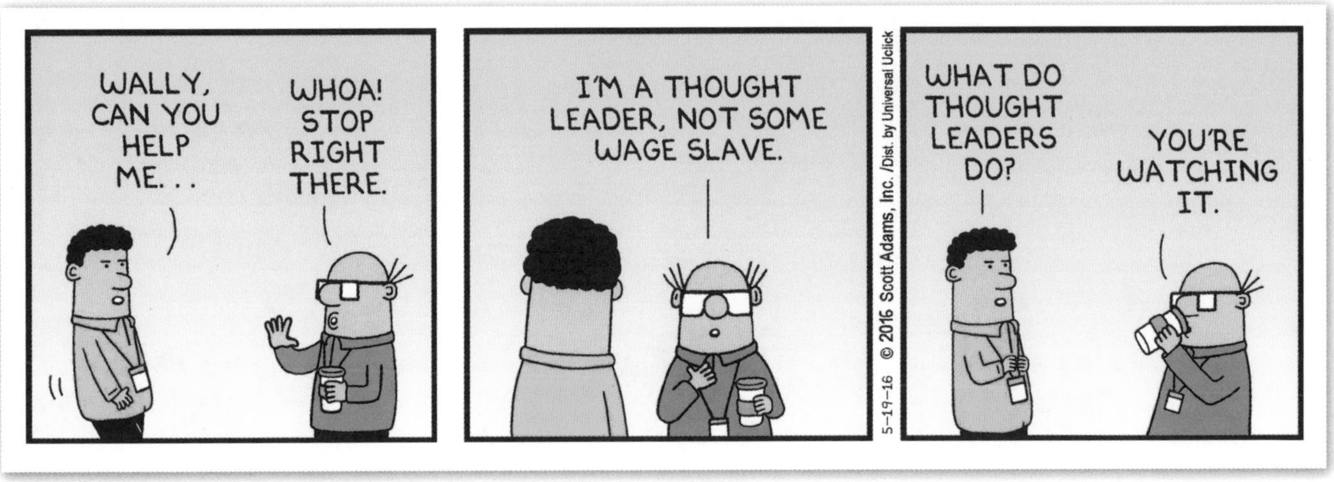
WALLY, CAN YOU HELP ME. . .
WHOA! STOP RIGHT THERE.
I'M A THOUGHT LEADER, NOT SOME WAGE SLAVE.
5-19-16 © 2016 Scott Adams, Inc. /Dist. by Universal Uclick
WHAT DO THOUGHT LEADERS DO?
YOU'RE WATCHING IT.

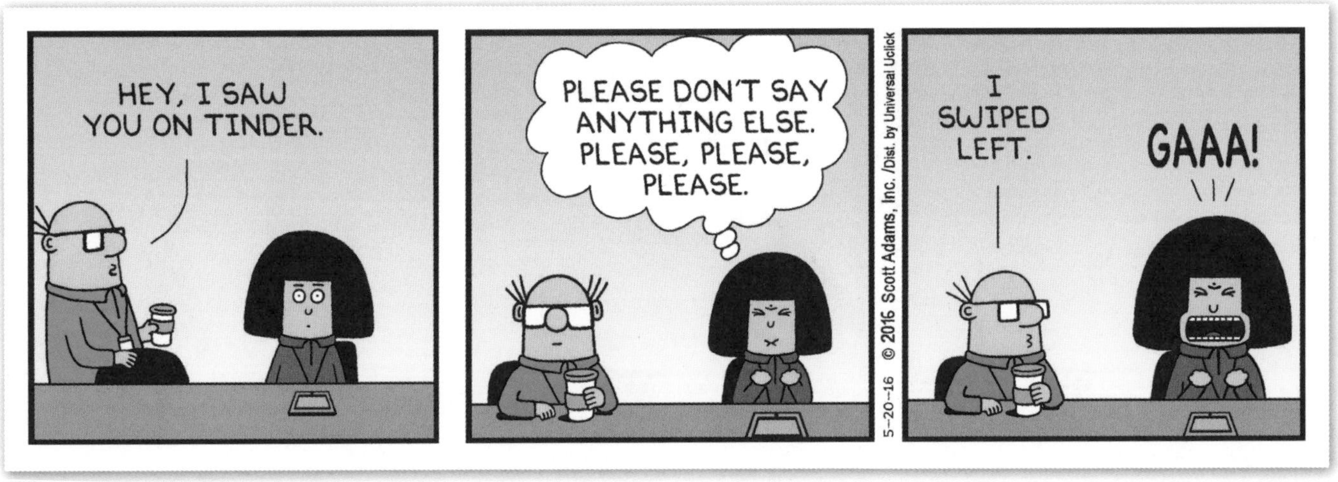
HEY, I SAW YOU ON TINDER.
PLEASE DON'T SAY ANYTHING ELSE. PLEASE, PLEASE, PLEASE.
5-20-16 © 2016 Scott Adams, Inc. /Dist. by Universal Uclick
I SWIPED LEFT.
GAAA!

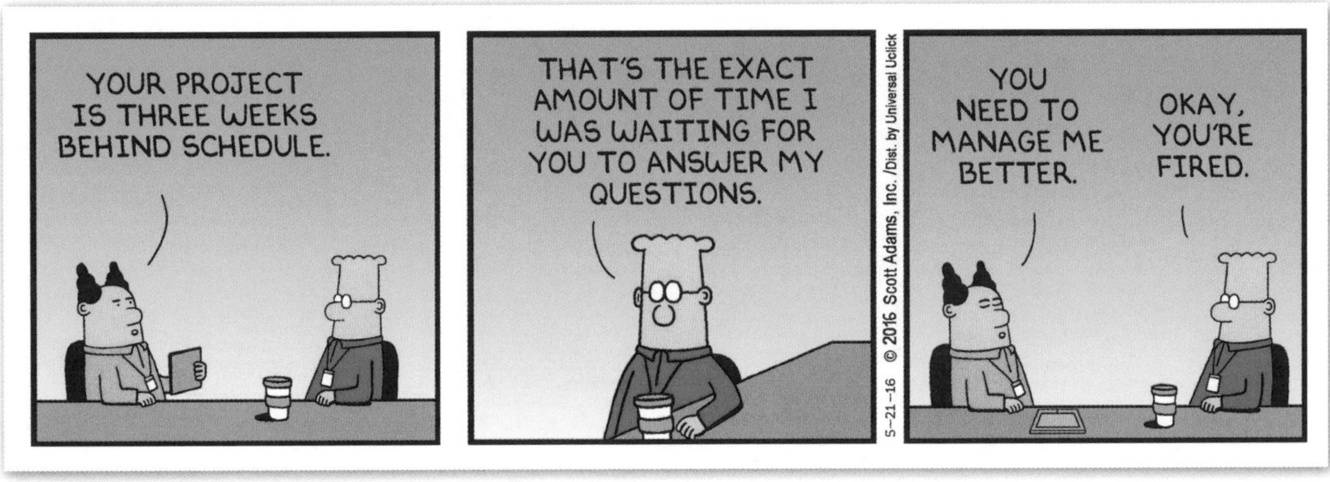
YOUR PROJECT IS THREE WEEKS BEHIND SCHEDULE.
THAT'S THE EXACT AMOUNT OF TIME I WAS WAITING FOR YOU TO ANSWER MY QUESTIONS.
5-21-16 © 2016 Scott Adams, Inc. /Dist. by Universal Uclick
YOU NEED TO MANAGE ME BETTER.
OKAY, YOU'RE FIRED.

DO YOU WANT TO GO TO DINNER AND A MOVIE WITH ME ON FRIDAY?

THAT PLAN IS POORLY CONCEIVED.

THE BEST TIME TO WATCH A MOVIE IS ALSO THE BEST TIME TO EAT.

AND WHAT ARE THE ODDS WE WANT TO SEE THE SAME MOVIE?

YOU'RE A PICKY EATER, SO IT WOULD BE A NIGHTMARE TO DECIDE WHERE WE BOTH WANT TO EAT.

ONE OF US WOULD HAVE TO COMPROMISE, AND I ASSUME IT WOULD BE ME.

I'M OFFENDED BY YOUR OFFER TO SUBOPTIMIZE MY FRIDAY EXPERIENCE.

DO YOU HAVE A BETTER OPTION?

NOPE. SEE YOU FRIDAY.

© 2016 Scott Adams, Inc./Dist. by Universal Uclick

5-22-16

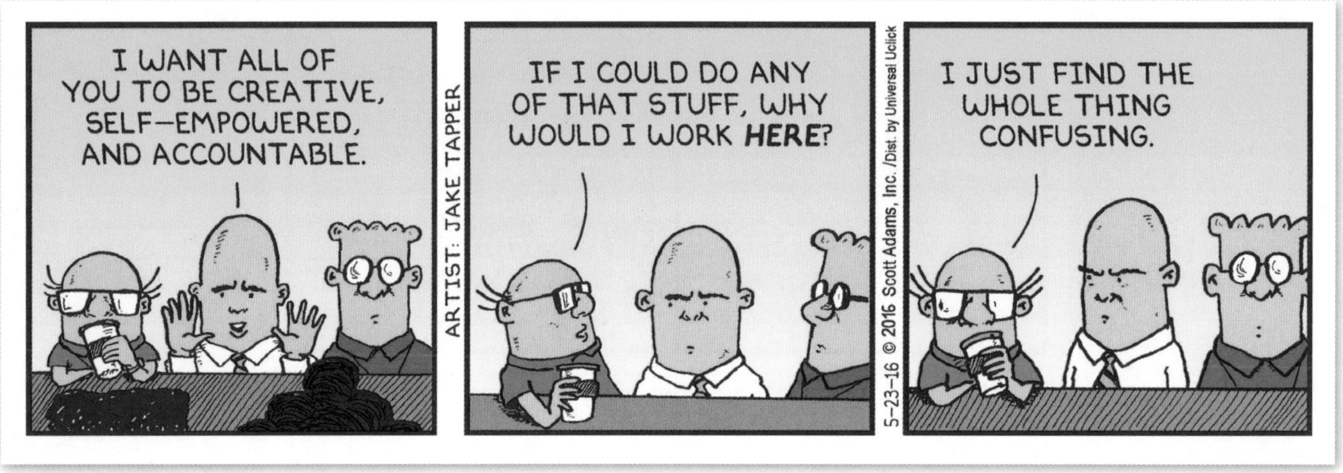
I WANT ALL OF YOU TO BE CREATIVE, SELF—EMPOWERED, AND ACCOUNTABLE.
ARTIST: JAKE TAPPER
IF I COULD DO ANY OF THAT STUFF, WHY WOULD I WORK **HERE**?
5-23-16 © 2016 Scott Adams, Inc. /Dist. by Universal Uclick
I JUST FIND THE WHOLE THING CONFUSING.

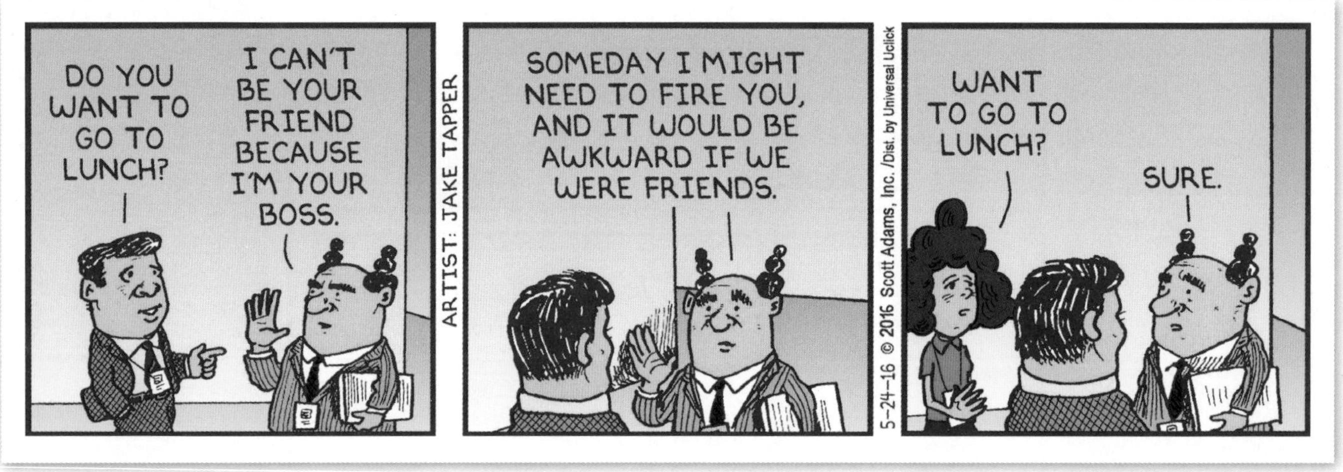
DO YOU WANT TO GO TO LUNCH?
I CAN'T BE YOUR FRIEND BECAUSE I'M YOUR BOSS.
ARTIST: JAKE TAPPER
SOMEDAY I MIGHT NEED TO FIRE YOU, AND IT WOULD BE AWKWARD IF WE WERE FRIENDS.
5-24-16 © 2016 Scott Adams, Inc. /Dist. by Universal Uclick
WANT TO GO TO LUNCH?
SURE.

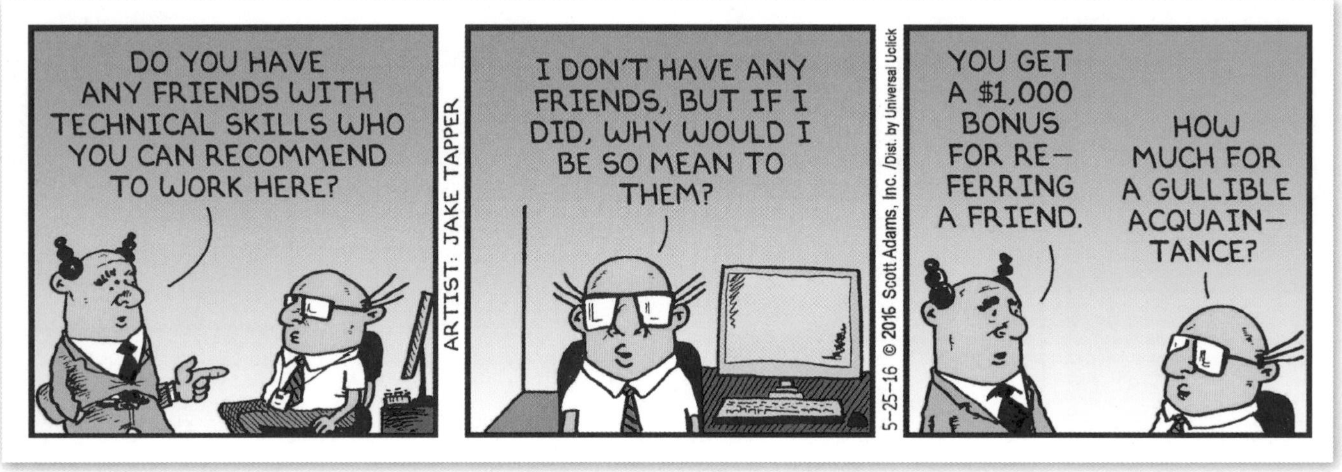
DO YOU HAVE ANY FRIENDS WITH TECHNICAL SKILLS WHO YOU CAN RECOMMEND TO WORK HERE?
ARTIST: JAKE TAPPER
I DON'T HAVE ANY FRIENDS, BUT IF I DID, WHY WOULD I BE SO MEAN TO THEM?
5-25-16 © 2016 Scott Adams, Inc. /Dist. by Universal Uclick
YOU GET A $1,000 BONUS FOR RE—FERRING A FRIEND.
HOW MUCH FOR A GULLIBLE ACQUAIN—TANCE?

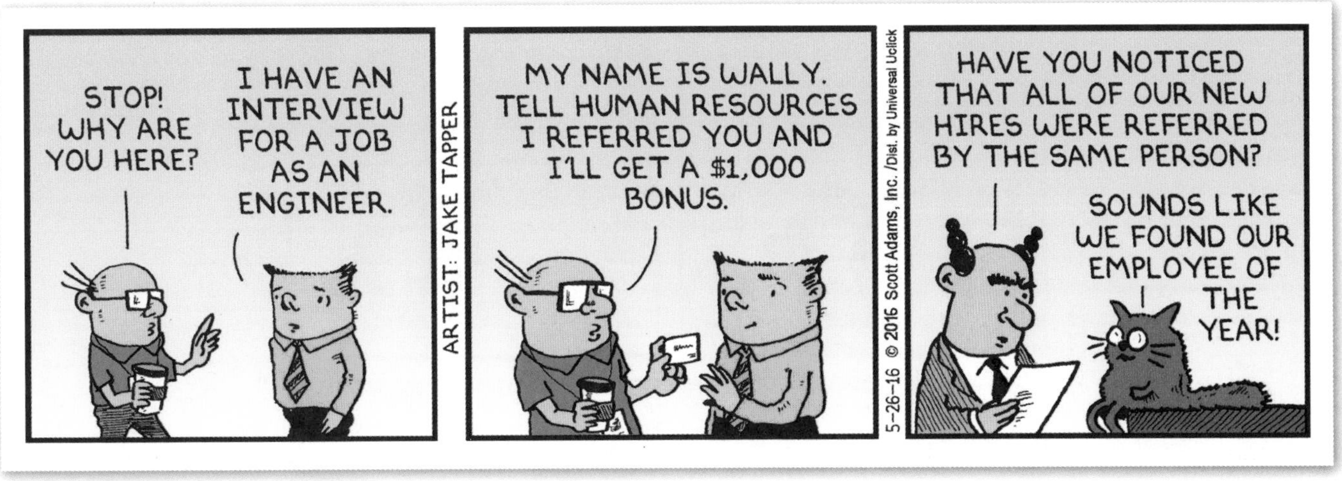
STOP! WHY ARE YOU HERE?
I HAVE AN INTERVIEW FOR A JOB AS AN ENGINEER.
ARTIST: JAKE TAPPER
MY NAME IS WALLY. TELL HUMAN RESOURCES I REFERRED YOU AND I'LL GET A $1,000 BONUS.
5-26-16 © 2016 Scott Adams, Inc. /Dist. by Universal Uclick
HAVE YOU NOTICED THAT ALL OF OUR NEW HIRES WERE REFERRED BY THE SAME PERSON?
SOUNDS LIKE WE FOUND OUR EMPLOYEE OF THE YEAR!

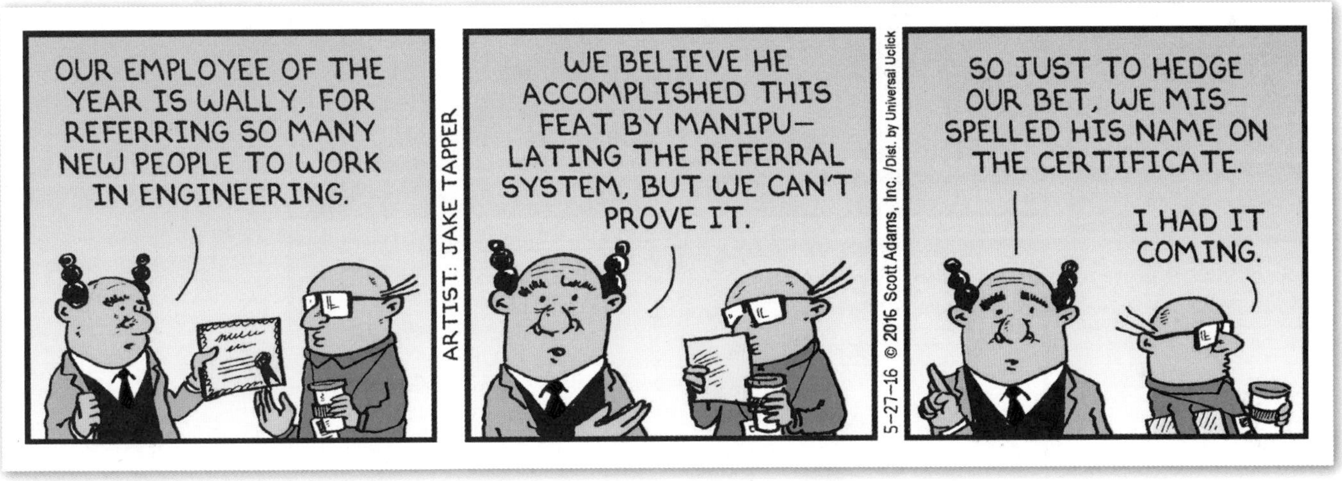
OUR EMPLOYEE OF THE YEAR IS WALLY, FOR REFERRING SO MANY NEW PEOPLE TO WORK IN ENGINEERING.
ARTIST: JAKE TAPPER
WE BELIEVE HE ACCOMPLISHED THIS FEAT BY MANIPU-LATING THE REFERRAL SYSTEM, BUT WE CAN'T PROVE IT.
5-27-16 © 2016 Scott Adams, Inc. /Dist. by Universal Uclick
SO JUST TO HEDGE OUR BET, WE MIS-SPELLED HIS NAME ON THE CERTIFICATE.
I HAD IT COMING.

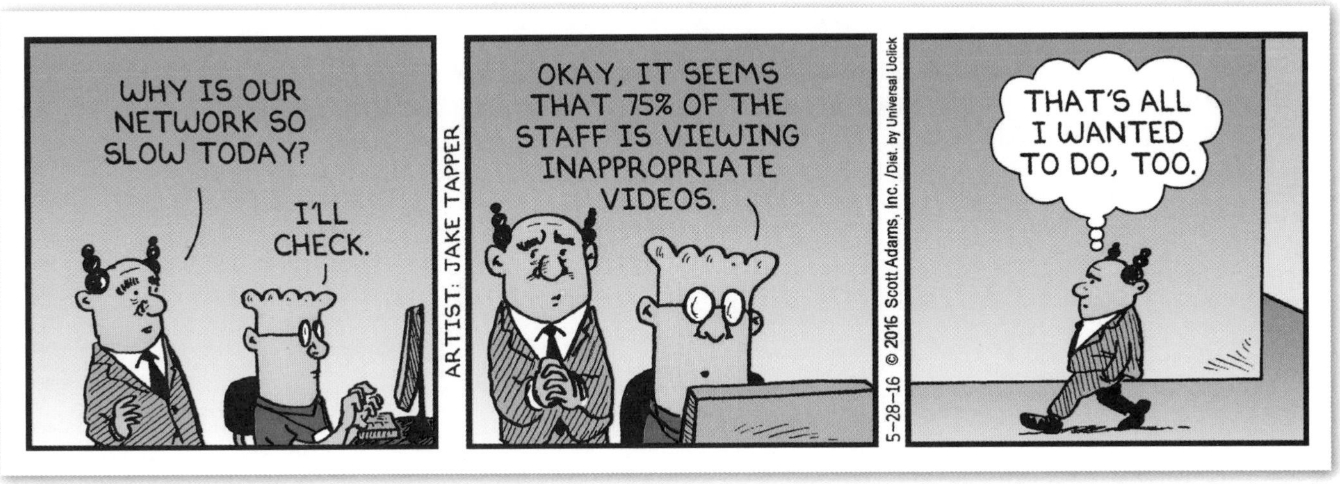
WHY IS OUR NETWORK SO SLOW TODAY?
I'LL CHECK.
ARTIST: JAKE TAPPER
OKAY, IT SEEMS THAT 75% OF THE STAFF IS VIEWING INAPPROPRIATE VIDEOS.
5-28-16 © 2016 Scott Adams, Inc. /Dist. by Universal Uclick
THAT'S ALL I WANTED TO DO, TOO.

DID YOU FINISH THE SLIDE DECK?

I TRIED, BUT IT WAS IMPOSSIBLE.

SOME IDIOT IN A NEARBY CUBICLE WAS CLIPPING HIS NAILS.

IT WAS LIKE TORTURE.

CLIP, CLIP, CLIP, CLIP, CLIP.

I COULDN'T THINK WITH THAT NOISE POLLUTING THE OFFICE AIR.

I THOUGHT IT ENDED, BUT THEN I HEARD SHOES AND SOCKS COME OFF.

IT WAS MY WORST NIGHTMARE.

OKAY, WHATEVER.

WALLY, DID YOU FINISH YOUR TASKS?

I TRIED, BUT THEN I NOTICED THAT MY NAILS WERE UNEVEN.

5-29-16

© 2016 Scott Adams, Inc./Dist. by Universal Uclick

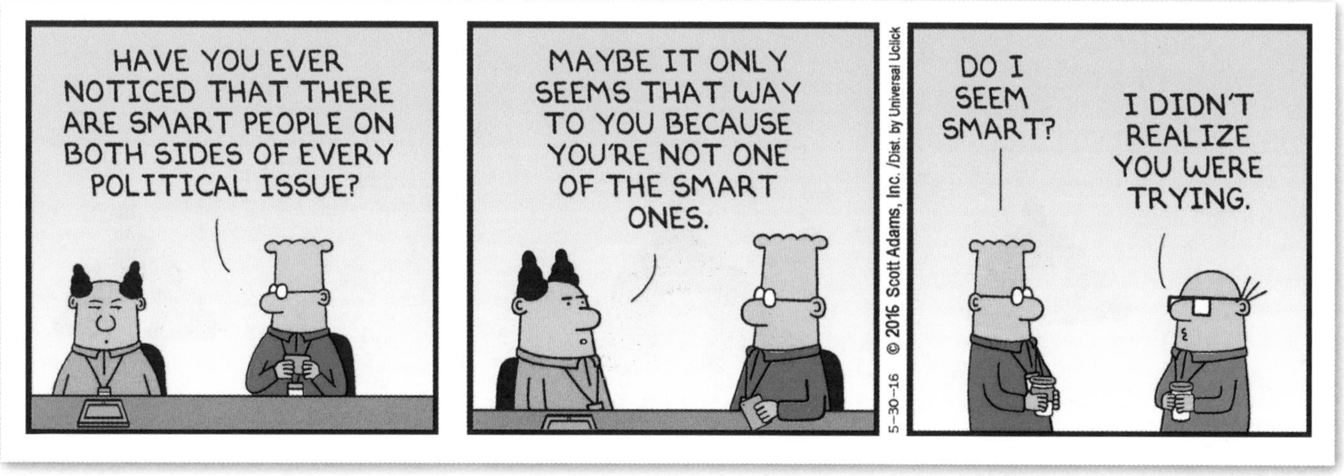
HAVE YOU EVER NOTICED THAT THERE ARE SMART PEOPLE ON BOTH SIDES OF EVERY POLITICAL ISSUE?
MAYBE IT ONLY SEEMS THAT WAY TO YOU BECAUSE YOU'RE NOT ONE OF THE SMART ONES.
5-30-16 © 2016 Scott Adams, Inc. /Dist. by Universal Uclick
DO I SEEM SMART?
I DIDN'T REALIZE YOU WERE TRYING.

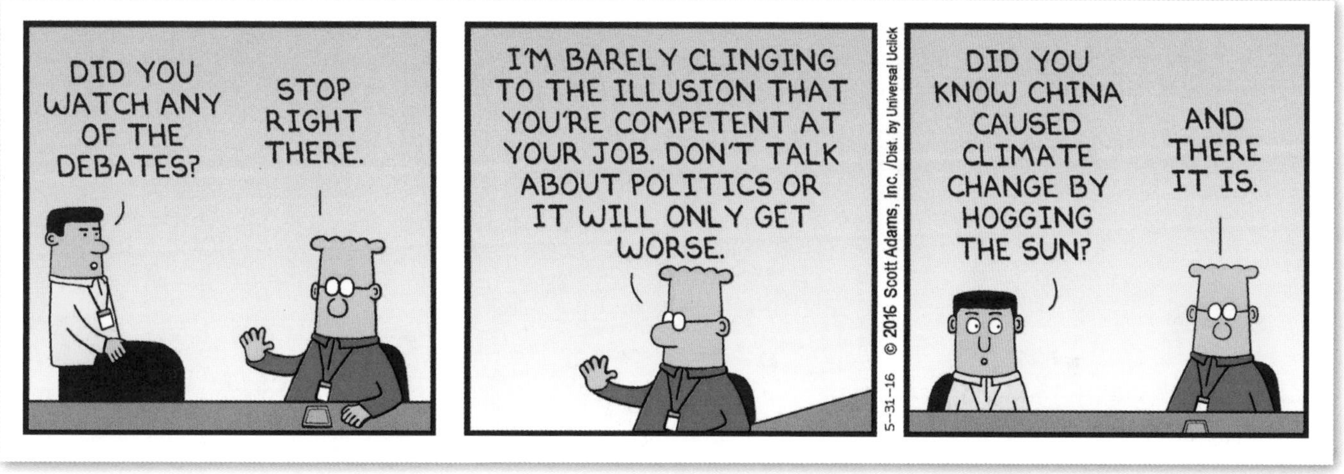
DID YOU WATCH ANY OF THE DEBATES?
STOP RIGHT THERE.
I'M BARELY CLINGING TO THE ILLUSION THAT YOU'RE COMPETENT AT YOUR JOB. DON'T TALK ABOUT POLITICS OR IT WILL ONLY GET WORSE.
5-31-16 © 2016 Scott Adams, Inc. /Dist. by Universal Uclick
DID YOU KNOW CHINA CAUSED CLIMATE CHANGE BY HOGGING THE SUN?
AND THERE IT IS.

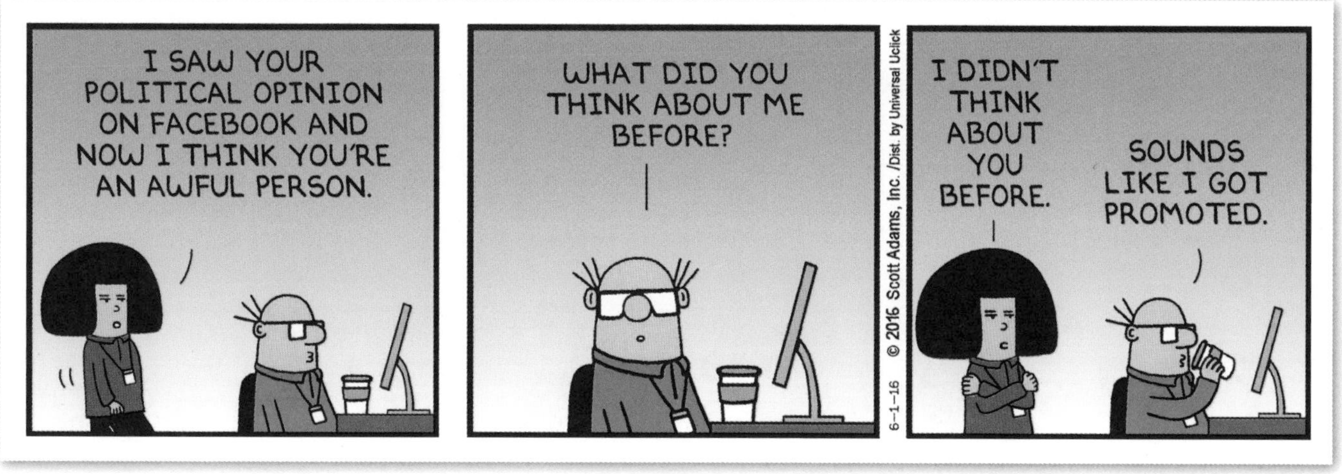
I SAW YOUR POLITICAL OPINION ON FACEBOOK AND NOW I THINK YOU'RE AN AWFUL PERSON.
WHAT DID YOU THINK ABOUT ME BEFORE?
6-1-16 © 2016 Scott Adams, Inc. /Dist. by Universal Uclick
I DIDN'T THINK ABOUT YOU BEFORE.
SOUNDS LIKE I GOT PROMOTED.

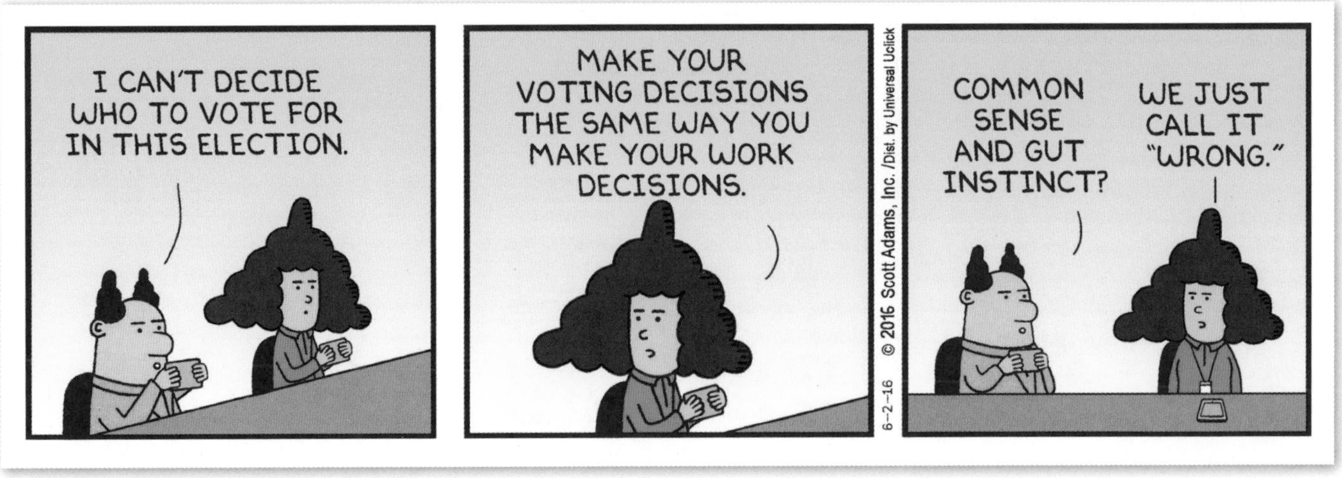
I CAN'T DECIDE WHO TO VOTE FOR IN THIS ELECTION.
MAKE YOUR VOTING DECISIONS THE SAME WAY YOU MAKE YOUR WORK DECISIONS.
6-2-16 © 2016 Scott Adams, Inc. /Dist. by Universal Uclick
COMMON SENSE AND GUT INSTINCT?
WE JUST CALL IT "WRONG."

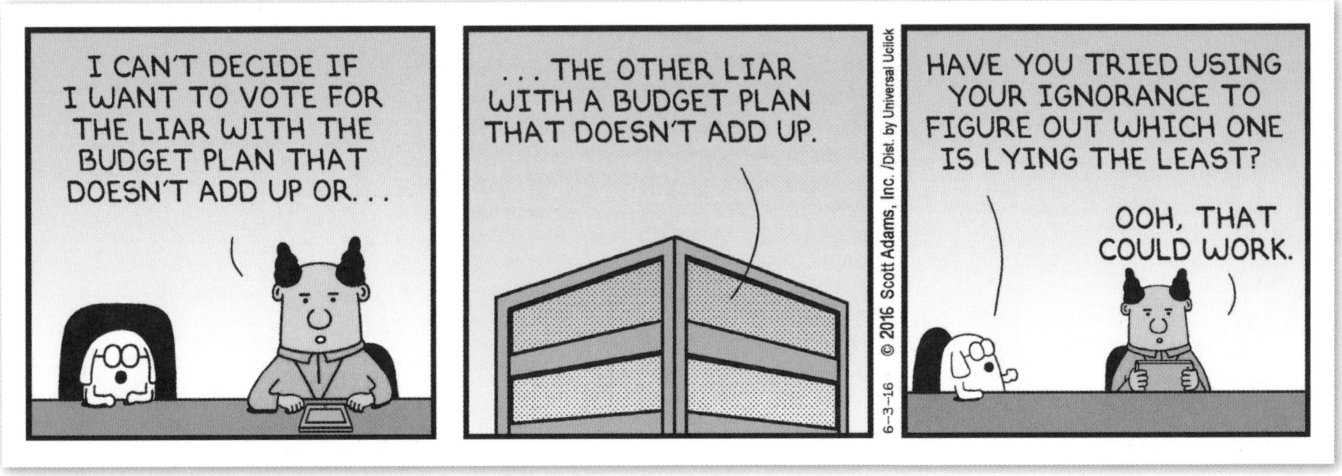
I CAN'T DECIDE IF I WANT TO VOTE FOR THE LIAR WITH THE BUDGET PLAN THAT DOESN'T ADD UP OR. . .
. . . THE OTHER LIAR WITH A BUDGET PLAN THAT DOESN'T ADD UP.
6-3-16 © 2016 Scott Adams, Inc. /Dist. by Universal Uclick
HAVE YOU TRIED USING YOUR IGNORANCE TO FIGURE OUT WHICH ONE IS LYING THE LEAST?
OOH, THAT COULD WORK.

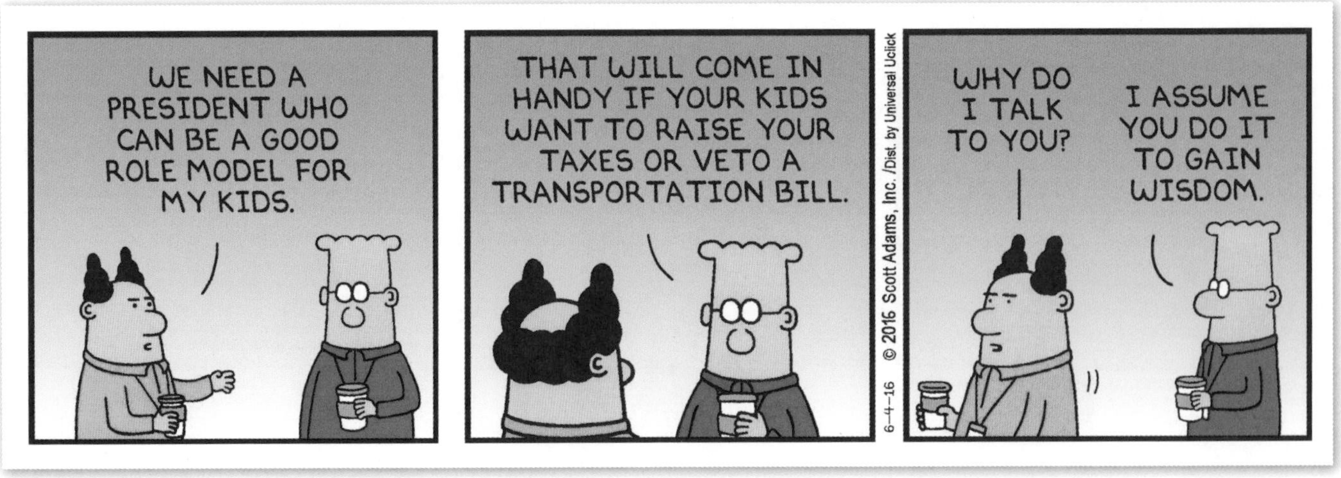
WE NEED A PRESIDENT WHO CAN BE A GOOD ROLE MODEL FOR MY KIDS.
THAT WILL COME IN HANDY IF YOUR KIDS WANT TO RAISE YOUR TAXES OR VETO A TRANSPORTATION BILL.
6-4-16 © 2016 Scott Adams, Inc. /Dist. by Universal Uclick
WHY DO I TALK TO YOU?
I ASSUME YOU DO IT TO GAIN WISDOM.

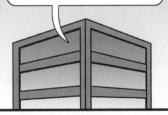

DID YOU SEE THE VIRAL VIDEO OF THE KITTEN RIDING A ZEBRA?
I KNOW WHERE THIS IS HEADING AND I DON'T LIKE IT.
YOU'RE GOING TO SPEND THE NEXT TEN MINUTES LOOKING FOR THAT VIDEO ON YOUR PHONE WHILE WE WAIT.
© 2016 Scott Adams, Inc./Dist. by Universal Uclick
IT WILL ONLY TAKE A SECOND.
AND SO IT BEGINS.
HERE IT IS. NO, WAIT. DANG. WRONG ONE. OKAY, HERE IT IS. OOPS, NO, WRONG ONE.
TEN MINUTES LATER
WHAT DO YOU THINK?
I CAN'T SEE IT BECAUSE YOU KEEP MOVING.
I WOULD LET YOU HOLD IT, BUT I DON'T WANT YOUR GERMS ON MY PHONE.
6-5-16
THERE ARE A LOT OF UNSATISFYING PARTS TO THIS INTERACTION.
NOW MY COFFEE IS COLD.

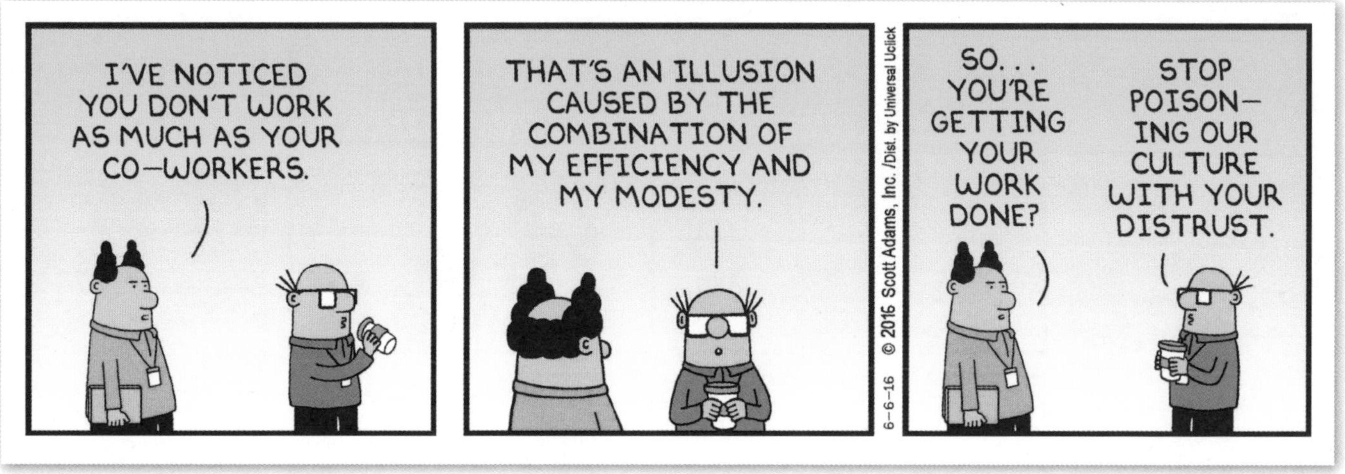
I'VE NOTICED YOU DON'T WORK AS MUCH AS YOUR CO-WORKERS.
THAT'S AN ILLUSION CAUSED BY THE COMBINATION OF MY EFFICIENCY AND MY MODESTY.
6-6-16 © 2016 Scott Adams, Inc. /Dist. by Universal Uclick
SO... YOU'RE GETTING YOUR WORK DONE?
STOP POISON-ING OUR CULTURE WITH YOUR DISTRUST.

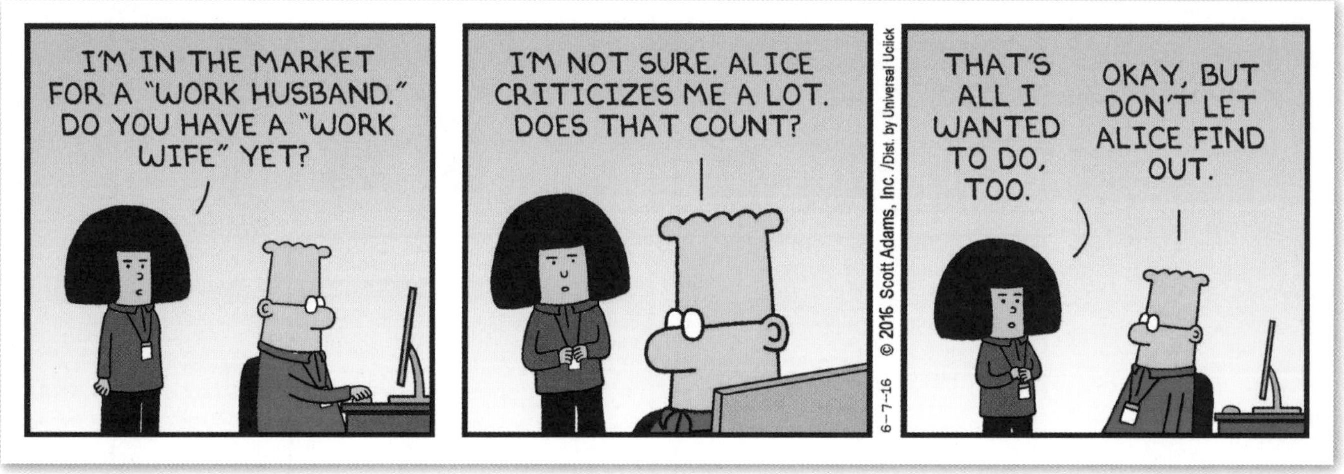
I'M IN THE MARKET FOR A "WORK HUSBAND." DO YOU HAVE A "WORK WIFE" YET?
I'M NOT SURE. ALICE CRITICIZES ME A LOT. DOES THAT COUNT?
6-7-16 © 2016 Scott Adams, Inc. /Dist. by Universal Uclick
THAT'S ALL I WANTED TO DO, TOO.
OKAY, BUT DON'T LET ALICE FIND OUT.

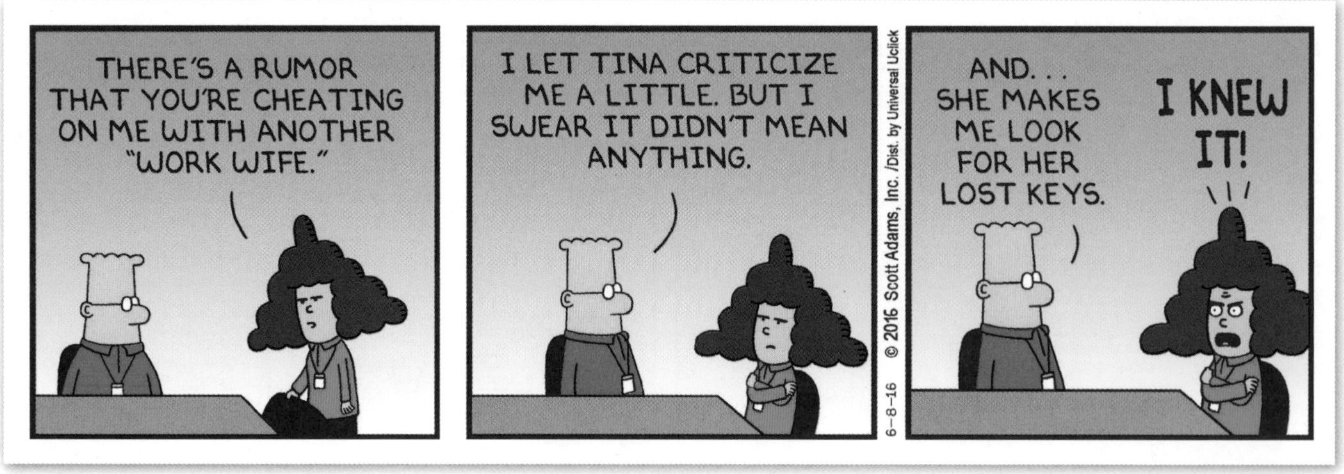
THERE'S A RUMOR THAT YOU'RE CHEATING ON ME WITH ANOTHER "WORK WIFE."
I LET TINA CRITICIZE ME A LITTLE. BUT I SWEAR IT DIDN'T MEAN ANYTHING.
6-8-16 © 2016 Scott Adams, Inc. /Dist. by Universal Uclick
AND... SHE MAKES ME LOOK FOR HER LOST KEYS.
I KNEW IT!

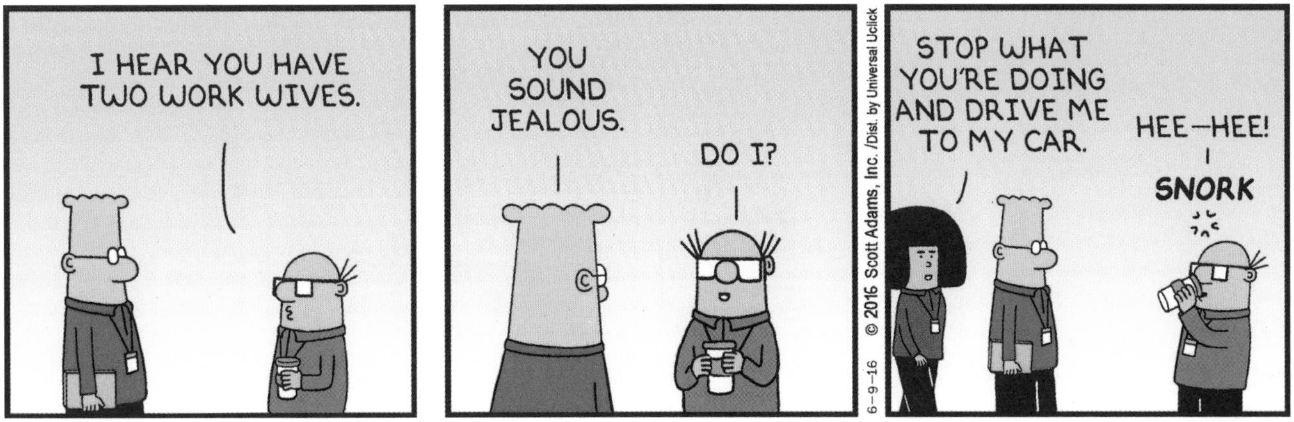
I HEAR YOU HAVE TWO WORK WIVES.
YOU SOUND JEALOUS.
DO I?
STOP WHAT YOU'RE DOING AND DRIVE ME TO MY CAR.
HEE—HEE!
SNORK
© 2016 Scott Adams, Inc. /Dist. by Universal Uclick
6-9-16

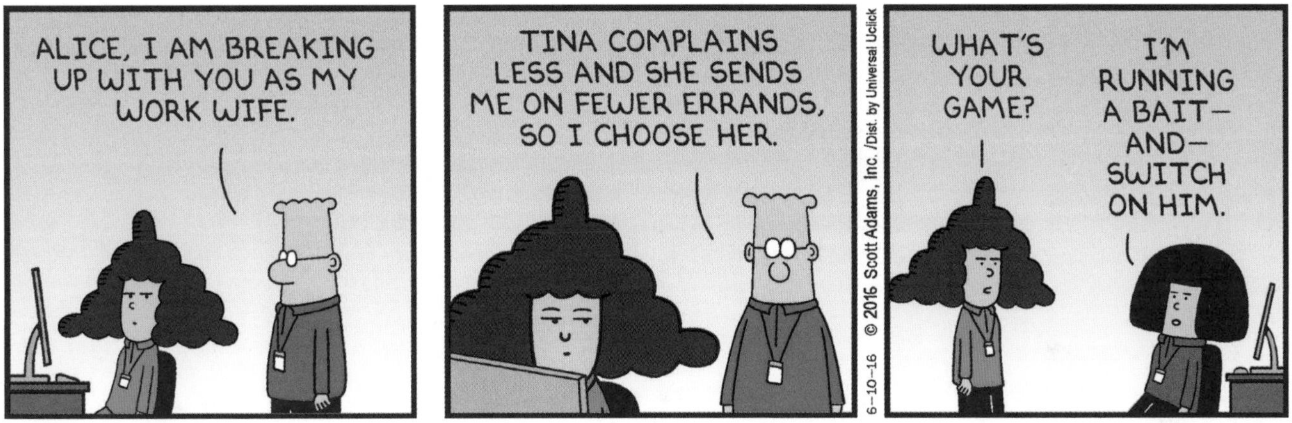
ALICE, I AM BREAKING UP WITH YOU AS MY WORK WIFE.
TINA COMPLAINS LESS AND SHE SENDS ME ON FEWER ERRANDS, SO I CHOOSE HER.
WHAT'S YOUR GAME?
I'M RUNNING A BAIT—AND—SWITCH ON HIM.
© 2016 Scott Adams, Inc. /Dist. by Universal Uclick
6-10-16

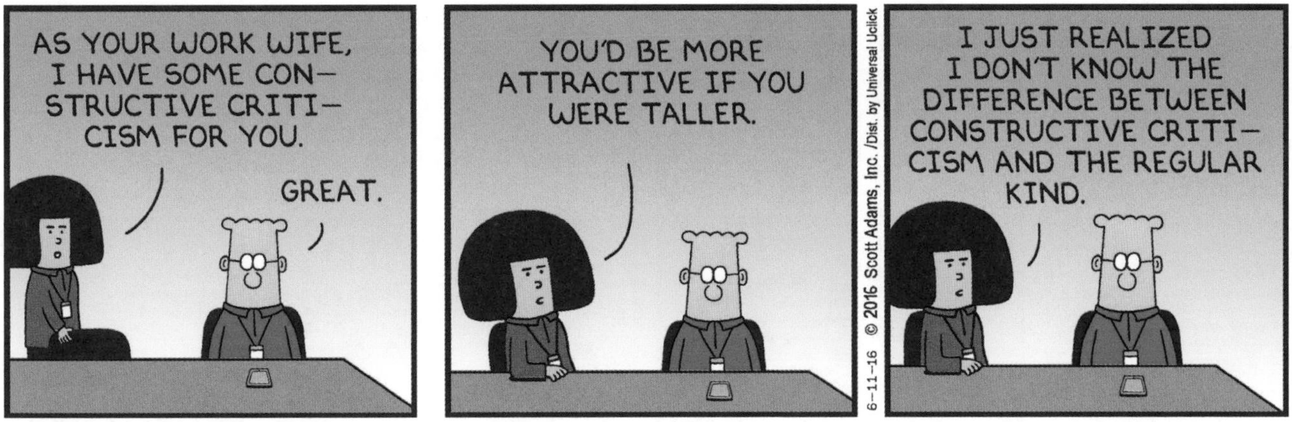
AS YOUR WORK WIFE, I HAVE SOME CON—STRUCTIVE CRITI—CISM FOR YOU.
GREAT.
YOU'D BE MORE ATTRACTIVE IF YOU WERE TALLER.
I JUST REALIZED I DON'T KNOW THE DIFFERENCE BETWEEN CONSTRUCTIVE CRITI—CISM AND THE REGULAR KIND.
© 2016 Scott Adams, Inc. /Dist. by Universal Uclick
6-11-16

I SIMPLIFIED THE USER INTERFACE AS YOU SUGGESTED.
YOU WANTED ONE BUTTON TO DO ELEVEN DIFFERENT FUNCTIONS.
IT WASN'T EASY, BUT I THINK YOU'LL BE PLEASED.
IF YOU WANT TO TURN UP THE VOLUME. . .
YOU HOLD THE BUTTON FOR EXACTLY FIVE SECONDS. . .
THEN DOUBLE-TAP, AND DOUBLE-TAP AGAIN. THEN HOLD FOR EXACTLY SIX SECONDS.
THEN PRESS IT ALL THE WAY DOWN, THEN HALFWAY UP, THEN 27% BACK DOWN. AND HOLD FOR NINE SECONDS.
OR YOU COULD ADMIT THAT YOU DON'T KNOW ANYTHING ABOUT INTERFACE DESIGN.
NEVER!
© 2016 Scott Adams, Inc./Dist. by Universal Uclick
6-12-16

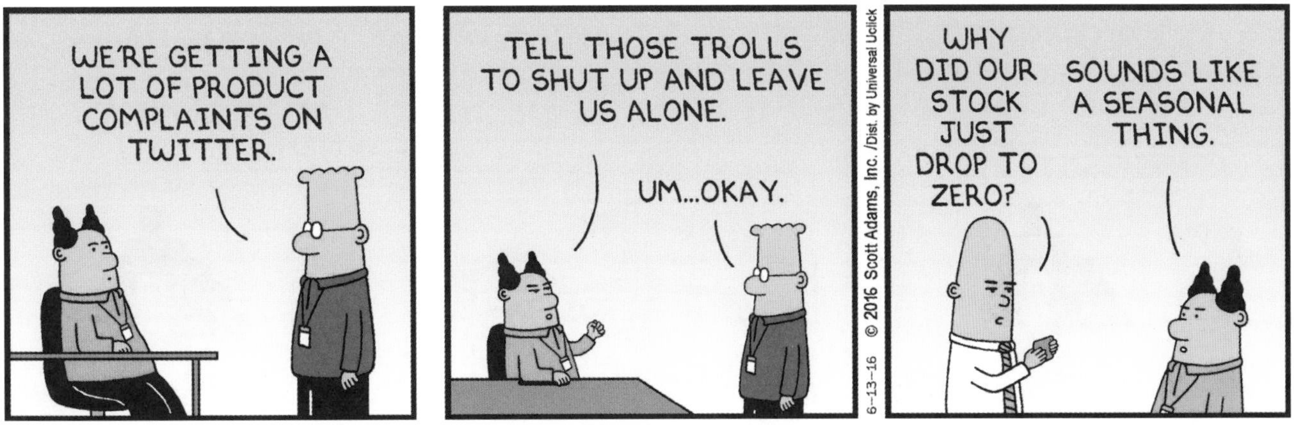
WE'RE GETTING A LOT OF PRODUCT COMPLAINTS ON TWITTER.
TELL THOSE TROLLS TO SHUT UP AND LEAVE US ALONE.
UM...OKAY.
6-13-16 © 2016 Scott Adams, Inc. /Dist. by Universal Uclick
WHY DID OUR STOCK JUST DROP TO ZERO?
SOUNDS LIKE A SEASONAL THING.

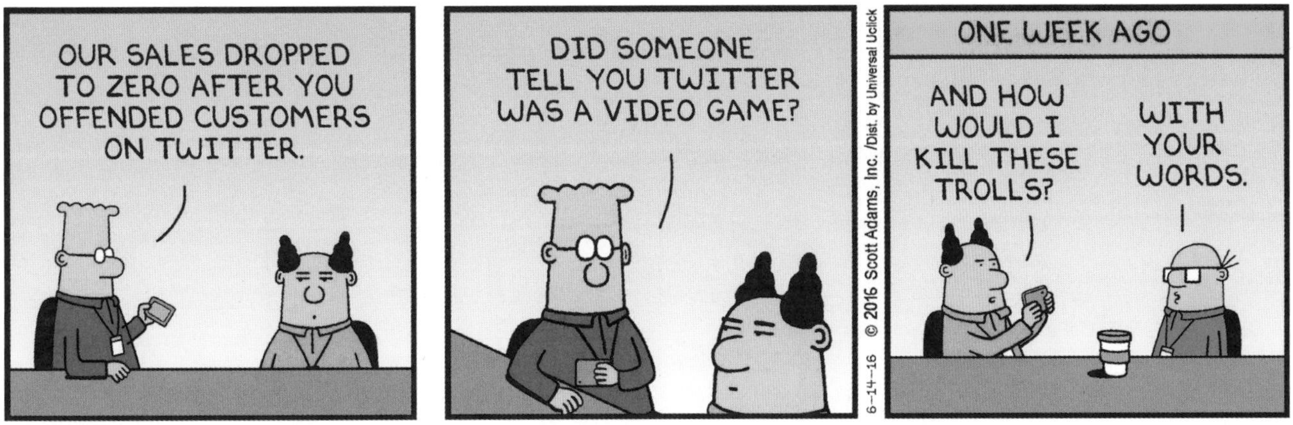
OUR SALES DROPPED TO ZERO AFTER YOU OFFENDED CUSTOMERS ON TWITTER.
DID SOMEONE TELL YOU TWITTER WAS A VIDEO GAME?
6-14-16 © 2016 Scott Adams, Inc. /Dist. by Universal Uclick
ONE WEEK AGO
AND HOW WOULD I KILL THESE TROLLS?
WITH YOUR WORDS.

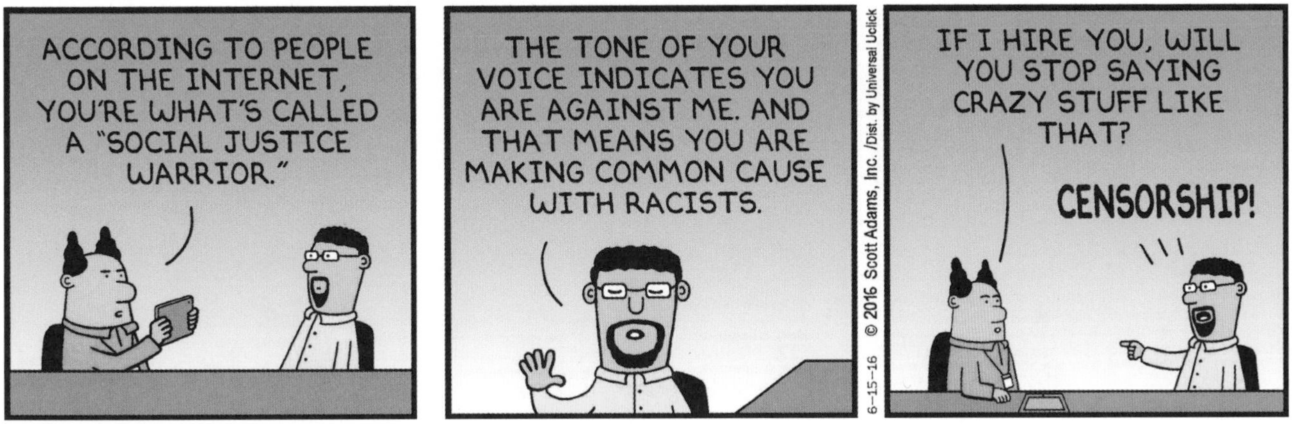
ACCORDING TO PEOPLE ON THE INTERNET, YOU'RE WHAT'S CALLED A "SOCIAL JUSTICE WARRIOR."
THE TONE OF YOUR VOICE INDICATES YOU ARE AGAINST ME. AND THAT MEANS YOU ARE MAKING COMMON CAUSE WITH RACISTS.
6-15-16 © 2016 Scott Adams, Inc. /Dist. by Universal Uclick
IF I HIRE YOU, WILL YOU STOP SAYING CRAZY STUFF LIKE THAT?
CENSORSHIP!

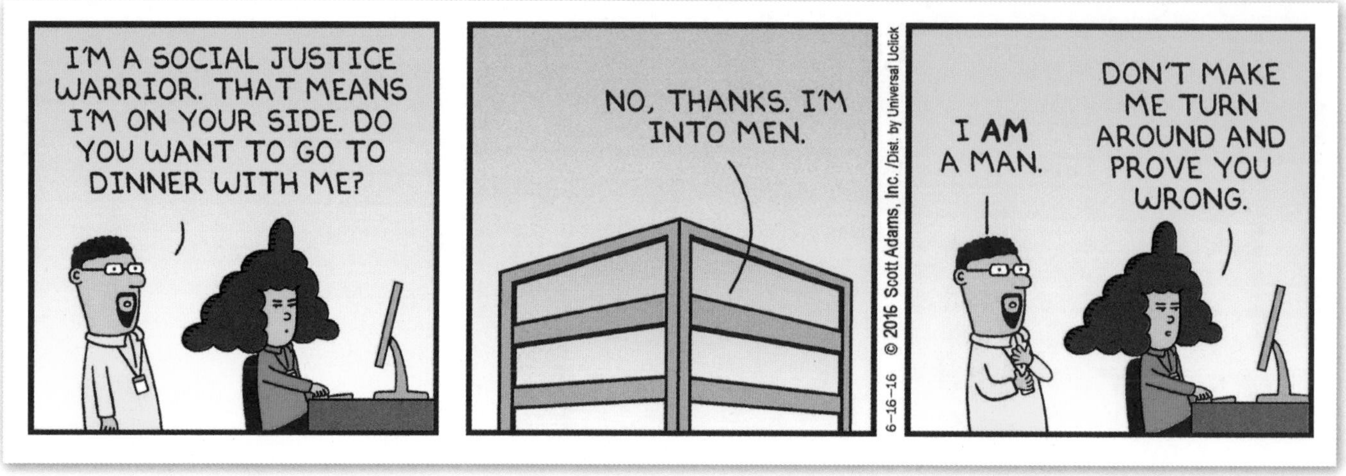
I'M A SOCIAL JUSTICE WARRIOR. THAT MEANS I'M ON YOUR SIDE. DO YOU WANT TO GO TO DINNER WITH ME?
NO, THANKS. I'M INTO MEN.
I **AM** A MAN.
DON'T MAKE ME TURN AROUND AND PROVE YOU WRONG.
6-16-16 © 2016 Scott Adams, Inc. /Dist. by Universal Uclick

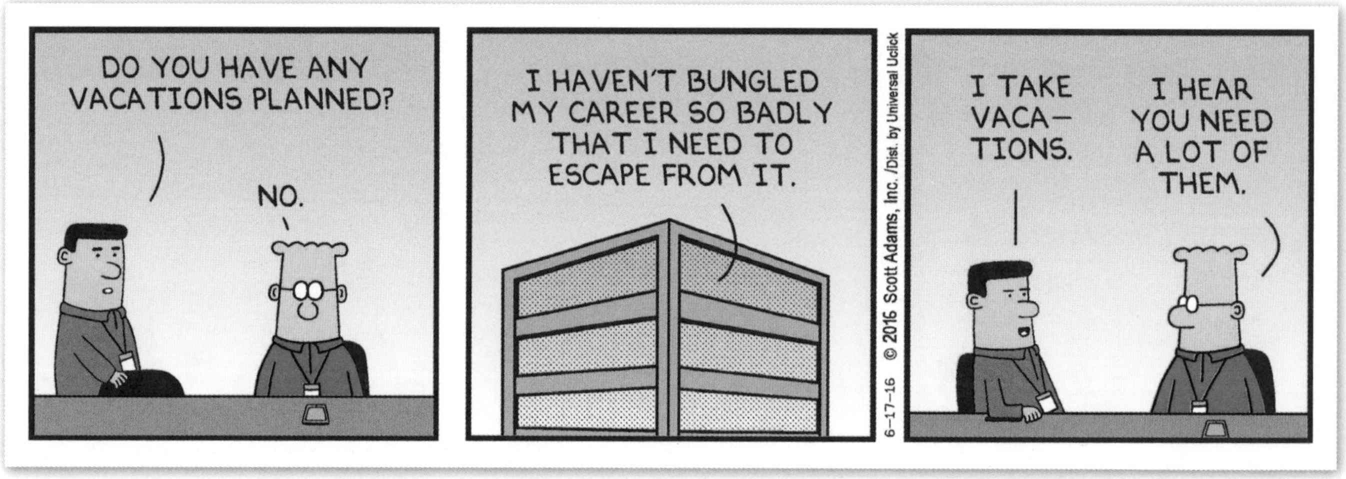
DO YOU HAVE ANY VACATIONS PLANNED?
NO.
I HAVEN'T BUNGLED MY CAREER SO BADLY THAT I NEED TO ESCAPE FROM IT.
I TAKE VACA-TIONS.
I HEAR YOU NEED A LOT OF THEM.
6-17-16 © 2016 Scott Adams, Inc. /Dist. by Universal Uclick

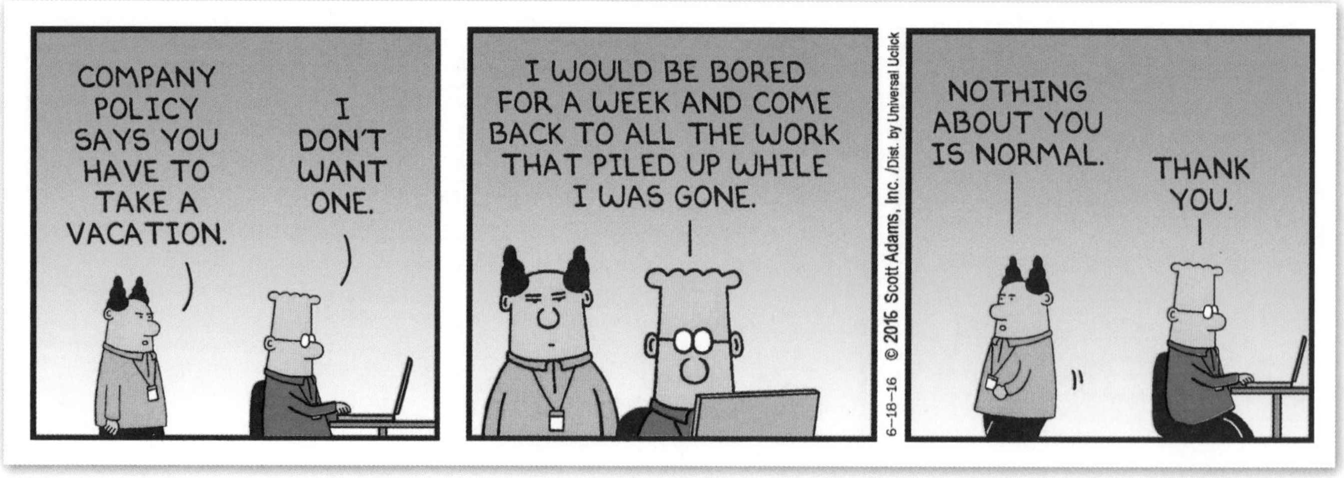
COMPANY POLICY SAYS YOU HAVE TO TAKE A VACATION.
I DON'T WANT ONE.
I WOULD BE BORED FOR A WEEK AND COME BACK TO ALL THE WORK THAT PILED UP WHILE I WAS GONE.
NOTHING ABOUT YOU IS NORMAL.
THANK YOU.
6-18-16 © 2016 Scott Adams, Inc. /Dist. by Universal Uclick

THE ROBOT WILL BE SITTING IN FOR ME WHEN I'M ON VACATION.
YOU CAN'T HAVE A ROBOT IN CHARGE OF HUMANS!
I GOT THIS.
I SEE YOU OWN A MOBILE PHONE.
SO?
THEN YOU ARE ALREADY A SLAVE TO A MACHINE.
NO, I'M NOT!
PING!
YOU CAN PROVE YOU HAVE FREE WILL BY NOT LOOKING AT THAT MESSAGE.
GAAA!!! YOU'RE ALREADY BETTER THAN OUR HUMAN BOSS!
© 2016 Scott Adams, Inc./Dist. by Universal Uclick
6-19-16

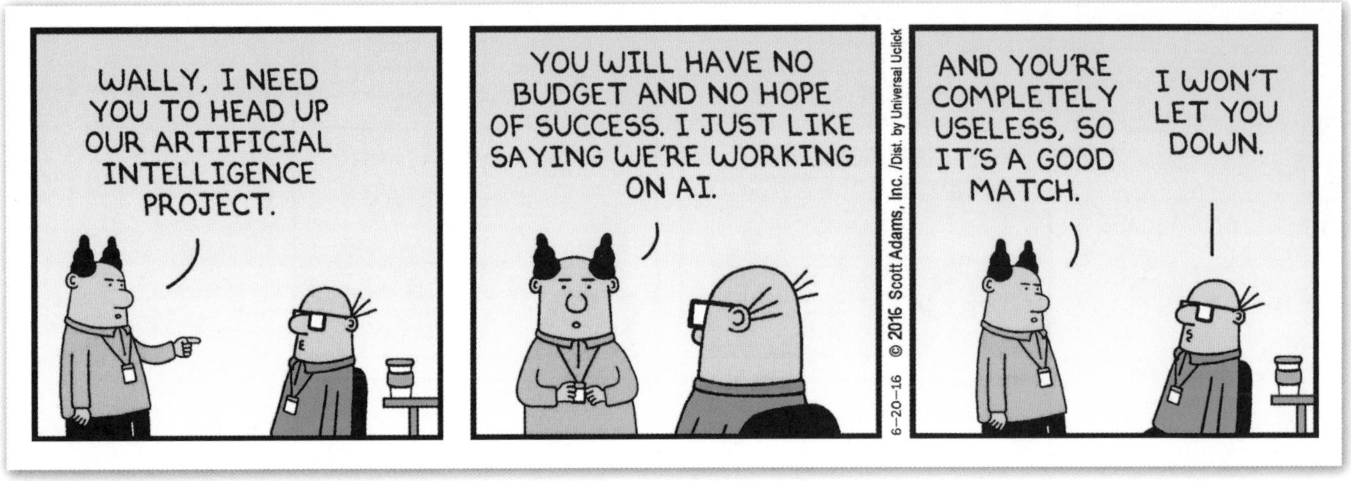
WALLY, I NEED YOU TO HEAD UP OUR ARTIFICIAL INTELLIGENCE PROJECT.
YOU WILL HAVE NO BUDGET AND NO HOPE OF SUCCESS. I JUST LIKE SAYING WE'RE WORKING ON AI.
AND YOU'RE COMPLETELY USELESS, SO IT'S A GOOD MATCH.
I WON'T LET YOU DOWN.
6-20-16 © 2016 Scott Adams, Inc. /Dist. by Universal Uclick

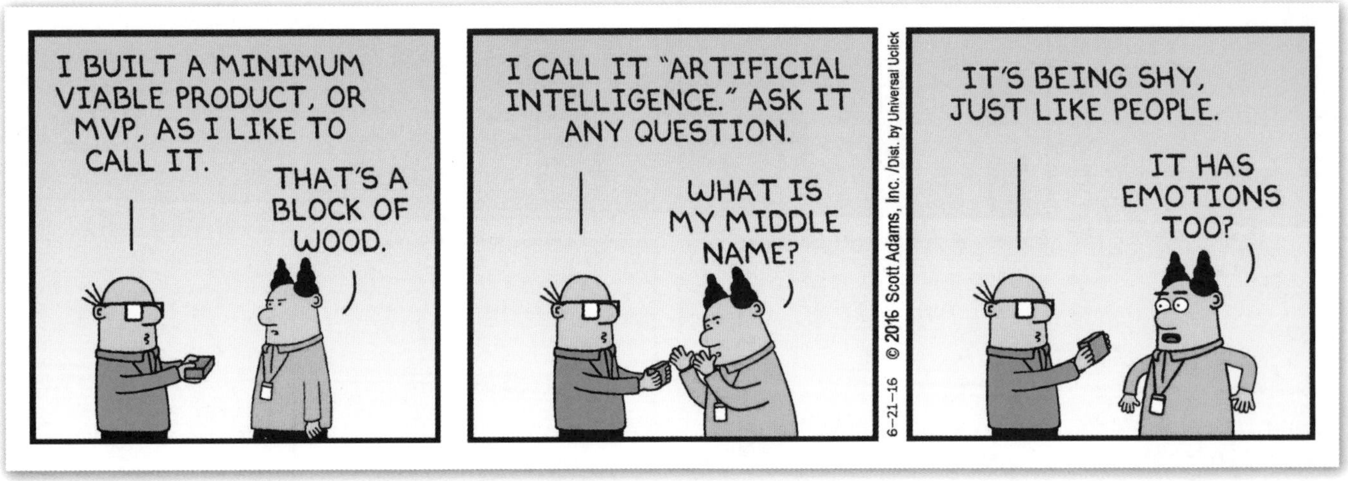
I BUILT A MINIMUM VIABLE PRODUCT, OR MVP, AS I LIKE TO CALL IT.
THAT'S A BLOCK OF WOOD.
I CALL IT "ARTIFICIAL INTELLIGENCE." ASK IT ANY QUESTION.
WHAT IS MY MIDDLE NAME?
IT'S BEING SHY, JUST LIKE PEOPLE.
IT HAS EMOTIONS TOO?
6-21-16 © 2016 Scott Adams, Inc. /Dist. by Universal Uclick

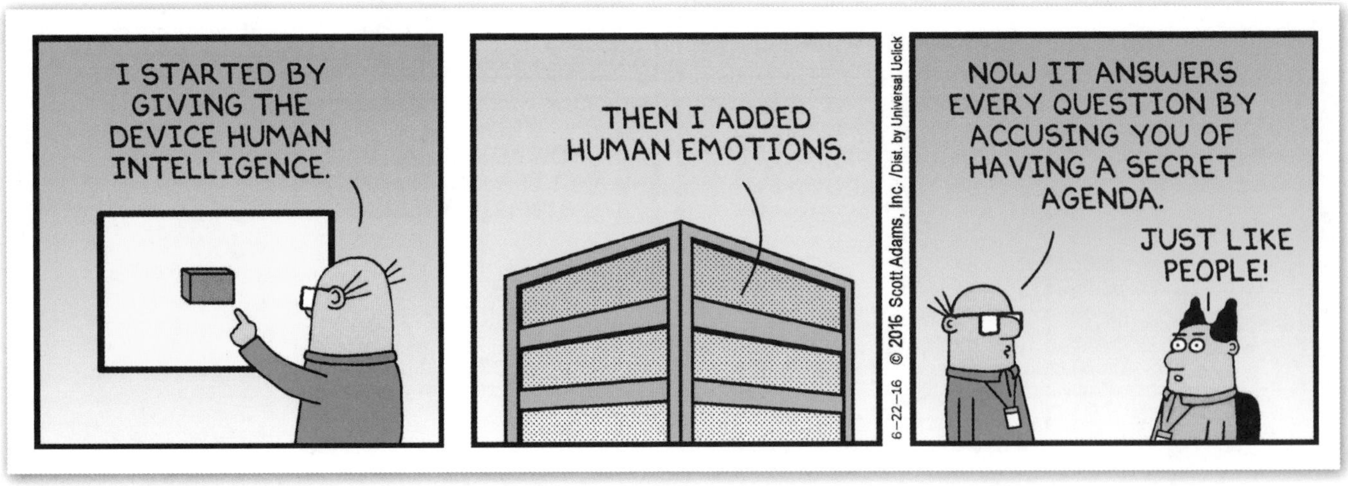
I STARTED BY GIVING THE DEVICE HUMAN INTELLIGENCE.
THEN I ADDED HUMAN EMOTIONS.
NOW IT ANSWERS EVERY QUESTION BY ACCUSING YOU OF HAVING A SECRET AGENDA.
JUST LIKE PEOPLE!
6-22-16 © 2016 Scott Adams, Inc. /Dist. by Universal Uclick

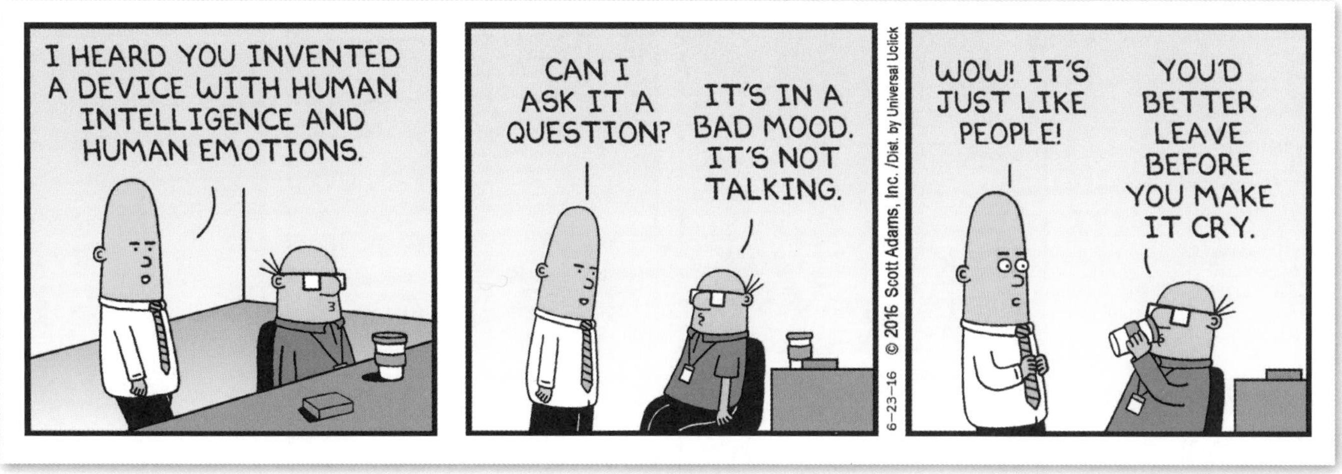
I HEARD YOU INVENTED A DEVICE WITH HUMAN INTELLIGENCE AND HUMAN EMOTIONS.
CAN I ASK IT A QUESTION?
IT'S IN A BAD MOOD. IT'S NOT TALKING.
6-23-16 © 2016 Scott Adams, Inc. /Dist. by Universal Uclick
WOW! IT'S JUST LIKE PEOPLE!
YOU'D BETTER LEAVE BEFORE YOU MAKE IT CRY.

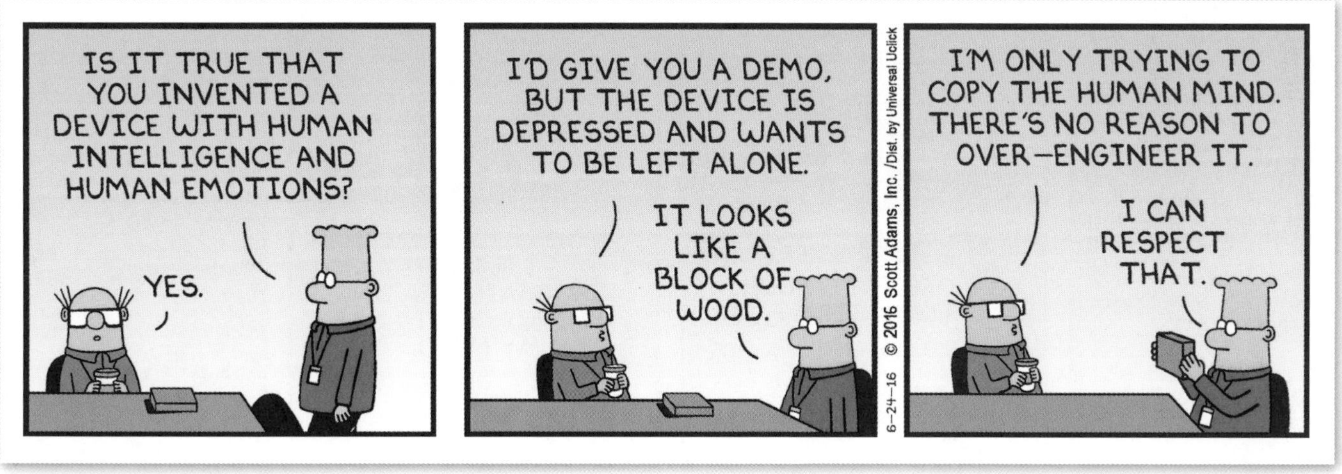
IS IT TRUE THAT YOU INVENTED A DEVICE WITH HUMAN INTELLIGENCE AND HUMAN EMOTIONS?
YES.
I'D GIVE YOU A DEMO, BUT THE DEVICE IS DEPRESSED AND WANTS TO BE LEFT ALONE.
IT LOOKS LIKE A BLOCK OF WOOD.
6-24-16 © 2016 Scott Adams, Inc. /Dist. by Universal Uclick
I'M ONLY TRYING TO COPY THE HUMAN MIND. THERE'S NO REASON TO OVER-ENGINEER IT.
I CAN RESPECT THAT.

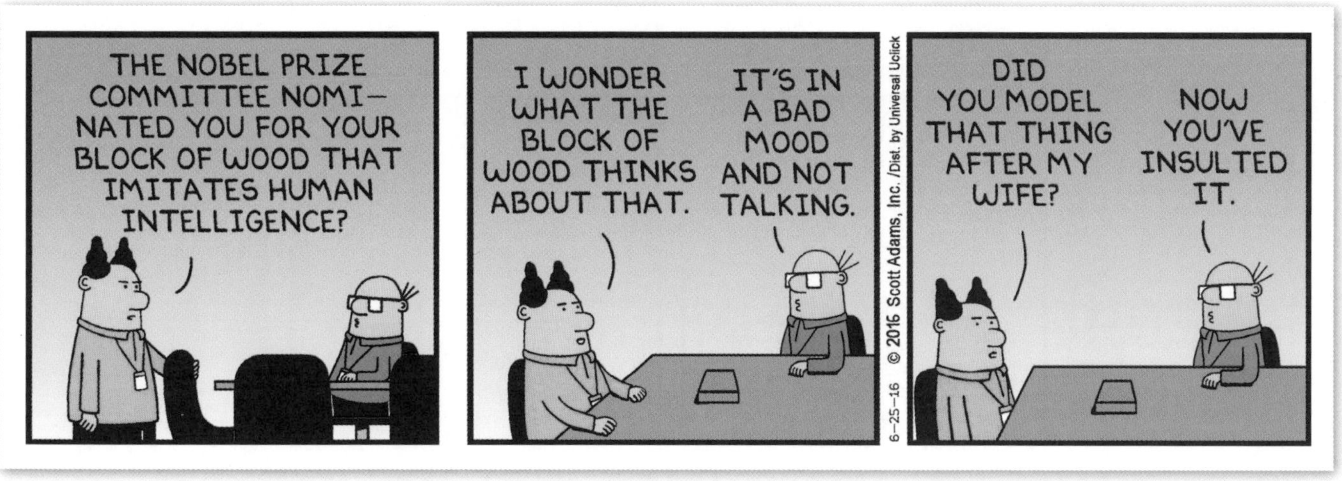
THE NOBEL PRIZE COMMITTEE NOMI-NATED YOU FOR YOUR BLOCK OF WOOD THAT IMITATES HUMAN INTELLIGENCE?
I WONDER WHAT THE BLOCK OF WOOD THINKS ABOUT THAT.
IT'S IN A BAD MOOD AND NOT TALKING.
6-25-16 © 2016 Scott Adams, Inc. /Dist. by Universal Uclick
DID YOU MODEL THAT THING AFTER MY WIFE?
NOW YOU'VE INSULTED IT.

DO YOU HAVE ANY LONG-TERM GOALS?
JUST DEATH.
DEATH ISN'T A GOAL.
IT'S THE BEST KIND.
THIS WAY, I CAN GO OUT AS A WINNER.
WITH MY LAST BREATH, I PLAN TO DO A FIST PUMP AND YELL, "I DID IT!"
WHAT'S **YOUR** LONG-TERM PLAN?
I PLAN TO USE BRAIN IMAGING TECHNOLOGY TO MAP MY MIND.
THEN I'LL CREATE A DIGITAL COPY OF MYSELF TO LIVE FOREVER IN A SOFT-WARE SIMULATION.
UNLESS I ALREADY DID.
GIVE YOURSELF A FIST PUMP, JUST IN CASE.
© 2016 Scott Adams, Inc./Dist. by Universal Uclick
6-26-16

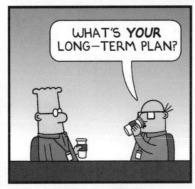

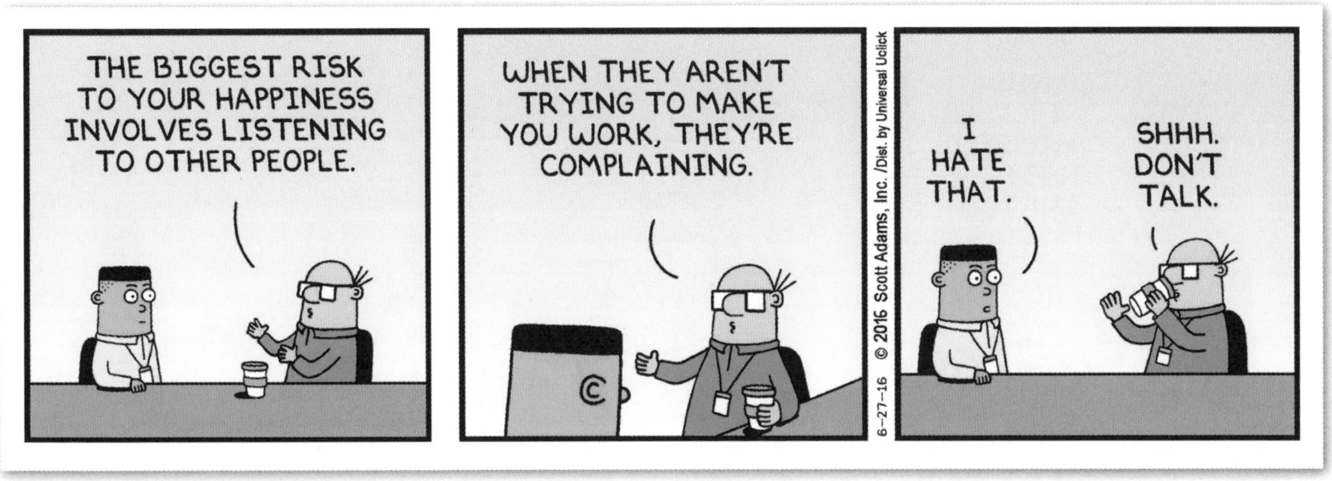
THE BIGGEST RISK TO YOUR HAPPINESS INVOLVES LISTENING TO OTHER PEOPLE.
WHEN THEY AREN'T TRYING TO MAKE YOU WORK, THEY'RE COMPLAINING.
6-27-16 © 2016 Scott Adams, Inc. /Dist. by Universal Uclick
I HATE THAT.
SHHH. DON'T TALK.

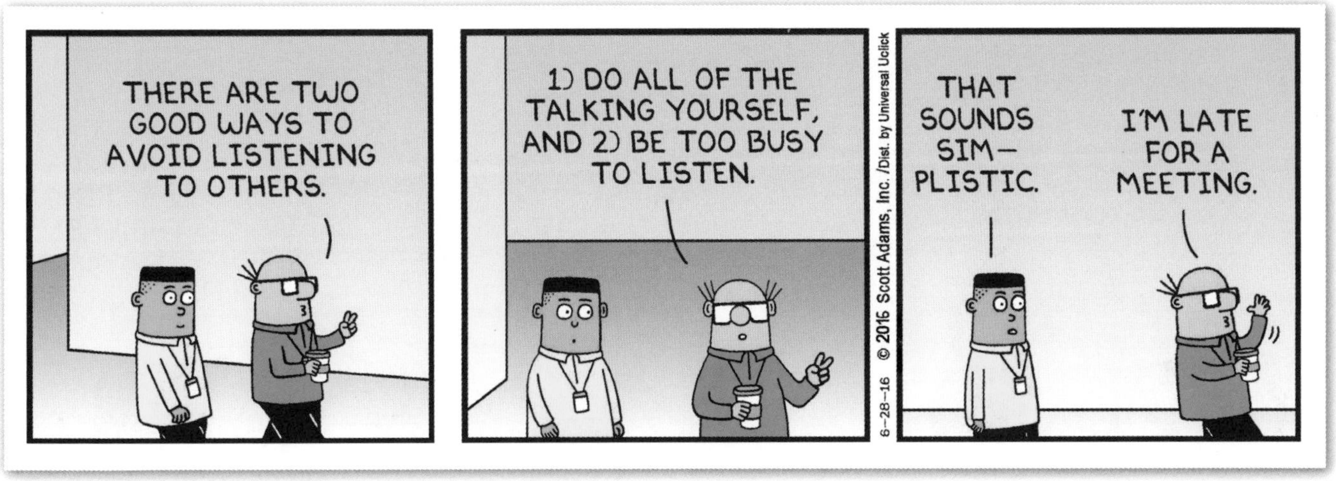
THERE ARE TWO GOOD WAYS TO AVOID LISTENING TO OTHERS.
1) DO ALL OF THE TALKING YOURSELF, AND 2) BE TOO BUSY TO LISTEN.
6-28-16 © 2016 Scott Adams, Inc. /Dist. by Universal Uclick
THAT SOUNDS SIM-PLISTIC.
I'M LATE FOR A MEETING.

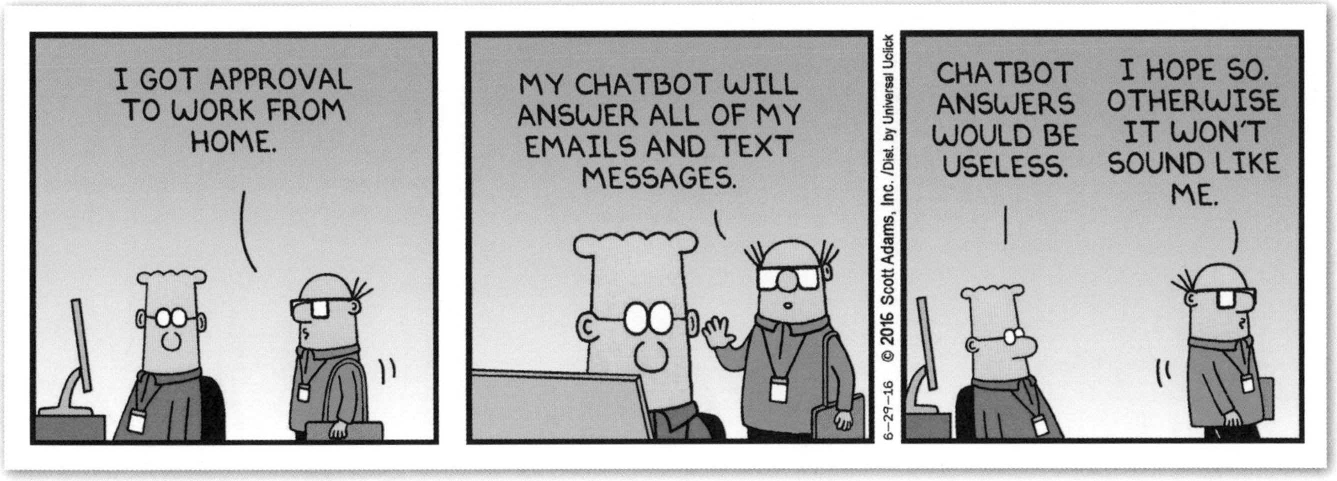
I GOT APPROVAL TO WORK FROM HOME.
MY CHATBOT WILL ANSWER ALL OF MY EMAILS AND TEXT MESSAGES.
6-29-16 © 2016 Scott Adams, Inc. /Dist. by Universal Uclick
CHATBOT ANSWERS WOULD BE USELESS.
I HOPE SO. OTHERWISE IT WON'T SOUND LIKE ME.

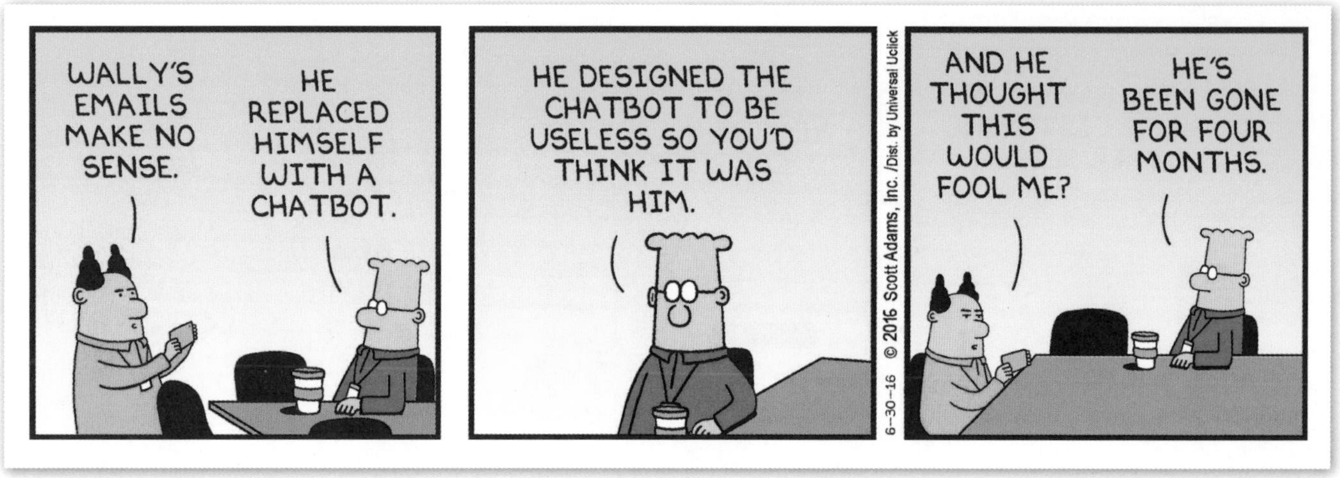
WALLY'S EMAILS MAKE NO SENSE.
HE REPLACED HIMSELF WITH A CHATBOT.
HE DESIGNED THE CHATBOT TO BE USELESS SO YOU'D THINK IT WAS HIM.
6-30-16 © 2016 Scott Adams, Inc. /Dist. by Universal Uclick
AND HE THOUGHT THIS WOULD FOOL ME?
HE'S BEEN GONE FOR FOUR MONTHS.

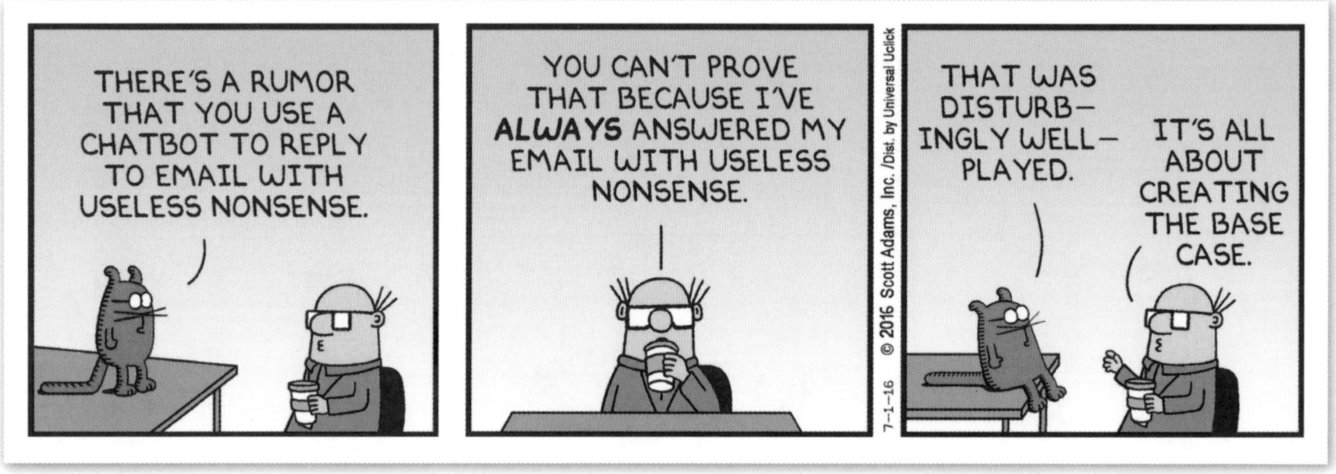
THERE'S A RUMOR THAT YOU USE A CHATBOT TO REPLY TO EMAIL WITH USELESS NONSENSE.
YOU CAN'T PROVE THAT BECAUSE I'VE **ALWAYS** ANSWERED MY EMAIL WITH USELESS NONSENSE.
7-1-16 © 2016 Scott Adams, Inc. /Dist. by Universal Uclick
THAT WAS DISTURB-INGLY WELL-PLAYED.
IT'S ALL ABOUT CREATING THE BASE CASE.

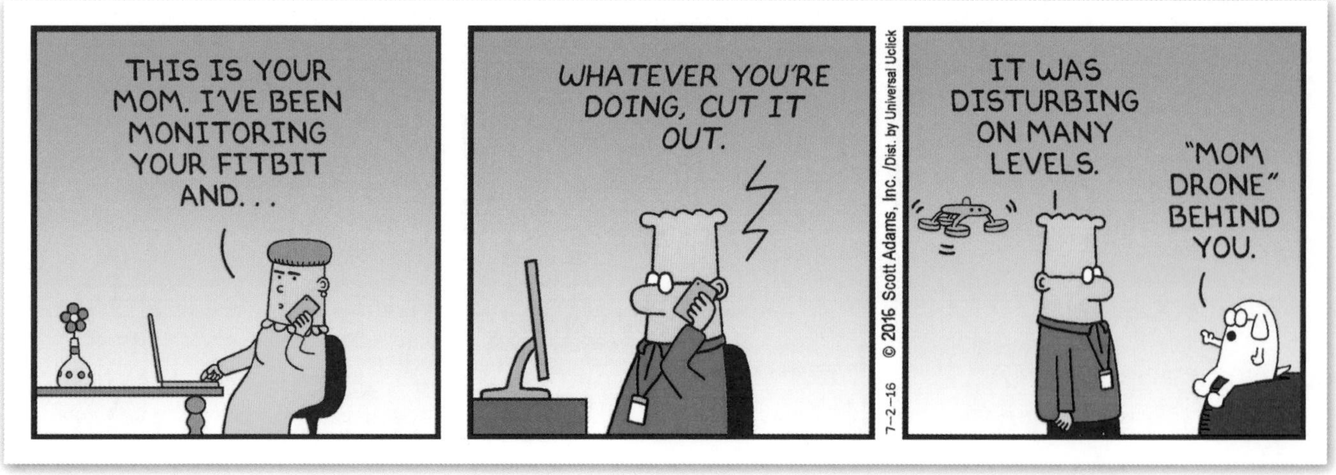
THIS IS YOUR MOM. I'VE BEEN MONITORING YOUR FITBIT AND. . .
WHATEVER YOU'RE DOING, CUT IT OUT.
7-2-16 © 2016 Scott Adams, Inc. /Dist. by Universal Uclick
IT WAS DISTURBING ON MANY LEVELS.
"MOM DRONE" BEHIND YOU.

SORRY I'M LATE. TRAFFIC WAS TERRIBLE.
ISN'T THE TRAFFIC FROM YOUR HOUSE ALWAYS TERRIBLE AT THIS TIME OF DAY?
EXACTLY! THAT'S WHY I'M LATE EVERY DAY.
DO YOU SEE ANY WAY YOU COULD FIX THAT?
I CAN'T CONTROL THE TRAFFIC.
YOU COULD LEAVE EARLIER.
THEN I WOULDN'T GET ENOUGH SLEEP.
YOU COULD GO TO BED EARLIER.
THEN I WOULDN'T HAVE TIME TO WATCH NETFLIX UNTIL TWO IN THE MORNING.
DO YOU WANT ME TO HATE MY LIFE?
I DIDN'T UNTIL NOW.
© 2016 Scott Adams, Inc./Dist. by Universal Uclick
7-3-16

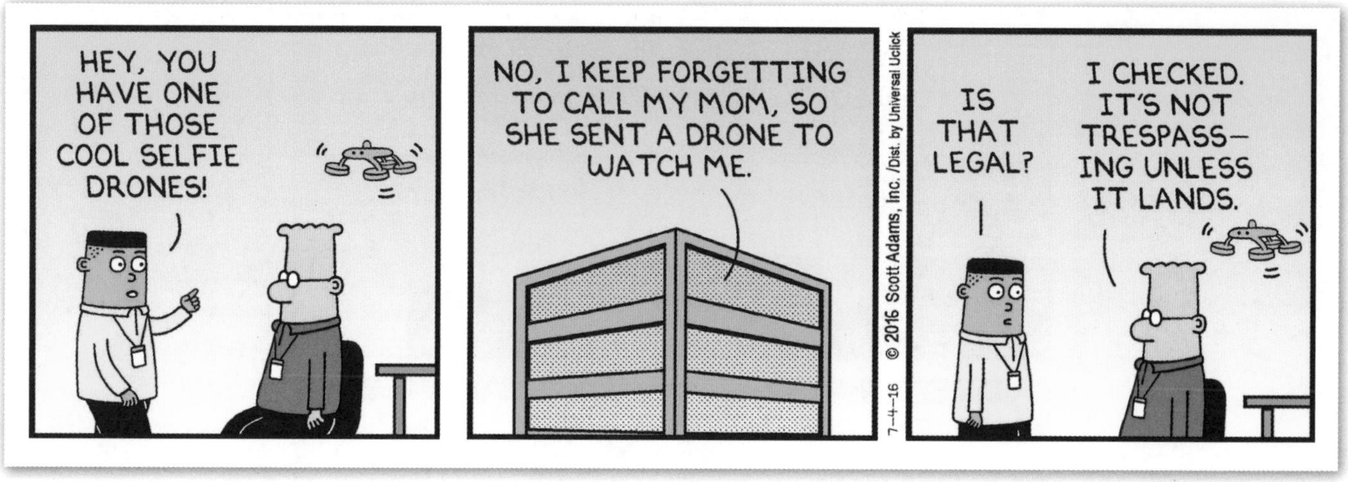
HEY, YOU HAVE ONE OF THOSE COOL SELFIE DRONES!
NO, I KEEP FORGETTING TO CALL MY MOM, SO SHE SENT A DRONE TO WATCH ME.
7-4-16 © 2016 Scott Adams, Inc. /Dist. by Universal Uclick
IS THAT LEGAL?
I CHECKED. IT'S NOT TRESPASS-ING UNLESS IT LANDS.

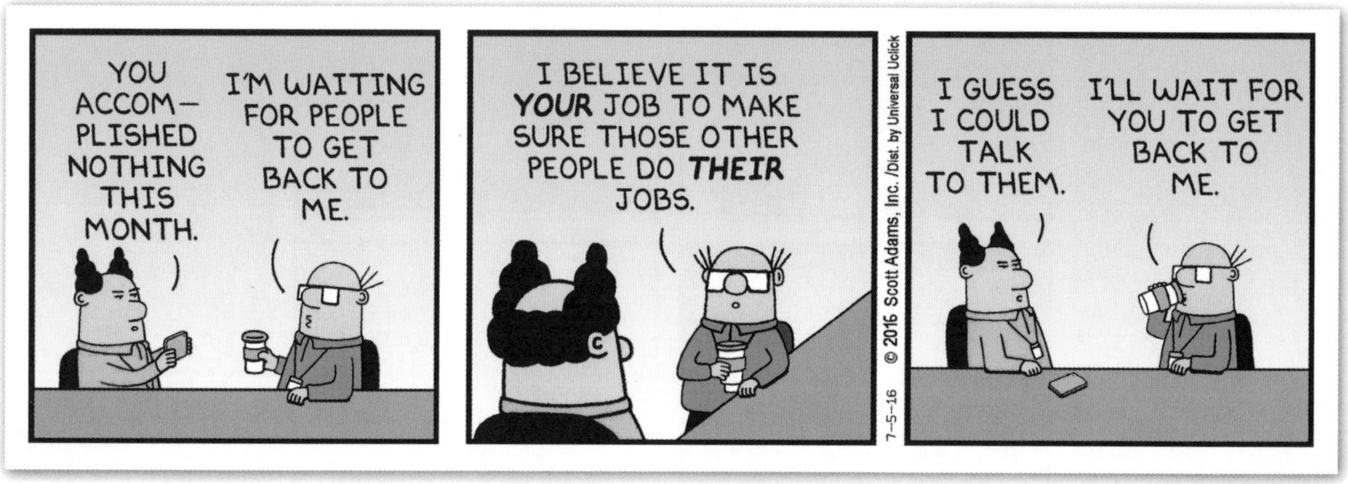
YOU ACCOM-PLISHED NOTHING THIS MONTH.
I'M WAITING FOR PEOPLE TO GET BACK TO ME.
I BELIEVE IT IS ***YOUR*** JOB TO MAKE SURE THOSE OTHER PEOPLE DO ***THEIR*** JOBS.
7-5-16 © 2016 Scott Adams, Inc. /Dist. by Universal Uclick
I GUESS I COULD TALK TO THEM.
I'LL WAIT FOR YOU TO GET BACK TO ME.

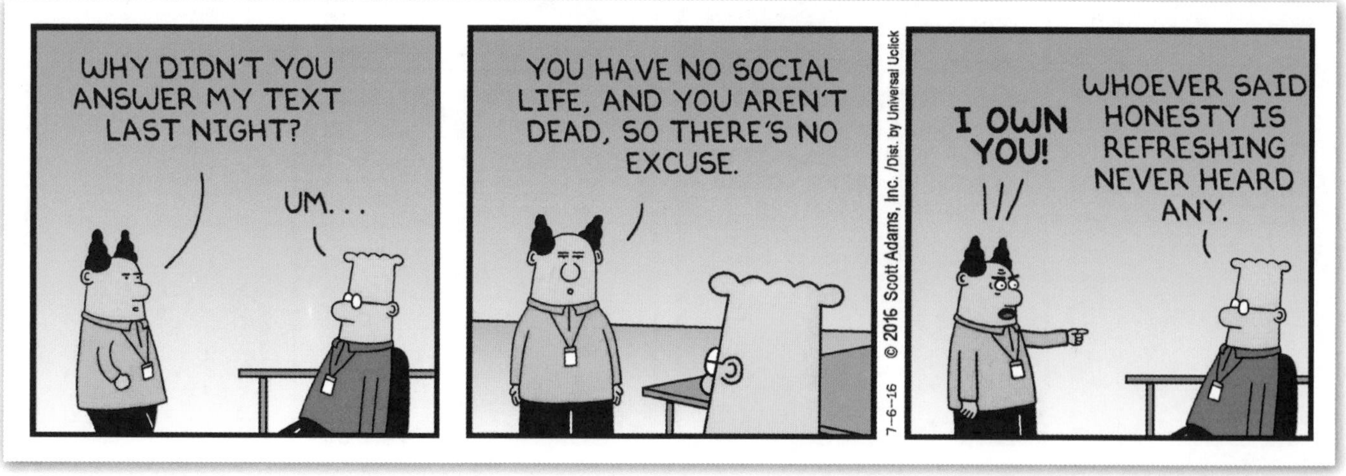
WHY DIDN'T YOU ANSWER MY TEXT LAST NIGHT?
UM. . .
YOU HAVE NO SOCIAL LIFE, AND YOU AREN'T DEAD, SO THERE'S NO EXCUSE.
7-6-16 © 2016 Scott Adams, Inc. /Dist. by Universal Uclick
I OWN YOU!
WHOEVER SAID HONESTY IS REFRESHING NEVER HEARD ANY.

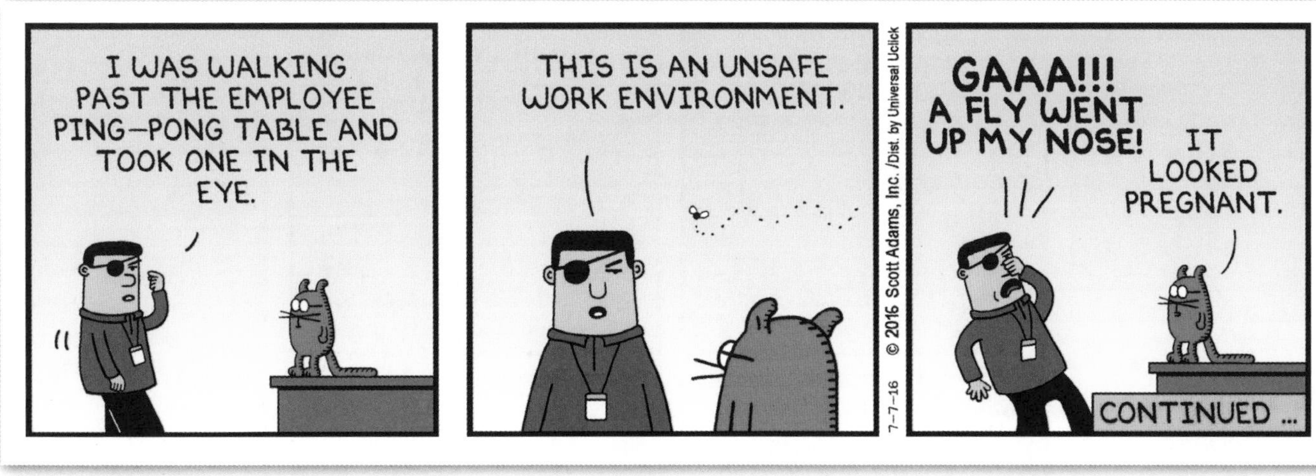
I WAS WALKING PAST THE EMPLOYEE PING-PONG TABLE AND TOOK ONE IN THE EYE.
THIS IS AN UNSAFE WORK ENVIRONMENT.
GAAA!!! A FLY WENT UP MY NOSE!
IT LOOKED PREGNANT.
CONTINUED ...
7-7-16 © 2016 Scott Adams, Inc. /Dist. by Universal Uclick

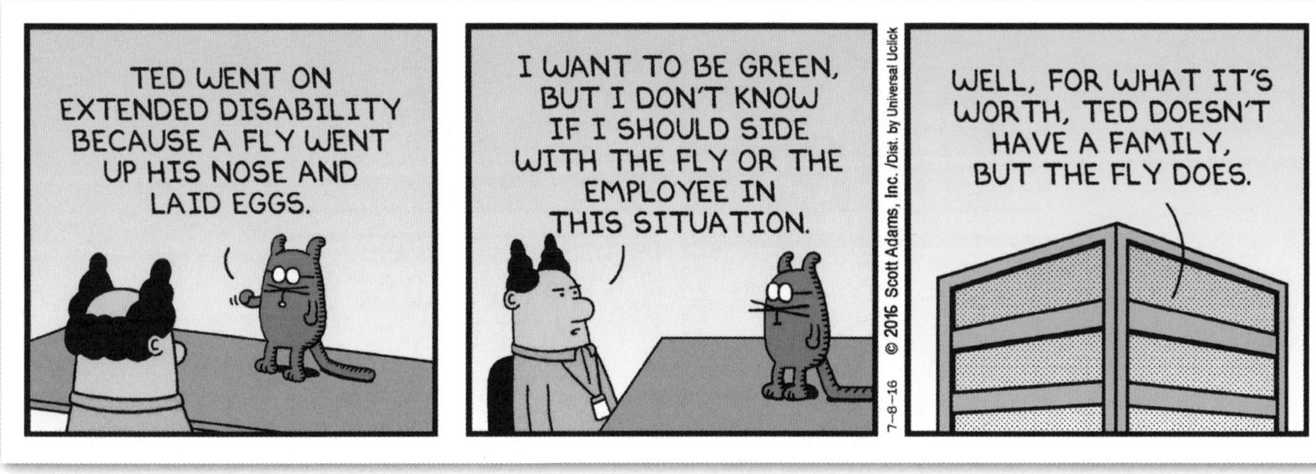
TED WENT ON EXTENDED DISABILITY BECAUSE A FLY WENT UP HIS NOSE AND LAID EGGS.
I WANT TO BE GREEN, BUT I DON'T KNOW IF I SHOULD SIDE WITH THE FLY OR THE EMPLOYEE IN THIS SITUATION.
WELL, FOR WHAT IT'S WORTH, TED DOESN'T HAVE A FAMILY, BUT THE FLY DOES.
7-8-16 © 2016 Scott Adams, Inc. /Dist. by Universal Uclick

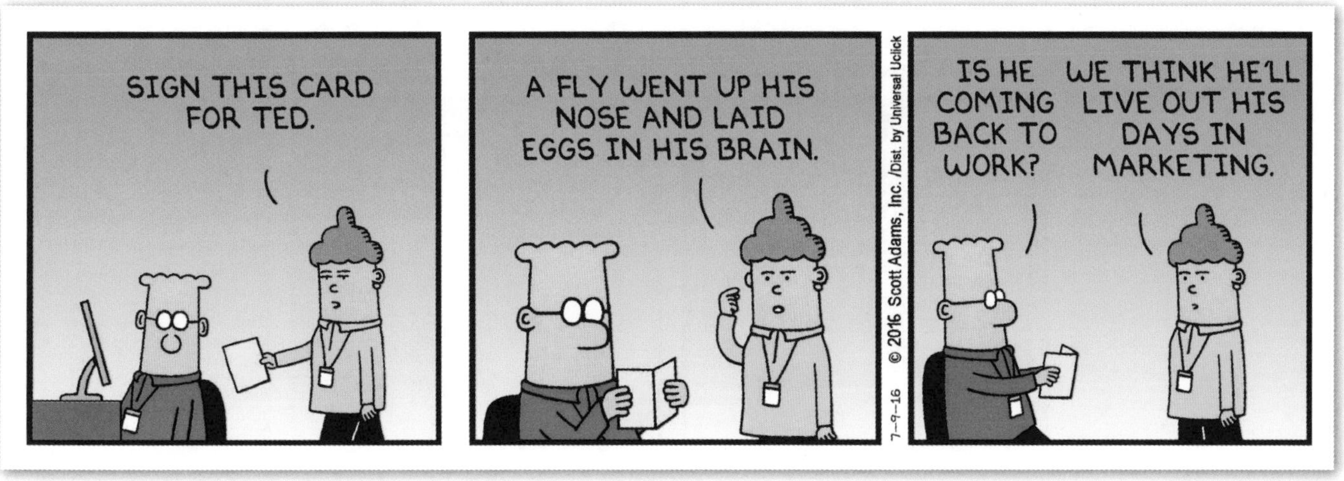
SIGN THIS CARD FOR TED.
A FLY WENT UP HIS NOSE AND LAID EGGS IN HIS BRAIN.
IS HE COMING BACK TO WORK?
WE THINK HE'LL LIVE OUT HIS DAYS IN MARKETING.
7-9-16 © 2016 Scott Adams, Inc. /Dist. by Universal Uclick

I HAVE TOO MUCH WORK, AND IT'S STRESSING ME OUT.
I'VE BEEN READING ABOUT THIS SORT OF SITUATION.
TRY WRITING DOWN ALL THE THINGS THAT MAKE YOU FEEL GRATEFUL.
THAT WOULD BE MORE WORK!
FOR YOUR ANGER ISSUES, TRY KEEPING A JOURNAL OF ALL THE TIMES YOU LOSE YOUR TEMPER.
THAT WOULD BE MORE WORK!
HAS ANYONE EVER TAKEN YOUR ADVICE?
DO YOU KNOW THE GUY IN MARKETING WITH THE EYE PATCH?
HE FOLLOWED YOUR ADVICE?
HALF OF IT.
© 2016 Scott Adams, Inc./Dist. by Universal Uclick
7-10-16

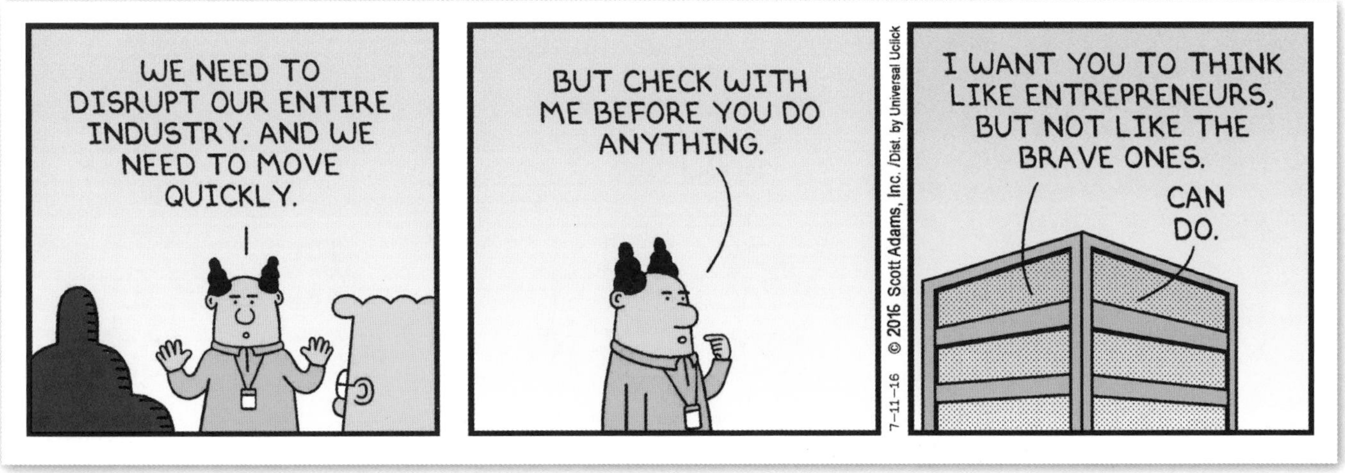
WE NEED TO DISRUPT OUR ENTIRE INDUSTRY. AND WE NEED TO MOVE QUICKLY.
BUT CHECK WITH ME BEFORE YOU DO ANYTHING.
I WANT YOU TO THINK LIKE ENTREPRENEURS, BUT NOT LIKE THE BRAVE ONES.
CAN DO.
7-11-16 © 2016 Scott Adams, Inc. /Dist. by Universal Uclick

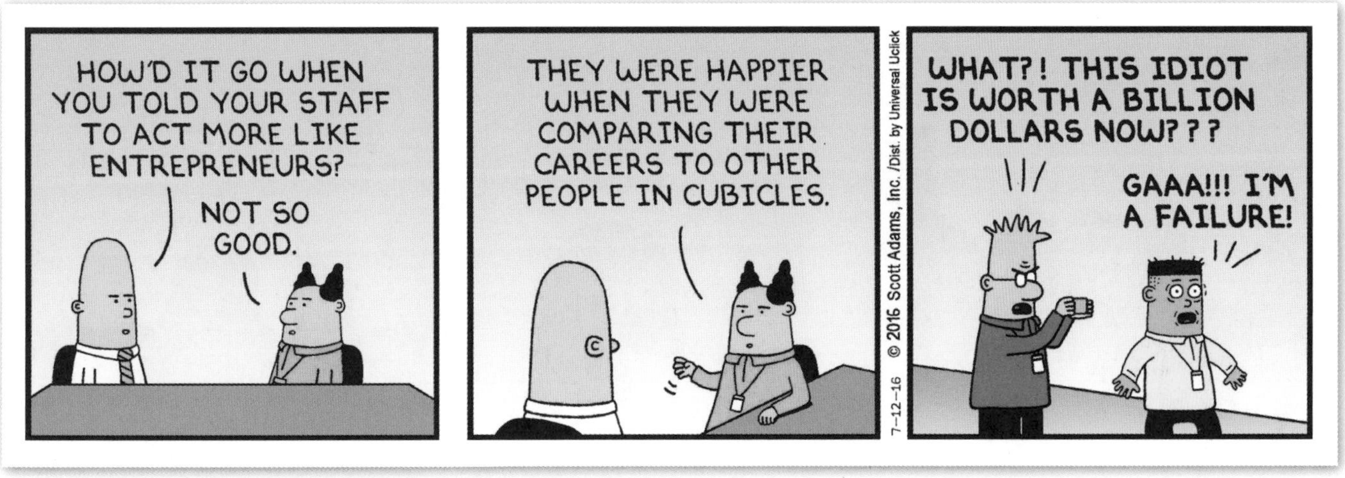
HOW'D IT GO WHEN YOU TOLD YOUR STAFF TO ACT MORE LIKE ENTREPRENEURS?
NOT SO GOOD.
THEY WERE HAPPIER WHEN THEY WERE COMPARING THEIR CAREERS TO OTHER PEOPLE IN CUBICLES.
WHAT?! THIS IDIOT IS WORTH A BILLION DOLLARS NOW???
GAAA!!! I'M A FAILURE!
7-12-16 © 2016 Scott Adams, Inc. /Dist. by Universal Uclick

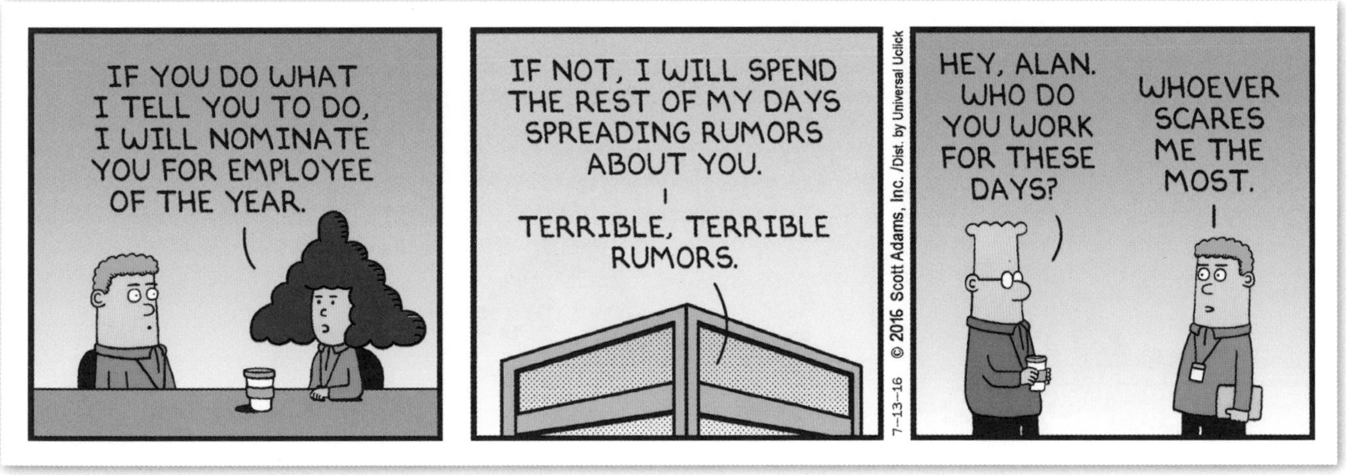
IF YOU DO WHAT I TELL YOU TO DO, I WILL NOMINATE YOU FOR EMPLOYEE OF THE YEAR.
IF NOT, I WILL SPEND THE REST OF MY DAYS SPREADING RUMORS ABOUT YOU.
TERRIBLE, TERRIBLE RUMORS.
HEY, ALAN. WHO DO YOU WORK FOR THESE DAYS?
WHOEVER SCARES ME THE MOST.
7-13-16 © 2016 Scott Adams, Inc. /Dist. by Universal Uclick

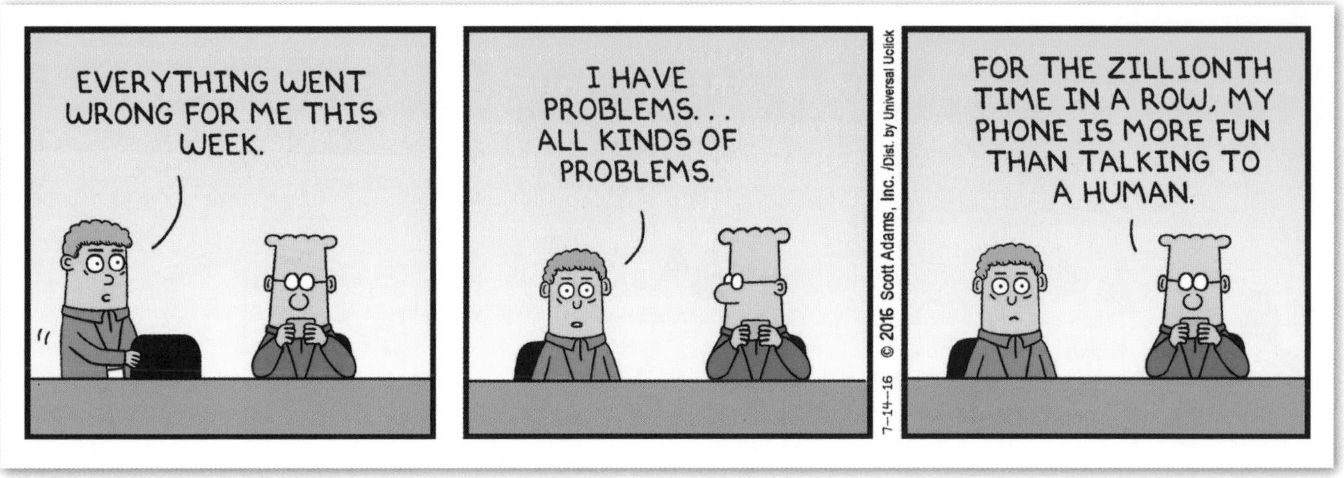
EVERYTHING WENT WRONG FOR ME THIS WEEK.
I HAVE PROBLEMS. . . ALL KINDS OF PROBLEMS.
FOR THE ZILLIONTH TIME IN A ROW, MY PHONE IS MORE FUN THAN TALKING TO A HUMAN.
7-14-16 © 2016 Scott Adams, Inc. /Dist. by Universal Uclick

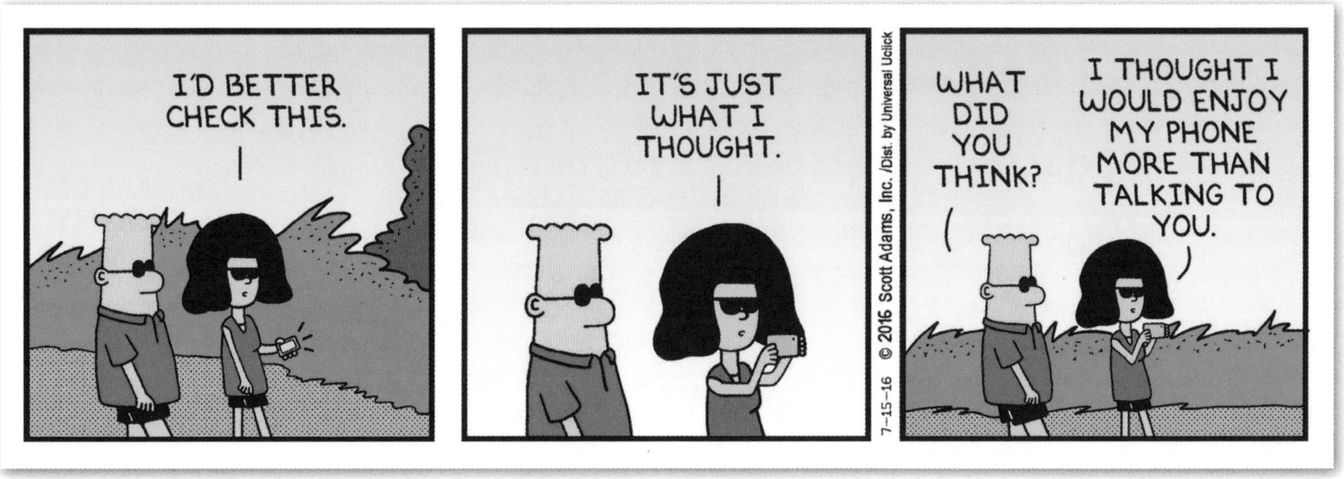
I'D BETTER CHECK THIS.
IT'S JUST WHAT I THOUGHT.
WHAT DID YOU THINK?
I THOUGHT I WOULD ENJOY MY PHONE MORE THAN TALKING TO YOU.
7-15-16 © 2016 Scott Adams, Inc. /Dist. by Universal Uclick

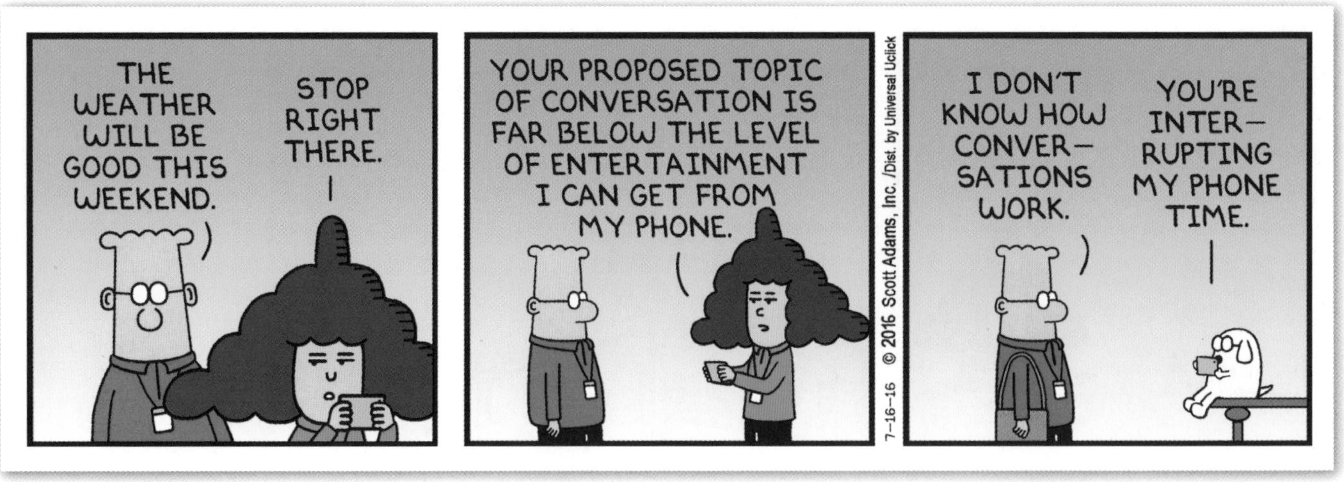
THE WEATHER WILL BE GOOD THIS WEEKEND.
STOP RIGHT THERE.
YOUR PROPOSED TOPIC OF CONVERSATION IS FAR BELOW THE LEVEL OF ENTERTAINMENT I CAN GET FROM MY PHONE.
I DON'T KNOW HOW CONVER-SATIONS WORK.
YOU'RE INTER-RUPTING MY PHONE TIME.
7-16-16 © 2016 Scott Adams, Inc. /Dist. by Universal Uclick

I LOVE LIVING IN A WORLD WHERE EVERYTHING I NEED TO KNOW IS ON THE INTERNET.
I'LL JUST HOP OVER TO YOUTUBE AND LEARN HOW TO USE MY NEW APP.
PERFECT! I CAN CHOOSE FROM OVER A HUNDRED DIFFERENT TUTORIALS!
IT WILL ONLY TAKE ME AN HOUR OR SO TO FIGURE OUT WHICH ONE REFERS TO MY VERSION OF THE SOFTWARE.
ONE HOUR LATER
GAAA!!! THESE VIDEOS ARE POORLY LABELED!
TWO HOURS LATER
GAAA!!! THIS GUY TALKS TOO SLOWLY! GET TO THE POINT!
THREE HOURS LATER
GAAA!!! WHY ARE MY MENU OPTIONS DIFFERENT FROM THE TUTORIAL?
I HATE LIVING IN A WORLD WHERE EVERYTHING I NEED TO KNOW IS ON THE INTERNET.
© 2016 Scott Adams, Inc./Dist. by Universal Uclick
7-17-16

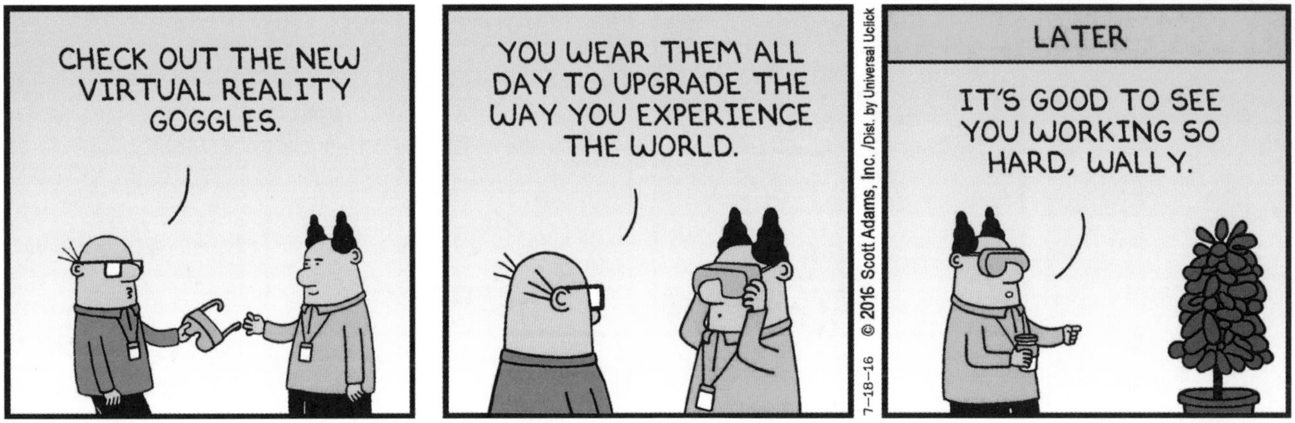
CHECK OUT THE NEW VIRTUAL REALITY GOGGLES.
YOU WEAR THEM ALL DAY TO UPGRADE THE WAY YOU EXPERIENCE THE WORLD.
7-18-16 © 2016 Scott Adams, Inc. /Dist. by Universal Uclick
LATER
IT'S GOOD TO SEE YOU WORKING SO HARD, WALLY.

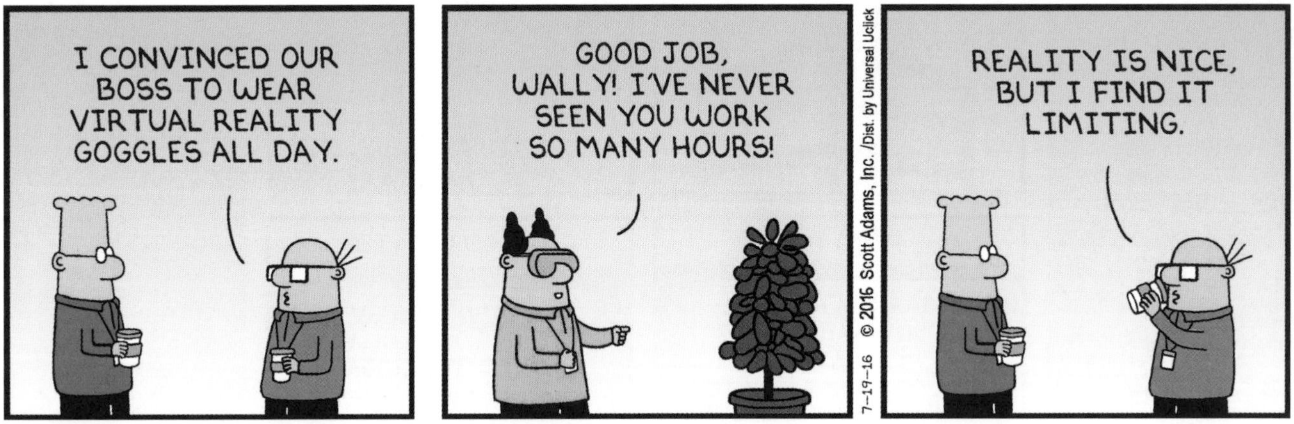
I CONVINCED OUR BOSS TO WEAR VIRTUAL REALITY GOGGLES ALL DAY.
GOOD JOB, WALLY! I'VE NEVER SEEN YOU WORK SO MANY HOURS!
7-19-16 © 2016 Scott Adams, Inc. /Dist. by Universal Uclick
REALITY IS NICE, BUT I FIND IT LIMITING.

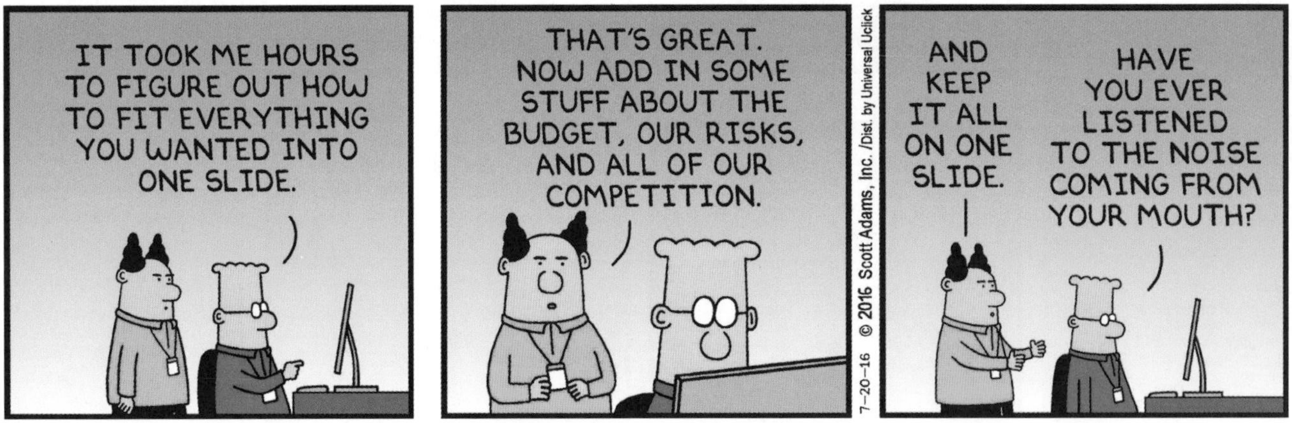
IT TOOK ME HOURS TO FIGURE OUT HOW TO FIT EVERYTHING YOU WANTED INTO ONE SLIDE.
THAT'S GREAT. NOW ADD IN SOME STUFF ABOUT THE BUDGET, OUR RISKS, AND ALL OF OUR COMPETITION.
7-20-16 © 2016 Scott Adams, Inc. /Dist. by Universal Uclick
AND KEEP IT ALL ON ONE SLIDE.
HAVE YOU EVER LISTENED TO THE NOISE COMING FROM YOUR MOUTH?

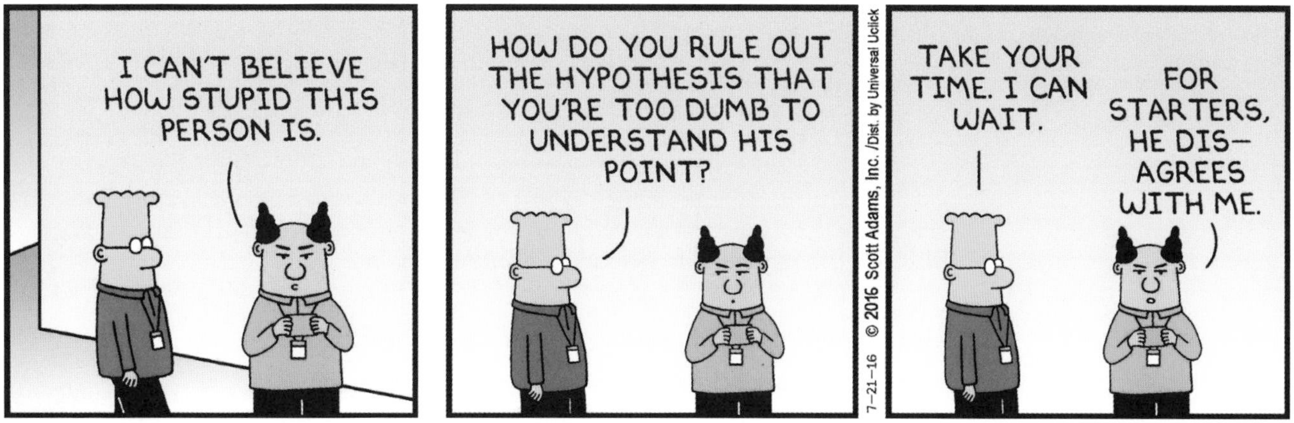
I CAN'T BELIEVE HOW STUPID THIS PERSON IS.
HOW DO YOU RULE OUT THE HYPOTHESIS THAT YOU'RE TOO DUMB TO UNDERSTAND HIS POINT?
7-21-16 © 2016 Scott Adams, Inc. /Dist. by Universal Uclick
TAKE YOUR TIME. I CAN WAIT.
FOR STARTERS, HE DIS-AGREES WITH ME.

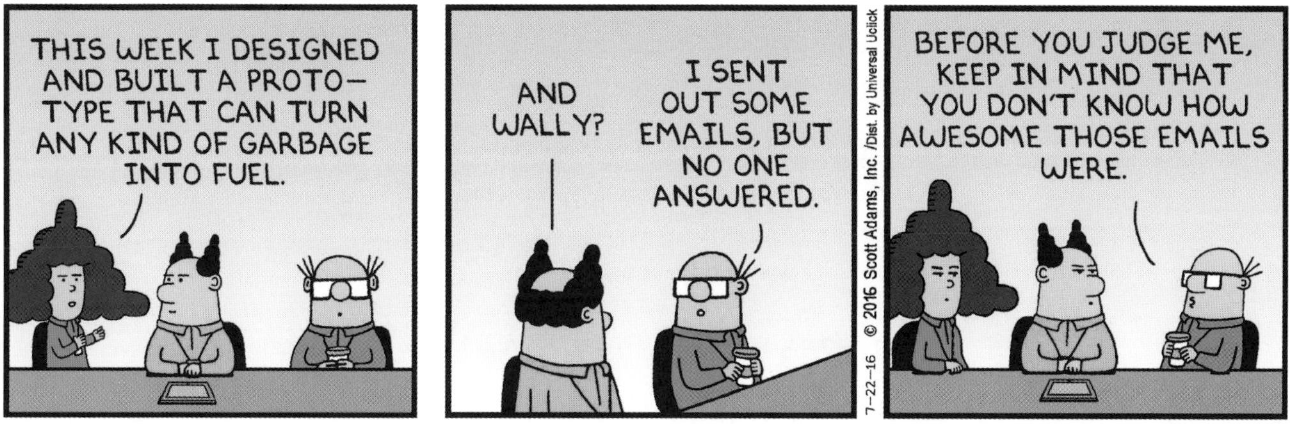
THIS WEEK I DESIGNED AND BUILT A PROTO-TYPE THAT CAN TURN ANY KIND OF GARBAGE INTO FUEL.
AND WALLY?
I SENT OUT SOME EMAILS, BUT NO ONE ANSWERED.
7-22-16 © 2016 Scott Adams, Inc. /Dist. by Universal Uclick
BEFORE YOU JUDGE ME, KEEP IN MIND THAT YOU DON'T KNOW HOW AWESOME THOSE EMAILS WERE.

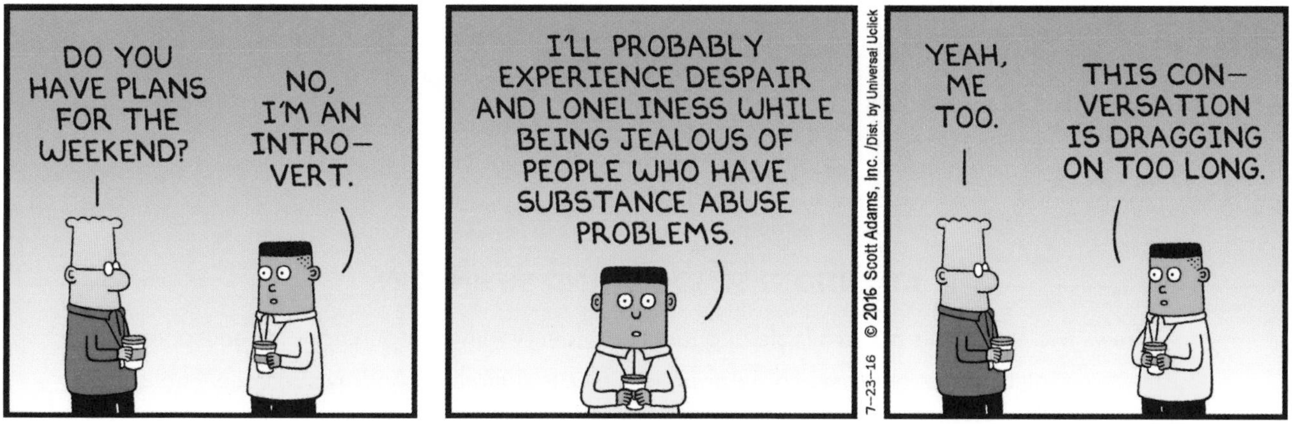
DO YOU HAVE PLANS FOR THE WEEKEND?
NO, I'M AN INTRO-VERT.
I'LL PROBABLY EXPERIENCE DESPAIR AND LONELINESS WHILE BEING JEALOUS OF PEOPLE WHO HAVE SUBSTANCE ABUSE PROBLEMS.
7-23-16 © 2016 Scott Adams, Inc. /Dist. by Universal Uclick
YEAH, ME TOO.
THIS CON-VERSATION IS DRAGGING ON TOO LONG.

Andrews McMeel Publishing
a division of Andrews McMeel Universal
1130 Walnut Street, Kansas City, Missouri 64106

www.andrewsmcmeel.com

16 17 18 19 20 SDB 10 9 8 7 6 5 4 3 2 1

ISBN: 978-1-4494-7196-5

Library of Congress Control Number: 2016930987

www.dilbert.com

ATTENTION: SCHOOLS AND BUSINESSES

Andrews McMeel books are available at quantity discounts with bulk purchase for educational,
business, or sales promotional use. For information, please e-mail the Andrews McMeel Publishing
Special Sales Department: specialsales@amuniversal.com.